OCT 0 8 2010

D0425919

Withdrawn/ABCL

THE OTHER SIDE OF THE MOUNTAIN
BRIDGING THE GREAT DIVIDES

THE OTHER SIDE OF THE MOUNTAIN
BRIDGING THE GREAT DIVIDES

The Friendship Force Story
Foreword By Jimmy and Rosalynn Carter

The Friendship Force

In Friendship,
Charlene
Terrell

Charlene Terrell

3 9075 03689700 4

Copyright © 1997

ISBN 1-883793-24-6

Library of Congress Catalog Number
97-60689

Charlene Terrell
162 Big Canoe
Big Canoe, GA 30143

WOLFE PUBLISHING
P.O. Box 8036
Fernandina Beach, FL 32035-8036

ACKNOWLEDGMENTS

I am very grateful to President Jimmy Carter and Rosalynn Carter for writing the foreword to The Other Side of the Mountain. My special thanks go to Mrs. Carter for allocating time to answer questions and express her views.

Thanks to everyone who helped, including these special people:

William L. "Bill" Davenport, a great writer and a great friend;

Fred Tallant, for detecting all the manuscript flaws I missed;

Kathleen Ingram, who rescued me each time the computer balked;

Wayne and Eleanor Van Tilburg who shared great stories and photos;

Bettye and Harold Brown, who opened their home and hearts and made available their vast collection of Friendship Force photos;

Nina Hill who discovered the perfect cover photo and to Colorview Publications, Ltd. for allowing the use of this great photograph;

Gerald and Helen Weekes who shared their stories and their enthusiasm;

Tony and Jenny Coates and Bill Lamkin who loaned several key photographs; Beverlie Reilman who shared her knowledge and to Inger Rice, George Brown, Boyd Lyons, Harriet Kuhr, Susan Smith, Hulett Smith; Claudia Oldenburg, Svetlana Lebedva, Levy Tavares, Claude Armendariz, Vickie Sterling, Sarah Wynn, Richard Falk, Jimmy Allen and Sam Ayoub for their help.

Old friends Winnie and Derek Bell (England) shared memories and photos, as did Margaret and Lou Chester, Eleanor Eyman, Donnis Bauman and Sandy and Nelson Dussault and
to Carolyn Smith from whom I gained much insight;

Susan Smith and Max and Carol Jennings who shared their moving experiences as they offered aid and friendship to the shattered people of Sarajevo in Bosnia-Herzegovina;

And to Wayne Smith who had confidence in me as I struggled to tell The Friendship Force story as well as he has lived it...

And to Dave most of all.

CONTENTS

Introduction   i-iv

1   The Dreamer   1-10

2   The Architects   11-14

3   The Engineers   15-20

4   Trial, Tribulation and Triumph   21-30

5   The Vision Expands   31-50

6   The Builders   51-64

7   Uncharted Waters   65-68

8   Philanthropist Meets Peacemaker   69-72

9   Old Enemies - New Friends   73-84

10   New Builders - Old Lands   85-108

11   A New Arms Treaty?   109-126

12   When the World Sings Together   127-136

13   It May Take a Camel To Build A
     Difficult Bridge   137-148

14   Young Ambassadors Bridge   149-160
     Old Divides

15   A Time To Act   161-168

16   A Path to a Friend's House is
     ·Never Long   169-186

17   Friendship - A Fearful Idea?   187-198

18   A Bridge Called Georgia-   199-214
          To-Georgia

19   A Magic Force?   215-226

20   You Can Make A Difference   227-246

21   A Bridge Called Friend-   247-258
          To-Friend

22   Job Description For   259-268
          Ambassadors of Friendship

23   Friendship: A Space Where   269-274
          Change Can Take Place

24   Friendship In Action   275-290

25   Ordeal or Opportunity?   291-300

26   Enemies No More   301-308

27   Vietnam: A Bridge Too Far?   309-318

28   Urgent Missions to Troubled   319-330
          Lands

29   Winning the Peace   331-338

Friendship Force Leaders and Facts   341-351

Surname and Place Name Index

Rosalynn Carter and the author

FOREWORD

In March of 1977, soon after we entered the White House, our friend Wayne Smith asked if we would work with him to establish a new international organization called The Friendship Force. We readily agreed, and in July 1977, the first exchange took place between Atlanta, Georgia, and Newcastle upon Tyne, England. Now, 20 years later, we look back with great pride on the accomplishments of The Friendship Force. Over 500,000 people from 60 nations have participated as ambassadors and hosts, and millions more have developed and maintained rewarding friendships.

In *The Other Side of the Mountain*, author Charlene Terrell describes the amazing power of "people-to-people diplomacy" in the true stories of ordinary men and women who have reached out to those in other lands and found their lives forever enriched. Ultimately even governments can be affected by the climate of peace and good will fostered by Friendship Force experiences.

Charlene Terrell stresses that individual friendships, multiplied many times over, can bridge the great divides that separate us, including race, religion, culture, politics, language, fear and ignorance. With a view to *The Other Side of the Mountain*, she encourages all of us to extend the hand of friendship across the nations and build a better world, one person at a time.

In Friendship,

Jimmy Carter   Rosalynn Carter

Author's Note

The story related in the introduction to The Other Side of the Mountain is not intended to preview the book, but rather to introduce the powerful idea which is central to this intriguing account of love in action.

Charlene Terrell
Big Canoe, Georgia

Introduction

What can one person do? Most people ask themselves this questions when they are faced with overwhelming circumstances, seemingly beyond their control. More than anything else, this book addresses this difficult question and provides an answer which hundreds and thousands of people have found to be true over the past two decades. Some of their stories are told in this book and they will warm your heart and show that *you CAN make a difference* in this tired, battered old world.

These stories make up the history and the heartbeat of an international organization called The Friendship Force. They are the stories of some of the thousands of volunteers who have reached out their hands in friendship to people in another land, people who were often of a different race, culture, and religion and who spoke another language. To their surprise, they found hands reaching back to clasp their own and discovered they were more alike than different.

The good that has been done through the volunteers of The Friendship Force cannot be measured, but the world would be much worse off if they had never worked together under The Friendship

Force banner, proclaiming that *A world of friends is a world of peace* and *You CAN make a difference!*

But what can one person do? Years ago, Dr. Albert Schweitzer gave his answer from his jungle hospital in Gabon, Africa. "Seek always to do some good everywhere," he advised. Dr. Schweitzer practiced what he preached and he passed along his philosophy to many, including my friend, Dr. Silvia Brandalise of Campinas, Brazil, a remarkable person whom I met through Dr. Wayne Smith of The Friendship Force. Here is her story.

Brazil, 1959. Young Silvia Regina lived in Sao Paulo and she dreamed of becoming a doctor. Family and friends gently discouraged Silvia and suggested other career choices, but she dreamed on and prayed for an answer—or at least for an encouraging word.

"One fortunate day, I happened to read a magazine article," Silvia recalled. "It was about the legendary Dr. Albert Schweitzer and his jungle hospital in far-away Gabon in equatorial Africa. I was electrified—this was my answer! I sat down and immediately wrote to Dr. Schweitzer, pouring out my hopes, dreams and fears. Instinctively, I knew this good man would understand everything, but would he receive my letter? Could he find the precious time to respond to what

I'd laboriously written in both French and English? The article said he was already in his eighties and still carried a heavy work load."

In time, a letter came bearing the postmark of Lambarene. It was dictated to one of Dr. Schweitzer's assistants, a Dutch nurse. The letter said he really believed Silvia should follow her dream and he wished her "...the best for...your studies, your plans and your future." He described his own work with enthusiasm and even enclosed a photo of the Ugowe River with this notation:

"Here you see the place where the small pirogues (canoes) arrive, bringing us their patients. Sometimes they come from very far and have a long and tiring journey behind them when they arrive."

The nurse added this final paragraph: "Dr. Schweitzer is still working from morning until late at night, organizing everything and helping where his help is needed. He regrets he cannot write this letter himself, but after so many years, writing so many nights in the light of his old petrol lamp, his eyes are very tired." (In truth, Dr. Schwietzer was almost blind.)

Silvia never doubted that she would become a doctor after the wonderful letter arrived. "It was my inspiration all through medical school," she said. "At each low point, I would retrieve the letter and read it again. I often visualized Dr. Schweitzer there in the jungle working past midnight, although he was an old man. My load would then seem lighter and my problems diminished."

During Silvia's last year of medical school, Dr. Schweitzer received the Nobel Prize for his work in medicine. Soon-to-be *Doctor* Silvia Brandalise, wrote another letter, congratulating him on receiving this high honor and thanking him for his encouraging letter. Another warm response came back. It was accompanied by a photo of Dr. Schweitzer in a pirogue on the Ugowe. Now Silvia possessed two letters and photos from Dr. Schweitzer!

Although I had little money, I felt very rich indeed," she told me.

Medical school was only a small step. "Aunt Silvia," as she's known by her young patients, soon had throngs of sick children coming to be treated. An unusually high number suffered from leukemia and other cancers. The desperate need for a modern hospital where children's lives could be saved haunted Silvia. She wondered and worried for a short time, then she scraped together just enough money to rent an old house and began a small, ill-equipped treatment center. Her days soon became as long and busy as Dr. Schweitzer's days had been at the jungle hospital. Many children were helped, but far too many had to be turned away. Dr. Silvia's dream for a larger hospital seemed remote, if not impossible. However, about this time, her work came to the attention of a private foundation.

The chief executive of this organization came to Campinas to see the young doctor and her tiny facility where very sick children were made well again. After he saw the good which was accomplished and the great need remaining, he recommended to his board that Dr. Silvia be awarded one million dollars to build a children's hospital.

Silvia said, "I was overcome with joy and wanted to find a way to express my gratitude to this kind man, but how? Quite suddenly, I knew what I would do. I immediately boxed up my treasures—the photos and letters from Dr. Schweitzer." With a simple letter of explanation, Silvia happily sent these prized possessions to her benefactor.

Time passed and the hospital was built. It quickly became an oasis of healing and a model to be copied in other Brazilian cities. The children occupied Dr. Silvia's every waking moment. No child was turned away because their family could not pay. There were many of these cases and expenses were climbing much faster than revenues.

"One night I was in my office looking glumly at the stack of unopened mail. Most of it was bills," Dr. Silvia recalls. "I sighed and began to open the envelopes. One packet was marked 'priority mail.' I opened it last, but no overdue bill was there to greet me. It was the precious letters from Dr. Schweitzer and the photos as well! The head of the foundation had written to say he could not bear to keep these items because they would never belong anywhere but here...in the hospital with the children."

Thanks to two brief encouraging letters from a good man who took time to counsel a young woman, the hospital has grown to more than twice its original size and includes a bone marrow transplant unit. Thousands of young lives have been spared because Dr. Schweitzer did what he could and Dr. Silvia followed his example.

You can make a difference. Read these stories in *The Other Side of the Mountain* and learn what you can do to wage peace in the world. We can't all be a Dr. Schweitzer or Dr. Brandalise, but I can attest that an involvement in the Friendship Force can change your life.

Charlene Terrell
Big Canoe, Georgia

"Goofy" doesn't look like little Sylvain Julmy nor does he come from Switzerland nor does he speak French, but Sylvain doesn't mind. Wouldn't it be a brighter world if everyone would cultivate the same attitude as this innocent child?

Chapter 1
The Dreamer

You never really understand a person until you consider things from his point of view.
—**Harper Lee,** *To Kill a Mockingbird* **(Harper Collins).**

This story began more than six decades ago in South Charleston, West Virginia, a suburb of Charleston, the state capital. The occasion was the birth of a child on July 19, 1934, in the midst of the Great Depression. The baby was given the ordinary name of David Wayne Smith. Dark clouds of the coming world war were already forming over Europe and Asia and the lean year of 1934 was not a time to inspire optimism for world survival, much less world peace.

Because of unhappy family circumstances, little Wayne Smith was soon placed in the full time care of his grandparents. His grandmother, whom he called "Mee-maw," was a McGill with roots back in Donegal, Ireland. Myrtle McGill Smith was widowed early in life but she later met and married Vincinzo Tiago Muscatello, an immigrant from Locri, a village near the bottom of Italy's boot. Jimmy, as he was called, was ambitious, though poorly educated, and soon after arriving in the United States, he followed an older brother to West Virginia to work in the coal mines.

As a child, Wayne Smith loved his doting grandmother and step-grandfather and considered them to be the mother and father of his heart. He called Jimmy Muscatello "Pee-paw" and it was plain to see that the Italian immigrant and the little boy loved each other with all their hearts.

Muscatello built his first house, dubbed 'The Shanty' by Mee-maw. Little by little, the structure grew as Pee-paw added rooms. Later he built another building a short distance away, calling it his *ristorante*. (His customers called it a beer joint.) Mee-maw and Pee-paw built three rooms to the rear of the beer joint and the addition became their home. Meanwhile, Wayne's parents moved into The Shanty where they lived with his siblings, a younger sister and brother.

Wayne Smith was an observant child and learned much from Pee-paw and Mee-maw, as they worked together in the family business.

The venture sprang from Muscatello's ability to grow fine grapes and to make equally fine wine. From Italy he also brought an ability to cook up mounds of savory spaghetti and meatballs, Muscatello style.

Smith began working in the beer joint at an early age and he soon became a shrewd observer of the patrons and their often rough way of life. His beloved grandparents taught him to accept people as they were, but they also quietly pointed out the harm caused by those who drank up their paychecks or were unfaithful to their wives. More than anything else they wanted their grandson to lead a productive life. They started early by teaching him how to work hard. One of Smith's earliest memories was of serving beer to the customers and of becoming something of a pool shark after Pee-paw added a room with pool tables.

Years later Smith said: "Sometimes I'd ask people if they wanted to see a trick shot. I'd show them a trick and after they admitted it was pretty good. I'd ask them to play with me for a dollar. They'd get angry after they were soundly beaten by a little kid. I paid for my first bicycle that way," he added. "Of course, I gave up hustling a long time ago," he confessed with a twinkle in his eye.

The beer joint and pool hall fronted on US Route 60 and young Wayne, watching cars whiz by on a summer's night, often wondered wistfully who these people were and where they were going—and why. Once a truck driver named Jack Fisher stopped by for a meal. "Mister, what's on the other side of that mountain," asked eight-year-old Smith, pointing across the Kanawha River to the ridge beyond.

"Another mountain," Fisher replied.

"What's on the other side of *that* mountain," Smith persisted.

"Just another mountain," Fisher grunted.

The boy said more eagerly, "Well, if you go on the other side of that mountain and the next mountain and then a third mountain, what will you see?"

"Well, I guess there's another mountain and maybe a river," was the answer.

Years later Wayne Smith admitted that his conversation with Jack Fisher had piqued his curiosity and inspired his dreams about a time when he could see for himself who and what were on the other side of all those mountains—and beyond.

During his boyhood days, Wayne Smith showed no sign of becoming one who would grace the world stage. He was quiet and introspective, but he was also an achiever and a hard working student, involved in many school activities. He played first trumpet in the school band. It was through the band that he met a pretty co-ed named

Carolyn Heaster, the girl who would become his wife when he was nineteen and she only eighteen. Today Carolyn laughs and says: "Wayne played first chair trumpet and I played second chair trumpet. And it's been that way ever since!"

Another duty Smith's grandparents required of him was church attendance. They were tolerant and didn't care which church he chose so Smith visited all the churches in town. After he and Carolyn started dating, he went only to the Presbyterian church because she worshipped there.

Smith's grandparents encouraged him to go to college and perhaps get a business degree. They envisioned the day he would be able to open the biggest beer parlor and pool room in West Virginia. But Wayne had recently become a Christian and had other dreams. Following his marriage to Carolyn he began working full time at Union Carbide's research laboratory.

In 1954, in the landmark case of *Brown v. Board of Education of Topeka*, the US Supreme Court ruled that racial segregation was in violation of the rights guaranteed in the Constitution. While others engaged in heated debate over the high court's ruling, Wayne Smith was attending night classes at Morris Harvey College, now Charleston University. The school was not located near Union Carbide, so Smith began to look at other options. The school most convenient to his workplace was West Virginia State College, a land-grant college for black students. The faculty was also black with the exception of one lone professor.

When Smith decided to take a closer look at West Virginia State he discovered that its academic staff had outstanding credentials. He applied for admission and was accepted. As the only white student in an otherwise all-black college, any prejudice Smith might have harbored was soon wiped away. He became "color blind," a remarkable and rare occurrence in the racially tense 1950's and 60's. Smith may have been the first white student in the United States to practice desegregation—in reverse.

Smith's decision to attend West Virginia State probably came easier because he had a paper route while he was still in junior high school which included the section of town where most black people lived. It was then that Wayne Smith found that black customers, just as white customers, possessed both virtues and vices. In both cases, some paid promptly and some didn't; some drank a lot and some were sober; some were hard-working and some were not. It was a lesson he never forgot.

Smith worked hard at West Virginia State and graduated *summa cum laude*. By this time, he felt a calling to the ministry and enrolled in Union Theological Seminary in Richmond, Virginia. The year was 1957 and David, the Smiths' first child, was born in the spring. At seminary Smith was ultimately voted the best overall student based on his "fidelity to God, his diligence to study and his compatibility with his classmates." He graduated in 1961 with a Bachelor of Divinity degree.

After seminary Smith returned to West Virginia where he became the pastor of Elk Hills Presbyterian Church of Charleston for two years. He left that church to apply for a missionary post in Brazil. The Presbyterian Mission Board members interviewed Smith but initially failed to recommend him for the job, feeling that he was "too naive" and "hopelessly and unrealistically idealistic." But Wayne Smith's stubbornness and power of persuasion overcame their doubts and soon he and his family boarded a ship bound for Brazil. It was August 28, 1963, and the Smiths now had four small children: David, Steve, Andy and Susan, age five months.

In language school Wayne and Carolyn studied hard to learn Portuguese. Both did well but Wayne was determined to excel. "I would walk about four miles to the middle of Campinas to practice speaking Portuguese. I'd go from store to store to engage shopkeepers in conversation. I made a lot of friends that way," Smith said. "And some of those people are still friends today."

Carolyn explained that they were required to be in language school for five hours each day and to complete a lot of homework. "They wouldn't send us out into the mission field unless we became fluent in the language," she remembered.

————

The Smiths were ultimately sent to Taguatinga, one of the satellite cities built for many of the workers hired to construct the new national capital of Brasilia. Carolyn vividly remembers their first look at their Taguatinga home.

"Though we had lived very modestly in Campinas, nothing we had seen of Brazil at that point had prepared us for Taguatinga. I was very shocked when we arrived," she said. "I have seen poor people and bad housing, having grown up in West Virginia, but I had never seen anything like this. It was like the *favelas* (slums) in Rio de Janeiro, only this *favela* was not on a mountainside. It was just row after row of makeshift shelters. They were made of sticks, boards, cardboard, plastic, rusty tin, tar paper—anything that might be used to construct a little shelter. These huts had no running water and open ditches carried the sewage.

"Our little house was better than most because it had been built by a missionary who was there before us. The kitchen was tiny and it was easy to touch both walls by extending your arms but, if you did that, you received an electrical shock due to faulty wiring. We had electricity some of the time. The streets were not paved and they became red muddy bogs when it rained. The rest of the time, everything was coated in red dust. You can't imagine the flies and mosquitoes," Carolyn said. "Although we had screens on our windows they were everywhere. Our children were all small—David was six, Steve, five Andy, three and Susie was in diapers. All of us were crammed into this tiny house.

"We had a concrete cistern in the front yard," Carolyn continued. "Once a week a water truck brought water that had been pumped from a creek in the vicinity. The water was just as it had been drawn, with all kind of trash, mud, leaves—and even fish! We had one filter where water flowed from the cistern and another at the point water entered the house, but the water was still not potable. We boiled all our water.

"We had a huge metal basin and the kids bathed in that. Wayne and I bathed in it too, but we stood in the basin and poured water over us in a primitive attempt at showering.

"When it rained, water would come in around the light fixtures and we kept buckets on the floor to catch some of the water.

"There was a bakery and an open air market nearby. I shopped every day. There were flies on everything at the market and I often brought home ground beef to make spaghetti sauce or chili. I would cook it until it boiled and soon flies would float to the top. I would skim them off and finish cooking the meal.

"The kids were sick a lot, especially with diarrhea, fevers and vomiting. Once a year we went back to Campinas to get our physicals. Dr. John Lane treated the missionary families and he would medicate us to get rid of worms and other parasites we had acquired during the year. Once Wayne was seriously ill with hepatitis. Dr. Lane sternly ordered him to stay in bed and rest for six months. For Wayne, that was an impossible thing to do. Later on I was very sick with what we think was meningitis..

"But on the positive side, it was good to see the people of Taguatinga so happy to have a church," Carolyn added. "And our kids had fun. The boys remember those days with fondness."

"Taguatinga was a city of about 100,000 when we arrived," Wayne Smith said. "We had responsibility for five different churches as well as food distribution programs, clothing programs and for opening schools to improve adult literacy."

Smith was not content to work alone as an outsider. He began to go to Brasilia to meet political leaders in the Congress. "I reasoned that the work in this huge country was too much for a handful of missionaries," he recalled. "We needed help from the top to really make an impact.

"One day in 1965, I stopped a man in the halls of Congress. I said 'Excuse me, are you a member of Congress?'

"He said, 'Yes, what can I do for you? Are you from my state?'

"When I told him I was from the United States, he was very surprised.

"'Well,' he said, 'then you must have been born here because you speak the language so fluently.'

"When I told him I'd only been in Brazil for eighteen months, he was amazed."

"How *did* you learn to speak Portuguese so well?" asked the senator.

Smith told him about the language school he had attended in Campinas and explained that the teaching method employed there was superb. He asked the congressman if he spoke English and when he admitted that regretfully he did not, Smith offered to become his English teacher. Furthermore, Smith promised on the spot that he would teach the congressman—plus five of his colleagues—at no charge. All Smith asked was a room in the Congress Building for a classroom.

The congressman smiled knowingly. "Ah, yes...I understand now," he said, "You're with the CIA, aren't you?"

Smith told him that he was not with any government organization, but was a Protestant missionary working in Taguatinga.

"Of course!" cried the Congressman. "I get it. I'm Catholic and you're trying to proselytize me."

"No, no," Smith replied. "Here's the deal; if you want to learn English, give me three hours a week and promise to do some homework outside class and I will never bring up the matter of religion in class. Now, *after* class, if *you* bring up the subject, then we'll speak about religion in Portuguese. But I will never mention the word in class."

The congressman agreed and a class called "Learning to Think in English" was organized. Smith was addressed as 'Professor' instead of

Reverendo. The class soon grew and, ultimately, 150 members of congress were taking his course. However, Smith soon became more than a professor. Many times after class he would be invited to take coffee with one of his students. Conversations often began with "Reverendo, my child has this problem...." or "My wife is ill and...." In this manner, the pool shark-turned-minister from the hills of West Virginia became the "unofficial chaplain" of the Brazilian Congress.

Wayne Smith won respect because he ministered to the people whether they were Catholic, Protestant, Spiritualist or agnostic. Out of chats over coffee, a Bible class emerged; however, Smith merely organized the class. He wanted the class members to confront their own beliefs and ideas, so he insisted that the congressmen share the teaching responsibilities among themselves.

The Smith family in Brazil: Andy, Carolyn, Steve, Wayne, Susan and David.

Carolyn Smith said that after two years in Taguatinga they were allowed to move into the new city of Brasilia. "Thankfully, this apartment had running water. It was small, but it was an improvement. Wayne helped start a school in Brasilia. At first, it was just kindergarten and the first grade and every year or so, two more grades were added. By the time we left, there were eight grades. With the help of volunteers, we were able to set up a two-hour program after each school day. The parents got involved and we had classes, including sewing, cooking swimming, arts and crafts, sports, volley ball and other games. This was at the *Escola Americana*, but it was not just Americans who came. We had English, French, Brazilians and anyone else who could afford the small tuition. Wayne also started a church for English speaking people. He often invited people to our home and we entertained his prayer group once a week."

Before Wayne Smith left Brazil he also organized the Christian Leadership Movement of Brazil (1967) and the first President's Prayer Luncheon and various Governors' Prayer Groups.

The Smith family moved back to the United States in 1970. A year or so earlier, Dr. Vernon S. Broyles, Jr. had visited Brazil and was highly impressed with the Smiths' work. Broyles, long-time minister of North Avenue Presbyterian Church in Atlanta, corresponded often with the missionary. When the elder pastor learned the Smith family was coming home, he asked Wayne if he would become the North Avenue church's "minister to the community." Smith accepted and on January 9, 1971, he arrived in Atlanta.

Jimmy Carter became Governor of Georgia in 1971, and Wayne Smith heard his inaugural address. When Carter said the time had come for racial discrimination in Georgia to end and that while he was governor, desegregation would be accomplished, Smith was instantly attracted to the peanut farmer from Plains. Smith had plans to meet all the community and state leaders and he vowed that Governor Carter would be at the top of his list. Within ten weeks the two had met.

During a 1972 conversation with Carter, he posed a question which the Governor found intriguing. "Would you be interested in meeting a friend of mine who is President of the Brazilian Congress?" he asked.

Carter admitted it sounded quite interesting, but wanted to know just what Smith had in mind.

"Well, since you've never been to Brazil, I think if you went there to meet this man, he would be very happy to take you into his home. Doors would be open to you that might never open if you went in some official capacity. Besides, I know you will enjoy meeting my friend. He is a fine person and has been in my home many times when we lived in Brazil. I will be happy to act as an interpreter and to arrange your itinerary.

Governor and Mrs. Carter made the journey and were delighted that Wayne had scheduled time for them to visit with ordinary people as well as with prominent leaders and government officials. Years later, Mrs. Carter said: "It was a wonderful trip. Wayne wanted us to love Brazil and the Brazilian people as much as he did. And today we still have many friends in that lovely country."

Following the visit to Brazil, Governor and Mrs. Carter went on to Argentina and Costa Rica on a trade mission. Traveling with them was Louis Truman, Chairman of the Georgia Department of Industry and Trade, and his associate Jack Welch.

The successful trip prompted Wayne Smith to discuss another idea with the Carters. He jotted down some notes about a new plan for people-to-people diplomacy involving citizens of Brazil and the State of Georgia. He broached the idea to Governor and Mrs. Carter and they responded with enthusiasm.

Wayne Smith was off and running. In 1973, the idea was tested further when two hundred Georgians flew to Brazil on a chartered flight and two hundred Brazilians got on the same plane to go back to Atlanta. In both countries, the people were hosted in private homes for ten days. At Smith's prompting, volunteers in both countries handled all the details of this major undertaking. Mrs. Carter was one of those on the flight to Brazil while Governor Carter hosted Brazilians at the Governor's Mansion.

The Georgia to Pernambuco, Brazil, citizens' exchange was so successful that it was continued annually through an organization called Partners of the Americas.

Wayne Smith was very pleased—but he was far from satisfied. "This exchange proved what I had already learned. Once a base of understanding exists between people, then things like race, culture, religion and language are less likely to become stumbling blocks. This is what I mean when I talk about people-to-people diplomacy," he explained.

During 1971-1975, Smith also founded METANOIA, a religious social services center in Atlanta which aided teenage runaways, ex-offenders, high school dropouts and those in need of emergency financial help. In 1975, another job opportunity came Smith's way when Atlanta developer Tom Cousins asked him to become Assistant to the Chairman of Cousins Properties, Inc. Smith accepted and went on to become vice-president of personnel, promotions and marketing of the Omni, Atlanta's first multi-purpose office-coliseum complex. In addition, Smith was the interim pastor of the Newnan Presbyterian Church and also served as Chaplain of the Atlanta Hawks basketball team.

Now, after struggling to get his education, making a commitment to a Christian vocation and honing it in the jungles of Brazil, Wayne Smith had firmed up the direction his dream should take. He saw that person-to-person diplomacy based on friendship offered a unique opportunity to contribute to world peace. Wayne had attracted persons of influence with his initiative and commitment. He had confidence in himself to direct a world-wide program. He was prepared to get on with the job.

President Jimmy Carter announces the formation of The Friendship Force on March 1, 1977, at a White House conferences with state governors.

Chapter 2
The Architects

The invasion of armies can be resisted, but not an idea whose time has come.
—Victor Hugo

Governor Jimmy Carter wanted to be President of the United States. Many scoffed at his chance of attaining the ultimate office, but Wayne Smith was not among them. When Tom Cousins told him, "Carter doesn't have a ghost of a chance," Smith politely disagreed. He strongly believed that his friend would be elected, and months before James Earl Carter was elected as the 39th President of the United States, an idea which Smith had long pondered took shape in his mind. On July 18, 1976, Smith sketched out his grand design and drove to Plains, Georgia, to deliver it to Jimmy and Rosalynn. They were away on the campaign trail, but the bold outline of Smith's plan was left with Lillian Carter, mother of the soon-to-be president. In part, it declared:

In a similar fashion as Georgia has led in beginning state-to-state citizens' exchanges, I would like to see the entire United States involved in a mass citizens exchange with the entire world. It is possible for all 50 of our States to engage in such ventures. These exchanges can be with the entire world, not only in Latin America. Just imagine! —A planeload of people from Wyoming living in the homes of Bulgarians! Citizens of Ohio traveling to and staying in homes of the people of India! And of course, the citizens of those countries return on the same plane to stay for two weeks in homes in Wyoming and Ohio. Imagine a day...a day when on national TV you launch 50 planes at one time, at the same moment, and 200 people from 50 states (10,000) lift off on their way to 50 different nations. Those 10,000 people are met by 10,000 hosts and the plane returns with 200 citizens of 50 different lands who are met by 10,000 Americans. What friendships! What understanding! What peace! All could be generated with such a **Friendship Force**.

Governor, there are many details which need to be worked out, but which can be worked out. It has been done before on a small scale. It can be done in a magnificent way now.

Let your administration be known as the one which, while recognizing the value of government-to-government relationships, began something new and fine in international relationships. Let your administration be known as one which helped the people of the world to know other people of the world by actually visiting them in their homes.

On July 23, 1976, Smith was elated to receive this handwritten response from Rosalynn Carter:

Mrs. Jimmy Carter
Plains, Georgia 31780

Dear Wayne,

I'm sorry we didn't get to see you when you were in Plains—and we both appreciate your letters.

Jimmy liked your suggestion for the...[Friendship Force] program and is planning to pursue it if elected. Maybe you and I can work on it together!

Sincerely,
Rosalynn
July 23, 1976

Wayne Smith later told a reporter: "Two very unexpected events occurred in 1976: it snowed in Miami and Jimmy Carter was elected President."

Carter was inaugurated on January 20, 1977, and Smith had lunch with the President and First Lady at the White House on January 27. On a napkin, he busily scribbled notes and diagrams for an organization called The Friendship Force.

"You see," Smith explained excitedly, "The Friendship Force will be built like a three-legged stool. One leg is a city outside the USA. The second leg is a city within the USA. The third leg is The Friendship Force in Atlanta (soon known as Friendship Force International). These three legs are partners who work closely together—yet separately and independently—for stability and success. Friendship Force International is responsible for finding flight directors and training them to perform their tasks. Friendship Force International is also legally responsible for the operation of the overall organization and has the task of putting the two exchange cities into contact with each other and to aid them in carrying out their exchanges through training and encouragement. The two cities have the responsibility of following The Friendship Force procedures and actually causing the exchange to happen. Together, the two cities and Friendship Force International create an environment where the seeds of friendship can be planted and grown."

When Smith finished, President Carter asked his wife what she thought about the idea.

"I think we ought to do it!" she responded enthusiastically.

The President agreed and asked Wayne and Rosalynn to continue the meeting and to work out the plan in detail. The Carters pledged their personal support, without getting the government involved on any level.

"We'll give you no money—and no orders," President Carter promised.

On February 15, 1977, Wayne Smith sent a letter to Rosalynn Carter at The White House. He wrote that an attorney had been hired to incorporate The Friendship Force as a non-profit organization in the state of Georgia. Smith asked Mrs. Carter if she would serve as president of the organization, allowing him to serve as vice-president.

Smith also reported that the management of Omni International had agreed to give The Friendship Force an office in its complex until the organization was "officially chartered and has funds to pay rent." Smith added that Wade Seal, who had worked on the Georgia and Pernambuco, Brazil, exchanges, had agreed to serve as the paid National Director of The Friendship Force "...along the organizational lines which I showed you in the White House last Friday."

Mrs. Carter declined to serve as president of the new organization, but agreed to serve as its honorary chairperson. Wayne Smith became the president and, true to their word, the Carters gave immediate support to The Friendship Force. On March 1, 1976, at a banquet at The White House, the Carters hosted governors of the fifty states and their spouses. The President asked for their personal support in getting the organization off the ground.

"I want to see ties of our country with other countries—large and very small, powerful and weak, very friendly and not-so-friendly—strengthened," Carter told them. "I think it will be an exciting thing. This is the kind of involvement that each of us can have that is a little above and beyond the government."

Many of the governors responded immediately, including Governor Robert Ray of Iowa and his wife Billie Ray. Also responding were Governor James Hunt of North Carolina and his wife Carolyn and Governor and Mrs. John D. Rockefeller of West Virginia. Later the Hunts served jointly as state directors, as did the Rockefellers. Governor Dixy Lee Ray appointed her sister Marion Reid as director for Washington State. Response by the governors was so immediate and so positive that within six months, The Friendship Force had directors for most of the fifty states and a few US territories.

A number of state directors appointed by the governors were still active a decade later: Charlotte Blackmon of Alabama; Barbara Weinberg of Connecticut; Joseph Grubbs of Iowa, (and later in North Carolina); Richard Falk of Minnesota; Blanche Judge of Montana; Bert Lindsay of New Mexico; Inger Rice of Virginia and Louise Palumbo of West Virginia. Gladys Warren of Oklahoma served until her untimely death in 1984.

On St. Patrick's Day, March 17, 1977, The Friendship Force was officially chartered. Again, Rosalynn Carter wrote to Wayne Smith to express her strong belief in the fledgling Friendship Force:

Jimmy and I are very happy to assist you in providing the leadership for The Friendship Force. This project will receive a good deal of my time and my complete support, because I am confident it will promote peace in the world.

The minister, turned citizen diplomat, the President and the First Lady had completed the organization's design. It was time to begin the quest and to see how far the force of friendship could go to cross barriers of race, culture, nationality, religion, politics, age, language and class. Would the force prove to be too weak to span these great and age-old divides?

Chapter 3
The Engineers

---◆---

Faith is believing something in advance which will only make sense in reverse.
—**Philip Yancey**, *Finding God in Unexpected Places*, (Moorings Press)

The Friendship Force was a legal reality first and it soon became both an operational reality and a great challenge. President Wayne Smith and Executive Director Wade Seal worked with a small staff in Atlanta to arrange the "maiden exchange" and to create support for The Friendship Force worldwide. Carolyn Clarke, Project Coordinator, flew to the United Kingdom to select a partner for Atlanta in the very first exchange which was scheduled for July 4th. This exchange would be the model to copy, to build upon and to serve as an example of how future exchanges would function. It was an adventure and a learning process all rolled into one.

It was difficult for Carolyn Clarke to select a city in the United Kingdom to pair with Atlanta, but Newcastle upon Tyne, England, finally was selected. Perhaps the way was paved by President Carter's earlier visit when he stood before a Newcastle audience in May, 1977, and greeted them with the Geordie expression, "Howay the lads!" (Translation: "How about our great soccer team!" The term 'Geordie' probably originated in 1745 when King George II of England was the object of a rebellion started by Bonnie Prince Charles, who came out of exile in France, stopped in Scotland to rally the Clans and proceeded to take over much of Northern England. He was finally ousted, but during the occupation, the people of Newcastlle remained steadfastly loyal to King George II, hence the name 'Geordie, an English derivative of George. The unusual dialect often spoken in Newcastle is also called Geordie)

The people were elated by the familiar greeting and the warm feelings for the President generated that day would later spread to include The Friendship Force. Furthermore, Theresa Russell, former

Lord Mayoress of Newcastle and a very optimistic and enthusiastic Briton, engineered a fabulous welcome for Carolyn Clarke.

When the exchange was announced, headlines proclaimed: "Atlanta, Here We Come—It's Official!" and "Geordies Ready for a Taste of Dixie." The excitement continued to build and back at headquarters, feverish activity reigned.

A program began to emerge under the guidance of the Board of Directors (later to become the Board of Trustees). Founder Wayne Smith, businessman Ralph Birdsong and attorney John Wallace of Atlanta and Hulett Smith, former governor of West Virginia were the first on the board. (Governor Smith was the first asked and he accepted immediately.)

On April 22, 1977, the official purpose of The Friendship Force was stated: "To provide, largely through volunteer efforts, a means by which the people of the United States and other countries can meet and develop friendship and understanding among each other. It is our belief that the knowledge, understanding and friendships developed through personal contacts with the people of different countries will promote the cause of world peace."

Following the lead of President and Mrs. Carter, The Friendship Force voted neither to neither accept nor request financial support from the United States or any other government. But how would the corporation be financed? According to calculations by Smith and his advisors, enough profit from shorter flights to Europe would bring in much of the operating capital. For additional funds, The Friendship Force would rely on "...grants from corporations and foundations and, to a lesser degree, from individual philanthropists." It was also hoped that an advisory council would be formed from leaders around the globe and that they would undertake fund-raising campaigns to benefit the organization. State directors were expected to raise funds for their state's expenses. Those who traveled were to be called ambassadors and they would pay an induction fee plus $250 for their exchange visit, regardless of the destination.

Wayne Smith was spending his considerable energies on two levels: he became pastor of the Decatur (Georgia) Presbyterian Church, and he was very much involved in the pilot exchange and in spreading the word about The Friendship Force. Wade Seal and the small staff worked with make-shift equipment in designing program concepts and manuals to instruct volunteers and staff in exchange-planning procedures.

Privately, President and Mrs. Carter spoke to various heads of state and supplied Wayne with names of those who should be contacted in other countries.

Wayne Smith insisted that the philosophy of The Friendship Force would be that WHERE people traveled was not important, but that WHY they were going would make the important difference. To insure this, after the first exchange, ambassadors were not to be told where they were going. They would be told to bring only one piece of luggage and to return home with the same single bag. It was made clear that Friendship Force exchanges were not tourist trips or shopping excursions. The motto of "You CAN make a difference" was adopted.

Students at Georgia State University volunteered to write the first public relations manual.Help also came from the King and Spalding law firm; Delta Airlines; Charles F. Kettering Foundation; Trust Company Bank; Cousins Properties and the International City Corp. The Coca Cola Company made the first gift in April ($10,000) and gifts then came from Arthur Andersen & Co.; Charles F. Kettering Foundation; the Armand Hammer and Trebor Foundations; Walter Rich Memorial Fund; Marshall Trust; Coronet Industries; Life of Georgia; Atlanta Coca Cola Bottling Company; Fuqua Industries; the Allen Foundation and Fred Darragh and members of the Korean Businessmen's Association. The combined initial gifts amounted to $148,000.

Volunteers were soon enlisted to help in the office. They shared card tables in a storage room and made do with very little equipment. Some of these early volunteers were Penny Campbell, Ann Hare, Norma Hassinger, Betty Hull, Anne Jackson, Bobbie Jones, Pat Ku and Beverlie Reilman. Reilman remembered that volunteer efforts were coordinated by Jan Hudgins and Gracie Phillips and that J. Walter Drake, a young Atlanta attorney, was the flight director for the first exchange.

The first exchange left amid much fanfare and excitement in both countries. The charter flight (Delta Airlines) brought 381 goodwill ambassadors to Atlanta. Awaiting them was a red carpet reception with music, flags, and welcome speeches by Governor George Busbee, State Director Jasper Dorsey, Wayne Smith and others. The next day the plane left carrying 381 Georgians to Newcastle. They were greeted there with the same enthusiasm offered to their countrymen by Georgians. For ten days, friendship was celebrated. In years to come, memories of the initial receptions slowly fade, but the friends made and families embraced—numbering over 2,200 people—would never be forgotten. Lessons learned would endure as well. The Georgians found

Wayne Smith escorts Theresa Russell of Newcastle from the chartered plane on the first Friendship Force exchange.

that far from being snobbish, cold and unfriendly, the Geordies were warm, outgoing and down-to-earth. Likewise, the Geordies found that the Georgians were not brash, overly-proud of their country or rude, but were interested in them, eager to be friends and delighted to be in England and to try all things English.

As Winnie and Derek Bell of the Newcastle area said later: "One surprising thing that we experienced as a family was the sheer joy that we felt each time we opened our lives and our homes to people from other countries and other cultures. Without The Friendship Force our paths would never have crossed. Long after the exchanges are over, we are continually delighted by letters, post cards and small gifts which remind us again and again of what happens when people reach out in friendship to strangers," Winnie Bell added, a touch of awe in her voice.

Wayne Smiths supplied one of his favorite stories about this first exchange. "This involved a poor black woman from Decatur," Smith recalled. "Her name is Myrtis Davis and she is a great lady and a great ambassador. She was a cook and was so poor she could pay only fifty dollars of the fee. While in England, she lived in the home of a middle-class white family, the home of a woman who was a cook at a college. Mrs. Davis was welcomed and treated very well by this family and she was even able to see Queen Elizabeth and Prince Philip. It blew her mind.

"The problem arose when it was her turn to be a host," Smith said. "She called us and said, 'I can't let those people stay in my house. My home isn't as good as theirs. They'll be embarrassed, and so will I.'

"Well, she told the members of her church about her problem and they went over and painted her house, built an extra room with a bath and even bought lawn furniture. Then they had a big picnic when the British guests arrived, two hundred blacks and two whites had a marvelous time together."

Although The Friendship Force is not connected with any religious movement, Wayne Smith confessed that he sees the organization as his personal ministry and believes he was called to it by God. "My mission now," Smith told a reporter, "is the same as it was in the church: to build a better relationship between people and also between people and God. God is love, and friendship is part of love.

"However, we have three 'no-no's' in The Friendship Force," he added: "No commercialism, no tourism and no partisan politics."

When the Geordies arrived at the airport to head home, Chip Carter, son of President and Mrs. Carter, was there to greet them and to bring a written message of farewell from his mother. It read: "I regret so much that I cannot be with you today as you return to Newcastle from my home state of Georgia. You are the pioneers of The Friendship Force and that makes you very valuable. I hope that the friendships you have made here and the friendships made by our people who are in England will now draw our countries even closer together. You have enriched our lives and our culture by coming here. Please return again and again."

The quest to make friends on the other side of many mountains had just begun.
(The Tetons, photo by Gene Bantekas used by permission.)

Chapter 4
Trial, Tribulation and Triumph

◆

*Most of our high and noble objectives are not reached unless there is
first a time of struggle...and pain. And sometimes you lose ground—a
lot of ground—before you ever get there.* —**Dr. Vernon S. Broyles**

Fueled by optimism generated by the first "wildly successful"
exchange, membership of the advisory council continued to grow. By
the end of 1977, the council included co-chairpersons Bert and LaBelle
Lance, world heavyweight boxing champion Muhammad Ali,
businessman Smith Bagley; developer Tom Cousins; actor Kirk
Douglas; resort owner Bunny Grossinger; philanthropist Armand
Hammer, US Senator Mark Hatfield; industrialist M.B. Seretean;
former West Virginia governor Hulett Smith and US Representative
Jim Wright. David Frost was also an early supporter who served
briefly as National Director for England. These high-profile
individuals had the duties of "advising the Board, promoting the
program, raising funds for its operation and providing visibility and
credibility at a high national and international level."

Wayne Smith used the first exchange as an opportunity to visit
contacts and officials in American embassies in Denmark, Germany,
Netherlands, Luxembourg, France, Italy, Switzerland, Spain and
Portugal.

J. Walter Drake, an Atlanta attorney, traveled to Ireland, England,
Germany, Denmark, Israel and Egypt on behalf of The Friendship
Force. His mission was to find individuals capable and willing to serve
as exchange leaders. Americo Ciuffardi of Atlanta (formerly of
Venezuela) traveled throughout South and Central America for the
same purpose. In 1977, Wade Seal went to Canada and Ron Condon,
on loan from Delta Airlines, traveled to Brazil while Tom Deardorff,
public information officer for The Friendship Force, visited Costa Rica
and Carolyn Clarke made still other development-oriented trips.
Concurrently, Clarke and assistants Marcia Dworetz and Doug
Jackson were spending much time with committee organization and
planning for the first exchanges.

State and national directors were charged with selecting exchange cities and flight directors within their area and to assist in fund-raising and promotion at state and national levels. Executive Wade Seal and his staff were responsible for "activation and pairing of exchange cities; aircraft charters; financial accounting; training of all state and national leaders; fund-raising support and response to public inquiries and other public relations."

World boxing champion Muhammad Ali and Wayne Smith greet people during the first exchange.

Only $22,000 in foundation grants was received during 1977 prompting The Friendship Force to hold a major 'gifts luncheon.' Although $200,000 was projected, only $10,000 was realized. Dr. Armand Hammer was later responsible for a private exhibit at the High Museum of Art in Atlanta and Muhammad Ali "challenged" local dignitaries to "get in the ring with me." The Ali event featured Atlanta's Public Safety Commissioner Reginald Eaves, sports announcer Skip Carey and Atlanta radio and television personalities Neal Boortz, Ron Sailor, Harmon Wages, Steve Somers and Jim Viondi. Hal Lamar of WAOK Radio was the Master of Ceremonies.

Much reliance was placed on the Ali bout, but it netted only $1,500 due to the heavy cost of promoting the event. However, some key benefits of these fund-raisers were good press coverage and more public recognition for The Friendship Force. As big financial successes, they were serious disappointments. Although Hammer's two-month exhibition of his collection entitled "Four Centuries of Masterpieces" opened at the High Museum with an exclusive reception for private patrons, including Rosalynn Carter as a special guest, The Friendship Force only netted $40,000.

In October, The Civil Aeronautics Board finally granted an important CAB waiver, allowing the organization to operate beyond the restrictions normally governing charters. The waiver was effective through December 1980; however, The Friendship Force was required to post a $200,000 bond to protect advance charter payments of US participants. They also had to enter into a contract with each ambassador and much paperwork had to be filed quarterly with the CAB. The paperwork was burdensome and the large bond was a tremendous and unexpected obstacle. Finally a number of supporters guaranteed the full amount, using letters of credit. These important backers were M.B. Seretean; Armand Hammer; Delta Airlines; Walter Wattles of Frank B. Hall Co.; board members Ralph Birdsong, Hulett Smith, Wayne Smith and John Wallace, plus Advisory Council member Bunny Grossinger.

Upon learning of the CAB waiver, travel agents in The United States became concerned that the organization would be allowed to compete unfairly with them. They cited the CAB waiver as an example of what they perceived to be special assistance from President Jimmy Carter. The Friendship Force withstood a series of mostly negative articles in *Travel Weekly* until Wayne Smith granted the magazine an interview. He explained the organization's goals, denied Carter's involvement in the waiver and explained why The Friendship Force was not a tourist organization.

At the close of 1977, Wade Seal and eight others on the organization's international headquarters staff shared a salary budget of $171,600, a modest payroll, considering all the organization had accomplished in the first ten-months. The Friendship Force had established volunteer organizations in forty-five states, four territories and the District of Columbia. They had also established volunteer organizations in countries around the world and had achieved high levels of public visibility and recognition in the United States. Three exchanges had been completed with great success: the Atlanta-Newcastle pilot exchange, Des Moines, Iowa-Dublin, Ireland and Caracas, Venezuela-Nashville, Tennessee. After the pilot exchange, destinations were not announced until the first workshop meeting prior to departure. The reason for the mystery was to prevent people from signing up only because of the low price of $250. The Friendship Force wanted only those committed to the idea of people-to-people diplomacy, regardless of the destination.

Funding had been secured to sustain operations for the year. The first National Conference of The Friendship Force was held in Washington and thirty-six State Directors attended training sessions during the conference. First Lady Rosalynn Carter hosted a White House reception for the attendees.

The Friendship Force applied for and received tax-exempt status from the Internal Revenue Service, certifying the organization as a non-profit organization. An international headquarters staff with appropriate skills to implement exchanges was in place.

"We have demonstrated our potential to achieve a long range goal of hundreds of exchanges per year involving hundreds of thousands of people around the world," Wayne Smith declared.

However, the lack of successful fund-raising soon led to grave concerns at Friendship Force headquarters. Instead of optimism, caution became the watchword. It became necessary to place on hold a much-needed computer system for flight administration designed by Arthur Andersen & Co. at a cost of $28,500.

The Force Fades

By March 1, 1978, financial problems threatened Smith's vision of world friendship, despite a successful fourth exchange involving Hartford and Tel Aviv with a record 850 persons traveling as ambassadors and 2,500 serving as hosts. Exchange number five between Harrisburg, Pennsylvania, and Mexico City, made a total of

3,414 people traveling as Friendship Force ambassadors and involving approximately 6,212 hosts. Nevertheless, the serious cash flow problem continued to build.

Wayne Smith lamented to the Board of Trustees, saying "We formally incorporated The Friendship Force on March 17, 1977. It is ironic that on March 17, 1978, we will be out of funds and faced with terminating The Friendship Force if a solution is not found."

Despite a positive cash flow of $115,000 generated on the five flights completed, the organization had been generally unsuccessful in appeals to fund-raising prospects. On April 3, 1978, Wayne Smith received a gloomy letter from Executive Director Wade Seal. The last paragraph concluded:

Wayne, you know that the staff and I have been totally dedicated to the success of The Friendship Force. It is with much sorrow that I come to the realization that this great program cannot continue to be expanded and shared with people of the world. But we must be responsible in dealing with the realities of our current situation. I need the concurrence and authorization of you, our Chairperson, and our Trustees to begin preparation of a termination plan, to be implemented on April 15, if we have not received the necessary funds.

Copies of Seal's letter were sent to Rosalynn Carter, Bert Lance, Hulett Smith and John Wallace. Two days later, John Wallace, legal counsel for the organization, sent a confidential memorandum to Wayne Smith and Rosalynn Carter. Wallace painted a bleak financial picture, indicating that only $25,000 remained in the bank against an unsecured bank debt of $150,000. An outstanding pledge of $50,000 had not yet been paid. In the aggregate, four flights scheduled for May should produce a profit, but summer flights would lose money, resulting in an overall deficit. Office overhead was fixed at $35,000 a month. Wallace concluded that "...if we are forced to wind-down the program, I believe we can do so and pay the bank most of what we owe."

One primary concern to Wallace and to Wayne Smith was that closing the doors of The Friendship Force would reflect badly on the Carter White House. As Wallace put it: "Our failure...would, at least in the short run, reflect badly on the Administration. There are many in the country who are eager to say that yet another project started by Georgians has failed because we do not know how to do things."

Upon receipt of Wallace's letter, Wayne Smith struggled mightily to come up with a plan that would rescue The Friendship Force. He wrote several drafts of a proposal to Rosalynn Carter. Those drafts, still in his files, poignantly reveal the struggle going on inside his mind. The crumpled state of the paper, heavy black marks through many words, crossed out sentences and paragraphs, illustrated how Smith grappled to find just the right phrase to convey his strong feelings. He listed strengths and weaknesses of the organization but came back to the same conclusion: The Friendship Force would not succeed without an immediate infusion of capital.

Smith concluded that the $250 fee, though very attractive, had basic drawbacks. Several times The Friendship Force management had found themselves in a very compromising position of forcing profitable flights to operate on schedule while canceling or delaying unprofitable flights. Only from the Eastern seaboard could flights to Europe break even and this sort of juggling did not contribute to the goals of The Friendship Force. It became apparent that something had to be done at the conclusion of the Hartford-Tel Aviv exchange. Due to the great distance between the cities, the exchange produced a loss of $43,000. The Friendship Force management anticipated this loss, but would not dishonor their commitment by canceling the exchange.

On April 28, 1978, a memorandum entitled Financial Condition/Richmond-Genoa Flight was sent to the board of trustees. Fees were already collected from 190 Genoa ambassadors ($48,545) and deposited in the Bank of America in Genoa. The bank was on strike and was unable to confirm to Bank of America US that the money was being held. The airline company demanded full payment of $64,687 that very day. Wade Seal, author of the earlier memorandum, stated that M.B. Seretean had agreed to loan $35,000, but that operating accounts and emergency payroll funds would have to be used to come up with the money due. After making the payment, The Friendship Force would be down to only $500 in its operating account. Seal also stated that the entire staff had been given a thirty-day notice. He told the employees that unless money came in soon, they should prepare themselves to become unemployed.

Furthermore, a payment for the Tacoma-Olympia/Seoul upcoming exchange would be due on May 1st. After paying funds collected to date, The Friendship Force bank account would still be short $73,185.76. Seal placed the responsibility for the cash shortages on recruitment problems and slow remittance by The Friendship Force's foreign committees.

In the first week of May, headlines in the Atlanta newspapers declared: " Friendship Force Fades" and "The Force' Still With Them As Friendship Force Staff Departs." When the telephone rang at headquarters, the caller heard, "I'm sorry, but The Friendship Force is phasing down its national operations. Most of us are...leaving today, so you'll have to get here before five p.m.

The Light Still Shines!

But The Friendship Force was simply too dear to its architects to let it die without a fight and the press had not yet realized that the one thing most abhorrent to Rosalynn Carter was defeat. For this strong woman, defeat was not an acceptable alternative. She decided that The Friendship Force was far too important to discontinue its mission. She telephoned Wayne Smith, telling him the organization must go on. Smith jubilantly called Billie Cheney Speed, an editor at The Atlanta Journal-Constitution.

"Our leader says the sun will shine," he told her. "The First Lady promised to help open some private financial doors for the program and she has suggestions for a new, less expensive method of operation. We're going to continue," he declared firmly.

The next day the headlines changed from sad news to: "First Lady Helps Friendship Force Avert Shutdown." The office remained open.

Rosalynn Carter then asked financial consultants for the Rockefeller Brothers Fund to review The Friendship Force operations and to propose a reorganization. In late July, a very favorable report was presented to The Friendship Force Board of Trustees and Mrs. Carter by Bill Moody and Stephen Rhinesmith. These analysts felt that The Friendship Force could survive under the guidelines they presented. The reorganization plan was adopted. Mrs. Carter pledged to continue her role and to ask Paul Austin, President of Coca Cola, to raise enough money to allow The Friendship Force to reinstate five exchanges in the fall. Induction fees were raised to $300 and Stan Humphries replaced Wade Seal as Executive Director. Seal remained as a volunteer consultant.

Exchanges continued on schedule and glowing reports began to come in to Friendship Force headquarters.

In 1977, Marijane Brown of Washington state saw a small advertisement regarding a new organization called The Friendship Force. Marijane responded with an inquiry for more information and received a letter of invitation to a meeting in Olympia, Washington, at the Governor's mansion. Marijane invited Eleanor Van Tilburg, her best friend, to accompany her.

Years later, Marijane and Eleanor explained what happened next. "I agreed to go because the meeting was at the Governor's mansion," Eleanor frankly admitted. "The State Director was Marion Reid, sister of our Governor Dixy Lee Ray. Well, after that meeting, we both became very enthusiastic about the 'mystery trip' Mrs. Reid told us about that day. "

"Eleanor volunteered to compile a demographic study of her area, a required task to be completed before we received applications," Marijane said. "The idea was to send ambassadors who represented a broad range of vocations and walks of life. I think my husband Hal and I were chosen because we were farmers as well as teachers."

Marijane Brown became the applications and hosts director for the first exchange. The participants only knew that a reciprocal exchange was planned involving 250 ambassadors from Washington state and they would be paired with hosts in an unknown country. American hosts would be arranged to receive the same number of ambassadors traveling from the unknown country. Applications poured in and it was finally time for the first orientation meeting.

Eleanor said, "It was amazing to us that people would sign up to go somewhere although they did not know where they were going until the first meeting. We met at a hotel and both hosts and ambassadors were there, a total of over four hundred people. The suspense was terrific. Finally everyone was seated and the room became quiet.

"Three people bearing flags walked slowly and stately down the aisle. One carried our state flag, one carried the American flag and another carried the flag of the 'mystery' country. Finally, an envelope was opened and this brief message from Rosalynn Carter was read: 'Greetings!' I am pleased to announce that your destination will be...Korea!'"

Dr. Wayne Van Tilburg later recalled the response. "Everyone was so excited and happy. We were cheering and laughing and hugging each other—all except one. Lyle Bowers was there with his wife Kaye and he was very unhappy. 'I'm not going to Korea and there's no way anyone can persuade me to go to there,' he said firmly. 'I spent my time there in the Korean War and I didn't like it then and I'm NOT going now.'

"Kaye was devastated," Dr. Van Tilburg said. "She tried to change his mind and we all talked to him. It took several days of persuasion before he finally said, 'All right. I'll go, but I'm NOT going to get involved. I'll go, but just for Kaye's sake.'"

Several workshops were held before the Washington ambassadors departed. Marijane Brown took a practical approach to educate herself and her fellow ambassadors. "I went to an Oriental market in town and asked the grocer if he was Korean. Fortunately, he was President of the Korean Society in Vancouver. I asked him if he could help us by speaking about his country at a workshop meeting. He said he would do better and he arranged for the Korean Society members to cook a typical meal for us.

"They cooked all one Friday night and all day Saturday getting ready for our evening dinner meeting. They came dressed in beautiful native costumes and there were more Koreans than Americans at the dinner. They served a wonderful and elaborate meal. They also graciously offered advice and answered our many questions. I have since gotten to know these kind people very well and I visited several of their families in Korea when I went on my second exchange."

In June 1978, the group left for Seoul. The Van Tilburgs traveled with their fourteen-year-old daughter Jennifer. Eleanor Van Tilburg said, "Wayne and I decided from the start that if we were going to be involved, our four children should be involved, too.

"After the months of planning, you can't imagine how excited we felt to finally be in Seoul. It was like a dream come true. Our hosts, Mr. and Mrs. Kim, met us with their son Kangki, who served as our guide and interpreter during the visit. They were lovely people with a great sense of humor.

Marijane Brown added, "When we landed, there were three brothers in our host family who met us and took us first to a hotel to take a shower and a nap, a wonderful courtesy after a flight of more than twelve hours. After we rested, we met them for lunch. Ten minutes after we met, one brother taught me two essential phrases in Korean: 'I love you' and 'Cheers.' He assured me that these few words were all I really needed to know. It was during that first meeting that my husband Hal and I gave this cheerful smiling Korean brother his nickname. We called him 'Jolly Boy,' a name he liked very much."

The days sped by happily until right before the exchange ended. About seventy ambassadors were suddenly stricken with a virus, accompanied by diarrhea, nausea and vomiting. Dr. Van Tilburg said, "The media learned about the illness back in the states and headlines screamed **MYSTERY VIRUS HITS KOREAN TOUR.** The virus was over long before the dramatic media coverage ended. Most were well by the time the plane landed in Seattle; however, epidemiologists were there to greet us and to examine the sick."

To the astonishment of everyone, including his wife, Lyle Bowers had the time of his life with his new Korean friends and he came home filled with great enthusiasm for The Friendship Force. "He could scarcely wait until their Korean hosts could visit them," Eleanor Van Tilburg said. Her husband added: "Lyle was probably the biggest convert to The Friendship Force philosophy that I've ever seen. And his hosts couldn't even speak English!"

In September, 1978, Hanyang University in Seoul, Korea, bestowed an honorary doctorate degree on Wayne Smith for "life-long devotion to the religious mission and to the advancement of human welfare, and particularly his outstanding contributions in promoting friendly relations between the Republic of Korea and the United States of America."

Later in September, an elated Stan Humphries startled the staff at Friendship Force International by rushing around shouting: "Glory Hallelujah! The Coke machine is working! We just received gifts totaling $22,500 through Paul Austin's contacts with corporations."

If Stan Humphries was excited, Wayne Smith was ecstatic. And by the end of 1978, 10,948 ambassadors had visited in host homes in 12 countries. It was estimated that total new friendships exceeded 36,568. And news headlines echoed the joy, proclaiming: "Friendship Force is Alive and Well."

Christa Jamka, a twenty-seven year old teacher from West Berlin, stared at President Jimmy Carter in disbelief as he strode into the huge chartered jetliner which had just touched down at Dulles International Airport outside of Washington, DC

"Hello folks! Welcome to the United States," Carter said, flashing his well-known grin as he and the First Lady moved down the narrow aisle of the plane, shaking hands with everyone aboard.

It was election night, 1978, and neither Christa nor any of the other 253 West Berliners who had just arrived as Friendship Force ambassadors had expected such a welcome to American soil.

Wayne Smith said, "This gesture by the Carters showed their dedication to and support of The Friendship Force, which they helped launch two years ago.

Chapter 5
The Vision Expands

◆

For without understanding there can be no friends in an uncertain and perilous world.
—**George V. Allen**, former US Assistant Secretary of State for near Eastern and African Affairs.

On January 1, 1979, Wayne Smith resigned as pastor of the Decatur Presbyterian Church to assume full-time responsibilities as president and chief executive officer of The Friendship Force. It was a decision to which Smith had given much thought. "I finally realized that...from this point on, my life's work would be The Friendship Force," he said.

True to his word, Wayne Smith threw his considerable energy into promoting the idea that The Friendship Force is simply a means for ordinary citizens to help bridge the great divides of race, religion, culture, politics and class—divides which cannot be bridged by diplomats who meet across a conference table in a political setting without ever really knowing each other's countrymen. Smith maintained that ordinary people, living in the homes of citizens of other countries and getting to know them around kitchen tables, can find common ground on which to build lasting friendships. "We're more alike than we are different," he said. "And if enough people around the world become friends, we can bridge the huge chasms which divide us, one friendship at a time."

The Friendship Force was ready to expand and one of the first steps was to increase development in over a dozen countries, especially in the United Kingdom, West Germany and Korea. The board of directors was expanded, as was the international advisory council. When the board met in the first quarter of 1979, they approved a maximum of twenty-seven exchanges for the year.

A flight directors' manual was prepared and mailed to exchange leaders. The manual laid out descriptions of duties for each subcommittee involved in an exchange. Much had been learned from the three exchanges in 1977, and sixteen more in 1978. Staffers at

Friendship Force International were well aware that more training and planning was needed and in February of 1979, a small conference to achieve this end was held at the Atlanta offices. Representatives from Scotland, England, Venezuela and Salt Lake City met to plan their exchanges.

Wayne Smith and the board of directors were keenly mindful of the debts owed by The Friendship Force and were able to reduce by half the indebtedness to Trust Company Bank.. All current expenses were paid and other obligations held over from the 1977 deficit and a bank loan guaranteed by the Armand Hammer Foundation were rescheduled to be repaid over three years.

Wayne Smith continued to rack up air miles as he knocked on doors in many countries, including, Guatemala, Costa Rica, Germany, Dublin, France, Italy, Switzerland and Denmark, where he worked to gain landing rights. But Smith was not content to knock on friendly doors alone. His sights were higher and his intentions bolder and in

Wayne Smith explains another idea. Georgia's Lt. Governor Zell Miller (later Governor) is seated at the head of the table.

32

June, Smith traveled to Beirut, Lebanon, to introduce The Friendship Force to Palestine Liberation Organization Chairman Yasser Arafat.

Years later, Wayne and Carolyn Smith told of that unlikely meeting.

"Just before I resigned as pastor of the Decatur Presbyterian Church," Wayne said, "I got a call from Yussef al-Bandak who told me he was a Palestinian Christian visiting Atlanta and would like to see me.

"I'll see anyone, so I told him to come over. He came and began to tell me of the plight of his people. He explained that he was born in Bethlehem and was descended from a long line of Christians. He knew of my friendship with the Carters and he asked me to travel to Lebanon to meet the Chairman of the PLO, Yasser Arafat. He also wanted me to acquaint myself personally with the plight of the Palestinians and then return to report what I saw—good, bad or indifferent—to the President. He told me he was authorized to make this offer by Yasser Arafat and that my wife was also invited.

"Now Beirut was a powder keg in those days, but it was still possible for Americans to visit the city; although it was very, very difficult to do so. I didn't accept Yussef al-Bandek's offer but I promised I would at least think about it.

"I thought it over and prayed about it. I also talked it over with Carolyn. Finally, I phoned Mr. al-Bandek and told him I could not promise that I would talk to President Carter about this, but if his leader wanted to take the time to arrange for me to see the situation for my own edification, then Carolyn and I would make the trip. You see, because of The Friendship Force, I wanted to encourage friendship with all people throughout the world, even in a land as strife-torn as Lebanon."

The Smiths left Atlanta in June 1979, at the invitation and expense of the Government of Palestine. First they flew to Greece where they easily obtained a ticket to Beirut. Carolyn Smith recalled that once they were at the gate, things changed.

"We were told that since we had no visa, it would be impossible for us to go to Beirut because we would not be allowed to enter the country. I couldn't believe it, but Wayne finally convinced the officials at the airport that he was expected in Beirut. First they called in a Palestinian official who worked there and Wayne met with him. The official ultimately became convinced that we actually had business in

Beirut, so he cleared us through. We both knew things were bad in Lebanon, but neither of us realized just how bad," Carolyn said.

"When we landed, I was shocked to see the bombed out Beirut Airport terminal. In the distance we could hear gunfire and explosions. It was just like being in a war movie, except the firepower was coming from very real weapons of destruction. But you know Wayne," she sighed. "He does not take danger seriously."

They were met at the airport by Yussef al Bandak and an assistant named Mustafa. Although they had no visa to enter Lebanon, they were cleared though rapidly and were driven to the Beirut International Hotel in a black Mercedes with dark tinted bulletproof windows. Carolyn said, "Our hotel was on what was once a beautiful beach. However, we were warned not to go out on the balcony outside our room. We were also told never to leave the hotel for any reason unless they escorted us. As if to accent this grim warning, the sounds of warfare in the distance seemed to grow stronger."

Nevertheless, the Smiths' first act was to go directly to the United States ambassador's office to pay a call on John Gunther Dean. Dean had formerly served as US Ambassador to Denmark when The Friendship Force exchange between Copenhagen and Westchester County, New York, occurred. Ambassador Dean was well acquainted with The Friendship Force and upon learning of Wayne Smith's plan for an exchange between Beirut and St. Louis, he explained that, while he favored such an exchange, there were many difficulties.

"First of all, you must realize that the United States government does not recognize Palestine as a government," Dean said. "However, the Palestine Liberation Organization (PLO) is recognized officially by the UN and over one hundred countries throughout the world as the legitimate governmental representative of the Palestinian people and the PLO was given official observer status by the UN in 1974."

The ambassador also told Smith that visas would be granted to Palestinians provided they were not members of any official Palestinian organization. Such Palestinians could visit America only on a travel card issued by the government of Lebanon.

The second concern of Ambassador Dean was more serious. "Security for visiting Americans cannot be guaranteed in Beirut," he warned. "The real problem is Beirut itself," he added. "It is torn by strife and Christians and Muslims are still fighting in spite of intervention by the Syrians who are attempting to maintain order in the city. If any exchange takes place, the PLO must agree to take full responsibility for the safety of the Americans.

"As for the PLO, it transferred its headquarters to Lebanon in 1970, after being expelled from Jordan. As you have seen, much of Lebanon is in ruins. The war between Muslims and Christians which began in 1975 killed sixty thousand Lebanese in two years. Killing goes on here on a daily basis. You see, we have the Maronite Christians, Sunnite and Shi'ite Muslims, Greek Orthodox and Armenian Catholics, and Druze and Greek Orthodox. Most Lebanese are Arabs and Palestinians make up only ten percent of the population. None of the religious groups trusts the others," Dean sighed. "Perhaps Jordan might be a better place for an exchange," he advised.

At the conclusion of the Smiths' courtesy call, Ambassador Dean insisted that they be driven around in the Embassy car, which was said to be bullet proof. It was quickly pointed out that it was, too, because there was a mark on the back screen where a bullet had made a dent, but had been deflected.

"The next day we traveled from our hotel to the Presidential Palace on the other side of town to call on President Elias Sarkis," Smith said. "This meeting was arranged by Ambassador Dean. As we traveled through the bustling city, we soon discovered that confusion reigned. We were stopped at six different checkpoints by six different factions just on this one trip across town. Instead of going the direct route to the Presidential Palace, which would have taken about fifteen minutes, the driver took us on a winding route that took over an hour," Smith said.

"We soon realized that it was difficult to tell who—if anyone—was really in charge, but it was obvious that all the factions were actively vying for power. It was absolutely chaotic."

This chaos Smith described began after the civil war broke out in 1975. The center of Lebanon was carved up into a checkerboard of fiefdoms and private armies, each with ideas about who was right and who should be eliminated.

"We finally arrived and were received by President Sarkis," Smith said. "I told him about The Friendship Force and of our desire to have an exchange between his people and people in the United States. I asked if it would be possible to accomplish this by a chartered plane. (Sarkis was a Christian, but there were several different Christian groups in the city.) He was perplexed by my proposition. He remained silent for several minutes before he said, 'Do you want an exchange with the Lebanese or do you want it with Palestinians or do you just want it with people who live in Lebanon? We have all of these possibilities.'"

Before Smith could answer, the glass windows started shaking and the walls trembled. The Smiths feared it was an earthquake, but Sarkis didn't seem alarmed. When the shaking stopped, he pointed skyward, sighed and said, "Our friends, the Israelis." Only then did the Americans realize that the tremor was the result of sonic booms from Israeli jets.

Wayne Smith continued, "After collecting my thoughts once more, I told President Sarkis that we wanted the exchange with people who live in Lebanon and that we did not care about their background, religious preference or otherwise. I explained that our goal was to initiate friendship with people everywhere.

"Well, we can do that," Sarkis answered, "but it may be difficult to include any Palestinians together with the citizens of Lebanon."

The Smiths spent the next three days in Beirut, observing a clamorous mix of modern and ancient—automobiles and camels, the call to prayer for the faithful and jackals howling in the hills. "But the city was mostly a series of bombed out buildings," Carolyn Smith recalled. "Everything was awfully 'cloak and dagger.'"

Arafat soon sent escorts to guide them, making certain they saw hospitals, orphanages and bomb sites. Some months later, Wayne Smith saw these same sights in Israel where he was informed of the death toll of innocent Israeli civilians. Both sides suffered and both hated the effects of these conflicts. Unfortunately, they seemed to hate each other even more. At times Wayne Smith, the eternal optimist, doubted that peace would ever come to such a confused and troubled land.

Nevertheless, he still believed that The Friendship Force could continue to put people together and then, with hope and prayer, they would realize that love is stronger than hate and that friendship is a form of love. Smith says "Although there is within the human heart a tendency to self-destruct, there is a stronger power and that's the power of love. That's what we're counting on to happen through The Friendship Force and its exchanges."

Finally, the Smiths were told that Chairman Arafat would see them.. About three in the afternoon, his assistants came for them at the hotel and took them to a nondescript apartment building. They had already learned that Yasser Arafat circulated from place to place and that he was not always in Beirut. In fact, he rarely stayed in one place

36

more than several hours. Since he could not afford to settle down anywhere in treacherous Beirut, Arafat was hosted in various apartments all around the country as he moved from place to place each day.

"We entered a modestly furnished suite, one where ordinary people might live," Smith recalled. "Present were several maids and three or four women who were cooking and serving. There were also Arafat's assistants, the Chairman himself and Carolyn and me.

The Smiths could scarcely believe they were face to face with this slightly pop-eyed, paunchy man who always wore a Palestinian headdress and was perpetually in need of a shave. Despite his five-feet, four-inch height, this man, called *Al-Khityar*—"the Old Man"—by his followers, was instantly charming and exuded confidence and charisma.

"He had beautiful eyes," Carolyn said. "They were both lively and sad at the same time."

Arafat invited the Smiths to talk during a meal.

"The meal was served and what a feast it was!" Smith exclaimed. "Course after course, unhurried, with plenty of time to talk. Chairman Arafat spoke English very well and the conversation never lagged. Looking back on it now, I marvel that Yasser Arafat, then thought of by many as just another terrorist, has recently won the Nobel Peace Prize! However, his transition from guerrilla to peacemaker has not been easy.

"We talked and talked and quickly established a rapport. It was evident that we sincerely liked each other as people. I told him that he was not at all like he was often portrayed.

"'And how is that?' he asked.

"Well," I said, "like the kind of monster who eats a baby for breakfast every morning. He found that portrayal to be so ridiculous as to be amusing and he laughed out loud."

"How can I change this image?" Arafat asked.

"I told him he might began by shaving now and then and that I would send him an electric razor if he wished. We were to a point where I could be that frank with him.

"He only laughed again and refused the offer."

"I like the way I look," Arafat declared.

"Over all, Carolyn and I found Yasser Arafat to be very intelligent and very personable," Smith said. "He had a sparkle in his eye and an eagerness to hear my ideas about friendship world wide. You see, he was elected President of the Palestinians by the *Diaspora*. Back in 1948 when the United Nations decreed the creation of the state of

Israel, the Palestinians stood back because they didn't have any weapons to join with the other Arab countries who vowed to 'throw the Jews back into the sea.' Of course, when the Palestinians left their homes to escape the war with Israel, they found that they could not return after Israel prevailed. *Diaspora* is Greek for "those dispersed," so Arafat was elected by his people—dispersed people who no longer occupy the land they call Palestine. This situation has continued to create a real danger and the fear has remained that an Arab-Israeli conflict could trigger another global war. So we talked about these things and I found Arafat's comments to be both moderate and reasonable. Of course, we were just talking as two men...not in any international forum and Arafat wished to make a good impression

"We must find a way to live with Israel and they must find a way to live with us," Arafat stated. "'But we are a proud people. Yes, we did give up our land when we left and Israel won the war. We admit it. They won. Nevertheless, what are we to do? We are people without a land. We need a spot where we can say we have our government and where we can issue our own passports - like you're talking about in The Friendship Force."

Smith asked Arafat just where he thought that spot would be.

"Well, How about Bethlehem?" he responded. "It's an Arab city, basically. Or Jericho? There's land enough for us all. And we must get along somehow. You see, the defeat of Egypt, Syria and Jordan in the war with Israel in 1967, opened this period of disunity. It is difficult for the West to understand the great need of an uprooted urban population such as ours to have our own place in this region."

"We talked on like that for a long time," said Smith. "Arafat never asked me to plead his case to Jimmy Carter when I went back to the United States. It is interesting that since that day, Carter has met with Arafat. If Carter had been elected to a second term, perhaps there would have been another Camp David Accord, this time regarding the Palestinian question.

"I will never forget the last conversation with Yasser Arafat," Smith said. "It came at the end of our long meal. It was time for coffee. Arafat gave an eye signal and the coffee appeared. With another eye signal one of his aides brought me a lovely mother of pearl case containing a Bible, complete with Old and New Testament. There was a mother-of-pearl cross on top.

"Mr. Chairman, I said, it is wonderful that you've met with me and let me see what your people are like. You've hosted me at a magnificent dinner. Now you've honored me by giving me this gift, a gift that any Christian would cherish. But I'm very embarrassed that I have no gift for you. However, I was in Japan a few months ago and they've got a new product on the market. It's something called a digital wrist watch and it has all kind of interesting features. I see that you're not wearing a watch, I said as I removed my watch. Here, Mr. Chairman. Although this watch is used, it has been used for only a short time and only by me. Will you please take this watch and put it on your left wrist. Your left arm is the one closest to your heart and when you look at that watch in the future, please recognize that there is someone in America who knows that the time for justice and peace is NOW and that that person is praying for you.

"Arafat received my watch as if it were a ton of platinum. He put it on his wrist and called everyone—the women, his aides—and he said 'Look, look what my brother Wayne has given me! You have touched my heart,' he said to me. Then he said, 'Let's have another coffee.'

"After a few moments, he turned to me and said, 'You know, brother Wayne, you should have a watch. I see you're not wearing one.' One of his servants immediately came to me with boxes of very expensive watches—Rolexes, Piagets, all kind of expensive brands. He said, 'Please! Take any or all of these. Although they are costly, none of these are more precious than the watch I'm now wearing.'

"Well, when Arafat saw the look on my face he knew that I could not—and would not—take one of those watches. Arafat hesitated. Then he sighed and said, 'I really ought not to do it, but I will. You see, a very dear friend of mine gave me *this* watch, the one I'm wearing now. He took it off and said, 'If you would like to have the most precious watch of all, take this one and put it on the wrist of the left arm, the one closest to your heart. Look at it from time to time and think when you see it that the time for justice and peace has come for the Palestinians, for the Israelis, for the Americans.

"As Wayne took back his watch, Arafat said, "And know that someone here who is not of your faith, but who believes in God, is praying for you.""

Crossroads

While the Smiths were waiting for the plane to take them back to the United States, Wayne Smith was pensive. He recorded his thoughts as follows:

"As things look at this writing, I am uncertain about what should be done concerning an exchange with the people of Palestine. I think we should proceed one step at a time. If a potential flight director could be found, I think he should come to Atlanta where we can continue...conversation. I must check with some of the Friendship Force directors and with the US State Department.

"I believe The Friendship Force stands at a crossroads: we can either decide to set exchanges which have some danger—both physical or political—attached to them, or we can continue to build exchanges, as safely as possible, in places where there already is a good deal of friendship and understanding. The taking of the first option could mean the end of The Friendship Force. To take the second option exclusively could mean The Friendship Force will gradually be diluted into a glorified travel club."

In 1979, others traveling on behalf of The Friendship Force to cultivate new exchange opportunities were Stan Humphries who went to Mexico City and Inger Rice, State Director of Virginia, who met with Imelda Marcos in the Philippines. The exchange specialists at Friendship Force International in Atlanta were also busy. Marcia Dworetz, Howard Chadwick and Kathleen Eagen were planning on-site training in procedures so that new leaders would know how best to motivate others to participate in Friendship Force exchanges. Rita Trivellato was working along the same lines in Italy.

Alan Redhead of England was hired as an Associate Director of Development and he was charged with training, scheduling and recruiting in the United Kingdom and Ireland.

There were still problems to face, but now the Friendship Force International staff had assistance from fifty volunteers coordinated by Betty Hull. There were eleven employees. Beverlie Reilman became executive assistant to Wayne Smith, with responsibility for program plans and written materials. Bobbie Jones succeeded Reilman as exchange coordinator.

In spite of a firm mandate from headquarters limiting purchases to one hundred dollars per person per exchange, the return baggage grew with each exchange. The mandate, designed to prevent Friendship Force exchanges from becoming tourist trips or shopping excursions, continued to be ignored by some and one group arrived at the airport with overweight baggage of four thousand pounds.

Flight coordinators' reports contained minor complaints, but they were insignificant when compared to the friendships made and the barriers bridged. Perhaps no one wrote more movingly of what was already called "The Friendship Force magic" than did Sally Friedman who traveled with her family to Piacenza, Italy. Her article "To Piacenza, With Love" appeared in the October 1979, issue of *South*

Jersey Monthly It merits repeating because Friedman's piece captured perfectly the essence of The Friendship Force ideals.

To Piacenza, With Love

By Sally Friedman

I watch my husband—my reserved, proper American husband—as he embraces another man in farewell.

I watch my daughters openly weeping as they cling to their "mama" in a village square on another continent in the early dawn light.

And the tears are rolling down my cheeks too, because none of us is quite ready to say good-bye. None of us is willing to let go of this extraordinary experience that has carried us halfway around the world to a little town in Italy called Piacenza.

And now I think back to how it all began....

The first notices appeared in the local papers during the chilly winter of early 1979. For those of us who read them with more than passing interest, the brief releases were intriguing. An organization that called itself "The Friendship Force" was seeking 250 residents of Camden and Burlington counties to participate in an exchange visit with an unnamed foreign country. Interested candidates were invited to attend a meeting in Cherry Hill.

We went to that first meeting. We sat fascinated as Sidney Z. Daroff, A business executive and volunteer chairman of The Friendship Force for South New Jersey, outlined the program. And by the time he was finished, we were hooked.

The Friendship Force made sense to us. It is a program based on the belief that international diplomacy begins with people—not career diplomats or statesmen, but printers and plumbers, lawyers and laborers. It allows them to come together, not in the hushed halls of lavish embassies, but in each other's homes.

And now it was South Jersey's turn to join The Friendship Force, and the five Friedmans—one father, three daughters and one slightly apprehensive mother—were going to get a unique opportunity to try their hands at statesmanship, family-style!

When you join The Friendship Force, you agree to go wherever you are sent, but you don't know where that will be until long after you have signed on the doted line and paid the required $370 per person.

You also began to beat the bushes for American host families who will take part in the exchange in a different but equally vital way. You seek those friends and neighbors who will open their homes and hearts to a planeload of foreign visitors arriving from the country you are visiting just as you are deplaning there.

We learned a lot about human nature during that search for host families. We learned that few people are eager to extend themselves when they think they are getting nothing in return. "Why should I?" our friends and neighbors demanded to know. And our answer—for the sake of international friendships—didn't move too many.

In the end, however, the right number of ambassadors and the right number of host families somehow, miraculously, surfaced.

In the end, the best side of human nature came shining forth as South Jersey prepared to launch its very first Friendship Force exchange.

The room was absolutely silent.

"You are being sent to...ITALY! announced Sid Daroff on an April evening, and pandemonium shook the rafters.

The geographical guessing game was over, and everyone was a winner. Italy—at last it was real. Italy—land of gondolas, golden wines, *la dolce vita!*

This was the night we first heard of a town called Piacenza. It was a name we would come to know intimately in the ensuing weeks and months.

Piacenza is a town the size of Camden and is in the Po Valley of Italy. While it has its share of castles and cathedrals, it is not a tourist city, particularly in late July, when the temperature soars and the humidity matches that of the steamy Delaware Valley.

But Piacenza is a town where people live and work and dream their dreams, a town eager to reach out to Americans from South Jersey who do the same.

As our orientation sessions began, we learned that Piacenzans were as likely to speak English as people in Cinnaminson were to speak fluent Italian.

Communism, we were told, was spreading throughout Italy, and Piacenza was not exempt from its influence. There was political unrest. There was a general ambiguity about the political future of small towns in Italy like Piacenza, and an urgent need to dispel the "ugly American" image in the place where we were to live as ambassadors for five summer days.

Hurdling the language barrier was the first challenge, and we tackled it through the early summer weeks, 254 Americans struggling with words and phrases that did NOT pour trippingly from our Yankee tongues. *Buon Giorno* (good morning) we intoned, at night sessions at Cinnaminson High School conducted by teacher and tour guide Nick

Pascale. *Sono molto lieto de fare la sua conoscenza* (I am very pleased to meet you) rang out in the empty school building.

"Practice—practice—practice!" urged Pascale. "You'll please your Italian hosts if you can say something in their language." So practice we did.

Invited lecturers spoke to ambassadors and to hosts about the Italian culture, of the country's rich history, of the Italian passion for music. Members of the Haddonfield Symphony and Chorale tuned up for their scheduled presentation in Piacenza as part of the cultural exchange.

Questions about how to dress and how not to, what to bring our Italian hosts as gifts and even the subtle differences in toilet facilities were fielded in those sessions. South Jersey was gearing to meet Piacenza head-on!

With it all—the briefings, the language lessons, the tips on tipping and the lore of current Italian folk heroes—254 Americans grew very silent as our charter plane dipped into the Milan airport on a steamy July night. Last minute linguists practiced words of greeting and phrase books peeked out of every pocket.

"I'm scared," 12-year-old Nancy whispered to me as we made our way through the mob scene at the Milan airport. And so were people much taller and older than Nancy as we gathered around Nick Pascale like lost children waiting to be claimed.

In our tour guide's hands was the list of names linking host families and ambassadors. "Jill and Amy Friedman," called out Pascale. I felt a momentary pang of maternal anxiety. Our family of five would not be housed together. Our two teenage daughters were on their own, while Nancy would remain with us.

There was a frantic reshuffling of family suitcases, then a scurry to find the right buses, buses that would deliver us to Piacenza and the unknown.

She sat at the front of Bus Number One on the ride from the Milan airport to town. It was my husband who stumbled on the fact that this Italian bus escort—this graceful, beautiful, smiling young woman—was to be our Piacenza hostess.

On that hour-long ride from Milan to Piacenza, our contact with Nadia Lavony began. All we could glean then was that her own husband was on a plane heading for America as part of the exchange—that she spoke little English—and that she seemed truly delighted that we were to be her guests. When she leaned over on that bumpy bus to kiss sleeping Nancy on each cheek, I knew we were going to make it!

Piacenza. Midnight. Suddenly, magically, a tiny town square an ocean away from home is filled with cheering, waving, laughing people holding American flags. They swarm around us in joyful welcome as we step down from our buses.

No Friendship Force ambassador will ever forget that night or that sight. None of us will ever forget the feelings that came flooding over us on that extraordinary evening when, after all the weeks and months of planning and worrying and waiting, The Friendship Force Exchange had truly begun!

In the mad scramble to unite guest and host which followed, a tall blond woman studied the number that Jill and Amy clutched. In a sudden wave of recognition, Marilena Ferrari was suddenly hugging our daughters, introducing her husband and children to us all, and gathering up their suitcases.

Perhaps she saw the look on my face as she began to lead them away. Perhaps she understood what I was feeling. But without a word being spoken, Marilena Ferrari took my hand and held it for a long moment in reassurance and friendship. "I will take care of them," that gesture promised. And the universal language of motherhood told me that she would.

That first night is now a blur, filtered through layers of time, but some things remain vivid.

Jill and Amy were gone. Last minute changes and crises in guest placements had delayed our departure for hours. But finally, sometime between two and four in the morning, Nadia Lavony escorted us through darkened streets to our Piacenza home.

We were prepared for anything—a tiny farm, a crowded house, an humble flat. We were NOT prepared for Nadia's luxury apartment, in a magnificent high-rise on the outskirts of Piacenza!

Polished marble floors—handsome paintings—rich furnishings greeted us, as Signora Lavony flung open the door. In our fatigue, it seemed a palace—but a palace without air conditioning. That first night, we were to learn that even the height of luxury in Piacenza does not come packaged in cool air.

We were to learn, too, that Italian street life and sounds begin early, and never quite stop. And we were destined to become quick studies in how to sleep through heat and laughter and the roar of motorcycles....

Our first Italian breakfast was served up in Nadia's tiny kitchen. No cereal. No pancakes. No eggs, just marvelously rich, dark coffee (one-half cup), rolls, and the pleasure of our hostess' company.

Nadia Lavony is a 34-year old civil servant married to a sweater manufacturer. At first glance, one might mistake her for a glamorous, sophisticated American woman. But one would be very wrong. Through Nadia, we were to glimpse the enormous charm and grace and gentility of a Piacenzan lady, in every sense of those words.

Haltingly, the communication began. We learned that, despite the appearance of great wealth in the Lavony apartment and life style, inflation in Italy necessitates her going out daily to her job in City Hall. And a strong need for independence makes that job important to Nadia.

"I need —how you say—be my own lady," Nadia told me one day, after we had swapped views on everything from American fashion (way behind Italian) to women's liberation (alive and well in Italy). "I do not want Enrico for all things...."

Like many women in Italy, Nadia Lavony walks a delicate tightrope in her daily life, balancing ancient tradition with a very contemporary outlook. She is home each day to prepare Enrico's main meal, the meal enjoyed traditionally in Italy at two in the afternoon. But she is also fiercely independent, determined to keep her job, and used to traveling to foreign places without her husband.

Despite her sophistication, Nadia Lavony is tradition-bound in her sense of obligation to home and hearth. She runs an immaculate and gracious home with no servants, and takes obvious pride in her gleaming floors and glowing furniture. Magnificent meals appeared magically, daily, from a tiny preparation area no American suburban woman would settle for. Those meals were an integral part of Nadia's culture, and our Piacenza experience.

Dinner—served at midday—was far more than a meal: It was an event, orchestrated not just by abundant food, but by fine china, gleaming crystal, and the ever-flowing wines that changed with each course. Most of all, that meal was a coming together time, as guests filled Nadia's table each day to share food, merriment, and the iron-bound tradition of a midday respite from worldly cares.

After several days of being literally wined and dined, we were convinced that the Lavonys' economic circumstances made this graceful event possible. Surely less-privileged Italian families did not stop everything in midday to head home for four-hour feasts and siestas. Most people probably just grabbed a bite on the run....

How wrong we were!

At the Ferrari flat, where Jill and Amy were housed a bit less lavishly than their parents and sister, the real differences in life-style were minimal.

Emilio Ferrari, a handsome Piacenza police officer recently promoted from traffic patrol to a more prestigious desk job, worked only mornings. His vivacious wife, Marilena, a hospital recreation aide, worked different hours. Emilio and Marilena are clearly part of Piacenza's middle—not leisure class.

But if a child's toy or sneaker occasionally decorated a chair at the Ferraris,' there was still a grace and gentility about their way of life that deeply impressed two American teenagers from Moorestown. Jill and Amy, along with the two young Ferrari children (Barbara, 12 and Vincenzo, 9), were caught up in a family life that invited warmth and openness, yes—but one which also dictated a greater distance and formality between parent and child.

The midday meal that we enjoyed with Nadia was duplicated at the Ferraris.' One significant difference was the language spoken at that meal. The Ferraris, unlike Nadia, knew no English. Our daughters were plunged into lively exchanges in Italian, and—miracle of miracles—they found themselves speaking the language in very short order!

In the evening, Italian youngsters gathered, not at malls or movies, but on the street. Jill and Amy joined them, and it was at those nocturnal gatherings that our daughters learned the greatest lesson of their trip: kids are kids wherever they may be on the globe.

In the dwindling light, the teenagers spoke of clothes and dating and parents and problems. Italian girls worry about boys. Italian boys worry about girls. They just worry in a different language.

Barbara Ferrari had posters of John Travolta plastered on her bedroom walls. The music she loved was the same music that vibrates through our house. Vincenzo and his sister fought and loved just like American kids. When she hit him with a hairbrush one morning and when he tattled on her, it was home sweet home.

And in the end, it was the likenesses, not the differences, that hit home. As they passed the days with a big-hearted policeman and his family, two American suburban girls learned that the language of caring is a universal one. The Ferraris scolded them, and guided them, and gently introduced them, not just to Italian supermarkets and swimming pools, castles and *casas*, but also to the warmth and comfort of family life far from the place they call home.

As the days rushed by and the week pushed inexorably toward Friday and departure, we were escorted to ancient *duomi* (cathedrals) and country castles that dot the Piacenza landscape. We shopped at open-air markets where stalls spilled over with food and shoes, paintings and pocketbooks, tasting discount shopping, Piacenza style, and relishing it!

We watched, deeply touched, as Cinnaminson Superintendent of Schools Dr. Richard Holtzman, Governor [Brendan T.] Byrne's state coordinator for The Friendship Force, read a proclamation from our governor to the people of Piacenza at an open-air concert on a summer night.

No effort was spared for our pleasure. When my husband, a Superior Court judge in Mount Holly, expressed a desire to see the courts of Piacenza, it was instantly arranged. When I asked to visit the newspaper (there is only one daily in Piacenza) not just one but four...tour guides showing us through Liberta from printing presses to patios.

And when we begged to give our hosts a breather by taking a day train to Switzerland, we were personally escorted on a six-hour car ride there.

In the end, nothing we saw—no ancient castle or magnificent church—astounded us more than the goodness and generosity of the people of Piacenza. "The guest is sacred," Nadia Lavony explained to us. And she and the Ferraris could not have demonstrated that concept more lovingly.

Our fairy-tale existence was not without its amusing flaws. In Nadia's apartment, there was one wastebasket. We carried our trash discreetly to that location under the sink many times each day. When we compared notes later with other American guests, we learned that we were not alone in our stealthy trash treks. Wastebaskets are simply not to be found in Italian households.

Our family shared one bath towel the entire week. We took showers infrequently and never quite got the hang of hand-held sprayers. Nor did we get too attached to Italian toilet tissue, which is a far cry from "squeezably soft!"

The language confusion occasionally reached riotous proportions. When Nadia kindly invited an American luncheon guest to douche in her bathroom, the astonished lady stayed in that room an appropriate amount of time before rejoining us. Alas, *douche* in Italian means to bathe....

Our last night in Piacenza was spent on a windswept hillside at the country home of a Piacenza professor. On that gala evening, we dined

47

on pressed duck and beef nerves (yes, beef nerves!) and experienced the delights of international hospitality. The wine flowed, the voices rose and fell in lively, if fragmented, conversation. After dark, we gathered on the professor's patio to share in song with a young American guest and her guitar.

"She'll be Comin' Round the Mountain," and "My Darling Clementine," swelled in the cool night air. So did a lively folk ballad of Piacenza. Americans and Italians sang out in harmony of a kind above and beyond the music. The words of "It's a Small World After All" were never more meaningful than they were on that bittersweet night of endings.

Only after we were on the plane for home did Jill, Amy and Nancy open the envelope the Ferrari family had pressed into their hands as we parted. That letter, written in an unsteady hand by people who had to piece together the English word by word, is our most cherished "souvenir" of our most cherished experience.

"To you, Amy, Nancy and Jill," it began. It spoke in touchingly fragmented English of the five shared days, of the storehouse of memories, of the special delights. And it ended with these words.

"We not to forget these days together in friendship. We hope you not us to forget...."

We never will, dear Ferraris.

Never."

An example of friendships which endured under less than desirable conditions occurred in 1979, when Friendship Force ambassadors from Washington State traveled to Korea. During their visit, South Korean President Park Chung-Hee was assassinated. This tragedy occurred near the end of the visit.

Eleanor van Tilburg of Washington said, "After living with the Korean people for two weeks, we were able to mourn with them with true empathy, especially since our country lost a president in the same manner during our lifetime. There were many armed guards around the city and many flags were flying. Other than that, the city moved as usual."

The Koreans later said they felt in their hearts the genuine sympathy and understanding from the Americans which reinforced the ties of friendship.

(Eleanor Tilburg traveled with her husband Dr. Wayne Tilburg and their sons Peter and Christopher.)

In a letter to Executive Director Stan Humphries, another ambassador said: "I was very interested in the change of attitude of some of the ambassadors. My husband did not care to go, but now that he has heard so much about it, he is most anxious to participate in an exchange.

"One ambassador was complaining to me on the flight that her family choice was not satisfactory because it included little children, whom she said she did not like. At the trip's end, she was completely won over. Another ambassador was going purely for the travel, but the graciousness of the people soon broadened her outlook and gave her a love and concern for the Korean people. Please keep up the good work you are doing."

Korea: Emerging Giant, Eager For International Friendships

A pretty Korean drapes a *humbok* around Hunter Biederman of Florida.

**Ian Thompson of Nebraska and a Guambiano Indian boy in Cali, Colombia.
(Photo by Joseph Omar Sarkar.)**

Chapter 6
The Builders

───────◆───────

*In the two years since its inception, The Friendship Force has
promoted the cause of international friendship from one end of the
earth to the other, scattering the seeds of grass-roots goodwill like a
globe-trotting Johnny Appleseed. And it all began as the idea of a
man who doesn't even like to travel.*
—*The Atlanta Constitution*, July 30, 1979, **Robert Lamb**,
Constitution Staff Writer

When 1980 began, Beverlie Reilman was busy at work at Friendship
Force International headquarters. It was primarily through her efforts
that a new community planning guide was mailed to Friendship Force
leaders across the country in January. The guide offered background
information and examples of good techniques tested earlier by local
committees in several states. The booklet also contained essays on
exchange planning. Procedures were tightened; new cities were paired
only with experienced ones; eight-member exchange committees were
given a full six months for planning and destinations were kept secret
until a sealed envelope was opened at induction time. The Friendship
Force received good publicity in *Parade* magazine in March in an
article by Sheila Moracarco. This generated many phone calls to
Friendship Force International.

Plans were under way for first exchanges with Brazil and
Colombia. A Friendship Force Festival was held in May in
Washington, DC. The Carters were on hand to greet ambassadors and
hosts from the cities of Sao Paulo and Sao Carlos, Brazil, and Cali,
Colombia, Charlotte, North Carolina and Dayton, Ohio. Exchanges
with the Brazilian cities were difficult at first because the Brazilian
government required a deposit of 16,000 *cruzeiros* (about $500 US)
from any citizen leaving the country. After several unsuccessful
attempts by Friendship Force International to persuade the government
to waive the requirement, the law was finally repealed.

Extensive planning was made for numerous exchanges involving
the United Kingdom during the year. Unfortunately, by April, it
appeared that Newcastle would have only half as many ambassadors

as it did in 1979. It did not seem likely that new cities in the UK would be developed as exchange sites for the year. Alan Redhead of England reported that "...the economic situation is biting deeply. Unemployment rates are high, particularly in those areas where we are attempting to develop, i.e. North East England, Strathclyde, South Wales. However, the reservoir of support in Newcastle is still there, but many of our Friendship Force club members and previous members are now traveling independently to meet friends made on previous exchanges."

While the small staff at Friendship Force International worked feverishly on many exchanges and new training techniques, Wayne Smith was busy knocking on important doors in high places. His chief aim was to gain entry to the USSR, a task he began the year before with letters to high-ranking officials and businessmen who might help him penetrate the Iron Curtain in a significant way. Smith first called on Dr. Armand Hammer. He then traveled to Washington, DC, where he met with Vladimir Zolotukhin, First Secretary of Cultural Affairs of the USSR. The Secretary listened, but made no comments. Smith was undaunted and wrote a letter to Zolotukhin in April 1980. Enclosed was information about The Friendship Force, but Smith didn't stop there. He plainly stated in his letter that his goal was "...a Friendship Force exchange between the people of the Soviet Union and the people of the United States." After explaining how the citizens' exchange would work, Smith dropped a big international name:

"Dr. Armand Hammer is a member of the Advisory Council of The Friendship Force. I would be hopeful that he would be willing to make a significant donation for the first Friendship Force exchange between our two countries since he has a particular love for both our countries.

"What I am saying , Professor Zolotukhin, is if there is a will on the part of your people—as I know there is a will on the part of the people of the United States—for a Friendship Force exchange, I am confident that we can work out all the problems."

Wayne Smith then told Zolotukhin that he would soon receive an invitation to attend a Friendship Force Festival on May 19, at the Pan American Union Building. "President and Mrs. Carter plan to attend this Festival," Smith said.

Zolotukhin declined to attend the Festival.

In May, Smith wrote to Gennady Fedosov, Secretary General of the USSR-USA Friendship Society in Moscow. Once again, the tone of the letter was bold and straightforward:

"Mr. Fedosov, I propose that a Friendship Force exchange be carried out between 250 ordinary citizens of the city of Tbilisi in your state of Georgia and the city of Atlanta in the USA state of Georgia during a period of two weeks this coming October."

Again Smith mentioned Dr. Armand Hammer and stated that Dr. Hammer had left some literature about The Friendship Force in the office of Mr. Brezhnev.

Would the force of friendship be able to penetrate the Iron Curtain as nothing else had done? That remained to be seen, but few Americans were as optimistic as Wayne Smith.

Meanwhile, The Friendship Force experienced some bad news concerning the much celebrated Cali-Dayton exchange. When it was time to return to their country, 28 of the 162 Colombian ambassadors failed to show up at the airport. The exchange directors were very upset in both Dayton and Cali. Jeanne Comer of Dayton worried that the media might use this news to cause much harm to The Friendship Force in Ohio before her local club became well-established.

When the Colombians checked in at the airport, Braniff Airlines officials were none too happy with their excess baggage, but they finally allowed each Colombian eighty pounds of baggage and a considerable amount of merchandise. After much negotiation, at least one motorcycle was allowed to be taken on the plane. The departure was almost two hours late.

Alvaro Gamboa Tasama, Director of The Friendship Force in Cali, wrote to Beverlie Reilman about his feelings concerning the deserters:

"Our committee was really hurted (sic) with the desertion of those 28 persons. I am very upset. A newspaper in USA and a Mr. Moyer from the Emigration and Nat. Service in Cincinnati says that we are emigrant smugglers! Ask Marcia [Marcia Dworetz at Friendship Force International] to tell you how hard I worked for the exchange. During the time the Americans were in Cali, I did not go to work in order to take care of the visitors.

"Many ambassadors from Cali—those who did not have a poor performance in the USA—said MUCHAS GRACIAS to me for allowing them to know your country under the auspices of The Force."

After this embarrassment, better screening was initiated; however, when more desertions followed on the second exchange, it became difficult for Colombian ambassadors to obtain visas for future exchanges.

Germany became very active in The Friendship Force during 1980 as Hanns-Peter Herz became the national director for that country. The West Berlin club hosted 120 delegates to The Fourth International Conference. Max Schmeling. world heavyweight boxing champion in 1932-1934, and the national chairman of The Friendship Force in Germany, greeted the delegates.

There were some American ambassadors who worried that those of the World War II generation might not be well received in German homes. There were some misgivings among American exchange directors as well. They feared that confrontations between ambassadors and hosts might mar the exchanges. Those fears proved to be unfounded.

Here is what one returning couple had to say about their Friendship Force experience in Germany:

"Thanks to our host family, we had the opportunity to enjoy their customs, cuisine and, most important, ask questions and get answers and exchange opinions with each other about our individual country's, history and present problems. They were considerate of our needs and their kindness was overwhelming. It was a very emotional good-bye. For a *Jewish* couple to go into a *non-Jewish* German home and ask honest questions of each other, yet form a deeply compatible relationship, was a tremendously rewarding experience."

On another exchange to Hamburg, Germany, Lucille Hendrickson from North Dakota, traveled with her husband where they were hosted in the home of Ilse and Gerhard Flechner. Upon their return to the United States, Lucille wrote a letter to Ilse and Gerhard which was published in *The Bismarck Tribune*. A portion of the heartwarming account follows:

Dear Gerhard and Ilse:

We will remember always our wonderful days with you in Hamburg.

You showed us your beautiful and interesting city and the surrounding countryside in a way no tourist can see it. But for all the beautiful landscapes and architectural, artistic and engineering wonders that we saw, we will treasure most getting to know you.

'Guten appetit' and 'A little bit for the stomach.' We'll remember your humor and how your eyes twinkled, Gerhard, as you said those words—which was often.

I think our favorite memory of you, Ilse, will be that late night you ran to hold the bus so that we would not have to wait forty minutes for the next one. You disappeared with the speed of a gazelle. Even when Gerhard explained that you had been a marathon runner in your girlhood and still belong to a gymnastics club, your fleetness of foot at more than sixty years astounded us. In fact, the stamina you and your countrymen have for walking put us American visitors to shame.

How good the food was, in the restaurants of your city and at your table. I have almost duplicated your tomato salad, Ilse. But alas, we have no blackberries in our garden to make your pudding.

We had been advised before we left Bismarck not to initiate the subject of World War II but, as we learned to know one another, how could those of our generation have avoided it? After all, that war was part of our youth and to a large extent, it set the pathway of our futures.

You said one day: 'There was a concentration camp near Hamburg—and we didn't know it.' We understood your need to speak of it, and we heard the sorrow and incredulity in your voice. To learn of its existence must have been a terrible shock to you—for we have never met a kinder, more gentle man than you, Gerhard.

Without you to guide us, we would not have visited the charming centuries-old farmhouse with a thatched roof and hand-painted wall tiles in Vier Lande. Nor climbed into the choir loft of that wonderful old church with the marvelous wood carvings and inlaid wood pews (in Altengamme). Who would have told us that the ornate wrought iron protuberances on the tops of the pews were hat stands to accommodate the stovepipe hats of the men of a bygone day—and that each man tried to outdo the other in making his the most elaborate.

Because we were your guests, we were privileged to tour and to be luncheon guests at the impressive senior center in your suburb of Bergedorf. Bismarck's senior citizens would be green with envy, especially over the pool.

If we had toured the countryside alone, we would not have turned off the highway and seen the locks at Scharzebek. What a marvel of engineering. We doubt, too, if we would have had a chance to see the folk festival at Finkenderfer.

Your garden. Such a little beauty spot. And how lovely it was of you to have a party there so we could meet some of your friends. Otto and Howard hit it off great, didn't they, exchanging experiences on hunting in Germany and in North Dakota.

As we grew to know one another better, we found more and more how similar our lifestyles and values are, didn't we? How we laughed that night while comparing German and American expressions, finding

55

so many that were similar. Like, 'stop running around like a chicken with its head cut off.'

We also liked the sharing of tables in your cafes. We met so many interesting people—like the two engineering students from India whom we visited with at Welcome·Point. Wasn't it amazing, our seeing them a week later in Munich, a city of more than a million people?

We will cherish always your celebration of our wedding anniversary the day before we left. The roses and candles on the table, the beautiful gift. Had we known that our store window wishing would prompt a special trip downtown [for you] to get that particular item for us, we never would have wished aloud. It was much too extravagant, but we love you for it.

On the bus, going south from Munich to see Neuschwanstein Castle, we had a middle-aged tour guide with a quaint manner of speech. Once in a while, she would drop pearls of wisdom. As we traveled through a particularly beautiful area, she said 'What the eyes see, no one can take from you.'

We could add a postscript to that after our visit with you: 'What the heart feels, that, too, no one can take away.'

(The Hendricksons were among 250 people who traveled with the Bismarck-Mandan, North Dakota Friendship Force club.}

Despite many glowing reports from Friendship Force ambassadors and hosts, those hearing about the organization for the first time were often skeptical, if not downright apprehensive. Many responded with astonishment when friends told them about The Friendship Force. "Wait a minute," they would say. "You mean we're supposed to pay our money and sign up for a trip and not know where we are going or with whom we're going to stay? And go into a perfect stranger's house in another country where they may not even speak English or have indoor plumbing? That's not *my* idea of a vacation."

When told that it indeed was not the typical vacation, but a real adventure and a chance to build yet one more bridge across the great divides which separate people and, maybe, just maybe, make the world a friendlier, more peaceful place, some individuals softened and ultimately made the leap of faith. They went on to make new friends and to have their own lives enriched in the process.

Letters which poured back into Friendship Force headquarters reaffirmed the power of exchanges many times over. Here is a sampling of positive comments:

"Language is not a problem as far as people-to-people private diplomacy is concerned," was a quote in the Daily Yomiuri, a large Tokyo daily newspaper. "This was demonstrated by 213 Japanese private ambassadors who went to the state of Montana, the US, May 14, for an eight-day stay under the exchange program of The Friendship Force."

First Lady of North Carolina, Carolyn Hunt, told a reporter, " The Friendship Force trip is go! With almost as much enthusiasm as NASA workers launching a space shot, we are planning this state's first international good will exchange, set for April 18."

And Millie Covington, flight director for the trip, said no one would be accepted as an ambassador if they were merely looking for... "a cheap way to travel. When people who qualify don't have enough money, we try to find a sponsor to help them with the money. Workers in some state agencies are collecting money to send deserving fellow employees," she added.

German ambassadors who visited North Dakota were delighted with their assigned destination—once they arrived. Erika Haack, thirty-six, of Hamburg was hosted by Toby and Margarete Wagner. For Erika, the rodeo was a new experience, but when asked about her chief impressions of the country, she said that people were willing to talk with her and were less introverted than "we Germans are with strangers. People here are friendly to everybody," she marveled. "I like the houses here," she added. "None of them are fenced in. You must realize that in Germany we do not compare a huge country like the USA with our smaller one. We compare the USA to Europe. But I can tell you this," Erika said, "German people feel friendly toward Americans."

Alvaro Gamboa Tasama, Director of The Friendship Force in Colombia, summed up his impressions of the exchange with Dayton, Ohio, in May:

"The people: Americans are generous, friendly, hospitable, open-minded, concerned about the way their government spends their money and are very worried about ecological themes. The people have a good sense of what it means to have a clean country and the avenues and streets are very clean.

"In the community: I saw a lot of people jogging around town—young and old people. Americans are proud of their flag, their national anthem, the McDonald's hamburgers, the ice cream, the President of the country, John Wayne and apple pie!!!!

"At the party in Washington, I enjoyed very much the Carters' Spanish. It was quite perfect. President Carter has a lot of charisma.

"WE LEARNED: to drink iced tea, to pray before having dinner and to smile.

"WE DISLIKED the association of Colombia with marijuana; no siestas in Dayton and to go home just when we start to know our hosts and they start to know us," Tasama said.

Perhaps the best advice that could be offered to someone who is new to The Friendship Force concept is to point them to the example set by Lois Wayland who traveled to Korea in 1980 .

Helen Grissom of Minneapolis wrote this about Lois, age eighty:

"Lois looked upon this flight as a great adventure, something new to experience. She knew that she would accept everything as it came and she didn't worry about anything because she was confident of her own ability and stamina to meet what might indeed be a different world for two weeks. She just knew in advance that this would be a thrilling experience in her life."

And how did Lois Wayland fare with her Korean hosts? "We took an instant liking to each other and we had great communication with each other—without words. It was surprising how well we communicated," Lois said.

In early January 1980, over a hundred persons attended a Friendship Force meeting in Smoketown, Pennsylvania. Eugene Witmer was the exchange director. They were told that a plane filled with 250 people would once again travel to a foreign country. All would be home-hosted and the exchange price was $479. The attendees were told that a like group would be coming back to their area where they would be home-hosted in the Lancaster area.

Before the departure, ambassadors and hosts attended workshops to prepare for the exchange. They were told that much effort would be made to match ambassadors with their foreign counterparts by age, occupation and hobbies.

In February Leo Shelley came home from his work as librarian at Millersville State College. He told his wife Ginger that one of his colleagues had signed up to be an ambassador for The Friendship Force. He further explained that she was expected to find a host family to entertain some foreign visitors for a week or two sometime in May. Ginger knew something about The Friendship Force from articles in the Lancaster newspaper. The couple discussed it and decided it would be a fun thing to do. In Ginger's words, this is what happened:

Our family waited excitedly to hear what country would be chosen for the exchange. Our daughter Sarah, age 5, was learning how to say "hello" in other languages at her nursery school. One day she came home excitedly and asked, 'Are our foreign friends going to come from *Bonjour, Buenos Dias, Guten Tag* or *Shalom?*' A few days later we were able to tell our children that our visitors were coming from *Guten Tag*.

We began to prepare for our visitors and went to the library to learn more about Germany. I had some German in college, but I remembered very little. Out came my old textbooks for a cram course in German, but I figured most Germans would know English.

We told The Friendship Force directors that we were interested in hosting a couple with young children. Finally the day came when the all-important paper arrived with the information about our German ambassadors. I anxiously ripped it open and stared in disbelief. Some mistake must have been made. Our ambassadors were a couple in their mid-sixties (we are half that age). The man was a commercial agent, but we had no idea what that meant. It didn't sound like anyone in the education field. Their interests were concerts, opera and theater; Leo and I can't sing a note. Then the real shock: neither of them spoke English!

After informing Leo of the apparent mistake, I called Lancaster headquarters to find out who our real ambassadors might be. They assured me that there had been no mistake and that Ursula and Egon Hahn were assigned to our family. They explained that they could not satisfy our requirements, but they were sure things would work out.

Finally, our family sat down and wrote a long letter introducing ourselves and telling them a bit about Lancaster County. We enclosed a photo of the children. How, I thought, would an older couple survive for a week in our home? Our active children, our wild cat named Margaret Thatcher, our busy schedule and early morning risings might seem somewhat annoying to our guests.

Before long the letter with a German postmark arrived. I quickly tore it open and found enclosed a postcard. On it were three sentences written in an attempt at English. Two of the sentences we could not figure out at all and neither could any of our neighbors. The third sentence said, "We also have a garden."

Finally the day came when the Berliners were to arrive at the Harrisburg International Airport. When we arrived...we became caught up in the anticipation of the crowd. I rehearsed the four or five German sentences I thought essential to begin this adventure. When the plane arrived, we tried to pick out Herr and Frau Hahn, but with no success. We resorted to the number system and I went to the area for Nos. 52 and 53. Before long I spotted them. Frau Hahn, an attractive young-looking-for-her-age woman, not much taller than my five-feet, two-inches, greeted me with a handshake and lots of German. By this time I had forgotten my few essential German greetings and just smiled a welcome.

Herr Hahn, a large man over six feet tall, bowed deeply and shook my hand. I tried to explain in very poor German that my husband was trying to find two other Germans who were going to ride to Lancaster with us.

After Leo found the other couple and loaded all the luggage, we were on our way. By then I had my wits about me and, by concentrating very hard, I could understand some of the German being spoken. The trip to Lancaster went very quickly. We dropped off the two ambassadors at our friends' home and continued on to our house.

We were greeted by wild Margaret Thatcher. Frau Hahn told us their daughter had a cat and, in fact, her daughter had married the cat's veterinarian. Herr Hahn said that maybe we should call Margaret Thatcher "Helmut Schmidt' for the week. Both apologized for their lack of English.

By bedtime, Leo and I felt that this adventure wasn't going to be so bad after all.

The next morning the house reverberated with the sounds of the William Tell Overture. Our seven year old son Penn had turned on the TV to see the Lone Ranger. What a way for our guests to be introduced to American life!

Although they could scarcely wait until the Hahns came downstairs, when the actual moment came, the children greeted our guests hesitantly. Sarah ran behind Mother when she first heard the unfamiliar sounds of another language. Penn, with some prompting, uttered a feeble *Guten Morgen* and shook hands, but at that point he would have obviously preferred to ride into the sunset with the Lone Ranger and Tonto. Fortunately, hungry tummies and curiosity soon urged the children to the breakfast table.

In the days which followed, we visited the usual Lancaster County sites. The Hahns enthusiasm and sense of wonder were contagious and we found ourselves rediscovering Lancaster and looking at our county with a new perspective. It was a surprise to realize how much we take for granted. The Hahns made us appreciate more fully our American freedoms.

Ursula had a relative living in Washington, DC, whom she had not seen since 1945. We took them to Washington to visit this relative and to see the sights. The days were busy with so many things to do and not enough time.

By the time that *Sie sinds* became *Du bists*, Ursula treated me as one of her daughters and she seemed to me to have many of the same qualities my mother had had. The bridge between proper European manners and our informalities were closed by warm embraces. Egon's sense of humor was a real delight. We discovered he knew two words of English. When talking about ancestry, I mentioned that I was *ein halb Englisch, ein viertel Schweiz and und ein viertel Deutsch.*

"Ah, so" he commented with a twinkle in his eye. *Du bist ein mixed pickle.*

Well, I had never thought of myself as a mixed pickle, but his comment made me remember that most Americans are indeed 'mixed pickles.'

The week went much too quickly. Many times we laughed with Ursula and Egon and sometimes we laughed at them. Sometimes we didn't understand a thing they were saying and yet, at other times, without saying a word, we understood each other completely. We listened to the story of their lives. Of Ursula's life on a farm that had been in her family for three hundred years and of their marriage on that farm thirty-six years ago. We heard about the war years when Egon served in the German army and of his surrender to the Americans and life in a POW camp. We heard of the Russians capturing Ursula's farm (now a part of Poland) and her flight from the Russians to Berlin. We listened in horror at how their baby son died from lack of medical care. They told us about their city of Berlin, their garden and their travels. They made us glad we had met them and had this opportunity to make them our friends.

When it was time for them to leave, they thanked us profusely for all we had done for them. I could not begin to tell them all they had done for us. No language spoken or written could express the knowledge and love we have gained and given during this Friendship Force Exchange.

On an organizational level, many positive things happened at Friendship Force International headquarters during 1980. One of the best ideas came from creative Beverlie Reilman who suggested that Friendship Force clubs be organized within communities. Reilman believed that clubs would provide support for program goals and would be a good way to spread the news about The Friendship Force. The Board approved the idea and guidelines were established for licensing clubs through Friendship Force International headquarters. Clubs were authorized to use the trade name and the logo of hands clasped in friendship.

In November, the CAB waiver was extended for five years, with two restrictions. The $200,000 bond had to continue and The Friendship Force was still required to enter into ambassador agreements with each traveler.

Near the end of the year, Claude Armendariz became Director of Finance of Friendship Force International. Armendariz, a native of Chiapas, Mexico, moved with his family to Mexico City in 1940 to escape a particularly virulent type of malaria which was plaguing Chiapas. He attended school in Mexico City for two years, then left to continue his education in the United States where he first studied English, then majored in accounting.

Armendariz met Wayne Smith in 1972 when Smith was working for North Avenue Presbyterian Church. When Smith, with the assistance of President and Mrs. Carter, organized The Friendship Force in 1977, Claude Armendariz was asked if he could help organize an accounting system.

"I helped them as a volunteer from April 1977, until September of that year. Before I accepted a full-time job with The Friendship Force in 1980, I had worked for 18 years as treasurer of an insurance company," said the soft spoken Armendariz .

President Carter narrowly missed being re-elected to a second term in 1980. There were concerns, especially from Friendship Force club members abroad, about the status of The Friendship Force after the Carters left Washington. Wayne Smith reminded the worriers that "The Friendship Force always has been a non-political organization. Its existence never has depended on any political endorsement but on the commitment of tens of thousands of people from all walks of life around the world to further the cause of world friendship. The Friendship Force always will be grateful to President and Mrs. Carter for launching us, but as Tim Ryan telexed from Dublin: 'We do not insist on Air Force One; we are quite happy to travel by covered wagon or by Irish hot air balloons.'"

Wayne Smith was not satisfied with the progress in 1980. Economic difficulties and increased world tensions meant that The

Friendship Force expanded much slower than expected. Nevertheless, Beverlie Reilman reported, "A total of $45,000 was paid on the deferred debts and the bank loan and the fund balance ("net worth" of nonprofit organizations) increased from $21,000 to $65,000. Exchange margins increased from $36 per ambassador to $42 in 1980. A record was set that would stand the entire decade: there were 10,856 ambassadors, 400 more than in 1979."

Hands working together bring hearts together.

"Girl From Impanema" at Boldrini Children's Hospital in Campinas, Brazil, during a Friendship Force exchange.

Chapter 7
UNCHARTED WATERS

If the Soviets and Americans can both put people into outer space, we ought to be able to put people from both countries into each other's kitchens. —**Wayne Smith**

In 1981, seventeen full charter flights were announced early in the year. The 1981 charter carrier was World Airways, but several exceptions to the charter plan were made. The first regular service was used in the Alabama-Cuernavaca/Guanajuato, Mexico, exchange.

Ambassadors from Birmingham and Atlanta had a "marvelous Friendship Force experience," according to Charlotte Blackmon, State Director of Alabama. Dr. Francisco Aguilar-Hernandez of Mexico and his family were very helpful in the 1981 exchange. Dr. Hernandez had been elected to The Friendship Force board of directors in 1980.

Since Wayne Smith's first visit to the Soviet Union on March 15, his thoughts often turned to that huge country. When he returned to the States, Smith wrote Gennady Fedosov of the Soviet/USA Friendship Society in Moscow, enclosing a lengthy proposal for his study. He asked Fedosov to consider a collaboration between his organization and The Friendship Force. Smith explained that his proposal was designed "to improve, through friendship, the environment for understanding between ordinary rank-and-file citizens of our two nations."

Before Smith traveled to Korea in 1981, he learned that the Korean government planned to purchase twenty-five F-16 planes at a cost of $25 million each. When Smith met with Korean leaders, he suggested that the government might amend the purchase order by one less plane. "With that $25 million savings, you could pay Korean Air Lines to transport Americans and Koreans at a very low cost, allowing many large exchanges between our people," Smith told them. "Don't you think money spent in this manner would produce long-term benefits far greater than the mere purchase of one more airplane?"

The novel idea caught the officials by surprise and they thought about it for a moment before responding. Then they discussed the matter in Korean. Ultimately they responded emphatically, declaring the suggestion as "a wonderful idea!" They promised to bring the subject up at the next cabinet meeting. Sadly, Smith's idea was never implemented.

Sometimes Friendship Force exchanges produce even more than friendships. Consider the exchange between Omaha and Seoul set for May. Dr. and Ms. Fred Youngblood agreed to host for the first time. They were the proud parents of four boys, but they had always wanted a daughter. They had even selected her name: Kathleen. They had inquired about adoption, but agencies were not encouraging, citing long lists of childless couples who would receive top priority.

Then they opened their home and their hearts to Dr. and Mrs. Do Young Kim. To the Youngbloods great surprise, they soon learned that Dr. Kim's family manages an adoption agency in Korea. When Bonnie and Fred told Dr. Kim and his wife of their desire to adopt a little girl, he said: "You want a little girl—I get one for you. She be pretty and she be smart!"

Still, the Youngbloods were afraid to hope. However, about a month after the visit, they received a call from a rather puzzled representative of the Children's Home Society of Minnesota. She explained that they usually placed children in Minnesota homes, but they were making an exception because proceedings had been originated in Korea, directing the placement of a child with the Youngbloods in Nebraska. In October, Fred and Bonnie were asked if they would adopt a five-year-old Korean girl! They were jubilant and accepted immediately.

Several years later, Bonnie Youngblood reported that "Kathleen is now a healthy little girl who loves pretty clothes and collects dolls. She is fluent in English. She is at first shy around strangers, but is soon chattering. Her big happy smile and trusting dark eyes capture your heart. She has made many friends at school.

"And in the words of Dr. Kim's promise: 'She be pretty and she be smart!.'"

(This story is based on an article in *Friendship* magazine by **Janey H. Ashley.**)

Wayne Smith outlined the specifics of another proposal to Gennady Fedosov, asking for a Friendship Force exchange between Leningrad and Des Moines, Iowa, from October 4-16, 1981. The proposal asked that 185 citizens from each city be allowed to travel and to live with families in private homes in the host countries. Each Soviet would pay six hundred rubles and each American, $875. This price would cover all expenses, since room and board would be furnished by the host families.

Smith offered an alternate proposal in which The Friendship Force would bring 185 American citizens to the Soviet Union each week for ten weeks in a row, beginning October 4, 1981, and continuing through December 6, for a total of 1,850 Americans visiting the Soviet Union, not for tourism, but for friendship. The proposal did not insist on home hosting, but provided that Americans would stay at Intourist Hotels. However, Smith suggested that Soviet citizens be allowed to mix and mingle with the Americans and to be able to get together daily for an event, such as a ballet or the opera.

Smith also wrote to United States Senator Mark Hatfield telling him of the proposal to Fedosov and asking Hatfield to lead one of the delegations, provided the second option was chosen by the Soviets. Correspondence and telephone calls continued throughout the summer months and into the fall. Smith was very frustrated when no agreement had been reached by year end.

Recruiting problems continued during 1981, because of increased travel costs and economic conditions. During the summer, the air traffic controllers went on strike, threatening existing exchanges. In many countries, currencies declined against the dollar. An exchange between Lancaster, Pennsylvania, and Cali, Colombia, was canceled because of the murder of a Lancaster missionary by Colombian terrorists. Riots in Korea caused the cancellation of a Salt Lake City-Korea exchange three days before the flight.

The Friendship Force Board published this statement regarding the canceled flights: "The safety and comfort of our ambassadors will be the prime factor. We regret that terrorism, riots and civil disturbances exist. More than ever, this unhappy world needs people like those we recruit and programs like those of The Friendship Force."

The first non-USA exchange took place in 1981 between Berlin, Germany, and Newcastle, England. The first intrastate exchange was between Virginia and Montana.

Public relations efforts increased. Ed Mann of Des Moines put together a Friendship Force slide story which was available to all clubs. At the International Conference in Newcastle in October, a public relations packet was distributed to leaders. Many of the items included were the result of a marketing survey undertaken in 1980 by volunteer Dr. Hall Duncan of Oklahoma State University and graduate students Margaret Gaeddert and Candy Low. Mac and Kay Sammons of Richmond were named to design a Friendship Force training program which was tested on United States Friendship Force leaders in September and on international Friendship Force leaders prior to the Newcastle conference.

In September Jimmy and Rosalynn Carter were honored in Japan at a breakfast meeting of business and government leaders. In his remarks, Carter said: "I believe with all my heart that when you come to our big cities and small villages and when we come to your metropolitan areas and lovely towns as well, our two peoples soon will discover how much they like each other and will form friendships which will be invaluable for our two countries."

While they were in Japan, the Carters met with Ryoichi Sasakawa, a Japanese philanthropist whose name would become very well-known to The Friendship Force in future years. The Carters were hosted by the Dentsu Corporation, an organization that would later offer financial and organizational skills to The Friendship Force.

By October 1981, Wayne Smith was able to write to his friend, Dr. Armand Hammer, to announce that The Friendship Force would have its first cultural exchange experience with the Soviet Union from February 1-9, 1982. This type of exchange did not involve home hosting and would ultimately be called first an interchange, then a mission.

Instead of home hosting, one hundred grass roots ambassadors were scheduled to participate in the interchange under the auspices of Intourist, a Soviet tourist agency, and they would fly to Moscow on Aeroflot, the state-run airline of the Soviet Union. The ambassadors would stay in hotels, but hoped to meet Soviet citizens during other planned activities. The diverse group was made up of many occupations and professions. Also included were former Governor of West Virginia Hulett Smith and his wife Mary Alice. The group would visit Moscow, Leningrad and Kiev.

Chapter 8
Philanthropist Meets Peacemaker

Every noble life leaves its fiber interwoven forever in the work of the world.
—Ruskin.

After World War II ended, Japan's Ryoichi Sasakawa scribbled these words in his dark, dank prison cell: "The most horrible sin on earth is killing, with war being the paramount example. The only way to allow the souls of the war dead to rest in peace is to bring about everlasting world peace, ridding the people on earth forever of the horror of war and building a heaven on earth where all people can live in harmony as brothers and sisters."

Sasakawa found a new meaning for his life during his years in Sugamo Prison where he was sent by the Allied Occupation Forces. He was a suspected war criminal because of his prior political leanings. It was in prison that he developed his personal philosophy: "The world is one family; all mankind are brothers and sisters."

Sasakawa was finally released from prison in 1949. Ultimately, he became very wealthy through his major role in the revitalization of Japan's shipping industry. Sasakawa later served as chairman of the Japan Shipbuilding Industry Foundation, a philanthropic organization he founded.

Several years before Wayne Smith ever heard of Ryoichi Sasakawa, he had a memorable meeting with his former boss, Tom Cousins.

"Wayne was very excited that day," Cousins said. "He said, 'Tom, I want to contact someone who will provide an endowment to The Friendship Force for at least $100 million dollars. Using only the interest on the funds, The Friendship Force could expand much more rapidly and develop contacts in many countries where friendship is sorely needed.'

"I made the mistake of thinking Wayne was joking, although I should have known better. I laughed and told him the idea was terrific, but how was he going to locate this rich benefactor?"

"Wayne just smiled and told me that God would provide such a person.

"I soon forgot about our conversation."

Months passed, and one day Wayne Smith read a magazine article about Ryoichi Sasakawa and the Japanese Shipbuilding Foundation. He immediately phoned Tom Cousins. "I have to talk with you right away," he said..

Cousins told him to come on over.

"Wayne came in with all the exuberance of a two-year old in a toy store," Cousins said. "He told me he knew where he would get the hundred million dollars. It would come from this Japanese man who sometimes gave money away through a foundation. I finally stopped Wayne and asked him what all of this had to do with me."

"I thought you might introduce me to Mr. Sasakawa," Wayne said.

"I don't know this man," Cousins said. "In fact, I've never heard of him. I have no more chance of getting an interview with him than you do. I hope you can find someone to help you, but I think the odds are against it ever happening."

"Wayne thanked me and left, but he was not the least bit discouraged. I thought no more about the conversation until some months later when the phone rang at my home one evening. When I mumbled hello, I heard Wayne say: 'Tom, guess where I am?'

"Of course, I had no idea and said so.

"Tom, I'm in Tokyo and I've met with Mr. Sasakawa! He told me he would give The Friendship Force one hundred million dollars as soon as his salvage company can raise a ship which sank with one of the Russian tsar's gold."

"I jokingly told Wayne that I'd heard people talk about how one day their ship would come *in* but this was the first time I'd heard of someone's ship coming *up*.

Wayne laughed and said he already had the first installment of $650,000 in hand.

"I shouldn't have been surprised," Cousins said, still shaking his head and chuckling at the memory. "I don't think anyone else I know could have accomplished this but Wayne Smith. I should have remembered what my pastor Dr. Vernon S. Broyles, Jr. said a long time ago. After first hearing Wayne's optimistic plans about many things, I phoned Dr. Broyles and asked if this guy Smith was for real.

"Dr. Broyles chuckled and said, 'Yes, Tom, he's for real—he's just different.'"

———————

After a jubilant Wayne Smith returned to Georgia, he told Cousins how he had gone to Sasakawa to discuss the needs of The Friendship Force. Smith had a strong sense that this was going to be a most interesting and momentous meeting and it certainly was.

After Smith's comments about The Friendship Force and the need to expand into countries like the USSR, Sasakawa asked a very direct question.

"How much money do you need" he wanted to know.

Smith didn't blink: "A hundred million dollars," he said.

Sasakawa didn't blink either. "What would you do with that much money? Would you put it in a bank account?"

"Well, yes...." Smith said tentatively.

Wayne Smith and Japan's Ryoichi Sasakawa.

"But you don't need it all at once?" Sasakawa prompted.

"No," Smith admitted.

Sasakawa smiled. "I have found that money is much like manure," he said slowly. "You see, Mr. Smith, if you just pile up a huge mound of fertilizer, it does little more than emit an awful smell and it's not only of little use, it's a nuisance. But when you take a little bit and spread it around, it makes things grow. How much is The Friendship Force's budget for this year?"

Smith replied that it was around $650,000.

"That much we will give," Sasakawa said. "Then we will see what happens to your growth. And if more is needed after that ... we have it."

Wayne Smith was elated. He immediately had a vision of expansion, enabling the program to grow rapidly as new countries became involved. Smith began to dream of other benefits, including grants which The Friendship Force might use to provide funds for dozens of people with real financial needs, allowing them to participate in exchanges or missions of friendship throughout the world. Smith could envision a time when many young people could participate in exchanges, thanks to The Friendship Force's ability to underwrite all or part of their travel costs.

———

On January 27, 1982, Ryoichi Sasakawa was welcomed to The Friendship Force Board of Directors. Later in the meeting Mr. Sasakawa was formally recognized for the gift from the Japanese Shipbuilding Industry Foundation in the amount of $650,000. The Board of Directors agreed to allocate the donation to a reserve fund of $350,000; another $150,000 for international development and $150,000 for additional support services.

Immediately, Friendship Force board members who had pledged their assets toward the CAB surety bond back in 1977, were released from those pledges. The Friendship Force could now cover its own bond. The last of the bank debt was settled in July and remaining old debts for legal and accounting services were paid later in the year and in early 1983.

After the January board meeting, Mr. Sasakawa, Wayne Smith and others flew to Washington to meet with President Ronald Reagan in the Oval Office. Upon hearing more about The Friendship Force, Reagan said, "It's about time we began to talk *with* people instead of just talking *about* them"

Chapter 9
Old Enemies - New Friends

Kind words may be short and easy to speak, but their echoes are
truly endless.
—Mother Teresa

On the heels of the historic board meeting, the first group of Friendship Force ambassadors to the Soviet Union departed on an historic venture of their own: one of making friends behind the Iron Curtain. Fifty ambassadors were from Des Moines, Iowa, and fifty were from other parts of the US. Wayne Smith, the dreamer, missionary and peacemaker from West Virginia was among them.

In a memorandum dated May 11, 1982, Wayne Smith explained how these interchanges were designed. In part, the memorandum said: "During a two-day stopover in Amsterdam, exchange directors will conduct seminars. Each ambassador will receive 250 calling cards which will be printed in Russian with this message:

THE FRIENDSHIP FORCE

I am Mr./Mrs. _____, a member of the delegation of The Friendship Force organization from the United States, and I bring you my heartfelt greetings. We have arrived in your beautiful country to meet your wonderful people. May the Soviet and American people always live in peace and friendship.

"The other side of the calling cards will be blank. Each ambassador may either take these cards to a printing shop or they may hand print their name, address and vocation on the blank side.

"Zoya Zarubina, known to many of you, helped me write this message and other Soviets who checked it agreed that it has the right psychological touch and that it is written in excellent Russian.

"Friendship Force International will also supply each local committee, at cost, *pens* and *pins* which are imprinted with "The Friendship Force" in both Russian and English.

"I think that all of you will be happy to hear that the Soviets are finally starting to talk with me about the possibility of actual exchanges for 1983. Zoya Zarubina and Gennady Fedosov are planning to attend our Sixth International Conference in Asheville, North Carolina, from October 3-6, to make the first beginnings along these lines," Smith said.

"Best wishes to each one of you as you prepare for one of the most fascinating experiences of your life!"

Although typical home-hosting was not possible, the first Soviet Interchange went well. Friendship Force ambassadors were challenged to make friends wherever they went. The schedule of carefully planned tours under the watchful eyes of Intourist guides made for limited opportunities for mixing with the man on the street, but many ambassadors still found ways to befriend Russians.

Jennifer, Chris and Peter Van Tilburg of Washington State traveled with their parents, Wayne and Eleanor Van Tilburg, on one interchange. The youngsters met several of their Russian counterparts on a beach. Later Wayne and Eleanor discovered that their children had dressed their newfound Russian friends in some of their American clothes so they could sneak them into the hotel and past the security guards. They were up half the night talking and laughing together.

According to Beverlie Reilman, "Ten more interchanges followed the first; the ambassadors were from Washington State, Missouri, Minnesota, Washington, DC, Utah, Kentucky, New England, North Carolina and Ohio, plus a repeat from Iowa. A total of 1,035 Americans traveled to Russia in that series. All but one group traveled through Finland and many made new friends in that country also."

Bettye Brown of Washington State said, "Sometimes people in the Soviet Union would stop and talk to us a little bit, but they would suddenly become frightened and hurry away." Her husband Harold added: "We wore small American flag pins and we took extras to give away. We couldn't keep a flag pinned on our clothing because so many Soviets wanted one. They were in great demand, which really surprised us. When we gave someone a pin, if they had anything to give us in return, they would, but if they had nothing, they'd just grab us and hug us and kiss us. I've never been kissed so much in my life!"

The Browns saw a darker side of Soviet life as they took a sixteen-hour train ride from Helsinki, Finland, to Moscow. "Now that was an experience," Bettye said. "We took food along because we were warned that there would be none on the train. We had enough food for everyone on the train and we gave what was left to the crew when we arrived in Moscow. At the border crossing, soldiers came aboard to search the train. We asked what they were looking for and they said 'Rabbits.' Of course, they meant stowaways. And during the night, we were locked in our compartment! Some of the young soldiers talked to us, but not when the older ones were around."

When a small group of Americans was leaving a church in Leningrad, an old woman approached and tugged on the sleeve of one American woman.

"She was about four feet tall, a typical *babushka*," Russian speaking Randy Bengfort of Des Moines said. "She said she didn't want us to make war on them and that they wanted peace."

This open obsession with war surprised many Friendship Force ambassadors. Sandy Freeman, a television talk show host from Atlanta said "They take it for granted that we want war. That's the Communist party line, and that's scary."

Someone asked Wayne Smith if he thinks the people-to-people exchanges will eliminate war. "No," he said. "However, these kinds of exchanges can eliminate fear, distrust and hatred, making a better environment for out governments to make these decisions."

During one of the interchanges to the USSR, Friendship Force ambassadors were standing in a long line to enter the Baptist church one gray winter morning. The weather was bitterly cold and light snow was falling. A brisk wind made it seem even colder. A Russian man, advanced in years, stood shivering in the cold for he had no winter coat or hat. He hoped to get inside where it was warmer. An American man had separated from the group and was at the end of the line when he noticed the old man's plight.

"Here, sir," he said as he removed his own coat and hat and handed them to the Russian. He held the coat as the old man slipped it on. With tears of gratitude in his eyes, the Russian looked wonderingly at the stranger. The two entered the church and their ways parted.

During the research for this book—fifteen years later—this story came to light as I chanced to read comments written in an unsigned ambassador's report. After relating the story, the ambassador added that the giver of the warm coat looked a lot like Wayne Smith.

When I asked Wayne to read this manuscript to check for inaccuracies which might have crept in during some of the midnight word processing, he crossed out this story and wrote **NO**! beside the paragraph. When I asked why, he was embarrassed and said he never meant for anyone to know about it and that the story was not something of great interest to others.

My friend is not often wrong, but this time is an exception.

―――――――――――

Interchanges in the USSR were not the only big news of 1982. In Japan, The Friendship Force received public service non-profit status and Billy Mosier of Montana was selected to serve as liaison between Friendship Force International and Japanese volunteers. Mike Yamano was the National Director for and The Friendship Force soon had five hundred members in Tokyo. It was time for Japan to form clubs in other areas and the Dentsu Corporation agreed to contribute organization, publicity and money to this endeavor. The Friendship Force of Japan soon organized clubs in Shimoda, Tokyo, Funabashi and six other locations. The Japanese clubs planned to offer five levels of English classes to members.

This precious child gave the peace sign without any prompting. Her new friend is Anne Skelley of Roanoke, Virginia.

Stanley Humphries resigned as executive vice-president in March and Boyd Lyons served as Acting Vice President. Ron Condon also resigned during the year and George Halstead, formerly of Finnair, was hired to take over travel and administration. Three of the directors were a great assets at Friendship Force International. They were: Claude Armendariz, head of finance; Beverlie Reilman, head of systems support and Bobbie Jones, head of exchange operations. These three dynamos directed the bustling activity at Friendship Force International with capability and dedication—and in the case of Bobbie Jones, with a big friendly smile of encouragement for everyone. Bobbie was already known as "the lady with the smile" to many Friendship Force members. Wayne Smith said "Bobbie is a key cog in the wheel that turns about two hundred exchanges a year for over thirty countries around the globe. Her responsibilities include the planning, directing and coordination of Friendship Force exchanges and missions."

"It's a big job and I love it," Bobbie said.

Kim Yong Song changed his name to Stephen Y. S. Kim and applied for a visa, pending a move to Atlanta. He was hired as head of planning.

In April 1982, the 100th exchange took place and July 4, marked the fifth anniversary of the first exchange, prompting President Ronald Reagan to send a congratulatory telegram.

During US Volunteer Week, The Friendship Force honored Charlotte Blackmon, Alabama; Juan Edgar Picado, Costa Rica; Richard Falk, Minnesota; Tae Wan Son, Korea; Alma McGovern and the late Betty Beahm of Albuquerque; Theresa Russell of Newcastle, England; Catherine Garst of Wisconsin, Rita Benzel of Berlin, Bud Seretean of Atlanta and Hanns-Peter Herz of Germany.

Following the Soviet Interchange of November 12-24, Exchange Director Mary Parker said, "Making friends with individual Soviets took much effort because our time was so filled by the Intourist schedule. Leaving off some of the tours and going off in two's and three's was important for making contact with Soviet citizens. Those of us who managed to do this were well rewarded. I wish everyone could have an opportunity to meet face to face with Soviet citizens. It would only help us along the road toward world peace. A man I met in a Leningrad coffee shop wrote in my travel diary '...to peace and friendship between the people of the USSR and USA.' Contacts like that were the highlight of my trip and I hope the goodwill created by these interchanges will...expand."

Girls from the Philippines teach little Brittany Johnson to sing with them.

Beverlie Reilman, Friendship Force International's volunteer historian, noted that "This year the USSR, the Netherlands, Philippines and Australia experienced The Friendship Force for the first time. Efforts to redevelop Mexico paid off and in the spring, Alabama ambassadors exchanged for the second time with Cuernavaca and Guanajuato. An exchange between Albuquerque and Chiapas in April had to be postponed when El Chiconal, a nearby volcano, erupted. However, New Mexico citizens collected $375 for volcano victims and for the new Friendship Force of Chiapas, which recovered to have its first exchange the following year."

In October 1982, Klaus Mierendorff of Hamburg, Germany was preparing for a sentimental journey—and an unlikely one at that. He had read about an organization called The Friendship Force. "Ambassadors are wanted for a trip to North America," it said. Although Mierendorff had never heard of The Friendship Force, the article sparked his interest. Why? Because Mierendorff was sent to Boston in mid-1943 as a twenty-year-old prisoner of war who had been captured in Africa. From Boston, he was sent by train to a POW camp in Opelika, Alabama. The war was still raging and no one knew when it would be over.

"With that in mind, we POWs reasoned that we had plenty of time to settle ourselves into our involuntary situation in our host country," Mierendorff recalled. "Many of us did this without complaint, because we understood that although our treatment was tough, it was fair."

After nearly a year in Alabama, Klaus was shipped to Camp Wheeler in Macon, Georgia. Finally, in November of 1944, Mierendorff found himself at a branch camp in Reidsville, Georgia. This would be an important transfer for the young POW, but just how important he did not realize at the time.

The story unfolds here in Klaus Mierendorff''s own words:

Photo shows Klaus (back row, third from right) and fellow prisoners of war at Camp Wheeler, Macon, Georgia,

In Reidsville we were assigned a great variety of jobs—the main one being wood cutting. In addition, harvesting had to be carried out. To that end, we were appropriately employed in the peanut and corn fields. These duties were the ones we particularly liked because we worked in groups of five to ten men. That meant we had closer contact with civilians than did the larger wood cutting groups.

Naturally we were very happy when the harvest season began, because we had heard about a group of farmers who, although it was prohibited, slipped extra food to their POW workers. Even today, I clearly remember an incident that I shall never forget as long as I live.

It was during the corn harvest season. As group leader and translator, I was assigned four POWs. We were picked up by a young American, hardly twenty years old, who drove a pick-up truck. It was October, a somewhat cool but wonderfully sunny day. After a forty-five-minute ride, we arrived on a farm in the middle of a forest.

A farmer stepped out of his small store which not only carried necessary foods, but also, as it seemed to us, the life-sustaining Coca-Cola. He greeted us warmly. His name was Mr. Moon, an older man with a weathered face and very friendly eyes. Near his shop stood a huge old tree, under which a wooden hut was situated and that was where raw ice was stored. One could see Mr. Moon's farmhouse, sitting on a small hill not too far away. It was brilliantly white with a porch and an ever-present rocking chair. Everything radiated peace and friendliness.

This farm became like home to us.

After Mr. Moon warmly welcomed us, we went to work. Each of us threw a large sack over his shoulder, in which we collected the ears of corn that were later stacked together in a pile. Mr. Moon worked with us and I was glad that we young guys were able to keep up with his quick, experienced pace. We worked in this manner until noon.

Mr. Moon drove us back to his store, and I proceeded to get our supplies from the icebox. As I was about to distribute the daily portions of white bread, peanut butter and jelly, Mr. Moon came over and asked what I was doing. When I explained what was only obvious, he told me to pack the bag away and come along with him. He took us to his farm house, gave us soap and a towel and suggested that we wash our hands before entering the house.

This surprised us, but not nearly as much as what was awaiting us. The dining table was set as for Christmas, with so many things that we hadn't eaten in a long tim —fried chicken, fish and our favorite—fruit cocktail. In addition, there were sweet potatoes, bread and cake. In short, a real feast. Mr. Moon wished us a hearty appetite and left the room.

We timidly seated ourselves at this wondrous table and didn't stop eating until the last plates were completely empty. I can't remember how long it took, but it must have been quite a while before we finished and returned to our boss for work. Curiously, he asked us whether the meal sufficed and then he treated each of us to a Coke. He gave each a pack of cigarettes as well.

The work which followed wasn't exactly easy on such full stomachs, but we kept our boss's tempo until he suggested at four p.m. that we take a break. We sat in the grass and enjoyed the sun and leisure and began a conversation. Still astounded at the hospitality of our boss, I couldn't help but ask him whey he was so generous, even though he had to pay the same for a POW worker as for a farm hand. In response, he mentioned that when he had asked for us at the Farmer's Union, a co-member had stressed the fact that one wasn't allowed to supply the POWs with food, cigarettes or drinks. The words of the union member had surprised him. Mr. Moon couldn't believe any workers should be badly treated in a land as rich as America. As far as he was concerned, he was a free citizen of this country and he wouldn't be told what he had to do or what he was allowed to do.

This open attitude really influenced us young Germans, as we had been brought up under an authoritarian regime and had never been exposed to this type of open thinking. In our environment, one could only do what the government permitted us to do.

I've never since experienced such a warm reception and I'm still thankful for my encounter with Mr. Moon," Mierendorff said.

Klaus Mierendorff's thoughts turned to his unforgettable experience when he read about The Friendship Force in a newspaper. "I had always wanted to see more of the country which accommodated me for over three years," he said.

Mierendorff's enthusiasm landed him the job of exchange director of a Friendship Force group which left Germany on October 24, 1982, bound for Winston-Salem, North Carolina.

Once the group arrived in North Carolina, Klaus Mierendorff was ecstatic about the reception which he described as "overwhelming." He was soon introduced to his hosts, Millie and Lee Hinshaw. "While Millie was busy arranging meetings, visits and sightseeing trips, Lee entertained me by, among other things, trying to fig- ure which beer, in my opinion, was the best American beer. (He knew I was a beer brewer by occupation.) We tested many beers before I settled upon Michelob," Klaus recalled.

Klaus Mierendorff now

Once his hosts learned of his POW experiences and his desire to revisit the old prison camps in Alabama and Georgia and hopefully to find out what had become of the Moon family, arrangements were made for Klaus to fly to Atlanta where he was met by Wilma Gray of Friendship Force International. Hosts in Atlanta were Ruth and Mac McLeod. "I also had the pleasure of having lunch with Wayne Smith and Bobbie Jones," Klaus recalled.

Thanks to the McLeods, Mierendorff soon went to Opelika and found the campsite and a few barracks still standing. Next, with help from Mac McLeod, Mierendorff rented a car and plotted his course on a map. Then he was off to Reidsville. By noon, he arrived and noticed a welcome sign with the greeting "Reidsville, Georgia—Friendship City USA."

Mierendorff remembered that the camp consisted of tents plus a kitchen and wash barracks built of wood. He also recalled that the POWs built a small church, according to the orders of the commanding officer. Klaus drove into Reidsville with mixed feelings, only to find that time had taken part of the town with it. Once-nice houses were boarded up and front yards had gone to seed. However, Klaus noted that the "townscape" was about the same. He finally found the spot where the camp must have stood, but the small church and the water tower that stood nearby no longer existed. From talking to elderly residents and the local insurance agent, he could learn nothing about Mr. Moon. Mierendorff regretted not finding some members of the family still living in the area, but Mr. Moon will always live in his heart and his memory. And thanks to some caring new Friendship Force friends, he was able to make a very sentimental journey in search of an old friend.

Another major event in 1982 was the establishment of a Sasakawa Fellowship Program for worthy ambassadors who simply could not afford to travel otherwise. The program was scheduled to be repeated in 1983.

By the end of 1982, thanks to the Sasakawa gift, The Friendship Force budget was enlarged to include many new areas. Tony Coates, Hugh White and John Luke were busy in the UK and Stanley Mooneyham worked to find leadership for The Friendship Force in China, Poland and Thailand.

In 1983, The Friendship Force offered three types of experiences, now that the huge charter flights were a thing of the past. In addition to exchanges with home hosting there were non-reciprocal exchanges outbound from the United States and there were interchanges planned with the USSR, China and Poland.

The Friendship Force of South Central Minnesota in Krakow, Poland, on a Friendship Interchange in December, 1983.

American ambassadors learn about Chinese cotton production.

Gerald Weekes of New Zealand calls his group of Friendship Force hosts and ambassadors together.

Two Friends, Henny Willemsen of The Netherlands and Tony Coates of the UK, have often worked together to promote The Friendship Force.

Chapter 10
New Builders - Old Lands

With friends there is no East or West;
There is no South or North.
But one great fellowship of love
Throughout the whole wide earth.
(Adapted from a hymn by **John Oxenham**.)

Wayne Smith visited beautiful New Zealand in the Pacific and fell in love with this unique two-island country. During his stay he met Gerald Weekes, a genial giant of a man and a public information officer for the city of Wanganui. Years later Weekes fondly recalled that meeting.

"I received some preliminary information on The Friendship Force and a letter from Wayne Smith telling me he would be coming to my city to seek an appointment with me," Weekes recalled. "We often received such requests and some of them were not legitimate; therefore, I tended to be a bit wary of all new proposals. Smith said he would be there on a Monday, but he telephoned me on a Sunday evening to schedule an appointment.

"It was not an ideal time because Helen and I had just returned from a major promotional tour for our city and we were very tired. Nevertheless, I told him to come to my office at 8:30 a.m., thinking I would see him quickly and get it over with before I tackled the full day's work awaiting me. I simply couldn't imagine what this Friendship Force business was all about or how it remotely related to me.

"The next morning Wayne Smith came in as scheduled and sat down. Basically he began by saying 'Have I got a deal for you!'

"How would you like a group...

"A group?"

"Yes, how would you like a group of people to come here to stay in private homes to promote friendship and understanding among our people."

"How many people?" Weekes asked warily.

"Well...a lot of people...do you think you could put together a group of people willing to host people from another country with the idea that they would become friends?"

"Well...yes, I'm sure I could, but...."

"Good!" Smith said.

"How many are coming?"

"Eighty people will be coming for a week."

"Eighty! For a week!

"Well, before I knew it, there was a knock on my door. It was my wife Helen telling me it was lunch time!" Weekes recalled. "Quick as a wink Wayne Smith piped up and said 'Shall we all go to lunch?'

"So we did and he kept talking about The Friendship Force. As we talked I began to see what an amazing organization this Friendship Force was. We went back to my office and continued talking and suddenly I realized it was three p.m. Wayne said he had a plane to catch in an hour, so my wife and our daughters took him to the airport.

"I reflected on everything he'd said on the way home and I realized that the reason I had wanted to know every little thing about The Friendship Force organization was because I was sold. Completely sold. And you know what? That meeting with Wayne Smith changed our lives."

The meeting changed a lot of lives in New Zealand and Australia. By 1996, there were twenty-three clubs in New Zealand and twenty-one in Australia. The Gerald Weekes International Club of the Year award was established in 1988.

The Friendship Force had operated primarily via the system of State and National Directors and by May 1983, the club system was becoming well established. In the USA, thirty-three clubs had been licensed with eight more in the embryonic state. Five overseas clubs were also licensed.

Also in May, the first mission to Mainland China was led by Wayne Smith and Janey Ashley of Omaha. This exchange was well received and greatly exceeded expectations. Ashley later wrote about her impressions of that vast land and its people.

"Millions of Chinese ride bicycles thorough the streets of Peking and Shanghai," Ashley said. "Tree-lined avenues are crowded with endless waves of blue, olive drab, gray and black Mao-coated figures. Street vendors' stalls throng the side streets selling many varieties of fresh produce.

"Daily life begins early in China and the streets are teeming with activity by five a.m. The slow, trance-like motions of *tai chi*, an ancient form of the martial arts, and individual meditation are practiced by many as they gather in front of buildings or in parks.

"Any Friendship Force story is a story of people. And certainly the masses of Chinese encountered by the ambassadors on the first Friendship Force Mission to China was the first and most lasting impression. For the Chinese, our group of seventy-six Nebraskans, two Iowans and four Georgians was massive too. The Chinese People's Association for Friendship with Foreign Countries, more accustomed to tour groups of four to twenty, had carefully organized a busy itinerary for us.

"Outdoor markets with their varied wares lined many streets and intrigued the ambassadors, who wished for more time to wander through the streets, mingle with the citizens and experience the sights and sounds and smells which are part of life for millions of Chinese. Whenever their busy schedule allowed, ambassadors did just that, frequently finding themselves surrounded by a growing crowd of Chinese as they presented little cards written in Chinese to explain their purpose. Many colorful green balloons that announced The Friendship Force in Chinese and English were given to solemn faced children, who...were often reminded by their parents to say 'thank you.' Frequently children are tended by grandparents, who push the babies and toddlers about the city and country roads in split bamboo carts similar to our baby buggies.

"Few are idle. Jobs are assigned. One young woman explained that it is not easy to change jobs because you must find other work, then get permission from the superior there before requesting a release from your present employer. It is unusual to ask for a change and even more unusual for it to be granted," she said.

"While true friendships were difficult to develop in such short time spans, friendly smiles, language cards, limited conversations and small gifts were rewarded with a warm response from the Chinese. A frequent topic was the change that has occurred since the cultural revolution. It seemed very important to the Chinese that this recent but slow progress be recognized.

"The most in-depth chances to communicate were experienced at briefings with the Chinese guides on the buses and at the receptions. Others met and talked with Chinese citizens, exchanging addresses and promises for further communication. Two ambassadors were invited in for tea after they met an elderly Chinese woman during an early morning stroll. Another ambassador had dinner with the family of a Chinese friend now living in Nebraska.

"I can say that the first group of Friendship Force ambassadors to visit the People's Republic of China found the experience surpassed their greatest expectations. For each there were unique adventures, special memories and a feeling of success in beginning the bond of friendship between Chinese and Americans—Friendship Force style."

A number of Americans received letters from some of the Chinese they encountered. In a note to Richard Marshall, Huang Ji wrote: "I'm very proud of having an American friend like you from the USA. Still can I recall the scene of conversation we had at the People's Park in Shanghai, through which was born firmly in my mind a good memory as well as a good impression of the people of the USA."

After Janey Ashley served as the director of the first interchange to the People's Republic of China, she moved from Nebraska to Atlanta to become an exchange coordinator with Friendship Force International.

Washington State globe-trotters Bettye and Harold Brown went to Berlin as ambassadors. They were hosted by a couple who had a cousin behind the Berlin Wall. When the wall was erected, the cousin was cut off from the rest of her kin in West Germany.

"While we were there, we went with our hosts to see this cousin," Bettye said. "It took about an hour by train. What a shock it was to see East Berlin after just having been in West Berlin. The Communist area was awful—the saddest, grayest place you've ever seen.

"Later we went back to East Berlin by car and witnessed first-hand the scrutiny given to people who were going from one side of the Wall to the other. When grain trucks came through, soldiers would climb on top carrying long poles with sharp spikes attached. They would jab the spikes down in the grain. If anyone was hiding beneath the grain, they would be killed or seriously wounded. We also saw the soldiers take cars apart looking for anyone trying to escape from the East.

"We tried to do a small amount of shopping in East Berlin," Bettye said. "I wanted a doll for my collection. We looked and looked and found only two very small ones. Our German friends pointed to one department store and with typical dry humor explained: 'Now in that store, if you don't want a TV, you go to the first floor; if you don't want a radio, go to the second floor and if you don't want a stove, go to the third floor....'"

In May 1983, The Friendship Force published the first issue of *Friendship* magazine, with William P. "Bill" Lamkin as editor and director of publications. He was assisted by Becky Bradshaw. Lamkin had previously served as news director and as editor and publisher of *Presbyterian Survey*. He was with the *Survey* for twenty-two years.

With six issues annually, *Friendship* magazine was a much-needed vehicle whereby volunteers could share their Friendship Force experiences with others throughout the growing network of clubs. The very first issue of the magazine contained a message from Wayne Smith in what became a regular column called "Friend To Friend."

The inaugural issue of the magazine was dedicated to Rosalynn Carter. In a salute to Mrs. Carter titled "The First Lady of Friendship," Wayne Smith said "Many people have had a hand in the making of The Friendship Force. Thousands of hosts and ambassadors have participated in Friendship Force exchanges since its beginning in March 1977, as a result of the efforts of hundreds of volunteer leaders in some thirty-five countries and thirty-five states in the USA...but no one has played a more important role than Rosalynn Carter. It truthfully can be said that without her initial sponsorship, involvement and dedication, The Friendship Force would not be a reality today.

"The role she has is that of aiding, advising and of opening doors. She continues to play this role to the point that, as this magazine is being formed, the Carters have recently returned from the Middle East and within two days of their return, Rosalynn wrote to say, 'Morocco is most interested in an exchange. I'll talk with you about it soon—and about Jordan.' She also met with Friendship Force volunteers in Egypt. She is constantly working for The Friendship Force, leading forcefully, quietly and effectively...."

By this time, things were beginning to look more promising in the USSR. Valery I. Zima, manager of the Intourist Travel Information office in the USA commented, "We have thousands of Americans who come to the Soviet Union every year for vacation and fun, but they come with the attitude of a tourist wanting the full value for their money. They are not governed by the idea of making Soviets understand Americans. But through The Friendship Force, large groups of Americans come with the idea of bringing the best of themselves and their feelings to the people," he continued. "They are able to share the good and bad about their life and, in turn, learn about the good and bad in the life of Soviets."

However, a serious incident in 1983 threatened to wipe out all gains made in the USSR. The first of a series of Missions to Moscow, led by lieutenant governors from around the country was to begin September 9, with Georgia's Zell Miller as the first leader in the series. The Missions to Moscow project was aborted nine days before the scheduled departure when a Korean Airlines plane was shot down by Soviet jets. US Congressman Larry McDonald of Georgia was one of the victims of the attack. Lieutenant Governor Mike Runnels from New Mexico immediately canceled the mission he was to lead beginning October 14.

This was a disturbing and costly turn of events for The Friendship Force; however, Wayne Smith told reporters that "...when the time is right for people-to-people contacts between citizens of the USA and the USSR, our missions will resume." Few shared Smith's optimism for a renewal of exchanges with the Soviet Union. It seemed as if the Iron Curtain had suddenly dropped and was drawn tightly shut once again.

In addition to the cancellation of the Missions to Moscow flights, an anticipated first exchange with Nigeria was canceled due to adverse changes in the political climate there. Charlotte Blackmon of Alabama and others had worked tirelessly to try to make the Nigerian exchange a reality and they were very disappointed with this failed effort.

The first of the all-European conferences was held in June in Holland. Delegates from England, Germany, Holland and Ireland attended. On September 1, the anniversary of the 1939 invasion of Poland by Nazi Germany, the first Friendship Force visitors from Madison, Wisconsin, left Berlin by train to enter Poland, using friendship to win the hearts of the Polish people. Zdzislaw Pawlik, General Secretary of the Polish Ecumenical Council in Warsaw, was host chairman for The Friendship Force Missions to Poland. The mission—dubbed "A Friendly Invasion"—was led by Margo Lindl, later to become a member of The Friendship Force Board of Trustees.

The Missions to Poland involved hosting for the American ambassadors, but only during the day. Each night the ambassadors returned to their hotel. Reverend Pawlik went to a great deal of trouble to match ambassadors with Polish Hosts who had an English speaking family member or members. This made vital communications flow well, much to the satisfaction of hosts and ambassadors alike. The first city visited was Czestochowa. Then, following a farewell dinner, the Wisconsin group left for Krakow.

Although Lindl later reported much confusion with the tour agency, with bus drivers and at border crossings, the first mission to Poland was a positive experience. One ambassador wrote: "The mission was the best time I ever had in my life. I'm sure we made many new friends, which was our goal."

Lindl summed up the mission experience with this: "With adverse and almost daily "crises" being faced by our sturdy group of ambassadors, a loss of morale could have been fatal! But instead, everyone rose to the true spirit of "flexibility." All became one in crises, one in joy and one in friendship."

Not all of the correspondence to Friendship Force International was positive. Wayne Smith received this stormy letter of protest from one couple who went on the first Friendship Force exchange to Egypt:

Dear Mr. Smith:

We have been royally taken in by the "Friendship Force." You have used us as Guinea Pigs and had us live like Guinea Pigs to satisfy one of your whims. For all the following reasons...we feel that we should be reimbursed for our six night stay at the Holiday Inn and three meals a day, not to mention our transportation.

For what we paid, you had us put up in huts of FILTH, DIRT, BUGS, COCKROACHES, CHICKENS AND GOATS. We were fed by our hosts from carts on the street.

Arriving at the Cairo airport was enough to make anyone take the next flight right back to the USA. Our host picked us up in a taxi because he was too poor to own a car and away we went to his tenement. As we entered his "home" we had to walk through...filth and up 5 flights of stairs. We soon discovered that an Egyptian's education and title does not reflect his home life. His home was filthy, one towel in the bathroom, no soap and no toilet paper could be flushed in the toilet. We had to put it in the waste basket and when the basket was full, he would then empty it into the street! The kitchen had not been cleaned or remodeled in at least 200 years!

I confronted your leader about this the next day and complained about our living conditions and reminded her of what we paid to make this trip. She only said, "You do not belong in The Friendship Force!"

Most of the people from Salt Lake City held a grudge against me for complaining. After we moved to the Holiday Inn, your leader did not call us even once to see how we were doing!"

I expect an answer and a check from The Friendship Force and an apology.

However, Wayne Smith also received the following letter from Paul Jones of Salt Lake City who was on the same exchange:

Dear Wayne,

After reading a copy of a letter sent to you by a couple...who stated that the Egyptian Friendship Force trip was a disaster, I had to reply to that letter and to you.

It's amazing! I took exactly the same trip they did and was placed in similar conditions and I can say without reservation, it was the most interesting, most gratifying, most exciting trip I have ever taken in my life...and I have been all over the world. I have stayed with a family in Venezuela who had five servants and, for a week, I slept on the floor in the flat of a taxicab driver in Berlin. The couple who wrote the letter apparently have no concept of what The Friendship Force is all about. It is not, as all of us have been told many, many times, a 'freebie luxury tour.' It is a golden opportunity to meet people in their environment and in their homes and to share their lifestyles and their problems, as well as their joys. This is a unique opportunity that I have not found anywhere else.

We learned in a hurry that dirt is not a negative concept in Egypt. There is dirt everywhere. In terms of dirt on the streets it is probably the dirtiest city I have ever visited. However, I didn't see a single hippie-type spaced out on dope, nor were the streets littered with drunks and transients as you find in many of our larger cities. Dirt there is a fact of life. So that's how it is—no big deal.

The most important thing we discovered was the friendliness and the generosity of these lovely people who somehow manage to survive on as little as a hundred dollars a month. As the poet Gibran said, *Generosity is not in giving me that which I need more than you do, but in giving me that which you need more than I do.* It was obvious that these people were being generous far beyond their means. They offered us all that they had...who could ask more!

One night in the middle of one of Cairo's busiest streets, their wreck of a car broke down. We laughed all the time we were pushing the car and dodging traffic.

Certainly there was dirt, certainly there was economic hardship and problems but they were nothing when compared to the beauty and warmth of these people. We were simply overwhelmed by these lovely people and the close family ties they held with all of their relatives. We became a part of their big happy Egyptian family.

Again to quote Gibran: *The only difference between the richest man and the poorest is but a day of hunger and an hour of thirst.* These people opened freely their home to us and as humble and meager as some of them may have been, they were offering us all they had to offer. I didn't hear of one single Egyptian family turning an ambassador out of his home because *they* couldn't take it.

I truly feel sorry for those who couldn't cope. Some people never seem to realize that friendship is not an opportunity, but a sweet responsibility. We personally feel that we not only made some life-long friends, but that in some small way we helped to dispel the myth of the "Ugly American" that is so prevalent around the world.

I find it amusing in a way that two couples could view the same trip and similar circumstances with such totally different perspectives.

Since the very first exchange in 1977, a very special Friendship Force relationship continued to develop between citizens of England and of the United States. Many people in England made a world of difference in those early Friendship Force. One couple, Tony and Jenny Coates of Riding Mill, Northumberland, threw their considerable energies and enthusiasm into The Friendship Force from the beginning.

"We almost missed the opportunity to participate in the very first exchange," Tony Coates said. "You see, over a thousand people signed up to travel or host. Late in the selection process, we discovered that our application had been received, but we had not been given the required appointment for an interview. That was quickly arranged and we were selected. We went to Atlanta on the first exchange in July 1977, and we're still good friends with the people who were our hosts. Jenny was expecting our first child at the time.

"When our daughter was born, we had several names selected, including 'Amy.' Since we had met President and Mrs. Carter through The Friendship Force and their daughter was named Amy, we named our daughter Amy also.

"We were completely sold on The Friendship Force. We hosted in 1978 and in 1980, I was exchange director for a group which went to Cheyenne, Wyoming, and I traveled with The Friendship Force to Berlin that same year. Unfortunately, Jenny couldn't go on either of those trips because she was expecting our second daughter Charlotte.

"Newcastle was chosen as the site for the 1981 Friendship Force International Conference and I was head of the committee. Following that experience, Wayne Smith asked me to go to Holland with some people to organize clubs there. I met Henny Willemsen, a great man and still a good friend, and he helped in getting the first clubs organized in The Netherlands."

Jenny Coates remembered a phone call she received in 1982. "When I answered the phone," she said. "I learned that Amy Carter was coming on an exchange, traveling with a Friendship Force group from Lancaster, Pennsylvania. We were asked to host Amy and her friend Cricket Kent. The girls were both fourteen.

"We also learned that Amy and Cricket would be traveling with seven members of the Secret Service. We were thirty years old at the time and this was quite exciting for our family.

"Before they arrived, Mrs. Carter called and instructed us to discipline the girls as if they were our own if they gave us any problems. She said they didn't expect us to treat the girls any differently just because Amy's father was once President of the United States."

Tony Coates added, "We were still quite in awe. It was thrilling to receive phone calls from Washington and to learn we would be hosting the former President's daughter. As it turned out, we had a great time with Amy and Cricket and everything went very smoothly. I think they enjoyed themselves quite a bit."

In interviews with several newspaper and TV reporters in Newcastle, Amy Carter said: "I have had to save my money to come here. I have been doing odd jobs like baby sitting and washing cars to earn part of the money." Amy also said her dad had told her that the people in Newcastle were very nice and that she and her friend would have fun while they were there.

One TV reporter said of the secret service men: "As we gather to meet Amy, they are searching politely but firmly, the camera cases of the gentlemen of the local press, many of whom are astonished by their presumption."

Amy Carter said, "I've made a list of places to see here. Before we came, we researched the area a bit—but it depends on Mr. and Mrs. Coates. I'm happy to go anywhere they want me to go."

Another newsman said: "Amy was soon romping with her friend Cricket and the two daughters of her hosts...posing for pictures, slipping down slides, cuddling and smiling."

"The Friendship Force works in an amazing manner," Tony Coates said. "You should be at the airport at the end of a visit. Hosts and ambassadors are crying all over the place. And the emotion is quite sincere because friendships, quite deep and lasting, can be made in a few day's time."

When asked how he thinks The Friendship Force of Newcastle became the first club to thrive and grow, Coates gives much credit to Theresa Russell, former Lord Mayoress of the city. "I remember when Theresa Russell was introducing a guest from South Korea," Coates chuckled. "She was up on the platform when she suddenly noticed that she was wearing one red shoe and one green one. She said, 'In case some of you are wondering about my shoes, I have another pair just like them at home.' She said that quick as a flash. She's such a quick thinker. She's been known to stop people on the street who aren't from the area and invite them for a cup of coffee or to lunch, selling Newcastle all the while. She has contacts all over the UK and some of those helped us with other clubs. Frankly, I think Newcastle was selected for the first exchange because of Theresa Russell's enthusiasm and power of persuasion. She loves Newcastle and it shows."

(Theresa Russell has often described The Friendship Force as "the biggest family going, full of warmth and love.")

Another early booster of The Friendship Force was Alan Redhead, information and publicity officer with the Newcastle City Council. He served as the Newcastle exchange director on the very first exchange.

Amy Carter makes friends with Amy Coates.

Angelica Tavares of Brazil changed her mind.

A shining example of Friendship Force magic in action is in the following essay written by Angelica Lino Goncalves Tavares of Sao Paulo, Brazil, daughter of Levy Tavares, one of Wayne Smith's closest friends:

From Disdain to Friendship

When the special bus stopped slowly in front of the Centro de Convencoes do Anhemi in Sao Paulo last May 17, 1983, and the party of "ambassadors" coming from Lancaster, Pennsylvania, prepared to get off, I thought my heart was going to jump out. The only thing I knew was the name of the couple we were going to receive as our guests, and nothing else. My letter to the "ambassadors" didn't reach them in time and I confess, it was better they didn't get it because it said nothing but a few conventional words of welcome.

I was involved with The Friendship Force reluctantly, only for Dad's sake. He was the exchange director and he put all his family members on the alert. He told us that in case any Brazilian family failed in coming through, then we would be ready to take their place. And that was what happened. A problem of illness in the chosen family transferred their expected guests to us. My father already had much responsibility, so I myself would have to take on bigger responsibilities because I could speak English fairly well.

I had two problems. First, I was not yet convinced of the objectives of The Friendship Force and second, I didn't like the *gringos*.

In the first case, because of all I had read about the program, I got the idea that a few crafty ones had discovered an intelligent way of combining tourism and politics through the program—unfurling the flag of fraternity among men as a pretense for their personal ambitions.

In the second case, as I already belonged to the Communist Party, I had learned to hate the American capitalism and the explorer imperialists!!! So, my disposition was not the best one to receive the group. However, as I was accompanying my father in his efforts, hurries and apprehensions, it wasn't fair for me to abandon him in such a difficulty.

The door of the bus opened and the first gringos began to come out. I was right! They were really clumsy people and so inelegant in their attire. Those red Bermudas reaching their knees, black shoes, long white socks, a purple shirt and a yellow cap made up the typical appearance of a North American. The women had the same ridiculous appearance, in their loose dresses, shoes with low heels, and a little colored hat with an inevitable little flower on its side. Speaking loudly, gesticulating as if they were the owners of the world, they started greeting us. And I thought to myself: "Ambassadors of what?" But soon I noticed the grim look of my father. He looked at me as if he were guessing my thoughts and then I smiled. "OK, Uncle Sam, I am here," I thought and with a broad smile, I went to meet the couple.

She was tall and blond with beautiful eyes and a likable complexion. He, a little shorter, seemed to be around fifty. Making an effort, I greeted them heartily, feeling that my initial task was fulfilled. Finally the luggage was in the car and I took them home. After the first meal together, I felt, for the first moment, a real approximation of their friendliness when I looked straight at the eyes of John and Mary, trying to discover who they really were behind that image. I had made up my mind about Americans through the years.

Just then Mary came over and put a charming red rose pin on my blouse, the symbol of Lancaster, her city. She kissed me on my face.

"There are moments," she said "in which, more than ever, we need the friendship of our fellow beings."

I saw tears in her eyes and immediately I associated the red color of the rose with her tears, thinking that while we belong to different races and have habits, traditions, religion and ways of living that are really different, there is no difference in our tears, or in our blood—be they occidental or oriental, black, white or yellow; Christians, Buddhists or Islamites; rich or poor; capitalist or communist. We are only human beings, created to live together in harmony, with our rights and wrongs, virtues and defects, with our accordance and discordance, but nothing that a cultured feeling of sincere and profound friendship isn't able to surpass or excel.

This reflection hit me fully and I couldn't sleep that night. However, in the morning, I was ready to go out with John and Mary. Not a single minute late, because I had already heard about the rigor and discipline of the North Americans concerning time and schedule. Soon we were riding about to show our guests the city of Sao Paulo.

Wonderful days ran on, and every moment and in every one of their gestures and words I found one more reason to admire and respect that couple. For years, I had been developing a false image about the North American people, but now that I was having the opportunity to have a close relationship with two of their representatives, that image was fading out, giving place to a friendship among us.

Today I understand the value of these exchanges, to which I began to devote a good part of my life, working as a volunteer. I have a new conception of life and this transformation of mine I owe to the experience I received by participating in The Friendship Force. The force of friendship in this one couple led me to an extraordinary experience of life.

The names of John and Mary are not their real names. There is a reason for this. The wife was suffering from leukemia and on a certain day, her husband told me, as a secret, that their trip to Brazil was a kind of farewell journey for them. They both wanted to enjoy together a trip abroad, preceding the big one to eternity which Mary would have to make some few months later.

The spirit of this couple—their meekness, their affection and tenderness, their generous friendship, their big example of faith—brought light to my way and I thank God for this.

At the time the group met to depart, my eyes were swollen because of so much crying and the words of Mary were still sounding clearly in my ears. *There are moments in which, more than ever, we need the friendship of our fellow beings*, she said. Now I could understand her. Now I could understand the meaning of and the reason for the existence of The Friendship Force.

They walked toward the bus in their red Bermudas, long socks and yellow caps, in their loose dresses, shoes with low heels and the ever-present little flower on the hats. I raised my hand in a last farewell. I could only stammer: *Good-bye, Mary; good-bye forever. Good-bye, gringos.*

President Ronald Reagan was portrayed as a warmonger in the USSR; however, in this speech in 1984, Reagan said some things that sounded a lot like what The Friendship Force founders had known and believed since the organization began:

Just suppose with me for a moment that an Ivan and an Anya could find themselves, oh, say, in a waiting room or sharing a shelter from the rain or a storm with a Jim and Sally. And suppose there was no language barrier to keep them from getting acquainted.

Would they then debate the differences between their respective governments? Or would they find themselves comparing notes about their children and what each other did for a living? Before they parted company, they would probably have touched on ambitions and hobbies and what they wanted for the children and problems of making ends meet.... They might even have decided they were all going to get together for dinner some evening soon.

Above all they would have proven that people don't make wars. People want to raise their children in a world without fear and without war. They want to have some of the good things over and above bare subsistence that make life worth living. They want to work at some craft, trade or profession that gives them satisfaction and a sense of worth. Their common interests cross all borders.

If the Soviet Government wants peace, then there will be peace. Together we can strengthen peace, reduce the level of arms and know in doing so that we have helped fulfill the hopes and dreams of those we represent and, indeed of people everywhere. Let us begin now."

When Stephen Y.S. Kim, Friendship Force Vice President for Development in the Far East, went to Bangkok in search of a leader, he was told by Prok Amranand, former Ambassador to the US, to contact Khunying Kanitha Wichiencharoen, Executive Secretary of the Thai-American Corporation. Khunying Kanitha had twice been decorated by the King of Thailand for her campaign for human rights. She was one of the best known and most respected professional women in Thailand. Despite her busy schedule, she accepted the task of organizing a Friendship Force Club in Thailand and of being the exchange director for the first incoming exchange in 1984. Club members in Iowa and Montana—103 strong—had nothing but praise for Khunying Kanitha's leadership..

Bill Lamkin, editor of *Friendship* magazine, joined 102 other Americans from Des Moines, Iowa, and Great Falls, Montana, to travel to far away Thailand, the land of smiles. He was hosted by Amarin Jugsujinda, his wife—nicknamed 'Poo'—and their three young children, Nan, Kong and Kay. From the start, the children called Lamkin "Uncle Bill," and fast and lasting friendships were quickly formed. This was true for the other ambassadors as well, many of whom wrote glowing descriptions of Thai hospitality.

Bill Lamkin's host said this was the first time the family had had a Westerner to live with them. They rearranged their own living quarters to make sure their honored guest had a room with a ceiling fan—the oldest daughter's room was given to Lamkin.

Like the other Friendship Force ambassadors, Lamkin was constantly delighted by ancient and exotic sights, such as the Emerald Buddha, the temple of Dawn and the old capital city of Aytutthya. Ambassadors and hosts enjoyed a grand evening reception at the home of US Ambassador John Guenther Dean. Dean was familiar with The Friendship Force from his former service as US Ambassador to Denmark and to Lebanon.

At the end of the Thailand adventure, Bill Lamkin said "The first Friendship Force exchange for Thailand is now history. It was a new idea for the Thais, but I left with the feeling that an exchange could not have failed there. After all, the Thai people have been friendship practitioners for centuries."

Connie McDonald of Great Falls, Montana, said she would describe the Thais in three words: "friendly, well-mannered and patient. Americans would do well to take a lesson from them," she added.

Eleanor and Paul Johnson, also from Great Falls, were honored guests at a Buddhist Funeral. Their Thai Host was invited to officiate at the ceremony and the family of the deceased also invited the visiting Americans. The Johnsons discovered that the chief monk already knew about The Friendship Force and was impressed by the organization's ideals.

India also had a first exchange in 1984, along with Sweden and Norway. Misha Radulovic tried to organize an exchange between Minnesota and Yugoslavia back in 1978 but the timing was not right. He assisted in activating Missions to Yugoslavia in 1984, this time with Des Moines.

Croatian grandmother weaves a gift for Harold and Bettye Brown.

Ireland was reactivated in 1984, a year after the Dublin club had disbanded. With much assistance from Bord Failte, the Irish Tourism Board, The Friendship Force organized a country-wide advertising campaign designed to assist with ambassadors in several Irish communities. This first year, ambassadors traveled to Ireland as part of a Friendship Force Mission. Ambassadors were hosted in bed and breakfast homes and farms, rather than in private homes. Constance Stapleton wrote of her encounter with new Irish friends and with her own newly-discovered Irish roots.

The Irish landscape is spectacular. Tidy towns with whitewashed and pastel-painted houses, some with thatch roofs held in place with wire. There is a refreshing lack of commercialization. Everywhere there are fenced-in yards full of flowers, varnished front doors with knobs in the center, often with a key left in the lock to let yourself in.

But the best of Ireland exists in her people. They smile and wave as you drive by, whether they know you or not. The Irish don't rush to meet tomorrow. They savor today, believing as my grandfather used to say, 'When God made time, he made a lot of it.'

Joe Clancy, our bus driver, not only explained Irish history and geography in depth as we went along, but also politics, economics, religion and sports.

"No matter how small a village," he explained "it will have a church, a school and a bar." We found the level of conversation in most pubs to be intellectually broader than most discussions at our college faculty get-togethers, but you don't have to drink to have a good time in Ireland and no pressure is put on you to do so.

Irishmen are in love with their words and never seem to be at a loss for them. "Every family I know has talkers and listeners," a young Irishman told me. "The listeners never talk and the talkers never stop."

The Irish are survivors who have outlasted many would-be conquerors and they have always known how to live well on little and to share what they have in style.

But best of all was the insight our hosts gave us in Irish values. Our first hosts, Ray and Mairead Maguire, never slapped the hand of eighteen-month-old Sarah. Instead of 'no!' they asked 'please?' giving her responsibility for the choice. It always worked. Their twins, David and Deidre, age nine, and Ann Marie, age seven, never argued over homework or chores and they entertained us in the evening with Irish dancing and tin whistle music.

Our Dublin hosts, Maudie and John Duffie, passed up the social hour before the farewell dinner so they could help their son Joseph with his homework. Therese Hayes, our Kenmare host, in addition to raising six children, running a bed-and-breakfast and helping her husband with a farm, also taught at the village school. Families work together, filling in for one another. When I became ill in Kenmare, fifteen-year-old Una became my nurse and companion.

Visiting Irish cousins affected me deeply. Seeing faces so much like those at home and hearing that my now-deceased grandfather spent much time talking about me, were presents for the heart. Having learned that my family is from Cork, I plan to come back and learn more.

As we prepared to leave, my cousins said "You really are one of our own."

I returned to America with a new sense of self and well-being, content to appreciate life and to live each moment. But I know just as sure as the swans and seagulls return with the tide to Kenmare each day that I'll go back—adding, as my Irish friends do, the blessing and phrase "God willing."

Friendly faces abound in Ireland.

The Friendship Force of Lincoln, Nebraska, was the first group to have an exchange with an Arab city in Israel. Seeds were sown for this exchange after Bill Lamkin made a short visit there a few years earlier. Lamkin met some of the local dignitaries, including a Druze sheik (also spelled Druse). The sheik asked Lamkin to convey his sympathy and heartfelt feelings toward the American hostages in Iran.

Lila Clawson wrote about her experience in *Friendship* magazine. Part of her story follows:

The dark robed Bedouin paused at the crest of the hill, dividing his attention between the goats he was herding and a group of picnickers several hundred feet below. He watched as we gathered up our cups and plates and began to remove stones from the hillside in a symbolic ground-clearing for a new House of Hope to be built overlooking the old town of Shefar'am in Galilee, Israel. We had come from four states—Nebraska, California, New Mexico and Minnesota—on the exchange in May with Shefar'am.

Shefar'am is the second largest Arab town in Galilee after Nazareth, ten miles to the east. We lived five days in our hosts' homes, met and talked with the neighbors and explored their town, which is built on seven hills, like Rome.

We walked narrow streets where donkeys share the right of way with tractors and Toyotas, Volkswagens and Mercedes.

We met with the mayor and two deputy mayors, one a Druze Sheik and the other the Shefar'am exchange director, Elias Jabbour. We later sat on long, low divans in the homes of two Druze sheiks and drank bitter Arabian coffee from tiny cups. We noted a cordial relationship between the Christians and the Druze. One of the sheiks explained that the Druze religion had existed since the tenth century when its founders broke away from Islam.

Elias Jabbour, founder of the House of Hope, is a former social worker and teacher. He was a deputy mayor of Shefar'am. He had been meeting on a regular basis with a group of Christian, Druze and Moslem students. The chief topic of every discussion was the possibility of acquiring a permanent meeting place where Arabs and Jews could exchange views in peaceful confrontations.

"The bravest person today is the one who brings peace, not the one who makes war," Jabbour said. "It is only by meeting each other and talking together that we can break down barriers that separate Arabs and Jews. That is why the House of Hope was founded. It provides a place where people can come together in a peaceful atmosphere to settle old problems and old differences without bloodshed."

The present House of Hope became a reality as a result of a visit Jabbour and some young people made in 1978. While on a peace mission in Germany, they were invited to come to England and visit Coventry, which was pulverized by the German Luftwaffe in November 1940. After that night of death and destruction, an Anglican priest, standing in the rubble of Coventry's largest cathedral, picked up three nails from the burning roof and shaped them into a cross. Instead of hatred and bitterness, he told his people they would strive from that day on for peace and reconciliation in the world.

Thus was born the Community of the Cross of Nails. In the intervening years, CCN chapters have been organized all over the world, all dedicated to peace and reconciliation. After Elias Jabbour heard this story, he helped form a chapter of CCN in Shefar'am.

On another exchange, Bettye Brown said: "Shefar'am perches on a rocky hillside. We were guests in Elias Jabbour's House of Hope, next door to a mosque. The big bell in the mosque starts ringing at four a.m. There's no sleeping then.

Another night we didn't get much sleep because a noisy wedding party was celebrating in the street. We got up and watched the festivities from our window. We were surprised to see that the dancers were all males. They danced and sang until after midnight.

"The next night, Elias was gone almost all night on a private peace mission. He was trying to keep two families from annihilating one another. Elias said the feud was over an incident which occurred ten years earlier. It seems that a man 'touched' a woman, offending another man in the process. The angry male was still seeking vengeance a decade later. Elias said that people in his land have very long memories and that they often carry grudges for years before they try to even the score.

"After we left Shefar'am, Elias traveled with us as our host and guide." Bettye said. "He baptized me and several other ambassadors in the Jordan River. It was a moving experience for us all."

In 1984, California became more active in The Friendship Force with good leadership for clubs in the San Francisco Bay area, San Diego and Brea. Baton Rouge and Morgan City, Louisiana each formed clubs and in Hawaii new clubs were formed in Kauai and Maui. El Paso and Austin organized clubs as did Binghamton, New York. In Massachusetts, new clubs were licensed in the Boston area (North Shore), Pioneer Valley and Westborough. Dover and Hannover were organizing and another club was forming in Connecticut.

Expansion continued throughout Japan and an office was established in Tokyo. In 1984 there were nine exchanges between non-US clubs: Tokyo and Taipei; Seoul and Manila; Pisa and Bristol; Niigata and Seoul; Arnhem and Newcastle, Bergen and Newcastle, Cardiff and Berlin, Cali and Hannover and Seoul and Berlin.

Two special events in 1984 were the 250th Friendship Force exchange which was between North Carolina and New Delhi, India, and the 350th exchange in November when St. Louis and Southern New Jersey members visited Mainland China.

In May, former President and Mrs. Carter visited Japan, the site of the first Asian-Pacific Regional Conference of The Friendship Force. Forty delegates from five Asian nations attended. In June, the second European conference met in Hannover with eight nations sending delegates.

The annual Friendship Force Conference in Rio de Janeiro attracted 388 delegates. Former President Jimmy Carter was the keynote speaker at the conference. He remarked that he was grateful for what The Friendship Force had done and he was excited about prospects for the future. More of his speech follows:

I think you can see that sometimes we can become too obsessed with a subject or something we like, to the exclusion of other things, The Friendship Force has taught us not to be too obsessed with our own immediate concerns and to recognize that within our own community, as well as communities completely different from ours, we can broaden the range of our hearts and broaden the range of our minds and not be obsessed with the things which, in the past, may have had a very selfish and narrowly focused intent.

The only thing I don't like about Wayne Smith is that I've never found a way to say "no" to him and actually make it stick. A lot of times I have said "no" to begin with, but before the conversation was over, somehow or other his original idea with which I disagreed seemed to me to be my *own* original idea. And eventually I found myself trying to talk Wayne into doing what he wanted me to do to begin with.

Because of The Friendship Force I am convinced that now Americans are seen in thirty or more nations as being not "ugly Americans" but as people of humility, not arrogance; people of peace, not belligerence; people of service, and not demands, people who want to extend the benefits of our own great wealth to others; people who want to share experiences in a mutually beneficial way.

I'm grateful for what all of you have done in the past—and are doing now. But I'm even more grateful and excited about what we can do together in the future.

At the conference, the new roving ambassador for 1985 was announced, the winner being Sajee Sudhikam of Bangkok, Thailand, who won the essay contest. "Volunteer of the Year" was Inger Rice of

Richmond, Virginia, who was presented the award by Theresa Russell, former Lord Mayoress of Newcastle, England, and a member of The Friendship Force Board of Directors. Inger had served as a State Director since 1977, when she was chosen by Governor Godwin of Virginia.

Inger Rice has an interesting story which may help to explain why she feels so much a part of The Friendship Force. When she was a child in her native Denmark, the Germans occupied her country. Inger, a Protestant, attended a Catholic School. One day she came home and told her mother she had decided to become a nun. Her mother was concerned about this decision and decided to keep Inger out of school the next day.

The day Inger missed school, the British Royal Air Force attacked German targets in Copenhagen. The lead bomber was hit by German anti-aircraft fire and its bombs, dropped prematurely, landed on her school. The other British planes in the formation followed suit and dropped their bombs on the school also. About five hundred children died that day.

Inger said she has always felt her life was spared for a reason. "I guess that's why I knock myself out doing volunteer work," Inger explained. In addition to service with The Friendship Force, Inger served as a member of the Virginia Commission for Children and Youth, which originated the idea for the International Year of the Child. She is the founder of Virginia Cultural Laureates, which gives the Great American awards and she has also served on the boards of the Richmond YMCA, the University of Richmond and the Virginia Museum Council.

Inger married Walter Rice in 1960. Rice was then a vice president and director of Reynolds Metals Company. He has also served as the United States' Ambassador to Australia.

Gladys Warren of Oklahoma died unexpectedly on October 28, 1984. She was one of the original group of State Directors and was a genuine Friendship Force friend and enthusiast A photograph of Gladys Warren at the White House with Honorary Chairperson Rosalynn Carter graced the cover of the November-December issue of *Friendship* magazine and Wayne Smith devoted his Friend to Friend column to her memory.

Fifty-one Sasakawa Fellowships were awarded during the year and one of those went to Anne Hausrath of Idaho. Anne was part of a group of quilters who made a special Peace Quilt which was delivered to the Soviet Embassy in Washington in 1982. The quilt was a gift to the ordinary citizens of the Soviet Union and was ultimately sent to the Soviet Women's Committee in Moscow for delivery to the Lithuanian city of Alytus (Also spelled Alitus) where it was supposed to be displayed.

Anne Hausrath was thrilled to receive a Sasakawa Fellowship, enabling her to travel to the Soviet Union with a group of fifty ambassadors led by Lieutenant Governor David Leroy. Anne and another quilter, Pat Hall, had two goals—they wanted to travel to Alytus to see the first Peace Quilt and they planned to present a second Peace .Quilt, made by the Boise Peace Quilt group. This second quilt was composed of tracings of drawings—images of children, flowers and mountains—sent by Soviet and American children. The women felt that this quilt was very special because it was symbolic of the combined hopes of parents everywhere—hopes that their children would grow up in a peaceful world. During the actual quilting process, many of the women involved felt they were symbolically stitching together a torn and divided world.

Delivering the new quilt to the location of the first one proved to be both a challenge and a study in determination. The challenge began when they learned that Alytus was a closed city to foreigners. They were then told that the first quilt was in Vilnius, a city in Lithuania which was not closed. After a week of frustration of threading their way through a bureaucratic maze, they found an Intourist representative who took their case to heart and helped them get their visas to go to Vilnius. After the initial frustration in Vilnius, they contacted Birute Boriesienne, head of the Soviet Women's Committee. She happily informed Anne and Pat that the first quilt had just arrived in Vilnius where it would be displayed as part of the 40th anniversary of their liberation from the Nazis. She also told them the Peace Museum was under construction and that when it was completed, the quilt would be on permanent display.

Later Ann Hausrath said: "Will the Peace Quilt experience make any difference? No one can predict what any of these personal experiences will mean in the broader tapestry of world diplomacy. But for those of us who participated, the value was in the doing."

There's peace in the valley, yet still more mountains to cross.
Photo by Kathleen Ingram used by permission.

Chapter 11
A New Arms Treaty?

Do the Russians Want a War?
Go ask the soldiers lying still
Beneath the birches on the hill
Go ask the sons who weep no more,
Ask, "Do the Russians want a war?"
—Evgeny Evtushenko, 1961

The first time I saw The Reverend Dr. David Wayne Smith was in late 1984. He was speaking from the pulpit of Big Canoe Chapel in North Georgia where he continues to serve as associate chaplain. As my husband Dave and I listened, we weren't at all sure we liked what we were hearing.

Smith began by telling of his plan to promote better understanding and harmony between people worldwide. Then he told of his latest plan to bring people from the USSR here. "They will be guests in our homes," he said. "When they arrive, let's greet them with ARMS—arms that hug, not arms that shoot."

Hug a Russian? Me? Not after my husband, retired Air Force Colonel Dave Terrell, spent over five years as a prisoner of war of one communist country in the Hanoi Hilton and other North Vietnamese prisons.

"Never!" I thought angrily.

Convinced that Smith's proposed A.R.M.S. program, the acronym for American Russian Mutual Survival, would never become a reality, we dismissed Wayne Smith's ideas as those of yet another idealistic and naive crusader. I remember marveling at how innocent this poor man must be to even *dream* of a time when Soviet officials would allow ordinary citizens to participate in a home-hosting exchange program in the camp of their perceived enemy

"The Soviets are no dummies," I reasoned. "They won't dare risk any defections or other potential embarrassments inherent in such a scheme."

How wrong I was. On May 8, 1985, the anniversary of the end of World War II in Europe, a group of thirty citizens from the Soviet Republic of Georgia came to our state of Georgia where they were greeted amid flashing cameras and glaring TV lighting. Music was provided by the Woodward Academy band at the Lockheed terminal at the Atlanta airport. Wayne Smith, through his brainchild organization, The Friendship Force, had actually succeeded in getting them here. Nevertheless, Dave and I were far from ready to embrace any Russians on the day ten of the Soviet Georgians arrived at Big Canoe, a North Georgia community where we and several hundred other families make our homes. (The other twenty Soviets left Atlanta for an excursion to Florida. Home-hosting was provided in Atlanta for a few days before they came to Big Canoe).

The visiting Georgians were hosted in the homes of our friends and neighbors and they all attended our tiny interdenominational Big Canoe Chapel on Sunday, May 12. Four of the Soviets took part in the service by singing a 12th Century Russian hymn.

Next Gela Charkviani, leader of the group and Deputy Chairman of the Georgian Friendship Society, added some excitement when he strode up to the microphone and pulled a wicked looking dagger from his vest. The "weapon" turned out to be a pen which he presented to former President Jimmy Carter's wife Rosalynn, who had come to Big Canoe for the occasion.

"I hope that gesture was the Soviet equivalent of burying the hatchet," I murmured to my husband.

As I glanced around the sea of smiling faces I saw former President Carter, a US Supreme Court Justice, hordes of camera crews and newspaper reporters and just about everybody in Big Canoe. People were crammed inside the sanctuary and the overflow crowd was sitting or standing on the decks, straining to hear and see. It was nothing short of amazing to see Americans and Soviets assembled in a house of worship in this obscure hamlet in the Blue Ridge Mountains.

That morning Gela Charkviani introduced others in the group including Violeta Dzhaparidze, a Tbilisi City Council member; Tamas Areshidze, cardiologist; Nodar Kikvadze, journalist and director of the Institute of Information, Georgia Academy of Sciences; Michail Guasalia, World War II hero and manager of a toy manufacturing plant; Georgi Kurtanidze, steel plant worker; Omar Chitaya, TV journalist, musician and singer; Michail Mtsuzavishvili, a choirmaster from Tbilisi, Nikolai Kapanadze, musician and singer and Tengiz Zaalishivilli, musician and singer. (Mr. and Mrs. Allya Konorezov traveled from Atlanta with the group. Mrs. Konorezov served as an interpreter.)

**Former President Jimmy Carter and Rosalynn Carter with two Soviet
Georgians in the historic visit to Georgia, USA, in 1985**

When President Carter spoke he described his and Leonid Brezhnev's exhilaration at the signing of the SALT II treaty. "We embraced and even exchanged kisses on the cheeks," Carter said. "Some of my opponents later criticized this move. But I'm convinced this is the kind of relationship that ought to exist between world leaders in working to remove the threat of a nuclear holocaust that could literally destroy this planet....

"My hope is that the harsh rhetoric and vituperation we've heard so much in recent years will soon be ended, and the hunger that exists in the hearts and minds of average citizens in both countries will soon be realized.... I'm grateful to all of you for this new vision of friendship and the use of arms to embrace and not to kill."

Near the close of the service the Chaplain, Dr. Vernon S. Broyles, Jr., said "What has happened today has touched chords in hearts that have not vibrated in a long time. To each Soviet Georgian I want to say that you have given us something we haven't had...your days here have been important to us. Our horizons have been broadened because you were here. Please know that as you go away that you are leaving those who now call you friends...."

The sense of history in the making was awesome that day. I wondered if those 'other' Georgians were feeling it too. My wondering was answered as people were exiting the chapel. A misty-eyed Tamaz

Areshidze, upon shaking President Jimmy Carter's hand, struggled to find proper words of expression in English. After a long handshake, he said "This has been the most remarkable day of my life."

Humorous things happened during the week, too. Before the Soviets arrived, the small community of Big Canoe was astir with activity. "We didn't know the difference between Russians and Georgians," Sandy Dussault said. "We went to Atlanta and bought a lot of Russian vodka. We also thought we would introduce them to the Peach State by making frozen peach daiquiris to impress them. We were reminded to give them food typical to North Georgia and, to us, that meant chicken.

Sandy's husband Nelson said, "Everywhere we took them during the three days they were here, they had chicken. They had it fried, stewed, baked, broiled, barbecued and fricasseed. Before they ate their last meal with us, our guest Michail Mtsuzavishvili, looked at us with a doleful expression and said, "Please, no more schiken (chicken)!"

"And when they were offered vodka, they turned it down," Sandy said. "They didn't drink much alcohol at all and when they did, they asked for wine. They thought our peach daiquiris were a strange kind of ice cream and they turned that down, too!"

Margaret and Lou Chester's guest was Tengiz Zaalishvili, one of the operatic tenors. "He spoke not one word of English," Margaret said. "One day when our guests had had several substantial meals and we were back home that evening, I offered Tengiz a midnight snack of dessert and coffee. He became very upset and we feared we had committed some breach of etiquette. He seemed so agitated that we called the interpreter and put Tengiz on the phone. He explained his problem to the interpreter and gave me the phone.

"The interpreter chuckled and said: 'He says: *No coffee, no tea, no orange juice, no dessert, no nothing. I just go to bed, please!*'"

As the Big Canoe hosts gathered to bid the visitors farewell, Gela Charkviani translated for Col. Michail Guasalia who said: "For us Georgians, this was not just three days spent in America. We were simply at home among our friends. We felt all the warmth here that we usually feel at home. We say 'thank you' from every one of us. We are leaving now, but all of you will be in our hearts forever. If we occupy a very small space in your hearts, we will be very grateful.

"The Colonel also says that now Georgians from both countries have tears in the eyes, but they are certainly tears of joy. We will be happy if this relationship becomes a tradition. We have a popular song called *Do the Russians Want a War*. If you are now convinced that neither we Georgians nor Russians want war, we are very grateful.

Before he got in the van to leave, Gela turned and smiled. "We love you," he said, "but without 'schiken!'

My original opinion of Wayne Smith's ideas changed that day, but I did not realize that far more important changes were taking place in the Kremlin under the new leadership of Mikhail Gorbachev. Soon we in America would add *perestroika* and *glasnost* to our vocabulary and, along with the rest of the world, we would soon wonder if the growing changes in the Soviet Union were for real. We had read what Charles McC. Mathias, Jr., a Senator from Maryland and a member of the Senate Foreign Relations Committee, had written in an article titled "Habitual Hatred—Unsound Policy." The senator said "Mutual understanding, leading to the erosion of Soviet rigidity through the contagion of exposure to freedom, is a distant dream, reachable, if at all, by very small steps."

Contagion of exposure to freedom.... Well, that was exactly what The Friendship Force was doing right here today in the foothills of the Blue Ridge Mountains. It was not "a distant dream, reachable, if at all by very small steps." It seemed like a big step to us, but was it a larger step for the Soviet visitors?

We wondered if the visitors were still certain about the evils of capitalism. When a reporter asked that question of Michael Mtsuzavishvili, he shrugged and said "So someone has more, someone has less. Should the relations of our two countries suffer because of this?"

Those conciliatory words were music to Wayne Smith's ears. But how did the Soviet ambassadors and their hosts hit it off? Eleanor Eyman of Big Canoe said this:

On May 10, the morning our Soviet Georgian visitors arrived at Big Canoe, I was reminded of the children on the first day at dancing school—boys on one side, girls on the other. As we waited beyond the marker Wayne Smith had delineated for us, we were mentally sorting them out. Which was the World War II hero, which the cardiologist? How would we converse? Would they like our food, would they like **us?**

We need not have worried. As Wayne gave us the signal to greet our guests, both groups moved quickly to pair off. I presented my guest with a single rose, a German custom I hoped would help us begin our dialogue with an international gesture of friendship.

From the time we boarded the bus for the ride to Dalton and Chattanooga, we found common ground. Violeta, called Viola, is a career woman, a city council member in Tbilisi. She explained a little of what that entails. I told her that I was a retired college library director. She showed me pictures of her husband and two children. Her husband is an engineer, as was mine. Her children love music, especially American jazz. I complimented her on her command of English.

Long before we arrived in Dalton, we were talking as easily as long-time friends. I pointed out anything I thought might be of interest, from fast-food shops to chicken houses. After Dalton, we went on to Chattanooga, Tennessee.

On the long ride home from Tennessee, the hosts sang old American standards. Our guests responded with ancient Georgian songs. Viola sang along with my Frank Sinatra cassettes. She also sang the old Negro spiritual *Ain' Go'n to Study War No Mo.'* We shopped at a music store and stopped by a marble shop. Back at home, I made coleslaw while Viola looked at dozens of catalogs. Before we knew it our visit was over. If there were any dry eyes at the farewell, I failed to see them.

In retrospect, it was a glorious, euphoric experience. So much said, so much not said. Do we few people make a difference in American-Soviet relationships? Yes, we do. We may not change the course of history, but we leave a mark. They sensed that, we sensed that. Who can say when a ripple will become a wave?

The Soviet guests and their interpreter traveled to Dalton, Georgia, where they were hosted by M B ."Bud" Seretean, Chairman of the Board of Coronet Industries of Dalton and Chairman of the Board of The Friendship Force. Seretean, the son of Romanian immigrants, is a highly successful and respected businessman.

"Two things have always appealed to me," Seretean said: number one is youth and number two is peace. I have always had an empathy for the poor because I was once poor. I also have empathy for minorities because of my own heritage. Of all the activities I am involved in, and have been involved with throughout the years, I have a special feeling about The Friendship Force. Participants in the program learn just how much we in the world do have in common with one another."

M.B. "Bud" Seretean

Seretean arranged tours of Coronet Industries' carpet mill during the afternoon of May 10, for the Soviet guests and their American hosts. Friday evening the A.R.M.S. participants were hosted by Seretean at a dinner party at his Missionary Ridge home in Chattanooga. Also attending were Mayor Gene Roberts, Vice-Mayor John Franklin and Frederick Obear, Chancellor of the University of Tennessee.

The Soviet musicians quickly found the piano and the Seretean home was soon filled with the sounds of Italian opera, Soviet Georgian folk songs and music from *Cabaret* —with a different accent.

Soviet Georgians entertain hosts at the Seretean home.

During the dinner conversation, Dr. Nodar Kikvadze, Director of the Center of Scientific Information for Social Sciences at a Georgian University, said what surprised him most about the Unites States was the kind hearts of the people. "We didn't know they would be so warm," he said, through Gela Charkviana who interpreted.

As the festivities continued, the 120 guests were treated to a performance of the University of Tennessee Singing Mocs who entertained with *One Voice, Will the Circle Be Unbroken, Down By the Riverside and Chattanooga Choo Choo.* The director was Glen Draper.

At the close of the evening Gela Charkviani said "Yes, we are different. Our philosophies and value scales are different. But our value scales overlap...we all value life, our children and our families. Today there's a danger that all these things will end. Our common enemy in World War II was fascism. Today's enemy is only a specter, but we can visualize what this specter called nuclear war might do to us all."

Violeta Dzhaparidze, a Tbilisi City Council member bids a fond farewell to Atlanta Council member Debby McCarty.

Everywhere the Soviets went, they were besieged by the media. Inevitably they were asked what impressed them the most about the United States. Speaking of his "new American friends," Michael Guasalia, a seventy-two- year-old toy plant manufacturer in Tbilisi and a retired Soviet army colonel, recalled how during World War II, he once embraced American soldiers after they had pushed the Nazis back. "Let's start where we left off," he said with a smile.

Cardiology professor, Dr. Tamaz Areshidze, said "...the surprising thing which I appreciate is the friendly relations we've established so quickly between our people and the American people, as well as the warm and friendly relations between the people of The Friendship Force.

After they left Big Canoe, the ten members traveled to Raleigh, North Carolina, before going on to Richmond, Virginia, and Washington, DC. In Raleigh, the group asked to see an example of rural America. They were also interested in meeting some senior citizens. Bobby and Penny Creech took five Soviets to Smithfield where they toured the Smithfield Senior Center. Pat Cunningham of the Johnston County Council on Aging was also present. "I was really impressed by their sincere and genuine interest," she said of the visitors. She also noted "patient and warm-hearted temperaments" that she had not expected from the Soviets.

The Soviet visitors were concerned about how Americans viewed their country and its people. "Most people here do not know much about Georgian culture, so of course, we are going to be stereotyped by what you hear on the news about us," Gela Charkviani said.

"Let me begin by telling you about our Republic of Georgia." he said. "First of all, it's not all snow. Our Georgia is like a Mediterranean country with a tropical climate and we are a big wine producer. Citrus fruits are grown in abundance in our country. People often ask me about the role of women in society," he continued. "Fifty-two percent of the judges and lawyers are women and sixty-five percent of the doctors are women. What many people in the United States don't understand is that the Soviet Union is a vast country of fifteen republics. Each has its own distinct individuality with different cultures and different languages.

"I am very glad to be a part of this Friendship Force so that hopefully a few people can see that there are common men in the USSR just like in the United States," Charkviani said. Charkviani also told the group about the terrific loss of life in the Soviet Union during World War II. "And no republic lost more men in ratio to the overall population than my own Republic of Georgia," he said. "We know about the horrors of war first-hand. That is why we are so happy to come in peace."

As the ten Georgians made their way to Washington, DC, they were hosted in Richmond at the home of Inger Rice, Friendship Force Volunteer of the Year, and her husband Walter, former US Ambassador to Australia. After a lovely dinner at the Rice home overlooking the James River, Bill Lamkin, editor of *Friendship* magazine, left the group to return to Atlanta.

Lamkin said, "When you travel with a group of people for a week, you get to know them pretty well. It was a sentimental moment that night in the spacious Rice living room as, one by one, I told the ten Soviets good-bye. When I embraced chain-smoking, overweight cardiologist Tamaz Areshidze, I sensed a heightened feeling of closeness between the two of us. I told him I would write to him and send some pictures."

Unexpectedly, Areshidze said, "I could look all over Soviet Georgia and US Georgia and never find a friend so good."

Atlanta Judge Clarence Cooper took his guest to court. She is Judge Ludmila Kuznetsova of Tbilisi, Georgia.

Once they were in Washington, DC, the Soviet Georgians got a big surprise from two of the USA Georgians they had seen a few days earlier. Nelson and Sandy Dussault were in Washington on business at the same time the Soviets were there.

The Soviets were in the Senate lunch room when the Dussaults entered. They were very surprised and pleased to see their new friends again. Nelson, ever the practical joker, walked over and threw a rubber chicken in the middle of the table. "At first, they just sat there in silence and then they realized what I had done," he said. "Everyone started laughing and we had a great time with the rubber 'schiken.' I guess they were thinking, 'These crazy Americans flew all the way to Washington just to deliver one last joke!'"

Holding the rubber "schiken" is Tbilisi citizen Michail Mtsuzavishvili. Nelson Dussault enjoys the joke.

Back at his home, Wayne Smith said: "For three wonderful days, Big Canoe became a microcosm of the world that everyone hopes and prays for. American and Soviets not only shared their lives with each other during those days, they thoroughly enjoyed each other's company.

"All of us who lived those days will never be the same again. We out-numbered the Soviets by a hundred to ten. If our common experience can be multiplied in both nations by two million on our side and two hundred million on their side, the world will live in peace. A world of friends is a world of peace. And why can't it happen? It can! We need to practice the words of that beautiful song *Let There Be Peace on Earth and Let It Begin With Me.*"

Bill Armstrong of Big Canoe added this: "Who knows—maybe fifty years from now history will record that nuclear disarmament was accomplished through a movement originated at Big Canoe, Georgia!"

It is also important to look at individual relationships formed during this important Friendship Force event. Phyllis Yancey and Martha Whitfield traveled to the Soviet Union in November 1982. Now they shared in home hosting Dr. Nodar Kikvadze, Professor of History at the Georgian Academy of Sciences in Tbilisi.

"Our adventures with Nodar included a walk around the neighborhood, two trips to the art museum, a tour of Duke University, a tennis game and a backyard cookout. But the most pleasant times were spent sitting around the table after meals conversing through phrase books and sign language.

"For the three of us, the rhythm of family life began to evolve. Nodar began helping clear the table after breakfast. He made sure that Martha didn't sleep too late. He became a back-seat driver and chastised me for exceeding the speed limit. Together, we planned the next day's activities and set the time for getting up and eating breakfast.

"I witnessed many touching scenes involving others.... I can still see the Soviets and their American hosts walking hand-in-hand up Franklin Street in Chapel Hill. I can still hear the laughter and hand-clapping as we danced together to the Georgian music. I can still feel the emotion experienced by Tom, a young man of twenty-three, and the retired Soviet Army Colonel, when Tom expressed his appreciation of the suffering of the Soviet people during World War II. The Soviet Georgians constantly let us know how much they appreciated our hospitality.

"At the end of three days...the Soviets had won our hearts and perhaps we had won theirs also," Phyllis said.

Another host, Mary Parker of Raleigh, spoke movingly of her guest Viola Dzhaparidze. "When we got into the hot car after walking along the shore of a lake, I complained about the heat. Viola simply put her arm across my shoulders and said, 'When beside a friend, everything is wonderful. The sun is wonderful, the heat is wonderful, cold is wonderful.'

"All the harsh rhetoric between leaders of both countries, all the misconceptions between our peoples and any differences in our own ideologies no longer mattered.

"We were simply two women meeting as friends."

During the exchange American hosts also learned that those from the Republic of Georgia did not wish to be called 'Russian,' which they are not. They preferred to be identified by their own country which they obviously loved dearly. When the group returned to their homes, Americans had still not actually hugged Russians. The future of a true Friendship Force exchange with Russians was still uncertain, but the successful exchange with Georgians gave Wayne Smith and other leaders much hope. The A.R.M.S. program would continue.

Wayne Smith really believed that what had occurred during this visit of only thirty carefully-selected (by the USSR) citizens to the United States was not a small step toward mutual understanding, but a very large leap. He kept traveling to the Soviet Union, pushing for regularly scheduled exchanges of citizens to begin. He hammered away on the theme of people-to-people diplomacy and argued that, if given a chance, it would succeed where conventional diplomacy had often failed.

He explained how he had cracked the hard veneer of Soviet rigidity. "When I first began this mission some years ago, I failed miserably by trying to debate the merits of democracy over communism. Of course, this tactic produced NO converts and the talks ended in a stalemate or worse. Then I looked for some common ground to use as a base for more constructive conversations. When I finally began to talk about the mutual fear which both of our nations have for each other and how we could get rid of the fear by eliminating the ignorance and misconceptions we have of each other, the Soviets became a lot more interested in listening. Once they agreed that fear was a major barrier to understanding and friendship, I was able to promote the idea of putting Soviet farmers, factory workers, doctors and plumbers into typical American homes. There, a different kind of diplomacy could take place around kitchen tables instead of conference tables."

When I asked Smith what on earth the Russians and Americans would have to talk about, he had a ready answer.

"Why they'll talk about their dogs and grandchildren; their vegetable gardens and recipes. From there they can learn to talk about their plans, hopes and dreams. In time, they can even learn to talk calmly about their differences."

"Okay," I agreed, "but what about the language barrier?"

He'd heard this question before. "You'd be surprised what tough barriers can be hurdled with a smile and some pantomiming," he told me. "Besides, if we really get this citizen exchange going, we might even learn enough of our respective languages to converse fairly well."

Dr. Wayne Van Tilburg and host Dr. Josef Bruner in Austria in 1985.

Bettye Brown and Host
(Language is unimportant if hearts do most of the talking.)

Dave and I didn't rush out to enroll in a Russian language course, but Wayne Smith kept on communicating. We didn't see much of him for a while, but we heard that he was off to far-away places. Moscow was often mentioned.

Although the visit of the thirty citizens from the Republic of Georgia was the highlight of 1985, other memorable events occurred. Twelve of the eighteen members of The Friendship Force Board of Directors gathered in Tokyo on June 3, for its semi-annual meeting. Mr. Ryoichi Sasakawa, chairman of the Japanese Shipbuilding Industry Foundation had invited the board to meet in his city.

Honorary Chairperson Rosalynn Carter presented a plaque to Mr. Sasakawa which cited his "outstanding international service and ...his dedication and generosity in building a world of peace and friendship."

In response, Sasakawa lauded The Friendship Force for its worldwide efforts in the cause of peace and understanding. "Many people and organizations talk about peace," he said, "while The Friendship Force effectively puts its words into action." He then announced his pledge of $650,000 in support of The Friendship Force in the coming year.

Rosalynn Carter presents a special award to Ryoichi Sasakawa.

The Friendship Force also received a big boost in Japan, thanks to mother and son, Miyeko Osanae, and Go Riju. Mrs. Osanae is one of the most popular TV script writers in Japan and her son is not only an accomplished script writer, but is a television star as well. Mrs. Osanae was deeply moved by the impact The Friendship Force can have in changing one's attitude toward other people and other countries through personal friendships. She experienced hosting in 1984 when she had Barbara Brugger and Anita Wright, two ambassadors from Atlanta, in her home.

As a result of these friendships, the mother and son team of script writers crafted a story based on a 1984 week-long visit of Michael Summers, who suffered from leukemia, and his mother. They were hosted by Mrs. Kelko Marui.

The story was written for a TV special to be aired on the Tokyo Broadcasting System and twenty-four affiliated stations throughout Japan. This prime-time TV drama was sponsored by the Coca-Cola Company of Japan. The drama, titled "Hello! Good-bye!" was broadcast to more than twenty million viewers. Stephen Kim, Vice President for Friendship Force Development in the Far East, brought this marvelous Friendship Force publicity to the attention of Friendship Force International and to *Friendship* magazine editor Bill Lamkin.

The successful visit of citizens of the Republic of Georgia sparked a great interest in their land, people and culture. In July, Atlanta syndicated columnist and well-known humorist Lewis Grizzard (now deceased) wrote about this interest in his regular column for the *Atlanta Journal* and the *Atlanta Constitution*.

He quoted Wayne Smith as saying: "Of all peoples, the Russians and Americans need to get along. If we can't get together, then we may all die together, the way it seems today.

"Don't get me wrong," Smith added." I do not agree with the Communist way of life. I'm three notches right of center, and some say I'm even more than that. But I've been to the Soviet Union six or seven times and I've met some mighty decent people over there. I'm not talking about people who represented their government. I'm talking about the everyday ordinary Russian citizen."

Grizzard explained that Smith was taking one hundred Americans to Russia in August. This group would visit Moscow and Leningrad and perhaps Vilnius (Lithuania), a small city near the Baltic Sea. "Incidentally, I'm going along and so is my stepbrother Ludlow Porch," Grizzard admitted. "If the Russians will provide the vodka, we'll bring the grits.

"We have to start somewhere," he concluded.

When August rolled around, Martha Pool, owner of a small-town newspaper in Jasper, Georgia, went on one of the Missions to Moscow. When she returned, she told of the contrast between the officials they met and the ordinary citizens.

"We met with representatives from the Department of Foreign Policy, Soviet Women's Committee, Radio Moscow, various journalists and carefully selected others," Pool said. "These meetings were intended to allow an exchange of ideas between us...and possibly get rid of the stereotypes we have of each other. The meetings usually resulted in the Soviets reciting practiced lines verbatim and dodging unpleasant (for them) questions or turning the lines of communication into a more advantageous (for them) direction.

"The hard-line Soviets who met with us have an unyielding distrust of the United States," she added.

"But there were times when we had casual contacts with the average everyday citizen. These people appeared to be pleased to meet citizens of the United States and wanted to share friendship. Such an experience occurred one afternoon as I was sitting on a park bench and watching a mother and her two small children. The children were eating ice cream cones as they shyly watched me, oblivious to the ice cream that rapidly melted and ran down their hands and arms—a sticky mess! The mother used a handkerchief, but the "sticky" remained. I tore open packets of pre-moistened towelettes and gave them to the young mother. She cleaned the little hands and arms while she repeated her thanks several times.

"In broken English, she asked me which part of the United States I came from. I gave her a card explaining in Russian that I was a member of The Friendship Force visiting her country. She smiled and nodded as she read the card and put it in her wallet. She hugged me and then left. The trip was worth the effort just to have one such experience.

"I asked a university student what she and her peers thought about citizens of the United States. Her answer: 'People with lots of money who can buy anything they want. People with no problems.'

"Russians have never known freedom as we know it, "Pool said. "Most Americans don't realize that as far back as recorded history goes, the Russians have been controlled and regimented by some form of autocracy. The liberation of serfs came in 1861, and the Revolution ending the tsarist rule came in 1917. The Russians have always accepted the form of government which controls their lives because 'that is the way it is.'

"Winston Churchill described the USSR this way: 'a riddle wrapped in a mystery inside an enigma.'"

During one Mission to Moscow, American ambassadors were amused when they realized that the driver of their Intourist bus was lost outside of Moscow. "We saw quite a lot of the countryside that we were not supposed to see," Bettye Brown said. "We thought it was the best tour of all. We saw lots of little children during the two hours we just wandered around."

Harold Brown said, "Someone finally asked the driver why she didn't telephone her office for directions. She said 'I would, but I don't even know where I am!'"

Chapter 12
When the World Sings Together

When asked what World War III would be like, Albert Einstein answered, "I don't know, but World War IV would be fought with sticks and stones as in prehistoric times!"
— Quoted by **Levy Tavares** in *Friendship* magazine, 1986

Home-hosting was not allowed in the USSR in 1985, however, the A.R.M.S. experiment in April worked so well that thirty-three Atlanta citizens traveled to Tbilisi in the Republic of Georgia in October and most were home hosted, a new gesture of goodwill on the part of the Soviets. Julie Powell, a young member from Georgia (USA), traveled as a Samantha Smith Scholarship Ambassador. Julie's father Josh Powell was also part of the group.

Wayne Smith recalled: "I will never forget the days I spent in Tbilisi as part of the delegation hosted by Soviet Georgians. We spent our time with our hosts—we laughed together, ate together, sang together and lived together. Josh Powell sings our theme song "Let There Be Peace on Earth," as well as anyone I know. It made me tingle all over and brought tears to my eyes as we sat around the table after dinner with an ordinary Soviet Georgian family and listened to these familiar words in a very unfamiliar setting:

> Let peace begin with me; let this be the moment now.
> With every step I take, let this be my solemn vow:
> To take each moment and live each moment
> In peace eternally
> Let there be peace on earth
> And let it begin with me.

Frank Garner, president of The Friendship Force of Atlanta, presented a handmade quilt to the city of Tbilisi on behalf of his club. The gift was accepted by Gela Charkviani.

Now, for the first time, Friendship Force ambassadors were allowed to stay with Soviet families because Soviet Georgians in May were home hosted by Americans. "The Georgian people were so happy to see us," said Levy Tavares of Sao Paulo, Brazil. "They are friendly, loving and happy people, but their music is reminiscent of their suffering. You see, we learned that their city of Tbilisi has been taken by enemies forty times and was destroyed twenty-six times.

"We also learned that friendship has a very special meaning to Georgians: a friend is more than a brother. We felt the intensity of their friendship during our entire stay in Tbilisi. They had prepared an extensive program—meetings, receptions and visits to historic places in the old city of Tbilisi, whose monastery dates back to the sixth century.

"The dinners were more like banquets, always with many friends and the toasts continued until late at night," Tavares continued. "We were aware that we belonged to different worlds, but the important thing was not our differences, but our similarities. This is the critical point. After meeting the Georgians, talking to them, living with them, feeling close to them and knowing their individual hopes and fears, I could not find one reason that would impede a peaceful coexistence based on mutual respect between people.

"By the time we left, I knew we had planted a small seed of friendship in very fertile soil," Tavares added.

In his pre-summit speech from the White House on November 14, 1985, President Reagan shared with the people of the United States and the world his hopes for his meeting with General Secretary Gorbachev of the Soviet Union. His mission, the President said, "...is a mission for peace."

"When we meet in Geneva our agenda will seek not just to avoid war, but to strengthen peace, prevent confrontation and remove sources of tension.

"Imagine how much we could accomplish and how the cause of peace would be served, if more individuals and families from our respective countries could come to know each other in a personal way.

"I feel the time is ripe for us to take bold new steps to open the way for our peoples to participate in an unprecedented way in the building of peace....

"Such proposals will not bridge our differences, but people-to-people contacts can build genuine constituencies for peace in both countries. After all, people don't start wars, governments do....

"We are proposing the broadest people-to-people exchanges in the history of American-Soviet relations.... Such exchanges can build in our societies thousands of coalitions for cooperation and peace. Governments can only do so much: once they get the ball rolling, they should step out of the way and let people get together to share, enjoy, help, listen and learn from each other, especially young people....

"A broadening of people-to-people exchanges can diminish the distrust and suspicion that separates our two peoples," the President said.

It was very interesting to Friendship Force leadership that many of the ideas in the President's speech had been incorporated in The Friendship Force at its inception.

In October 1985, citizens of Krems, Austria, hosted a group from the Southwest Washington Friendship Force Club led by exchange directors Eleanor and Wayne Van Tilburg. Monika Meyer, one of the Austrian hosts, almost refused the opportunity. She had good reasons for initially saying "no." Almost everyone in her family had the flu and her disabled six-year old showed signs of coming down with the nasty stuff as well. Moreover, her husband Michael was a minister with a hectic schedule.

Monika told Bumpfi Eigner, the Austrian Exchange Director, that she couldn't have a guest at this time. Eigner said he had some difficulties in getting enough lodgings for the guests from the United States. Monika softened a bit and said she would take a guest if he came up short. Luckily, the family was recovering form the flu before the Americans arrived and they decided they wanted to host someone after all.

When the news came that their ambassador was Ruby Shaw, a lady of seventy, Monika and her family were a bit disappointed. "The children had really wanted a student and there was a bit of grumbling as we left home to fetch our old lady," Monika said.

When Ruby Shaw found her hosts, her first words were "How nice of you to have an old woman like me in your house." The Meyers were astonished. They were all wondering how this woman had read their thoughts. But Ruby Shaw soon proved to be no ordinary seventy-year-old.

"Ruby was a marvel!" Monika said.

One of the children added, "She must have been ravishing when she was young."

"She still is," whispered another.

"Life with Ruby never got boring. Long talks, a thorough exchange of experiences, little silences in between, an understanding look now and again, cascades of laughter, much fun and a hug from time to time. Thus, Ruby conquered the vicarage and all its inhabitants," Monika said. We all hated to see her leave. I wish all conquests in the past would have been undertaken in this way! How much mankind could have been spared.

By the end of 1985, The Friendship Force reported first exchanges for Chile, East Germany and Northern Ireland, and 1986 began with much promise. The Twin Cities Exchange with Budapest, Hungary, and Vienna, Austria, departed on April 15. There was some doubt about this exchange departing on time; however, exchange director Linda Erickson wrote in her travel log: "Although this morning, April 15, is a clear and beautiful day for forty-three ambassadors to begin their exchange, tension runs high due to the US bombing of Libya last night. We were in the Friendship Force office in Atlanta early this morning to determine if the US State Department would recommend or even allow travel. None of our group canceled, but some considered it."

At the same time, a group of Atlanta ambassadors were agonizing over a planned exchange with Pau, France. Exchange Director Stuart Dorfman said the planning had gone very well and everyone was pleased to be heading for the lovely Bearn region. Suddenly, world tension mounted after it was determined that Libyan leader Muammar al Quaddafi was responsible for ordering the terrorist bombings of a West Berlin discotheque on April 5. On April 14, the United States sent warplanes to attack terrorist-related targets in Tripoli and Benghazi, Libya.

Suddenly Stuart Dorfman's phone began ringing off the hook. "Is the exchange still on?" they asked.

Dorfman met with his exchange committee to discuss whether to go or postpone. They debated for over two hours before deciding to go ahead. They tried to calm fearful ambassadors, telling them that they were not going anywhere near Libya and that chances were "extremely remote" that they would be put in harm's way.

More trouble loomed ahead. The next weekend the American Express office in Lyon, France, was bombed and a British businessman was assassinated. Lyon was only three hundred miles from Pau.

Dorfman began receiving calls of cancellations. However, thirty-one brave ambassadors stuck with the exchange and both they and their French hosts were very grateful that they did. Once they were in Pau, all the problems and worries of the past weeks disappeared.

Here is Stuart Dorfman's condensed version of what happened:

"Pau is a lovely city of about 95,000 people, nestled near the Pyrenees Mountains and only a one-and-a-half hour drive from the Atlantic coast.

"On the first day we visited Bayonne and the famous resort of Biarritz where we were guests at a reception given by the Mayor. As with all our group trips, we were accompanied by many of our new friends who would switch on different days, enabling us to get to know as many of them as possible.

"We were off again to Lourdes a few days later. Located in a beautiful mountain setting with the Pau River running alongside a lovely basilica, Lourdes gives hope to millions of the sick and infirm who visit, hoping for a 'miracle cure.' After Lourdes, it was high into the Pyrenees by winding and twisting roads for a picnic of French-bread sandwiches, hard-boiled eggs and fruit. Then suddenly and without warning, it happened! The 'terrorists' struck! Snowballs went whizzing past the heads of three American women. They turned and found themselves on the receiving end of this unprovoked attack launched by Francis Gentillet, one of the hosts. Undaunted, the women quickly retaliated. Although their snowballs lacked the velocity and range of those tossed by Francis, their sheer numbers finally forced their attacker down from his perch and back to the bus. None of us ever imagined we would be part of a picnic and snowball fight in the Pyrenees Mountains in May.

After days filled with tours of wineries and local restaurants, visits to chateaus and wine-tastings and free days to become better acquainted with new friends, the time flew by. As they left Pau, Dorfman said, "Thanks to our warm, caring French hosts, we never thought about the concerns we had before the exchange."

In July 1986, The Friendship Force of Lincoln, Nebraska, ventured into "uncharted waters." These Friendship Force members were the first to go on an exchange to Indonesia. Before their departure, they educated themselves about the far-away island country. They were amazed to learn that Indonesia is made up of more than thirteen thousand islands scattered over three thousand miles between the South China Sea and the Indian Ocean. *Bahasa*, they learned, was the national language, a necessary common tongue since over two hundred other languages and dialects are spoken throughout the islands. (The national motto of Indonesia is "Unity From Diversity.") Once known as the Dutch East Indies, everything changed when the Dutch were ousted by the Japanese in World War II. Following a time of struggle, Indonesia became a parliamentary democracy.

Members of The Friendship Force of Lincoln, Nebraska learn to dance a new way.

When they arrived in Jakarta, the bustling heart of Indonesia, they discovered preserved and restored gabled Dutch houses with doorsteps of black and white stone, walled gardens and red tile roofs.

They were delighted to learn that Poppy Hamim Penna, the Exchange Director and mother of twelve grown children, had made almost all the arrangements single handedly. She had recruited friends after explaining The Friendship Force to them. Poppy had apparently done a wonderful job of indoctrinating her friends because the Americans were welcomed like "long-lost family."

The ambassadors quickly found that knowing the friendly Indonesian people was the real way to learn about the country. For example, their hosts explained that there are thirty million Sundanese people in Indonesia. They are ninety-nine percent Muslim. The Sundanese came from other parts of Asia about two thousand years ago to settle the fertile land of West Java . Eighty percent of the Sundanese are farmers, working in rice paddies carefully terraced up steep volcanic hillsides.

"During the entire exchange there were parties in the evenings and calls on many relatives of host families, giving us a real insight into the culture of the Sundanese people," Alice Moore said. "Everywhere, whether with our families or in public, we were greeted with smiles. This was truly an immersion experience into a totally different culture from our own, introduced to us lovingly by our hosts."

In 1986, as in 1985, all Friendship Force experiences were called exchanges and most were not reciprocal. Groups of twenty or more were processed and leadership was either by an ambassador exchange director or a host exchange director. By 1986, almost fifteen percent of exchanges were between countries other than the United States., Colombia and Brazil exchanged for the first time and the 500th exchange occurred in April between East Central Florida and Wolfsburg, Germany. Although there were some cancellations in the Florida group because of fears of terrorism and anti-American feelings, these fears vanished the moment the Americans were "received with a wonderfully warm welcome," according to Laurel Grundish. The exchange turned out to be "fantastic, because we were determined to be flexible and tolerant and to keep in mind The Friendship Force purpose of making friends around the world," said Julia Sibley.

The third annual Asia-Pacific Conference was held June on 14-15 in Taipei, Taiwan. Dr. Han Lih-Wu was the featured speaker.

Dr. Han told the group how very essential it was to make friends today. "The world is becoming smaller and smaller," he said. "And at the same time the world is becoming more and more complicated and dangerous. It has become a dangerous place to live because of the forces that lead to conflict. On top of that, we have terrorism now present in the whole world," Dr. Han said. "It is not so easy to convert the enemy into a friend. It is only through a slow process of developing friendship on the basis of understanding that we may come to peace

---

(A story in *Friendship* magazine by Elizabeth Bowne is the basis for the following account of Violet's "sentimental journey.")

Violet Hada Hansen and her husband Frank were part of a Friendship Force group from Iowa, bound for Budapest, Hungary. When they got to the city of Debrecen, Violet told her husband that she would like to take a side trip following their stay in Budapest. She reasoned that since they had traveled such a long distance, it made sense for them to try to find the village of Kanyar. It was from there, his birthplace, that Samuel Hada, Vi's father, fled to Budapest before the beginning of World War II.

In the years before his death, Mr. Hada had revealed only a few details about his early life. Violet recalled his devoted memory of his mother, who married at seventeen and had seven children in fourteen years. She died of typhoid fever soon after the birth of her last child. Young Samuel, overwhelmed by grief and unable to accept a stepmother, ran away from home at age twelve. He walked two hundred miles to Budapest and apprenticed himself to a tailor, telling his employer that his parents were dead and he wanted to learn a trade.

Samuel grew to manhood and married Esther Nagy. In 1905, he came to the United States and found work as a tailor in West Pullman, Illinois, fifty miles from Chicago. After a few years he had saved enough money to send for his wife.

Vi and three sisters grew up in a household where they learned only a few words of Magyar, the Hungarian language. Their parents were fiercely proud to be Americans and her father wanted to forget the bitter memories of his youth.

However, some hint of Sam's whereabouts must have reached the village he had left behind because Vi remembered that in 1944, her father received a letter from the Hungarian consulate in Chicago telling him that his father had died, leaving him heir to vast estates. Sam refused to accept his inheritance because he did not wish to return to his native land. He suggested instead that the brother who was next in line should receive the property.

From that time on, no communication passed between the family so Vi was uncertain of the location of the village of Kanyar, knowing only that it was near the Soviet border. In Debrecen they found an English speaking taxi driver named Gusztav. Intrigued by her story, he agreed to help her in her search. First they must overcome a major problem. "There are two villages by that name," Gusztav said. "Tizna-Kanyar in the north and Kanyar in the south. Which way shall we go?"

Kanyar was only forty miles south of Debrecen, so they decided to try go there first. In the village, they located a church and received directions to the home of the minister. He invited them in, served brandy and studied his ledgers, but he found no record of a Hada family. However, he directed them back to Debrecen to a minister who might know something about Tiszna-Kanyar.

It was late at night when they completed the seventy-five-mile journey to Tizna-Kanyar, a quiet village. Everyone was asleep and the sound of the car caused a stir. Dogs began to bark, lights went on and people came out in their nightgowns and pajamas to see what was happening. Vi was directed to the minister's residence, a two-story house beyond a high fence. A car was parked in the driveway, but the pastor did not answer their knocks. When Gusztav blew the car horn, the neighbors called out and dogs protested the intrusion. Apparently the minister was the soundest sleeper in town.

Soon the villagers gathered with them and when a light finally went on upstairs, a cheer rose from the crowd. When the minister understood what they wanted he invited them into his study. His wife prepared hot sandwiches and brought in wine and brandy.

The beautifully handwritten old records revealed exciting information that Vi had never known. Her family dated back to 1180. In the year 1200, one ancestor was Proctor, adviser to King Bela III. Bela III was apparently a good king. He had six fingers on one hand, an oddity which was considered to be a sign of importance. His son married Proctor's daughter and Vi had descended from that line. The king gave land to one of Vi's early ancestors who founded Tizna-Kanyar. That relative became very wealthy and served as curate of the first Protestant church in the area.

From a cabinet in his study, the minister retrieved a pewter communion cup with the family name Hada and the year 1790 engraved on it. "As I held that cup, I felt a thrill beyond any I'd ever known," Vi said.

She was fascinated to learn that her grandfather had been a judge and she wondered about her father leaving such a heritage to become a tailor. Yet, she remembered that he was a proud, independent man who excelled at his trade and had made a good life for his own family.

The minister promised to write up a complete genealogy for Vi and to try to locate some cousins. His wife gave her a hand-woven, red tablecloth with a cross stitch design which had been made by a villager. It was typical of tablecloths given to ministers when they performed confirmations or weddings. The minister explained that they could not give her the pewter cup because it had served the church so long.

Vi says she and Ralph have traveled to many places, but it was this Friendship Force experience that helped make her dream of finding her Hungarian roots come true.

Can friendship be made here? (The author at The Kremlin.)

Chapter 13
It May Take a Camel to Build a Difficult Bridge

*The notion that we should face the Russians down in a silent war of
nerves, broken only by bursts of megaphone diplomacy, is based on a
misconception of our own values, of Soviet behavior, and of the
anxious aspirations of our own peoples.*
—Lord Carrington of the United Kingdom

Wherever Wayne Smith travels, he tells others about what it means to
be a member of The Friendship Force. He never communicated better
than with the following parable:

The Parable of the Eighteenth Camel

"A wealthy sultan died," Wayne Smith says, with a twinkle in his
eye. "He left behind three sons and seventeen camels. The instructions
in his will were that his first son was to receive one-half of his camels.
His second son was to receive one-third of his camels and his third son
was to receive one-ninth of them. But since it is impossible to divide
seventeen camels by two, three or nine, the sultan's heirs were about to
have a royal family feud!

"There was a very wise woman who lived in the same village. She
was asked to mediate the problem. After a little creative thinking she
told the three sons of the sultan that she had a solution. She herself
would donate a camel to the sultan's legacy so that the camels could be
divided evenly and fairly. The first son was given one-half of the 18
camels or nine. The second son was given one-third of the camels, or
six, The third son was given one-ninth, or two. Of course, the sum of
nine, six and two is seventeen. The wise woman took back the
eighteenth camel which she had donated to the cause and everyone left
happy.

"Wouldn't it be wonderful if we had more camels of the type
supplied by the wise woman in the story?" Smith asked. "Today's
world is in trouble because of people seeking their rights. Look at the
Middle East? Who is right and who is wrong? The Arabs? The Jews?
Look at Northern Ireland. Who is right and who is wrong? Look at that

bad relationship that may exist between yourself and another person. Who is right and who is wrong? In these cases, and probably in every situation where there is a bad relationship between people, there is right AND wrong on both sides.

"What is needed is an eighteenth camel. Some new element needs to be brought into the dispute which will help the litigants find a harmonious solution.

"Let me suggest some 'camels' which would help.

"One is the camel of *forgiveness*. We have all been wronged—all of us have wronged others. We all need forgiveness; we all need to forgive others. Too often, in the face of some affront done to us, our attitude is vengeance. There is even a popular saying: 'Don't get mad; get even!' Many people seem to think that taking vengeance on those who have wronged us will give us inner satisfaction. The opposite is the case. Taking vengeance on a person who has done us wrong is like spitting into the wind. Our venom comes back and spews all over us.

But what a difference forgiveness makes! We do ourselves a favor when we forgive those who have wronged us. How well I know this to be true. Once a person wronged me terribly. Day and night I thought of how I could have vengeance. The more I dwelt on the affront done to me the more sleep I lost, the less was my appetite and the more hostile I became with those about me who had done me no wrong. Then one day I noticed that the person who had wronged me was sleeping fine. He had his appetite. He seemed to be enjoying life. Finally I told him that he and I both knew that he had wronged me but I wanted him to know I forgave him. I do not know what it did for him. All I know is that my sleep, appetite and good humor returned.

Another 'camel'...is that of *understanding*. There is often hostility between people because they don't have all the facts. Will Rogers, the Oklahoma humorist, used to say that we are all ignorant—just on different subjects. How right he was. If we only knew what circumstances have caused people to act the way they do, it would be easier for us to get along with them. Frequently we make our judgments before we know their reasons behind the actions. Many a person has quoted the truism that states, 'There, but for the grace of God, go I.'

A third 'camel' worth having in our herd has the name of *friendship*. Friendship can establish a basis for the desire to reach amicable solutions to our differences. Often when I visit with Soviets, I find that our conversation goes from bad to worse in regard to the differences between communism and free enterprise. I believe very strongly in free enterprise. It has taken me time, but I am now convinced that there are Communists who actually do believe in the validity of their system. So what happens when two strangers with diametrically opposed ideologies come together? We argue. Nobody's mind is changed; often bitter feelings are stirred up.

Now I have discovered a better way to proceed. I begin with a sincere conviction that truth is stronger than a lie. Next I tell myself that I don't have all of the truth and neither does anyone else. I've got some of it. My polemic adversary has some too. And then I reaffirm that neither my adversary nor I have the desire to learn from each other until a positive relationship has been established between us. This relationship is called friendship. Once a person has become my friend, I still may not agree with him, but I will want to hear and understand his position.

In a world filled with rights and wrongs on every side, we all need to look for the eighteenth camel. *Forgiveness, understanding* and *friendship* are three of them.

In The Friendship Force, too, differences between our systems of government and our cultural backgrounds—and sometimes our past memories as adversaries—all vanish when we bring an eighteenth camel to the friendship.

The tenth birthday of The Friendship Force was celebrated in appropriate style. On Sunday, March first—ten years after President Carter announced the creation of the organization from the White House—Friendship Force President Wayne Smith and members of The Friendship Force International staff drove to Plains to celebrate with the Carters.

After attending services at the Carters' church, a birthday cake was shared with members of the congregation. Wayne Smith marked the occasion by presenting President and Mrs. Carter with the first copies of the tenth anniversary publication, *The Friendship Force Story: 1977-1987.*

At a more informal party held on March 2, at Friendship Force International in Atlanta, Smith unveiled a bust of Friendship Force benefactor, Ryoichi Sasakawa of Tokyo, Japan. The bust is on permanent display at the organization's headquarters.

In July 1987, Dave and I went on our first exchange, which was part of a Friendship Festival. We went to Newcastle, England, where we were hosted by a delightful family—Derek and Winnie Bell and their children, Alison and John. The Festival, which included home hosting, was also part of a year-long celebration of the tenth anniversary of The Friendship Force. People from countries around the world attended this event.

As Bill Lamkin wrote in *Friendship* magazine: "Pageantry, parades and plenty of hugs marked the tenth anniversary Friendship Force celebration July 2-8 in Newcastle upon Tyne, England." The Lord Mayor's Parade—an event scheduled for June—was delayed until July 4th, a national holiday for the Americans. Tony Coates, Regional Representative for The Friendship Force and the very able director of this Friendship Festival, jokingly noted that July 4th was 'the day when we English granted the American Colonies their independence.'"

The Lord Mayor's Friendship Parade in Newcastle upon Tyne, July, 1987.

Thousands lined the streets of Newcastle for the parade, normally called The Lord Mayor's Parade, but renamed The Lord Mayor's Friendship Parade for this special occasion. President and Mrs. Carter accompanied the Lord Mayor Stan Allan and his wife Evelyn in a horse drawn coach. Along the way, Mr. Carter left his seat and took the place of the footman on the back. He then took time to step down and shake hands with spectators along the way, causing some consternation among the Secret Service agents.

Former President Carter greets the crowd during the Friendship Parade.

It was quite a celebration indeed and Newcastle lived up to its name as the "world capital of friendship." About 620 ambassadors, hosts and special guests attended a banquet on evening of July 4th at the Newcastle Civic Centre. President and Mrs. Carter were there and the President praised The Friendship Force as "a guiding light, a beacon that can be not only instructional but inspirational to all those who seek friendship—and…love—and ultimately, world peace."

Honorary Chairperson Rosalynn Carter praised those in Newcastle for their hard work in arranging the Festival and in providing home-hosting for 255 visitors. She also introduced her mother, Mrs. Allie Smith, and noted that nine members of the Carter clan had traveled as Friendship Force ambassadors.

As a result of The Friendship Force," she said, "we now feel we have a vested interest in the future of individuals whose homes are in Brazil, Ireland, Germany and Russia. Through The Friendship Force, former strangers have become fast friends. And it is this ripple effect of strangers becoming friends that I believe will, in time, exert a powerful positive influence on this divided world of ours.

Friendship between strangers is the first step toward peace between countries, and friendship is something any of us can work toward, even the smallest child.

Back in 1978, I had the honor of welcoming a three-month-old Israeli baby who had accompanied her parents on a Friendship Force exchange to Hartford, Connecticut. Also participating in that exchange was a prominent Israeli diplomat. In my welcoming remarks to the arriving ambassadors and their Connecticut hosts, I reminded them that the baby girl, rather than the diplomat, was the most important ambassador in the group.

I told them that it was she and her contemporaries in Melbourne, Moscow and Milan, who will determine the fate of our very small planet. I can't imagine a better place for them to begin learning the lessons of peace than within the setting of The Friendship Force. In this environment, we learn much about each other, and although we have differences , we share one thing in common: the desire for peace.

As The Friendship Force celebrates ten years of bringing people together, Jimmy and I believe, more than ever, that this organization will make a difference in our world. My family and I are honored to begin yet another exciting decade as active members of The Friendship Force family.

Dr. Wayne Smith was one of the banquet speakers and he had good news.

"Beginning on September first of this year," he announced, "approval has been granted by the appropriate government agencies of both countries for a series of A.R.M.S. exchange programs between the Soviet Union and the United States."

The news was electrifying and drew a standing ovation.

Smith noted that this good news was made possible because of the success of that first exchange back in 1977, when 381 Geordies traveled from Newcastle to Atlanta and 381 Georgians went back on the same plane. "From then to now," Smith said, "look at what has happened. Here we are this evening with ten of the forty-five countries involved in The Friendship Force represented in this hall. And we are engaged in perhaps the most important thing there is in life: It's a form of love called friendship."

Smith said the occasion was also the opportunity to honor seven Friendship Force supporters by presenting them with awards. "First is

Rosalynn Carter who for ten years has maintained a steadfast fidelity to her pledge that she would devote a substantial amount of her personal time to The Friendship Force because she was confident it would promote peace in the world. She still is working toward that goal," Smith said.

"And to Jimmy Carter, whose commitment has never wavered. The Friendship Force is in existence—and is strong today—because this man stood with us from the beginning.

"M.B. "Bud" Seretean, our first Chairman of the Board of Directors, who has shared with us his business acumen, his experience and financial resources.

"Theresa Russell, member of the Newcastle City Council: Because of her leadership, her vitality and her very presence, we proved the concept of our program ten years ago."

Alan Redhead, Newcastle's first exchange director is honored as typifying Friendship Force volunteers...around the world," Smith said. "The Friendship Force was an unproved notion in 1977, and Alan not only made it work but proved it for all time."

Ryoichi Sasakawa was unable to attend. Of him Smith said, "Mr. Sasakawa, our philanthropist and benefactor, we thank for the gifts of wisdom and generosity he has given so magnanimously in support of international friendship.

"I also thank Robert D. Ray, Governor of Iowa, for the gifts of public and private leadership he has given so continuously in support of international friendship," Smith concluded. (Ray was unable to attend.)

As I listened to the speakers that July evening, I could not help but recall that day in 1984, when Dave and I sat in the church service in Big Canoe, Georgia, listening with utter disbelief to Wayne Smith, this 'naive' preacher, tell us that we should "hug a Russian." Since then we have slowly realized that *we* were the naive ones to have ever doubted the power of friendship in bridging the great divides that separate people across the world. Since 1984, we had hosted West Germans but we had never traveled before as Friendship Force ambassadors. Now we were on this exchange to England, still a bit naive. You see, we had expected to encounter the famous English reserve, all proper and stiff, and we thought our hosts might perhaps be a bit disdainful of their American 'cousins.' What we found was something else altogether.

It all began on the long flight across the Atlantic the evening of our departure. About midway, my husband experienced excruciating pain in his foot. The pain got worse and the foot swelled up twice as large as normal. He could not wear a shoe. When we arrived at our destination, his foot was so swollen until the skin was broken in places. I was too worried about Dave to think about how this situation would affect our waiting hosts.

When we changed planes in Amsterdam, Dave had to be assisted in a wheelchair. When we arrived in Newcastle, the plane parked on the tarmac. Dave could not walk down the steps, much less walk to the gate. A special lift took him off the plane and into a waiting wheelchair. There waiting for us were the Bells, Derek and Winnie. They were immediately warm and friendly and were ever so concerned about Dave's foot. They took charge of the situation as they quickly retrieved our luggage and helped my crippled husband to the car.

"Never, mind," they said. "We'll get everything all sorted out and get you to a doctor."

Once we were at their charming home in nearby Consett, Dave was whisked off to the doctor. Pills were prescribed after he was diagnosed as having gout. Alas, the pills were not effective, so the Bells called a private doctor and away they went again. This time Dave received what the English called a jab (to Americans, a shot) and he was much better soon, but still a bit lame. Our hosts' neighbors, Val and Frank Eastern, were hosting our friends, Jay and Gerry Wells. When the Easterns learned of Dave's problem, Val dashed over to a care facility for the elderly where her daughter worked and "pinched" a wheelchair for Dave so he wouldn't miss out on the big Fourth of July Friendship Parade..

Thanks to the Bells and their friendly neighbors, our first exchange was not spoiled. Winnie and Derek saw to it that we didn't miss a thing. When they learned of my affection for the famous James Herriot's books and my longing to see the Yorkshire Dales, they obliged. They took us to their favorite spots, including the old City of York where we walked on the historic wall that encircles part of the city, had lunch overlooking a stream and visited quaint little cobblestone streets on our way to see the stately York Minster. Winnie Bell's sister Margaret and her husband joined us for lunch and spent the afternoon with us.

Winnie and I spent one day doing laundry and exchanging family stories and travel experiences. The Bells were old hands at exchanges and, by example, they taught us how to host in true Friendship Force style: they made us feel like family. Derek pushed Dave in the wheelchair during the parade and we traveled together, went to Friendship Festival activities and visited Hadrian's Wall. They took us to some of their favorite historical sites and we enjoyed picnics along the way. They never seemed to hurry and were very eager to show us their England, an England we would have never seen as tourists.

As Winnie said so well: "When you travel with The Friendship Force, you see a country from the inside looking out instead of from the outside looking in." She also gave this good advice: "You have to put a lot of yourself into The Friendship Force," she said, "but you get much more in return."

So much for the English reserve—we never got a glimpse of it. Instead we found a lovely family in England, full of life and good humor. That family is now "our" family, too. After a one-week homestay, we were firmly under the spell of Friendship Force magic, thanks to Derek and Winnie Bell and their wonderful family and friends.

From September 1 to November 30, five Soviet delegations came to the United States to be hosted in homes in Texas, Louisiana, Georgia, Virginia, California, Iowa, Washington, Tennessee, Pennsylvania and West Virginia. Host families in New York and Wisconsin were on the waiting list for additional delegations.

During this same period, the United States sent three small groups to the Soviet Union. Most began their visit in Moscow and ended in Leningrad with a stop in between where they were actually home-hosted!

In December 1987, Wayne Smith received a call from the Soviet Embassy in Washington shortly before the historic summit meeting between President Reagan and General Secretary Mikhail Gorbachev. The call was to invite Smith to attend a group meeting to be held in connection with the summit.

"It was hinted that General Secretary Gorbachev had asked to hear my views!" Smith recalled.

Wayne Smith arrived in Washington on December 8, prepared to talk to Gorbachev about "peace on earth and goodwill among men."

"I arrived at the Embassy at 4:15 p.m.," he said. "There were a number of 'luminaries' there: Billy Graham, Paul Newman, John Denver, Henry Kissinger, Cyrus Vance, John Galbraith, Yoko Ono, Robert McNamara and about 50 others. When Gorbachev came into the room, I edged my way through the crowd and soon found myself shaking hands with this leader of the Socialist world, speaking to him about The Friendship Force. He was familiar with our organization and its work and thanked me for starting it. He said that we need to do more in getting our citizens to know each other.

"Mr. Gorbachev spoke to this august group for some forty minutes. As soon as he finished his monologue, he said, 'Well, I have come to this country not only to tell you what I think, but to hear what Americans think. We still have another forty minutes, so does anyone want to say anything to me?'

"I shot out of my chair and was the first up in the room. Mr. Gorbachev recognized me from the moments we had shared at the earlier reception. He smiled and indicated that the floor was mine. Here is what I remember saying to him," Smith wrote later.

"Mr. Gorbachev, most Americans like what you are saying. Many Americans even believe it. But, as you have said, the time now has come for us to put our words of friendship into action. I think that you and President Reagan have correctly identified the real problem that faces our nations. President Reagan has said: 'Nations do not distrust each other because they are armed; they are armed because they distrust each other.' Our problem is distrust. This comes from fear and ignorance and maybe, too, some legitimate reasons for distrust. However, we can never trust each other if we don't know each other.

"Mr. Gorbachev, you have said yourself that 'it is time for us to get rid of our myths about each other and see each other as we really are.' Fine. Let us begin. We need for your farmers, nurses, taxi drivers, firemen and every type of ordinary citizen to know our ordinary citizens. In like fashion, Americans need to know your people by going to your country and putting their feet under your people's tables and getting to know them one-on-one. When enough of this occurs, we can start having some mutual trust in each other.

"Governments can get rid of militia arms, but that won't bring us peace on earth and goodwill among men. Only people can reach out their arms to each other and become friends. When that happens, we can have a world of peace and goodwill because this will release love into our relationship, and this is the most powerful force in the world.

"Mr. Gorbachev, you have come to my country to meet with Mr. Reagan to reduce military arms. Good luck! But I want to extend to you an invitation to stay on for one more day so that you can talk about the real problem which divides your nation and mine. Come to Big Canoe, a little mountain community in North Georgia. Let's have a different type of 'summit.' We can hold it on top of a mountain. There are no mountains here in Washington —only monuments which for the main part record the failure of governments to give people

146

peace. Your government and mine know how to put people into space. My organization knows how to put people into kitchens. It is in kitchens, not space, that peace will be made. Come to my kitchen and let's have a cup of coffee together. I am sure that we can find a way to put people in kitchens.

"Few, if any, persons in all of history have had the opportunity which is yours Mr. Gorbachev. Seize it. Work on the real problem which you have identified. Peace is too important to be left in the hands of professional diplomats and political leaders alone. Let the people have a part. Let there be peace on earth and let it begin with all of us.

"With those words, I sat down.

"Mr. Gorbachev has not yet told me if he will come to Big Canoe to have that cup of coffee with me. But don't you bet against it. After all, there is an ancient prophecy which one day will be fulfilled. There really will be a time when there will be 'peace on earth and goodwill among men.' You and I and Mr. Gorbachev are all invited to help make this prophecy come true."

Secretary Mikhail Gorbachev and Wayne Smith in Moscow.

Rosalynn Carter, The First Lady of Friendship.

Chapter 14
Young Ambassadors Bridge Old Divides

There is no nobler calling on this earth than the seeking for peace.
—**President of the United States, Jimmy Carter**

In another Friend-to-Friend column, Wayne Smith said: "We are happy to dedicate this issue of *Friendship* magazine to the youth of the world. In the coming decade, one of the main emphases of The Friendship Force program will be that of getting more youth involved in our important mission of sowing seeds of friendship across the barriers which divide people.

"For some time," Smith continued, "we have been looking for a way that The Friendship Force can involve more people who are younger than the majority of our participants today. There are numerous reasons why younger people find it difficult to join a Friendship Force exchange. The high cost of international travel and having only vacation time available for travel are two such factors which make it harder for youth to meet other youth in our program.

"However, it is the youth of the world who will be making the decisions which will affect us all in just a few more years. If they can know each other now and learn how to live together in cooperation, there is hope that they can create a better world than their predecessors enjoyed."

Levy Tavares of Brazil is one of Wayne Smith's oldest and dearest friends. Tavares, a former member of the Brazilian Congress and a Protestant minister, met Smith in the halls of congress back in Smith's missionary days. Tavares became a Regional Representative of The Friendship Force and in 1987, his son Marcos Tavares traveled to Atlanta to work as a Friendship Force volunteer for several months. Wayne Smith had long ago identified one of the problems of The Friendship Force as being that of limited involvement of young people. In the following thoughtful article, Marcos Tavares shows why more young people who share his views are needed on every level of the organization.

Live Every Moment of Life

We live in a century of great technological advances in which science has dominated the human mind. The incredible results of these advances constantly flabbergast humanity.

In our age, when the distance between continents is unceasingly shrinking, the distance between human beings seems to be unfailingly increasing.

We apparently have no time to meet with each other anymore, nor even time for simply talking with those who are our closest friends. The daily 'rat-race,' the problems of just living from day-to-day and the difficulties that come along with 'progress' cause us to become more and more isolated and insensitive to what truly is important in the world about us.

We don't have time for anything. We read less. Our judgments become shallow and superficial. We cease reflecting deeply about life, simply getting caught up in the rhythm of our own provincial and materialistic existence. It is only with the greatest of difficulty that we are able to force ourselves to slow down. We have no time for ourselves — much less for others — in ways that permit us to show that we really do still have some semblance of human sensitivity left.

We are all brothers and sisters, yet we hardly know each other. We are children of the same Father, yet we rarely think of Him.

Now, at least, a large segment of the world has begun to be concerned about the estrangement that exists in the world today between people. At last, we have begun to search the road maps of life to try to find the highways that lead to love, to peace and to justice.

I have come to the conclusion that I can no longer remain silent. Silence is only a proof that a person is not interested in the world and its problems and opportunities. The effect of silence and indifference is to put distance between people.

Every means of communication—words spoken or gestures demonstrated—can serve as tools to help us build a better world. We need to be at work sowing seeds of love, kindness and understanding if we ever are going to fill in the vast vacuum that surrounds us all.

It is for all of this that I am a volunteer for this wonderful organization that is known as The Friendship Force. In it I see and live new experiences as I bridge cultural differences. It is where I learn more about humanity.

I march under the flag which unites all people who believe that the building of a better world depends on each one of us. Since the sun shines on each one of us, we all need to share our happiness with each other, because this is the way that our own happiness will be increased.

Each one of us has a mission in life. The ways we carry out our mission need not be grandiose. It is not through heroic acts or extraordinary inventions that our mission will be accomplished. What is necessary is that each one of us plays his own instrument in this orchestra called Life. As we bring to this orchestra whatever talent we have, we will find that the harmony we all seek will be ours as we make our contribution and leave the blending of our efforts to the Divine Conductor.

The following stories were also written by young Friendship Force ambassadors.

Chris Van Tilburg, Washington State.

"The planning for my first Friendship Force exchange to South Korea was carried out with strict attention to detail. My brother Pete and I anticipated chopsticks, bowing Orientals and an eighteen-hour flight. Travelers cheques and a one-suitcase limitation became...a reality. My parents were constantly repeating: 'You have to be FLEXIBLE.' We arrived in South Korea to a three-hour welcome ceremony, complete with succulent fried fish and sour kimchi (marinated vegetables). Pete fell asleep and had his picture in a national paper later that week—head back, mouth agape," Chris said, obviously relishing the memory.

"The most memorable part of our Korean exchange was the visit to P'anmunjom. This was the DMZ, where we witnessed the buffer zone between North and South Korea. We were in this building which had two rooms. One room was in one zone and one in the other. We were told not to touch the furniture in the North Korean side. This symbol of division and hostility made a big impression on us.

"Next, I remember Oulu, Finland, in 1981, when we were greeted warmly by Rita and Penti Lievonen," Chris continued. "They had an indoor pool, sauna and a two-person shower the size of a large bathroom. Pete and I took a swim one night by the light of the evening sky.... We jumped off the side into a huge air mattress. We didn't get in trouble for shouting and splashing because our Finnish brother was leading us.

"Mornings in Finland are still in my memory. Mornings which always began with a leisurely breakfast of fresh bread, farmer cheese, crunchy cucumbers and ripe tomatoes. Then a swim in the unheated pool and a dry in the sauna which refreshed our minds for the day. I can't remember having better mornings."

During the second week, the Lievonens, the Van Tilburg's host family, joined with their friends the Liebers and traveled in camping trailers with the Van Tilburgs, exploring Lapland and the Suomi lake region. There were eight children in the group and Chris remembered playing games, sharing music, magazines and laughs. "I still have the cassette Mona Lieber game me," he said. "One night our parents went cloudberry picking at midnight, but no one noticed the hour in the 'Land of the Midnight Sun.' The next morning, we had pancakes with the cloudberries. They were delicious."

Cloudberry picking in Finland. It is almost midnight, but that is no problem in the Land of the Midnight Sun.

By the time the Van Tilburgs traveled to Cairo in 1982, Chris was getting pretty good at practicing Friendship Force flexibility. Of Cairo he wrote, "Pete and I were intrigued by physically-jolting street smells of fresh, cooked and overripe pork and poultry. We were cautioned by our Exchange Director NOT to discuss religion while in Egypt, but our host Albert Aziz and his family were Coptic (Christian) and they and our parents had many conversations about religion. Pete and I just ate our eggplant stuffed with rice and meat and listened to the adults question each other, discuss religion and many other things and laugh together."

Of their cruise down the Nile following a week in the Aziz' home, Chris wrote "Pete and I had our own cabin with a porthole, shower, intercom and air conditioning.... The Valley of the Kings was truly fascinating. It seemed like a movie set, a museum and a barren wilderness all in one. We went back in time, exploring the ancient burial tombs, reading hieroglyphics and learning how to pronounce *Tutankhamen* correctly.

"The Soviet Union exchange in 1983 clarified the distinction between the Communist party and the people. I wish I had read more about the culture and communism before the trip.

"In 1985, I joined an exchange in Krems, Austria. We were in Waccau, a beautiful stretch of the Danube River. I tasted homemade Einsien root-schnapps and farm-fresh eggnog with my host, Dorothea Winkler. I exchanged guitar songs with another host, Josef Brunner, and played contemporary American songs after he played traditional Austrian folk ballads.

"After five continents, twenty-three countries and a B.S. degree, I can say that FLEXIBILITY is no longer a catchword for me, but an attitude. For a young, will-go-anywhere adventurer, exercising flexibility becomes far more important than impersonal bus tours; more than historical museums; more than making my train on time; more than a healthy travel budget. Especially when it draws an Egyptian laugh, a Soviet smile, an Austrian song or a swim with Pete and Ere in the Finnish midnight sun."

Chris agrees with his parents who often say of Friendship Force exchanges: "Tourists only collect things; we collect friends."

Jenelle Gallagher, USA
Jenelle Gallagher, age eleven, wrote about her travels with The Friendship Force, including places like New Zealand, Australia, Thailand and China (Hong Kong). Jenelle said she had many pen pals and that The Friendship Force had convinced her that making friends would indeed promote peace around the world.

Jami Prouty, USA
Jami Prouty of Omaha, age eleven, was the youngest of forty-three ambassadors who traveled to Nairobi, Kenya. She recalled that although the food was different, some things were the same as at home, such as spats between siblings and phone calls from friends. She was

surprised at how children her age talked about the same things that children in America discuss. "We also had fun trading books. The Kenyan people were very kind; they made me feel welcome in their homes and hearts," Jami added.

Jane of Kenya admires new beads. When Jane first spotted her ambassadors at the airport, she ran over, hugged them and said: "You're mine!"

Marlous de Haan, Arnhem, Holland

Marlous de Haan from Arnhem, Holland, traveled to North Carolina when she was eleven. She said her Friendship Force hosts treated her "like a daughter. They took me everywhere and they showed me and taught me many things. I went to school with girls my own age; saw an American football game; learned water skiing, ate crab and lobster; rode horses and saw beautiful nature. I was also on television and joined a potluck party for the first time in my life. I have since introduced potluck parties to my friends back in Holland.

"My experiences with The Friendship Force have been fantastic! I've been able to meet so many people from so many different cultures and places. Some of my memorable experiences include tubing on a river in Connecticut; open-air concerts in Atlanta preceded by a picnic where people even take candle holders to put on the tables; ice cream parties; raccoons in a garden; drinking coffee in a skyscraper; lifts on the outside of every building (they go so fast you get butterflies in your stomach) and a visit to the Houston Astrodome.

"But most of all, the warm, pure, beautiful and fantastic friendship between people! And the funny thing about being a host is that you learn things about your own country you never knew before, " Marlous said.

Amy Coates
Amy Coates, daughter of Regional Representative Tony Coates and his wife Jenny, wrote that "The Friendship Force has played an important role in my life, giving me experiences of other countries and people of the world."

Jenny and Tony Coates and daughters Charlotte and Amy with former President Jimmy Carter at Hadrian's Wall.

Ever practical, Amy added: "It also helps me in my geography work at school." She noted that her family had hosted quite a few people from other countries, including Dave and Dee Gustavson from San Francisco, California; Don and Tina McTaggart from New Zealand; Lothar Luehring from West Germany and Henny and Deinke Willemsen from Holland "But probably the most unusual person to me was a Japanese lady.... She was extremely kind and brought us sweets, pencils and a thick black pen.....

"The Carter family—President and Mrs. Carter and Amy—have all visited us. I was only four when Amy and her friend Cricket stayed with us in 1982. I do remember the publicity about the visit and what a fuss everyone made because our Christian names are the same. Then five years later, President and Mrs. Carter came to stay with us for the July Fourth weekend (American Independence Day). There was a big parade through Newcastle, which was part of the celebration of the tenth anniversary of The Friendship Force."

In summary, Amy concluded: "The Friendship Force has given me a great love for the USA and for Georgia in particular. It has been a very interesting organization to me and has given me many happy memories."

One of the first endeavors involving youth was detailed in *Friendship* magazine by Reno Domenico, a teacher and supervisor of Humanities for the Sterling High School District in New Jersey. This exchange was truly a youth exchange, including twelve students from Sterling High School in Somerdale; ten students from Mountain Lakes High School (also NJ); their teacher Lee Konetschny; exchange director Anita Ream and Reno Domenico.

This lively group flew to Moscow, had a quick tour of that city and then traveled to the Ukrainian capital of Kiev by train. Once in Kiev, they were greeted by students of School 125 and their families. The ambassadors were given flowers and the traditional Ukrainian bread.

Excerpts from Mr. Domenico's article follows.

"For students from Sterling and Mountain Lakes High Schools, the venture of a lifetime had really just begun," Domenico wrote. "For me, the highlight of the experience was the opportunity to teach for three days in School 125. Education was the primary objective of our visit to Kiev in the first place. Likewise, the opportunity of teaching in New Jersey ranked high with my host Valentina Chesakova and Talyana Mihalchuk (Mr. Konetschny's host), both Vice Principals of School 125.

"These two teachers were the keys to our success in the Soviet Union.... The central lesson I learned is that it is essential in an educationally based exchange to allow professionals to work directly together.... Everything, from teaching in School 125 to the social interaction with host families was...carried out. "For the students, the accelerated agenda made for quick bonding and a 'work is fun, fun is work' attitude.

"School 125 is exceptional in its own right," Domenico said. "In fact, all the schools I visited were sound institutions. The Soviet system is friendly and warm in its approach to the students. Great respect is given to the welfare of the children and the schools are relaxed, happy environments conducive to a positive learning experience. Discipline is fair, quickly enforced, judiciously used and professionally administered. Actually, very little need for discipline was ever observed.

"My carefully selected students performed exceptionally well. We decided together before we left that we expected excellence of each other.... The students worked diligently to prepare for the exchange and they didn't waste a minute in maximizing and intensifying the entire experience. Even as I write, they are still engaging in dialogue and analysis of their collective observations."

Here are some of the characteristics which the American teachers and the exchange director looked for in students chosen to participate as ambassadors to Kiev: "Flexible, optimistic, rugged, athletic and talented. In particular, the seniors served as a dynamic force, giving energy to the entire delegation." Dominico noted that the selection was not made solely on the basis of grades. "It was the quality of the personality that proved to be the most important asset the students brought with them to Kiev.

"The students of School 125 were intelligent and were aware of the American lifestyle. In fact, if it hadn't been for the English fluency of the Soviet faculty and students, communication would have been very difficult," Dominico noted. "What impressed me most about the young people of Kiev was that since their time was not dominated by after school jobs, they had more opportunity to pursue normal adolescent growth patterns resulting in significant cultural, intellectual and athletic development.

Dominico also wrote about encounters with other professionals, primarily because his host family arranged Sunday picnics with enough leisure time provided to discuss in depth the important issues in Soviet life, such as nationalism, socialism and a unified Germany. "We were working with the best and the brightest in Kiev," he added.

Dominico highly praised The Friendship Society of Kiev and its president, Boris Fouzic. He also praised Anita Reams of The Friendship Force of Northern New Jersey for her work with the students. Praise and thanks also went to Olga Prychka, The Friendship Force representative of South Jersey, and her husband for invaluable assistance and language instruction.

Students and Teachers From Kiev Visit The USA

The return exchange took place in May 1990, and it was a similar success story, although Dominico and Reams "found it difficult to match the warmth, professionalism, hospitality and excitement" seen earlier in Kiev.

Dominico told of the emotion following the return exchange when new friends from Kiev were about to depart: "A glance around the Dulles airport...revealed signs and advertisements signaling the upcoming Summit between the United States and the Soviet Union. As the American and Soviet students sang the verse from "We Shall Overcome" which begins: 'We shall live in peace,' I again concluded, as I had weeks before in Kiev, that these words, so beautifully expressed as a wish, would become a reality.

"As the singing continued, the host parents gathered closer and closer to the circle of students. Passengers, passers-by—all strangers—were drawn to the students. Airline attendants from Aeroflot, captivated by the strong bonding, dabbed their eyes. People applauded. A flight attendant hesitated to call the final boarding.

"As the last embraces and kisses were exchanged, Boris Fouzik called to us: 'Next year in Kiev!' We waited two more hours standing as an honor guard, determined not to leave until our friends winged out of sight. For me the only conclusion is now a truth. American and Soviet students, parents, teachers and families will never go to war with one another. I am convinced that through such exchanges, we shall live in peace someday," Reno Dominico concluded.

The somewhat elusive goal of finding more ways to include young participants in The Friendship Force was also achieved when a Georgia student choral group called CELEBRATE traveled to China. They were led by their principal at Crabapple Middle School, Dr. Doris Robertson.

The forty students and eighty adults who made the trip were welcomed into Beijing Middle School, the International School (Beijing), the Children's Palace in Shanghai and Guilin Middle School.

Doris Robertson said, "Crabapple parent Pete Hill's dedication to being a Friendship Force ambassador resulted in meaningful presentations to the principals in each school.

The Great Wall of China was impressive, but more impressive were the people.

He overwhelmed us by arriving in China with personalized letters for each school from former President Jimmy Carter, Georgia Governor Joe Frank Harris, Atlanta Mayor Maynard Jackson and baseball great Hank Aaron.

"Participation in these ceremonies with school heads in China was comparable to meeting the heads of state at a summit conference. When we shook hands at the conclusion of the ceremony, it was as if we were promising that our countries would live together in peace forever for the sake of our children. (Now we understand why The Friendship Force chose clasped hands as its symbol.)

"Each time we performed, the Chinese students enthralled us with their unbelievably talented performances, too. The talent in China touched our hearts. We have special remembrances of our students singing "Love in any Language" and "It's a Small World." When the younger Chinese singers sang "Auld Lang Syne," in perfect English...there was a moment in time when two diverse cultures were celebrated as one."

In Beijing, the young American students were amazed by the number of people on bicycles. They were awed by Tiananmen Square and when they first saw the Great Wall of China, completed over two hundred years before the birth of Christ.

They visited the Portman Center in Shanghai, designed by Atlantan John Portman, and saw Chinese acrobats perform. The Friendship Force ambassadors were guests in the Cao Yang Worker's quarters consisting of huge apartment complexes with many modest living quarters. It was in Shanghai that they encountered Children's Palaces, providing after-school care. Teachers seek to enhance each child's natural gifts in music and the arts.

After Shanghai, The Friendship Force ambassadors went on to Guilin and saw the spectacular mountains, honeycombed with caves in the Li River Valley.

Doris Robertson said, "While there was interest in sightseeing and shopping, Friendship Force ambassadors always remembered that their primary purpose was to promote friendship from Crabapple to China.

Chapter 15
A Time To Act

Perpetual optimism is a force multiplier.
—**Colin Powell**

Small groups of Americans and Soviets continued to shuttle back and forth between cities in both countries after Wayne Smith faced Mikhail Gorbachev in Washington, DC and spoke from his heart to the General Secretary. But the number of citizens involved fell far short of the large numbers Wayne Smith had repeatedly requested. Nevertheless, these exchange groups had been tremendously successful, convincing Smith more than ever that the A.R.M.S. program must expand.

In late May, Wayne and Carolyn left for New Zealand to attend a Friendship Force Festival in that lovely island country. Suddenly, things began to happen fast enough to make even Wayne Smith's head spin. Here is the incredible story from his computer 'diary:'

Visit to Moscow —June 1-4, 1988
On May 28, I was in New Zealand when I received a telephone call from my Atlanta office informing me that the USA/USSR Society in Moscow had called to request that I drop everything and go immediately to Moscow for meetings connected with the Summit between President Reagan and General Secretary Gorbachev. I was told that my expenses would be paid by the society and that I was urgently needed.

I left Auckland the evening of May 28, and flew back to Atlanta. On May 31, I flew to Washington and met with the First Secretary of the Soviet Embassy who obtained an instant visa for me and gave me my ticket to Moscow.

It was a fascinating journey. The Friendship Society of the USSR must have placed much importance on having me there to represent The Friendship Force at the Summit, because they flew me over and back on Pan American Airlines (first class) and installed me in a five room suite overlooking the Kremlin. A big Chaika limousine was put at my disposal for the entire visit. I mention these things only to underscore the importance that the Soviets placed on this visit. (Smith said that he had never before been accorded such treatment on his many previous trips to Moscow.)

Upon landing in Moscow, I was met by three representatives of the Friendship Society and was taken to the VIP room while one of them took my passport and cleared all formalities for me. The others took me into a private lounge for a cup of coffee.

St. Basil's Cathedral in Moscow

After checking into the Rossia Hotel, I was escorted to the headquarters of the Friendship Society to meet Valentina Tereskova, head of this organization and the first woman in space. She is also a member of the Supreme Soviet, the top echelon of the Soviet government. We had not met before. She is a charming intelligent and gracious woman, but tolerates no nonsense in her dealings with others.

After an hour's visit with Madame Tereskova there was just enough time to go back to the hotel for a few minutes and get ready to go to the Bolshoi Theater for the special program that had been prepared for President and Mrs. Reagan and General Secretary and Mrs. Gorbachev.

Madame Tereskova had reserved a seat for me on the very first row center of the theater. When the two national leaders and their wives came in, I was very proud to stand at attention with my hand over my heart as the Star Spangled Banner was played by the orchestra.

The next day I was taken to the Kremlin to meet with Mr. Gorbachev. I was told that over two hundred people had been invited from about sixty nations. I was asked to sit in the front row of the auditorium, directly in front of Mr. Gorbachev. Furthermore, it was requested that I be the first to speak.

Two other Americans were invited to be present. One of these was Susan Eisenhower, granddaughter of the former President, now the leader of a moderately conservative "think tank" located in Washington, DC. The other invitee was Jane Smith, the mother of school girl Samantha Smith who visited the Soviet Union a few years ago at the invitation of Yuri Andropov.

Mr. Gorbachev came into the auditorium at 3 p.m. and the meeting lasted until a little after 6 p.m. He began the meeting with a thirty minute exposition of his impressions of the Summit. When he asked for comments from those present, he nodded to me and I took the floor. I later learned that my comments (edited a little) were aired on national Soviet television that evening.

I spoke for about five minutes and said this:

"Good afternoon Mr. Gorbachev:

My name is Wayne Smith and I am the President of The Friendship Force. My name, 'Smith' is one of the most common names in my country and I consider myself to be representative of most Americans. I support my government and believe very strongly in our way of life. I am here at the invitation of the USSR/USA Society which is led by Valentina Tereskova.

Congratulations! You and President Reagan have concluded a fourth successful Summit. While many positive things have come from these Summits, perhaps the most important result is that you have proven the validity of what President Reagan said when you first met in 1985; namely, that it is better to talk *with* people than to talk *about* people. By talking to each other, you have also proven the validity of people-to-people diplomacy. I understand that Mr. Reagan has said that he no longer considers the Soviet Union to be 'the evil empire.' It is said that he has changed his mind because he has gotten to know you. This proves that personal contact can accomplish people-to-people diplomacy by dispelling ignorance and wrong ideas.

As you, Mr. Gorbachev, have intimated before, the problem between our two nations is not the fact that we have awesome arsenals of armaments. That is a symptom of our problem. Our problem is that our nations fear each other. This fear has been constructed on a garbage dump of ignorance. It is time that we threw out the garbage! As you have said, it is time that we got rid of our myths and see reality as it truly is.

Your meetings with President Reagan have made many of us in the world wonder if we should not have the same opportunity which you and my President have had. What I'm speaking of is that we should get to know each other on a personal basis also and thereby get rid of our ignorance and wrong impressions of each other.

It is true that a few thousand of our citizens visit each other's countries each year. But for the most part, these people are tourists, diplomats, academicians and bureaucrats. It is time that ordinary people get involved by spending a few days in each other's homes. We want your teachers, farmers and people from all walks of life to get to know us.

You will be happy to learn—and I think you already know—that under the auspices of The Friendship Society and The Friendship Force, hundreds of our citizens are making such visits each year. We need not only for hundreds of people to have these visits but for hundreds of thousands to do so. In this way we will eliminate our ignorance about each other and thereby lead to the eradication of the fears we have.

My organization has chapters in some 250 cities in nearly 50 nations. Just imagine what good things could happen if delegations of 50 citizens from each of these 250 communities could visit in Soviet homes for a week or two and if Soviets could return these visits and establish personal friendships by dwelling with these people in their homes for a few days. The Friendship Society and The Friendship Force have the ability to make this happen. We need your support.

When this occurs enough times, we will discover that 'a world of friends is a world of peace.'"

Gorbachev said: "Politics are lagging behind the technology of war. There is also the 'time factor' that needs to be considered. Now is the time for us to act, not just talk about acting."

That evening in my hotel room and before the television program aired, I typed out my impressions of Mr. Gorbachev during the three hour meeting between the General Secretary and those who engaged him in dialogue:

Candid, conciliatory, reasonable, patient, smiles a lot, good sense of humor, admits past mistakes of former regimes, intelligent, optimistic, personable, likable, flexible, articulate, informal, excellent communicator, enthusiastic, charismatic, has respect, confidence and admiration of his people, speaks from the head and from the heart, doesn't use slogans of the past, sincere, courteous, respectful of Ronald Reagan, does not engage in "US bashing." The man is frightening only in the respect that it is hard to find anything about him to criticize.

In the same computer diary, Smith concluded by expressing his impressions about the future of the A.R.M.S. program.

"I really believe that the Soviets are very, very interested in working with The Friendship Force in a vastly expanded exchange program. I think there is little chance that we will be duped into being facile instruments of Soviet propaganda. There are too many level-headed people on our Board of Directors to allow this to happen. I see that we have a great opportunity of exposing tens of thousands of Soviets to the West in a way they have never experienced before. I am convinced this will help them to want change even more than I think they want it now. It will also give Americans a chance to see the Soviet Union as it really is: like a person coming out of a pool of mud. The mud is still on the body, but it is dropping off slowly. But the direction away from the mud pool has been definitely set.

"It was agreed that two high-ranking representatives of the USSR/USA Society will come to a meeting of The Friendship Force that will be held in Gelsenkirchen (Federal Republic of Germany) from July 7 to 10. At that time we will finalize a plan that will be designed to allow this exchange of 20,000 Soviets with people of other countries.

Not everyone thought that The Friendship Force should be involved in any way with the USSR. In the early days, Wayne Smith received a carefully worded letter from the United States Information Agency in Washington, DC. On behalf of the USIA, Charles Z. Wick beseeched Smith to "please keep in mind that, very often, the Soviet propaganda apparatus portrays foreign advocates of peace as opponents of US Government policies, whether or not this is the case."

Wayne Smith also had some concern about his organization becoming a tool for disseminating Soviet propaganda. It was a natural reaction, as my husband and I ruefully recalled from our very first encounter with Smith in 1984.

In response to the letter, Smith agreed with Mr. Wick's statement that the Soviets "will always be at liberty to interpret as they please the statements of private or official Americans." Smith explained that The Friendship Force was not a part of any "peace movement" or nuclear freeze advocacy group. "However," Smith said, "we are convinced that truth is stronger than a lie and that an honest exchange of ideas between private persons will have good consequences."

"Before our participants travel to the Soviet Union, they first meet several times for orientation concerning Soviet life. One of these orientation sessions deals with the Soviet political system," Smith pointed out. "We attempt to go with eyes wide open, however, we do not go with a polemic attitude concerning politics. The Friendship Force position is the very simple one that we love our country, support our government and desire to establish personal friendships with ordinary citizens of all nations, including those in the Soviet Union."

Smith also told Mr. Wick that The Friendship Force, at the request of the FBI, routinely sends a list of all those who visit the USSR with The Friendship Force to the Bureau's Atlanta office. Smith further noted that he had attempted to get an appointment with Wick on three different occasions, to discuss the exchanges, but had not met with success in doing so. Smith indicated his willingness to meet with Wick and hear his counsel about the USSR program.

Earlier still, Wayne wrote an open letter to Samantha Smith in 1983. She was the young girl who wrote to Soviet President Yuri Andropov and asked that he not start a war. (Samantha was killed in a tragic plane crash a short time later.) Part of Wayne Smith's letter follows:

"...Samantha, Americans and Soviets are, just like you said, very much alike in some very important ways. For example, we all live on this small planet. If the government of one nation starts a war, citizens of both will pay the consequences. Citizens of both lands love their children and want them to live in peace in a better world than the one we now inhabit. In Russia, they cry real tears just as we do here. The Russians bleed and laugh and get hungry and tired just as we do. In all ways common to human beings, we are very much alike.

"My problem is that some people think that I, too, am naive and impractical for trying to do something about bridging the large gulf of ignorance between the people of the USA and the USSR.

"Just a few days ago, the Soviet Air Force shot down a Korean commercial airplane and 269 boys and girls and men and women were killed. People everywhere are saying that the Soviets are barbarians and uncivilized, that they are sub-human and that the rest of the world should have nothing to do with them. Right after these things were said, however, it was stated that the US government will continue to trade with the Soviets and to discuss an arms agreement with them. Certain airlines of the world have complained very strongly about this tragic destruction of the jetliner and have said they would not fly their planes to Russia anymore. At least for two weeks.

"One of those who died was Larry McDonald, a US Congressman from Georgia. Congressman McDonald once said something that I believe very much. He said that, "If we stand for nothing, we will fall for anything."

"Samantha...I stand for something, too. I believe that the world never has solved its problems with military arms and that it never will. I believe that the strongest force in the world is the force of love, of which friendship is an integral part. I believe we should get rid of our enemies by turning them into friends. We might be misunderstood by both Americans and Russians. We could be thought to be as naive as you have been accused of being. Some might even call us Communist sympathizers. I know this is not true.

"But there is a far greater risk. It is the risk of doing nothing."

Smith may also have remembered isolated criticism of the A.R.M.S. program when it began with the first Soviet Group visiting homes in 1985. In an Atlanta newspaper, one of those critics wrote: "...those of us in a position to know for sure realize that ONLY KGB agents are allowed to travel in the way these Soviets were. I am not declaring these recent visitors to be KGB agents, but the thought does occur when one remembers that this has held true for so many years and for so many visits. Spokesperson Garner made the statement that

'It makes you feel you have done something when you embrace a Soviet.' ...It certainly should, for by doing so you have 'embraced' a representative of a vicious, heartless murderous regime. And I repeat for the sake of emphasis, a regime that never changes, one that has said they will 'bury us,' and means it as much today as when said some years ago in the treacherous halls of the UN. To 'embrace' communists is to approve of the godless and inhumane way of life they espouse. Such an 'embrace' is much too deadly and God-offending to be morally correct," the complainer railed.

This writer who preached about a "godless and inhumane way of life" would be surprised to learn that many of the Soviet Georgians who made that first visit were Christians and that their country had embraced Christianity in the fourth century. He might also be surprised to learn that the people had continued to worship God, even when their churches were officially closed and they were forbidden to express their faith openly without suffering severe consequences.

"Deadly and God-offending?"

Fear and ignorance remain as prime breeding grounds for hatreds and ultimately, for wars.

Churches in Moscow undergo renovation after years of disuse.

Chapter 16
A Path To a Friend's House is Never Long

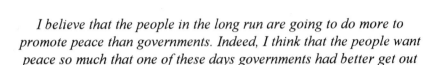

I believe that the people in the long run are going to do more to promote peace than governments. Indeed, I think that the people want peace so much that one of these days governments had better get out of the way and let them have it.
—President of the United States, Dwight David Eisenhower

Wayne Smith used another parable to describe what is required of each Friendship Force ambassador in order for the 'magic' of friendship to occur anywhere in the world..

"The land of Galilee is a living parable of life," Smith said. "Water descends from the mountains of Lebanon and fills the lovely Sea of Galilee. This lake is alive with fish and is a place of beauty. The Sea of Galilee surrenders its life-giving water to the Jordan River, and this river makes the entire valley fertile where it flows. The Jordan River empties into the Dead Sea. But the Dead Sea gives back nothing of what it receives. It keeps all the water that the Jordan River has deposited. It is a place of bitterness and death.

"Life is like this," he said. "We have been made to be loved and to love in return, if only we can find the courage to do it. I am convinced that we all want to be loved and that deep down we want to give back more than we take from life. If only we can have enough faith to believe that the losers in life are the *takers*, and the winners are those who always try to *give* more than they take."

Back in 1987, Friendship Force leaders in Washington State participated in a tribute to a team of Soviets on the anniversary of their trans-polar flight of peace and friendship. Forty-seven years earlier, their strange plane with bright red wings landed in Vancouver, Washington. The plane contained three Soviet fliers who had traveled six thousand miles non-stop across the North Pole, arriving in Vancouver after sixty-three hours and sixteen minutes.

One of those fliers, Colonel General Georgi Filipovich Baidukov, co-pilot of the epic flight, returned to visit a monument which the people of Vancouver erected to honor the Soviet aviators. The two other men on the flight are deceased. When the plane landed all those years ago, Pilot Igor Chkalov, said, "This is the route of peace and friendship and God forbid it if it is used for anything different.... On the red wings of this plane we have brought peace and friendship from the Soviet people to the American people."

Dr. Wayne Van Tilburg, President of The Friendship Force of Southwest Washington, and his wife Eleanor, were invited to participate in the ceremony as representatives of The Friendship Force.

Dr. Van Tilburg declared, "We must renew our efforts to promote friendship missions to the Soviet Union no matter what the political arena holds. I want my children to live in a world that doesn't present the fear of nuclear holocaust. Our hope lies in the children. I believe that if our children are able to meet Soviet children, we will have taken another step toward bridging that barrier that separates our two countries. Those who have been Friendship Force ambassadors or hosts know the value of sitting down and talking things over."

The Van Tilburgs hosted the Soviet visitors in their home and later recalled "...they continually expressed a strong desire for their children to grow up in a world of peace.

Following this special celebration, the Van Tilburgs fascination with the Soviet people grew and they were delighted to host the first delegation from Uzbekistan. It began when an A.R.M.S. delegation from that country traveled nearly 10,000 miles to share the spirit of friendship and peace with families in Washington State. Dr. Van Tilburg was the Exchange Director. During the visit, Fattah Teshabaiev, President of the Uzbek Friendship Society, agreed that "there is a lack of information on both sides about the lives of ordinary people in the two countries. During our visit we have had a chance to see the people of the United States who equally cherish peace."

In March 1988, it was time for the Van Tilburgs to see fascinating and exotic Uzbekistan for themselves.

Uzbekistan is located in central Asia and is bordered by the former Soviet Republics of Turkmenistan, Kazakhstan, Kyrgyzstan and Tajakistan. The Uzbeks descended from the great horse-riding nomadic tribes that once ruled central Asia. They joined the Mongol hordes to take part in the invasion of southern Russia in the 13th century. In the 14th century an Uzbek khan ruled the Great Horde. The Uzbeks captured much of the steppes north of the Amu Dorga River where they live today.

Eleanor Van Tilburg said "The region is a contrast of deserts, plains and snowcapped mountains. Cotton is the 'white gold' of the republic. She added: "This ancient land is known as 'a diamond in a sandy setting' but it is the people who add the sparkle. The hospitality extended to us was unbelievable. We came in contact with many kind and generous people, most of whom had never met an American before. We were exposed to their rich folklore, old customs and large families.

"Most of the people do not speak English, but prior arrangements were made in each city to have interpreters with us most of the time," she added. "Samarkand is one of the oldest cities in the world—over 2,500 years old. Caravans once traveled through Samarkand along the Silk Route from China to Europe. Today the city is a blend of East and West, old and new.

"Dr. Fattah Teshabaev planned the program for our visit. His assistant, Yakubjon Irgashev, was the personal escort for our eleven ambassadors. The itinerary could not have been better: a home-stay in Samarkand, an evening host in Bukhara, a home host in Tashkent and a day host in Almalyk. ...so many things happened until we began to expect the unexpected. In Samarkand, host families welcomed us at the airport with fresh flowers—at four in the morning! Together we explored this beautiful city where Genghis Khan, Shah-Zindeh and Tamerlane once lived. The mosques, mausoleums and *madrashahs* (religious schools) were magnificent with their blue tiled domes. We also visited a modern-day porcelain factory.

"By the time we reached the bazaar, many of the hosts and ambassadors were walking arm-in-arm. We were invited to taste the toasted apricot seeds or sample the mounds of sour cream. These markets have been a part of the cultural life of the region for generations. The men still dress in a *chappan* (robe) and *chust* (skullcap) and women are attired in brightly colored silk dresses.

"We were soon immersed in Uzbekistan family life, sharing traditions centered around meals and family. Meals began with the ritual of breaking a round loaf of bread and placing it around the table. We feasted on gifts from the land—fresh and dried fruits, tomatoes and cucumbers, rice pilaf, manty (meat filled dumplings} and shaslik (shiskabob).

"Throughout the meals there were toasts expressing friendship, peace and gratitude. These toasts were true expressions of love and a way to share feelings honestly for each other. After the meal, everyone retreated to a special area to sip tea and dance to Uzbek music.

Uzbek mother and child

Families presented guests with traditional robes and black skullcaps and with tea cups decorated with the cotton motif.

"Our role of ambassadors involved a busy, sometimes hectic schedule of meetings, press conferences, touring, visiting kindergartens and hospitals and a collective farm—and eating six meals a day!

"We were greeted by the mayors of Samarkand, Bukhara, Tashkent and Almalyk and by the presidium of the Supreme Soviet of Uzbek Soviet Socialist Republic (legislature). Many good ideas and much information came from discussions with these people, and we all agreed on the importance of knowing and understanding each other."

"Fattah said, 'We have some things alike, but we have differences so we can be ourselves.'

"...Tashkent, the capital, is known as a city of peace and friendship," Eleanor Van Tilburg said. "The city was destroyed by an earthquake in 1966 and was rebuilt with impressive modern buildings, wide streets and many parks and fountains. Monuments and fountains in the shape of cotton bolls adorn the streets and parks. The Uzbek rivers, which originate in the mountains, slow as they reach the dry lowlands, then dry up altogether in the flat sun-baked land containing salt marshes, sinkholes and caverns.

"We had lunch in the country one day and when we arrived at the place, we began a stroll though a forest of tall birch trees. Almost like a fairy tale, there in a glen was a table completely set. It was as if it had been magically lifted from someone's dining room. There was no one around but four Americans and ten Soviets who wanted to be friends."

Fairy tale dining in Uzbekistan. (Smiling Eleanor Van Tilburn and husband Wayne, Gennadei and Umida Atabaeva and Donna and John Marshall.)

"When it came time to go home, our new friends' eyes seemed to say, 'Don't go; I want to talk more; I want to know more; I want you to understand how I feel. These friends will always be in our hearts."

As part of the "Back to Basics" program for 1988, New Zealanders committed to go...well, somewhere. They learned of their destination only during the last organizational meeting prior to departure. For the forty-one "Kiwis," it was quite an adventure, but a puzzling one when they heard the name 'Big Canoe, USA.'

"We thought it was a joke at first," Joanna Bergman recalled. "Then we found out it was a place somewhere in the state of Georgia. We went to our maps, but there was no Big Canoe to be found. Some friends checked with travel agents and they came up with nothing. They said we were about to visit the unknown for sure. Finally one of our members called the Chamber of Commerce in Atlanta. The person who answered the phone didn't know about Big Canoe either!"

Of course, there is a Big Canoe. It is a secluded community nestled in the foothills of the ancient Blue Ridge Mountains, about fifty miles due north of Atlanta. My husband and I had agreed to host two of the New Zealanders and on February 12, we gathered with the other hosts at Big Canoe Chapel, anxiously awaiting the bus that would bring Joanna Bergman and Roy Johnson to us.

They arrived a bit late, but in high spirits. They were an amazing group and we instantly liked them because of their friendliness and of their positive attitudes. Anytime we asked if they would like to participate in an excursion or an event, the answer was always, "Why not!?"

The February weather was a bit gray, but we barely noticed, thanks to our sunny ambassador Joanna, who was "a live wire." She was quick with a quip and delighted us with her New Zealand expressions. Each morning when she came downstairs for breakfast, she would sing out: "Well! Are we a box of fluffy ducks this morning?" We liked that cheerful greeting so much until it soon became our own morning greeting.

Joanna also explained that New Zealand is home to three types of kiwi: the odd long-billed, flightless bird, their national symbol; the fuzzy coated green fruit and Kiwi, the slang for New Zealanders themselves.

We learned that our other ambassador, Roy Johnson, had built his own home and was interested in checking out Home Depot, a giant building materials store. Joanna and I tagged along as Dave and Roy inspected the warehouse-sized store. They were like children visiting a Disney theme park for the first time. Roy could not believe the prices of goods and merchandise, most of which were apparently much lower than comparable items in his country. Enthusiasm finally overcame poor Roy and he purchased a kitchen sink, amid hoots of disbelief from Joanna.

"I've heard of taking everything *but* the kitchen sink," she exclaimed, "but now you're taking that, too!"

After spending the morning at Home Depot, Joanna demanded equal time to shop at the mall. We never made it past the first shoe store. Joanna was Cinderella and the salesman was delighted to bring her shoes, shoes and more shoes. She may have broken a record for trying on shoes, but the clerks loved it as they gathered around just to hear her accent. Soon other shoppers were stopping as well. They received a crash course on both The Friendship Force and New Zealand, particularly Taupo, Joanna's home town. I don't think the mall shoppers will ever experience anything like it again. At least not until Joanna returns.

We stayed in the mountains most of the time and on one excursion we took Roy and Joanna to John's Mill, one of the few working grist mills remaining today. John Humphrey restored the mill and grinds corn each Saturday and Sunday. John was delighted to meet our guests and ran up to his house on the hill to get his guest book for them to sign. As John beamed at them good-naturedly, he said: "My goodness! New Zealand! Where did y'all learn to speak English?" That became our little joke that we often laughed about during the rest of their visit.

Roy Johnson watches John Humphrey grinding corn meal as in by-gone days.

Tom and Barbara Eubanks live in a rural community not far from Big Canoe. They agreed to host New Zealanders, but they were very worried about accommodating their guests because their home, the historic Cagle House, was in the midst of renovation. They had already moved into the house, but the construction in progress was something they could not hide.

"When our ambassadors Colin and Lynette Foote arrived, they were upset, but not because of the construction," Barbara said. "They were upset because they didn't bring work clothes so they could help us! They were sincere about it, too. We told them it wouldn't be fair for them to pay to come halfway around the world to perform manual labor. They responded with "What are friends for, if not to help other friends!"

Ah, those Kiwis. We loved them. Dave and I had come a long way from the day we dismissed Wayne Smith's notion of world peace through world friendships as that of an idealistic minister who didn't know what he was talking about. But Bob and Joan Herraman of Adelaide, Australia, took the art of making friends much farther when The Friendship Force inspired them to become friends to the poor in India.

Joan was a past president of The Friendship Force of Adelaide. She and her husband decided to extend themselves in friendship in India by volunteering to lend comfort to Mother Teresa's "poorest of the poor" at the Missionaries of Charity stations near Calcutta. Joan involved Friendship Force International staffers and The Friendship Force of Adelaide, whose members responded with contributions for the work in India. In December 1987, and again in January 1988, they worked with the poor and the ill, according to Joan's report in *Friendship* magazine.

It was in Howrah, a city of half a million on the outskirts of Calcutta, where Joan and Bob met a boy called Popaloo. "Both feet had been broken when he was a baby to make him more appealing as a beggar," Joan said. "As a result, the boy had cultivated 'heels' on the top of his feet. He was suffering from malnutrition and all the other usual things that go with living on the streets. He was obnoxious toward everyone and would hit the other boys. He wouldn't come near us."

"That first night we were at the YWCA and I said, 'We have a horrid child at Howrah. I can't stand him; he belts everyone and bites the little retarded boys.' A young American volunteer—a beautiful boy—said, 'How would you feel, Joan, if your mother had broken your feet when you were a baby so you could earn more money for her?'

"That," said Joan, "really made me think of how much our mother really loved us and was always telling us how wonderful our family was. So, the next day I thought I would make a big effort to like this boy. I cuddled him, even when he didn't want me to touch him. I sang to him and whispered to him—even when he couldn't understand a word I was saying."

Joan Herraman gives tender loving care.

Joan struggled hard to keep her promise as Popaloo maintained a tough outer shell.

"One day one of the Brothers said, 'Aunty, why do you always spend all the time with this boy?' I said, 'Because he needs love.' And he said, 'They all do.' I answered, 'Yes I know; but everyone dislikes Popaloo so much and the other boys are loved.'"

Joan persisted and by the end of the month, Popaloo would be waiting at the gate for her.

"He would put his arms around me and just hold on to me. He would kiss me and lay in my arms and go to sleep, even though he was thirteen-years-old," Joan recalled. "Popaloo began to show a dramatic change, to the point that he even began to feed the retarded boys and rub oil on the sick boys. He never hit or bit another person again."

Joan finally had to leave Popaloo, "still needing care."

She said "I'll never forget him and the lesson he taught me. Love is the most important ingredient needed in our lives. I know I must sound like an old preacher, but it was such a big lesson to me. We had the most rewarding experience of our lives there in India and we got much more from our work there than we put into it."

So, as Joan pointed out in her article in *Friendship* magazine: "Friendship spreads like ripples in a pond; once the 'pebble' of love and caring is dropped into the 'sea' of humanity, the effects spread endlessly in every direction."

Exotic locations are often thrilling, but the idea of The Friendship Force is not *where* one is going, but *why*? Wayne Smith says that unfortunately a number of potential Friendship Force "ambassadors" are actually tourists at heart and are more interested in the *where* instead of the *why*.

"Destination," he keeps telling people, "ought not to matter in our organization. Our purpose is simple: it is to create an environment in which seeds of friendship can be sown across the barriers that separate people."

And to Wayne Smith, creating such an environment should take place wherever friends are made. He can recite endless examples, as in the case of the exchange announced between people of Bristol, England, who were assigned the destination of Beckley, West Virginia, where they would spend their entire two weeks.

"Initially there was some consternation in Bristol about the destination," Smith said. "The Bristol ambassadors had just heard that the UK Club in Cardiff, Wales, had been assigned to San Diego,

California, and Las Vegas, Nevada, yet here they were, headed for an unknown town in West Virginia. Several ambassadors didn't realize there *was* a West Virginia. And not one of them had ever heard of Beckley. However, due to the magnificent leadership of Gerry Phillips-Hughes, a true Friendship Force believer who thoroughly understood that what Beckley had to offer was its people. She also knew the one purpose of the exchange was to make friends.

"BOTH groups had a wonderful experience," Smith said with a grin. "I was there in Beckley for that exchange. What a thrill it was for the Bristol ambassadors to see the name of their city displayed all over town welcoming them. The Governor of the state received them at a private reception in their honor. They even visited a coal mine, but best of all, they made friends.

"The same thing happened in San Diego and Las Vegas: the Welsh made friends...and that is the sole purpose of our organization. It doesn't make a whit of difference as to whether we visit people in one city or another. We are not going to visit a city. We are going to visit a person who lives in a city."

Smith was right and the Bristol to Beckley exchange was certainly proof. The Reverend Dr. Phil Leftwich of Beckley said, "We made friends with our guests and they made friends with one another. The British taught us how to make tea properly and we taught them to eat brown beans and cornbread. They tried to teach us how to speak proper English, and we educated them in how to greet their neighbors in Bristol with "how y'all doin'?"

Leftwich also told of how Peter Griffiths, one of the ambassadors, was united with an uncle he had never met before. This all took place with the help of his host, Bill Little. He also recalled the delight of local school children who were visited by the British guests. Peter Griffiths, who described Beckley as 'a quiet gentle place,' laughed loudly when one child asked, "Can British children understand what you're saying?"

Although the Bristol ambassadors had originally voiced trepidation about their destination, once they were in Beckley for a week and they had the option of leaving and touring other parts of the United States during the second week of their stay, most declined, opting to stay with second-week hosts right there in Beckley.

"We're having a delightful time," said Tom and Wyn David. "We hate the idea of leaving to go home."

In an article he wrote for *Friendship* Magazine, The Reverend Dr. Leftwich summed up the experience by saying: "Making friends. That really is what we're all about. The stereotypical wrappings loosely fall aside and the gifts of friendship are received with affection when hearts are opened and arms extended in love. The British came to Beckley and from now on, 'the latchstring will always be out' to our friends from Bristol!"

The twelfth annual international conference of The Friendship Force was celebrated in Veldhoven, Holland, in October 1988. Jimmy and Rosalynn Carter charmed the guests and spent time greeting delegates at the opening dinner. Prince Bernhard was on hand to open the conference. Beverlie Reilman described it as "the United Nations in microcosm" and it truly was that by representation: four hundred delegates attended from twenty-five nations and thirty-three states, enjoying friendships old and new from October 6-9.

Among those from the United States was television star Charlotte Rae. Wayne Smith introduced two distinguished visitors from the Soviet Union, Yuri Smirnov, Deputy Director of the Union of Friendship Societies of the Soviet Union, and his assistant, Natalie Semenikhina. Their presence must have been worth all those earlier and seemingly fruitless trips Wayne Smith had made to Moscow, trying each time to persuade those in power to allow The Friendship Force to become a reality in the Soviet Republics.

It was heartwarming to all when Smirnov said, "When we arrived here in Veldhoven and met members of The Friendship Force, we understood that there are many people in the world who pray for the same values and have common goals of peace, mutual understanding and contacts between people. We have a dream," Smirnov continued, "that at the next international conference that there will be Soviet flags among the flags of other countries."

Honorary Chairperson Rosalynn Carter expressed excitement about the Youth Festival planned for Taiwan, then slated for August 20-31, 1989. "There is no greater cause that we could work for—peace for ourselves, for our children and for our grandchildren," Mrs. Carter said. "You, through your efforts and dedication make The Friendship Force what it is; you make it work; you make it the force that it is for breaking down barriers that sometimes divide us as a people, a force that brings the world closer together.".

President Jimmy Carter also had a brief message in which he urged the delegates to continue spreading the word about The Friendship Force. "It wouldn't be enough for those of us who enjoy The Friendship Force to rest on our laurels and clutch this precious possession to our bosoms and not share it aggressively with others," he urged.

Conference attendees in Veldhoven discovered that Holland is a land of windmills and tulips—and friendly people.

Charlotte Rae had already been an ambassador and Wayne Smith said that first experience had been enough to convince her that she belonged in The Friendship Force. "Charlotte Rae has a heart of gold and much love for our organization," President Wayne Smith said. Smith then asked Rae to give her impressions of the conference.

"It blows my mind!" she said. "I hope you understand—from all over the world—what I mean. It's too good to be true. This is the force that is going to spread love and peace all over the world.

"It was marvelous being in Haren, Holland, during armistice time on my first exchange," she said. "I was moved by the way the whole town of Haren walked to the cemetery, grave to grave, acknowledging and talking and saying a prayer at each grave of those killed during World War II.

"President and Mrs. Carter are both truly guided spiritually," she said. "I mean, they know what it's all about. President Carter said it all when he made the point that as one gets older one has to re-evaluate what is going to make one feel really fulfilled in life. My hope is that we can spread the word...to more and more people, including more youth. If we can spread the word so everyone can begin to understand one another, care for one another and love one another, then they can't start a war—whoever 'they' are," Rae said.

American television personality Charlotte Rae is greeted by a Dutch host.

In 1988, the Reverend Nicasio Ortiz of Puerto Rico, received a call from a Spanish-speaking Brazilian. It was Levy Tavares, Regional Representative of The Friendship Force in Latin America. Tavares asked Ortiz if he had heard of The Friendship Force. When Ortiz said he had not, Tavares explained. When the phone conversation ended, Ortiz said he would be happy to meet with Levy and Wayne Smith who were already in Puerto Rico.

Later, Tavares explained how he chose to call Reverend Ortiz. He and Wayne Smith were in a motel in San Juan, trying to determine the right person to call on to help start The Friendship Force in Puerto Rico. "I looked for the listing for *Iglesias* in the telephone directory," Levy said. "Since Wayne and I are Presbyterians, I stopped when I found a Presbyterian church in Carolina, ten miles away. Since Wayne's wife's name is Carolyn, I told him that was a sign, telling us to phone the Reverend Ortiz."

"The Friendship Force story really impressed me," Ortiz said. After just one meeting with Tavares and Smith, he readily agreed to arrange for Puerto Ricans to host an inbound exchange. He traveled to Atlanta to receive further training at Friendship Force International and became even more enthusiastic He agreed to find hosts for twenty ambassadors who would arrive in 1989.

Nina Hill gives her Japanese host a warm hug as husband Loyd looks on.

Kyoko Sata makes new friends on an exchange between Niigata, Japan, and Nairobi, Kenya. The language is different, but their smiles spell friendship.

The 1988 Friendship Force exchange programs ended on December 20, when forty-one Japanese ambassadors from Niigata and Tokyo, returned home from their two week home stay with members of the Palm Beach and West Coast Florida clubs. This concluded a successful year where a total of 5,831 ambassadors traveled around the world to extend their arms in hugs and in friendship. In Japan, new clubs continued to be formed and by 1995, Japan had nineteen clubs.

In March, 1989, twenty ambassadors from Berlin, West Germany, arrived in Carolina, Puerto Rico, during Easter week, the busiest week of the year.

How did they fare? "We took them to church and included them in our normal home and church life," Ortiz recalled. "They had never been in church services where there is a big show of emotion and much enthusiasm during the singing and preaching. Ours is a happy demonstration of faith," he said. "I think they liked the experience," he added.

Ortiz said he knew the exchange was a big success because "the hosts said they would like very much to host again and they all agreed we should establish a Friendship Force club in Puerto Rico. "Our hosting experience with the Berliners was one from heart to heart, and so deep that it will last forever," he said.

The first Friendship Force International Youth Conference was held in 1989 in Taiwan, Republic of China, just outside Taipei. The event was hosted jointly by The Friendship Force and The China (Taiwan) Youth Corps, founded in 1952. This group is a private organization dedicated to helping youth with their intellectual and physical development.

"Will you be my friend?" Tanya Salas of Puerto Rico asks Marie Berner of West Berlin.

Lutz Marechall of West Berlin helps a new Puerto Rican friend up a hill.

Gertrude Scolzhauer of West Berlin with new Puerto Rican friend

Chapter 17
Friendship - A Fearful Idea?

◆

When we volunteered to host one or two guests...we wondered what in the world we would do with strangers for a whole week. That changed quickly to wondering how in the world we were going to find time to do all that we wanted to do with our new friends.
—Velma Smith, Orangeburg, South Carolina

Although The Friendship Force was into its second decade, it was still one of the best kept secrets in the world. There were over 250 Friendship Force clubs around the world and leaders at Friendship Force International constantly pondered how best to give the organization a higher profile—one that would attract hundreds of thousands instead of just thousands.

Not only was The Friendship Force unknown to many, it was often badly misunderstood. Apparently making friends with strangers is a fearful idea for many people all around the world. It seemed so simple to knowledgeable Friendship Force members who urged their friends to participate in exchanges. "This is a way you can have a personal impact on the world's future and be a positive part of building a bridge of friendship across the barriers which divide people," they said.

And many of those doubting friends answered back: "Yes, but suppose....we don't like our hosts or they don't like us? What if they don't speak our language and we don't speak theirs? If we can't communicate, what purpose have we served? And, maybe we won't like their food or maybe their homes won't be up to our standard of cleanliness? What if we got sick so far away from home?"

To the doubters, Wayne Smith offers some advice. "It takes a little courage and a lot of faith to be a Friendship Force ambassador," he encouraged. "You need to have faith that people who live in other cultures are more like you than they are different. And you need to believe that there is a potential friend out there who is willing to share his or her life with you. And you must always go with a spirit of adventure and confidence. With these attitudes, you will finish your Friendship Force experience with new friends," he promised.

Audrey Post, a staff writer for *The Macon Telegraph and Post* (Georgia) wrote a thoughtful article for *Friendship* magazine published in the second quarter, 1989. Post traveled to Hannover, Germany, where she was hosted by Andreas "Andy" Muschiol and Ilke Meyer-Delvendahl.

"The Hannover couple wanted everything about my stay to be perfect. I wanted to be the perfect guest. We got over that in a hurry!" Post said. "During our week together, the three of us shared our hopes, our dreams and our most embarrassing stories. We talked about world politics, the arms race and acid rain. They told Helmut Kohl jokes and I told Ronald Reagan jokes; you could switch names on most of them and they would still be funny. We ranted about drivers who don't use turn signals. We decided that Americans should get six weeks' paid vacation a year like Germans do. We agreed that ice cream is one of life's greatest pleasures.

"And we discovered that neither a different nationality, a different native tongue nor several years' difference in age mattered. We were more alike than different and discovering that common ground lent magic to sitting around the kitchen table."

And then Audrey Post made this very memorable and definable observation about The Friendship Force: *Experiencing the culture and heritage of Germany with German friends instead of a tour operator is like passing through a doorway instead of looking through a window.*

Post saw things to be sad about while she was in West Germany, especially when her hosts took her to the East German border to view the hated Berlin Wall. "The difference between the two Germanys were visible. In the village to the East, there were no window boxes filled with flowers, no automobiles, no people in the streets. It looked deserted, save a lone cat walking between houses. Seeing museum photographs of hollow-eyed refugees from the Soviet occupation zone flooding into Hannover at the end of World War II, and learning that a friend's mother had been among them, turned those refugees into real people.

"Visiting the memorial to concentration camp victims at Bergen-Belsen and hearing your host say softly, 'This is the shame of all Germans,' brought home the realization that those born long after the Third Reich ended have inherited its guilt. They, too, are victims.

"Ilse said, 'It's hard to believe our countries were at war not so very long ago. I hope the world has learned a lesson.'

"That lesson is what The Friendship Force is all about, "Post concluded. "A world of peace through a world of friends."

On May 23, 1989, Dr. Wayne Smith, President and founder of The Friendship Force and Assistant Chaplain of Big Canoe Chapel, received the prestigious Officers Cross of the Order of Merit from the Federal Republic of Germany. The award was presented to Dr. Smith by Herr Dr. Alexander Von Schmeling, Consul General of the Federal Republic of Germany. Dr. Smith received this honor at a special dinner held at the Peachtree Plaza Hotel in Atlanta. According to remarks read by Dr. Von Schmeling, the award was given to Dr. Smith for his work through The Friendship Force "...for actively contributing to the strength of friendship between Germany and the United States of America."

This award was presented on the 40th anniversary of the founding of the Federal Republic of Germany.

Wayne Smith spends a lot of time thinking about how The Friendship Force can expand. When he speaks to people who have not yet heard about the organization before, he often tells them the same thing he wrote in this "Friend To Friend" column:

"There are two paths to peace. One is called fear. The other is named friendship. The path of fear is a dangerous way to travel to peace. For example, the United States has a nuclear submarine system called Trident. Aboard this class of submarine are missiles called Polaris. There is more 'fire power' on just one Trident-class submarine than was expended in all of World War II.

"The path of fear levies a high toll," Smith says, warming to his subject. "It saps the financial resources of nations. Instead of spending money on education, medical research and the like, nations who walk the path of fear spend trillions of dollars on armies and armaments. And as sad as it makes me to admit it, I personally believe that a strong military is a necessity in the kind of world we live in, where no basis of universal trust exists among nations. When there is no trust, there is fear," Smith maintains. "And when fear abounds, it is necessary to be prepared to defend yourself.

"A curious thing to note about the path to peace called fear is that it is a dead-end street. Never in the history of humankind has this type of approach to peace ever taken those who traveled it to the desired destination. Warfare has always erupted.

"But," Smith smiles, "there is a second path to peace; it is named friendship. Unlike the path of fear, the path of friendship does not have as its destination a state where there is a simple lack of overt warfare. Friendship believes that peace is a positive value. Friendship involves sharing and cooperation. Friendship doesn't say, 'Stay away from me or I'll kill you.' It says, 'Come closer and I will embrace you and turn you into a friend.'

"The path to peace through friendship also has its dangers," Smith admits. "It requires that we trust others—and this is risky. We will be betrayed by some, because not everyone is trustworthy. But it is only by trusting others that they will trust us. Without trust, fear is a certainty.

"The path call friendship is costly, too. For one thing, it will cost us our prejudice. Prejudice is just a word that means we have 'prejudged' others. A terrible human inclination is to impute the worst to others, especially if they are strangers. We can never establish a friendship that will lead to peace if we always are thinking that others are devils. The truth is that other people are just about the way we are. They have good qualities and bad ones, too.

"The plain fact is that nations tread the path of fear in search of 'national security,'" Smith explains. "Nations are afraid they will lose their freedom or their economic advantage. Nations build arms to defend themselves against those whom they perceive to be threats.... Nations generally do not spend a great deal of effort in establishing trust with other nations," Smith says with a sad smile. "And yet, any real peace must be based on trust.

There are two paths to peace. Nations generally have taken the path named fear. Maybe that is all that nations can do, given the state of today's world. However, you and I can walk the path of friendship.

"If people will lead, nations will follow."

Despite Wayne Smith's convincing ways, there are those who still express strong doubts about the ability of The Friendship Force to have any lasting effect. The doubters reason that perhaps it is possible to visit a person in another country and be friends for a little while, but that friendship will soon fade because of the distance between the two.

These doubters should meet Gerry Earnest, past president of The Friendship Force club of the Bay Area in California. Gerry wrote the following letter to Friendship Force International after the October, 1989, earthquake.

"Following the devastation in the San Francisco Bay area, pictures of the damage flashed around the world.

"Three days after the earthquake, a call got through to our home and the operator asked if we spoke Estonian; because she was having difficulty understanding the incoming call. Moments later Helva came on the line, crying with relief to hear that we had come through the catastrophe without problems—and so had the rest of her Friendship Force friends in the Bay Area," Gerry said.

"Helva had been trying to contact us ever since the quake struck. She had stayed in our home last May and we were able to stay with her on an exchange in June. I can't explain how much her call meant to us.

"Members of our Bay Area Friendship Force club also received calls from the Netherlands, Germany, Korea, Ireland, Italy, Mexico, New Zealand, Chile, and many of our states. And those are just the places I have heard about," Gerry Earnest wrote.

"This experience dramatically illustrates how The Friendship Force provides a framework within which individual private citizens can meet, experience the common similarities that exist in our sometimes disparate cultures, yet truly forge bonds of friendship. Thank you Friendship Force."

On January 17, 1994, Daniel and Sylvia Postar were taking an early morning walk with another couple in their Los Angeles neighborhood. "The earth began to roll beneath us and we had to hold on to each other to keep from falling. Fortunately we were not hurt, but we later learned that our son Stanley's house burned to the ground since it was at the epicenter of the earthquake," Daniel Postar said.

In the tumultuous days following the quake, the Postars never dreamed that their former Friendship Force hosts, Sayoko and Katsuiku Okajima from Gifu, Japan, saw the devastation to Los Angeles on television and were frantically trying to reach them. Since the phone service was disrupted, they did not learn of the Postars safety for over a week.

The Postars had also hosted the Okajimas' daughter Asako. They remembered that she had photographed their son's home. They contacted Asako and asked her to make reprints of the photos, providing evidence of the damage for insurance purposes. The pictures were sent along with a check for three hundred dollars, payable to Stanley and Cathy Postar.

"Within the next two weeks we received letters from Friendship Force people we knew all over the world—Australia, New Zealand, England, Brazil and Thailand," Daniel Postar said. "All were interested in our welfare. Only through The Friendship Force can one make such wonderful friends."

Jim Sykes visited Lithuania with The Friendship Force and discovered what it really means to him to be a Lithuanian-American. His father emigrated to the United States around 1900 and in 1989, almost ninety years later, Sykes was in Vilnius, Lithuania. He found that the city offered vast green areas in its center. Where the Neris and Vilnia Rivers merge, he discovered that the old city had expanded into new suburbs, but without any of the sprawl, typical of city expansion. He watched city parks being used daily by people gathering to visit while their children and grandchildren played. "Television," marveled Sykes, "seems to have failed to change active, thoughtful Lithuanians into couch potatoes."

He was also pleased to find an openness to an exchange of views and an eagerness of the Lithuanians to learn about him and the other Friendship Force ambassadors from Madison, Wisconsin. "We did not spar over ideological differences...and I discovered that friendship begins at the personal level and is not at risk when unpretentious people share their homes and values."

Sykes was thrilled to learn that Lithuanians have a deep appreciation for their heritage and a love of art and music. He also learned that many older citizens had lived under the tsar, the Poles, the Fascists and now under Moscow, and that most wanted total independence. Sykes found no one who did not share Gorbachev's goals. He enjoyed his hosts and their friends and found that Vilnius reflected their progressive spirit. He rejoiced in the Lithuanians care of the natural environment.

"Across a wide ocean and ideological differences, eleven Madison area people discovered that we and our Vilnius hosts want peace, friendship and the opportunity to discover what makes us unique—and alike," Sykes said. "We've studied war far too long; now it's time to build peace, one friendship at a time, person to person, city to city."

Audrey Collins wrote about forty-one Japanese ambassadors who were hosted by South Florida families. "From the snow they left in Niigata to the sunshine of the Palm Beaches, hosts greeted ambassadors in friendship, putting old fears and misunderstandings behind them," she said.

Audrey was a bit taken aback when she learned that Takao and Takako, her ambassadors, also planned to bring their children, Keiko and Gota, aged three and six. "I had only two bedrooms and our grown son had just moved from Ohio to live with us," she said. "After all our corresponding, I just couldn't let Takao's family stay anywhere but with us. Chalk up another victory for flexibility, because The Friendship Force experience happened again! Even though I have seen it happen time and again, I continue to be amazed at the depth of feeling that can develop between people who were total strangers just seven short days before. It is difficult to explain this phenomenon to someone who has never experienced it.

"The Friendship Force of the Palm Beaches is a relatively new club," Audrey explained. "The experience of hosting was a 'first' for many of our members. Comments from ambassadors and hosts, almost without exception, were favorable. The hosts learned several important things about a Friendship Force exchange: Foremost, we learned that it is stepping out in friendship, not in fear, and then extending your hand in love, not hate. We also learned anew how knowledge and understanding banish ignorance.

M.E. "Bud" Seretean was the keynote speaker at the 13th International Conference held in Portland, Oregon, October 5-8, 1989. Seretean, the first Chairman of the Board, outlined challenges to Friendship Force members around the world. He also made a prediction about Wayne Smith.

"Wayne Smith, our founding visionary, has yet to discover an unfriendly country, to meet an unfriendly person or hear of a task that cannot be accomplished," he said. "In the early years of The Friendship Force I often expressed concerns to Wayne about proposed projects. Each time that I said something couldn't be done, he DID it.

"In 1983, Wayne envisioned a Friendship Force relationship with the USSR and its Eastern European allies—an extremely difficult task in those Cold War days, but one brought to fruition almost single-handedly by Wayne. And now he hopes to develop Friendship Force contacts with three countries with deep-seated unfriendly relations with the US and with most other countries in the rest of the world. These countries are Vietnam, Cuba and South Africa. And HE WILL DO IT," Seretean predicted.

Hanoi, Vietnam

On May 7, 1989, The Reverend Wayne Smith delivered a sermon at Big Canoe Chapel in the North Georgia foothills where he lives when he's not roaming the world, selling peace to people who need it badly. Although Wayne is well known at Big Canoe, he caught his neighbors completely off guard. You see, his sermon incorporated two recent visits he had made: one to Vietnam and one to Cuba. People sat up a little straighter in the pews and some leaned forward to make certain they didn't miss anything.

"Hanoi is a devastated place," Smith began. "There is no time in recent history that its citizens have not known war." He then presented a brief history lesson, recounting the many times the Vietnamese had suffered under the rule of numerous nations. Smith told of how the French were forced out of Vietnam in 1954.

"The late 1950's was a time when the United States was terrified of communism's spread," Smith said. "John Foster Dulles was preaching the doctrine of 'massive retaliation' against any nation which would threaten the American way of life. This was the time of Eisenhower and Nixon and the advocacy of the 'domino theory' which said that the United States would be the world's policeman for democracy and would use its might to keep one nation from falling into the communist sphere if it would effect its neighbors by causing them to fall under Soviet or Chinese domination."

Smith also reviewed the terrible time of the Vietnam War during which many Americans lost their lives. Others lost years of their lives as prisoners of war, many imprisoned in the old Hoa Lo Prison in Hanoi, called the "Hanoi Hilton," by Americans unfortunate enough to land there.

Smith talked about seeing the Hanoi Hilton, "The grim structure made me realize how lucky I was because my greatest discomfort in Vietnam had been that the kitchen staff at the Victory Hotel couldn't cook an egg to my liking."

Smith explained why he went to Vietnam, a bitter enemy of the United States almost two decades earlier.

"The Vietnam War ended fifteen years ago," Smith reminded the people." Everybody involved was a loser. Technically, South Vietnam lost that war, but North Vietnam lost too. Today, Hanoi is a basket case. Of all the nations of the world that I have visited, Vietnam is the poorest and has the lowest standard of living. For example, the clerk at the gift shop at the Victory Hotel is an intelligent woman, about thirty five. She is married and has children and speaks English fairly well.

She makes eleven dollars a month. My hard-boiled eggs, with a cup of coffee and a slice of stale bread, cost me half of her monthly salary.

"I went to Hanoi to look into the possibility of establishing a chapter of The Friendship Force there. Life goes on, you know. Fifty years ago, America was at war with the Germans and the Japanese. Today they are two of our staunchest allies. It seems to me that there is a great deal of healing that needs to take place between the people of America and the people of Vietnam. The governments of those nations certainly have many problems to straighten out. But, as Do Xuan said to me while I was in Hanoi: 'Let the people lead so the governments will follow.'

"My plan is that there soon will be a hundred Americans a month going to Vietnam for the simple purpose of trying to establish bridges of personal friendship with ordinary people there. Will it make any difference. You better believe that it will!

"I have seen what small beginnings can do. It was only four years ago that the very first group of eleven Soviets came to Big Canoe Chapel to make friends. Take a look at how that small beginning has expanded into incredible things that are happening between Americans and Soviet citizens. I assure you that both President Bush and President Gorbachev are aware of these efforts, because both have told me so. I am proud to tell you that in this calendar year alone there will be not just eleven people involved in this program, but nine hundred of us visiting each other who will stay a few days and nights in each other's homes. This can happen between Vietnam and the United States. It needs to happen because the wounds of war are still very sensitive. They will continue to pain both of us until we have placed the balm of friendship on each other's bruises," Smith said.

My husband, a former inmate of the Hanoi Hilton prison and other prisons like it scattered around Vietnam, occupied a seat in the Chapel that Sunday. When Wayne Smith said that many veterans of the Vietnam War would be invited to return to that country and see it again in peacetime, Dave whispered to me, "I hope he's not counting on *me* to go back."

Smith told the incredible story of how he and Levy Tavares of Brazil flew to Paris and then to Hanoi, not knowing a single person there. Once in Hanoi, Smith met Do Xuan Ohne with whom he established a personal rapport almost instantly. At that time, Ohne was the vice president of the Vietnam Society for Friendship with Foreigners. Ohne immediately agreed to the idea of citizens exchanges between the United States and his country. He also agreed that these exchanges would not be done to offer either an apology nor a justification for our nation's participation in the war. "It will simply be a visit designed to sow seeds of friendship across the barriers which divide us," Smith said. "As President Bush often says, 'Stay tuned.'"

Havana, Cuba.

Smith continued his astonishing sermon by telling friends and neighbors that he had also recently traveled to Havana for the same reasons that he went to Vietnam.

"I was favorably impressed by the natural beauty of Cuba and by the friendliness of the people," Smith recalled. "The position of the state is that you belong to society, not to yourself, much less to God. It was a sad thing for me to behold.

"I went to Cuba to establish a chapter of The Friendship Force. I met a Presbyterian minister named Orestes Gonzales, who decided to stay in Cuba under Castro. I met a Methodist minister and his wife. Once again, I learned that, as in many other journeys I have made, that some nations have bad systems with some good people in them, and some nations have better systems with bad people in them. And above all, I have learned that no nation has a perfect political system.

"A world of friends...and of peace...is surely a goal worthy of our efforts to befriend those isolated and separated from us for whatever reason," Smith said.

Did he succeed in establishing a Friendship Force club in Cuba?

Not yet.

Stay tuned.

Mark Johnson traveled to Brazil with a group of thirty-eight Friendship Force members of East Central Florida. "We were all first-timers to this massive land south of the equator and no one really knew what to expect. The chance to meet people from a different culture made me jump at the opportunity to travel to this country of coffee and Carnival.

"And from that first step, from the first handshake in a crowded airport in Sao Paulo to the last good-bye, the relationships built over the course of ten days will remain in my memory and my heart for a lifetime," Johnson said.

Johnson was hosted by Jose and Fluvia Kalmus who took him into their home and made him feel that he belonged. He was amazed that he felt so at ease in this strange land, living in the homes of two people he just met. "I was part of the family," he marveled. "They didn't change their lives in any way just because this rather large American had invaded their home. They welcomed me I was, accepted me in spite of my faults and answered all my dumb questions with humor and understanding. I thank them with all my heart for what they have taught me, a normally reclusive young man.

"Sitting down over dinner or a cool drink and talking about our differences, similarities, hopes, desires and dreams made me realize that once you get past ethnic and cultural differences, most everyone in this world is the same."

Richard Falk, State Director of The Friendship Force in Minnesota and a member of the Board of Directors of Friendship Force International, presented a heart pump machine to Dr. Alexander Savchenko, Surgical Director of the Byelorussian Research Institute of Cardiology in Minsk, USSR, during a 1989 exchange between Minsk and Minnesota. The heart pump, valued at $20,000 was donated by Bio-Medicus of Minneapolis.

WE ARE FREE!

Hand-printed in red, these words headlined a letter to Lewis Debo from a friend in East Germany.

Debo said, "I met Helmut and Renate Weihrauch on a Friendship Force mission from Iowa to Poland in 1985. In our exchange of letters during the years since then, Helmut has frequently asked questions about our organization and my participation. He has long hoped that his country could be included in home-stay exchanges. Perhaps now the doors can be opened. I am sending the text of his letter to share their good news with others in this wonderful organization of ours.

Dear friends of The Friendship Force:

Today on the 9th of November 1989, the borderline between East and West Germany and the wall in Berlin were opened. I believe you can imagine our feeling. The Germans are the happiest people in the world.

It's like a dream. Thousands of people were crossing the borderlines. The streets were congested by cars of the GDR (German Democratic Republic). I remembered the 13th of August 1961, when the terrible wall was erected. We wept because we were divided from friends and relatives. Our hearts were filled with wrath.

Now, after twenty-eight years, we weep again because we are so very, very happy. The 9th of November 1989, will be one of the most important days in our history.

For weeks we have demonstrated every Monday evening in the streets of Leipzig. Last Monday we were about 300,000 people. We succeeded in getting the right to travel. Now we want free elections and next Monday we shall demonstrate again.

This weekend our son Jens and stepdaughter Sylvia are going to Berlin to visit the West for the first time in their lives. In the meantime we were phoned by friends from West Germany who invited us to spend New Year's Eve with them. Thank goodness, now we can do it. At present we are not allowed to change money, but we hope this problem will be solved soon.

As you know we completely agree with the objectives of The Friendship Force to create peace and goodwill throughout the world by making personal friendships. We are so happy."

Andiry Yulykov Infui of Ukraine said, "The Friendship Force delegation visited the USSR in the spring of 1988. That was my introduction to the organization. When I first heard of a 'world of friends,' it sounded great. Then came the invitation to visit Americans in their homes. It was not the first time some members of our delegation of ten had traveled to the USA, but this experience was still unique because we would be living in American homes, thus having an insight into the real life of Americans.

Andiry wrote an article in *News from Ukraine* praising many Americans who had befriended him during this exchange. Using the English alphabet, he wrote of something or someone to praise from A to Z. He then joked that Americans should come to his country because in Ukraine, the alphabet has more letters than the English alphabet. "Come over here and get in touch with us, learn about us and pass this knowledge on," he said.

"A man is entitled to have his own independent thinking. This is what more and more people in my country are coming to realize. But one should learn from his friends or at least recognize their right to have their own way of thinking. In mutual trust and respect, we shall live on the opposite sides of the globe, but on a similar side of human endeavor. And if I'm able to convey to you, my American friends, at least a portion of what I learned from you—then this planet shall become a world of friends and that would really mean a world without wars.

Chapter 18
A Bridge Called 'Georgia-to-Georgia'

Guests in the home are gifts from God.
—Ancient proverb from the Republic of Georgia

The Berlin Wall came down and the Iron Curtain went up in 1989. Many astute people in high places openly voiced sincere beliefs that these events occurred in part because of The Friendship Force, whose legions of volunteers had been quietly building bridges of friendship across all barriers which normally separate people. In Tbilisi, Georgia, USSR, in 1989, large exchanges called "Georgia to Georgia" were initiated. Beverlie Reilman described the important first Georgia-to-Georgia exchange from the viewpoint of the busy staff at Friendship Force International.

"It was both a cause and a challenge. It was at once frustrating and exhilarating. It was a back-breaking task and a heart-rending occasion for joy," Reilman said. "It all began when a true Friendship Force exchange was announced between people of Georgia, USA, and Georgia, USSR. We will never be the same; the experience changed all of us."

Carolyn Smith, wife of founder Wayne Smith, said, "The excitement was electrifying. I had not seen such enthusiasm and joyfulness since the inaugural exchange with Newcastle, England."

"Wayne Smith was the exchange director for this history-making exchange. "He gave me as applications chairperson only three guidelines," Beverlie Reilman said. "We should attempt to recruit a cross-section of the state of Georgia; we should make selections fairly within each occupational category and we should make financial aid available to those with a financial need. It was just two and a half months to the scheduled departure date," she continued. "We had no idea that we would have such a huge response or that the logistics would come close to overwhelming us. We never dreamed that over a thousand people would come with deposit in hand to our interview sessions."

Channel 11-TV Public Service Announcements about the upcoming exchange prompted fifteen hundred callers to respond to the message center number. Committee member Alice Josephson and Beverlie Reilman retrieved each name and address; Mary Pace typed labels and mailed each one a flyer telling of the interview locations.

Meanwhile, another committee member, Barbara Bruegge, planned the interview sessions and recruited interviewers while Norma Hassinger arranged for host-greeters to be at four metro Atlanta locations on Saturday, Sunday and the following Wednesday. Elsewhere in Georgia, club representatives Jim Beeson in North Georgia, Mary Sarner in West Georgia and Fred Fuller in Macon set up interviews for the same February weekend.

"Never in twelve years had The Friendship Force experienced such a response," Reilman marveled. "People were lined up waiting for us at all locations; we ran out of forms, completely exhausted the interviewers and took in deposit checks so fast we were worried about recording them.

"The first step was to pre-select those candidates who had received a double sticker at the upper right of the form from their interviewer. We had asked interviewers to alert us to any super candidates who showed unusual enthusiasm, flexibility, personality and deep interests in the Soviet exchange. If this handful of people had so impressed their interviewers we knew they were the first ones we wanted on the trip. Other than members of the press, these were the only ones pre-selected," Reilman said. "Finally, the selection process ended and the applications committee members were very pleased that half of those chosen were under forty.

Then came the crucial period of making certain everything was in order—especially passports. Beverlie Reilman said "We had to enlist the help of Senator Nunn's office and a Passport/Visa service. Together with Wilma Gray, Wayne Smith's assistant, we saw signatures jumping over fences in our sleep.

"Ah well, whoever said a Friendship Force volunteer's day was to stop at eight hours," Reilman chuckled. "We racked up four and a half weeks of sixteen-hour days—every one of which was worth it when we saw 301 smiling faces board at the April 17th departure and the smiles and hugs when Soviet Georgians greeted their American hosts on April 18."

Where is this "other" Georgia?

This small republic, located in the southwestern corner of what was then the Soviet Union, lies between the Black and Caspian Seas.

Georgia has a population of around 5.2 million and the area has a long history of conflict. In ancient times this territory was known as Colchis, land of the Golden Fleece sought by Jason and the Argonauts. According to legend, Prometheus was bound on a mountain in Georgia.

Rich in agriculture and raw materials, Georgia has been the site of much violent conflict and, from this conflict, Georgians developed a commitment to cultural unity. One of the most important institutions of the republic has been the Georgian Orthodox Church. Another important symbol is the Georgian language. Georgians are unique in having their own language and alphabet, one of only fourteen alphabets in use in the world today. Although they were required to speak Russian, Georgian is their preferred language. In their universities, most teaching is in Georgian.

Using an old fable, Georgians explain how they came by the good fortune of living in such a lovely land. They say God decided one day to parcel out the lands of the world, but reserved the best land for himself. Finally, after all the others had long been gone, a Georgian representative arrived.

God said, "Why are you so long in coming?"

The Georgian answered, "I had guests in my home and I could not leave them."

God said, "For one who is such a good host, I will give you the land which I have reserved for myself." Georgians still repeat the fable to explain why their land is so rich, fertile and lovely to behold. The fable also indicates why these generous people have long been known for their marvelous hospitality..

After the USA Georgians returned, they were all generous in their praise of the land and the people. Most were awed by the hospitality and by the exotic culture they found there. They also were surprised that the capital of Tbilisi, located in the Kura River Valley and surrounded by the steep Caucasus Mountains, looked more like a Mediterranean style village. Although most people live in apartment buildings, everyone has a balcony they utilize to dry the laundry or to sit and watch the passing scene. Older buildings have red roof tiles so common in Mediterranean regions. For a small country, Georgia boasts many sculptors, artists, musicians, poets and writers.

At one end of Rusteveli Street was Lenin Square and there in front of the City Hall was a large statue of Lenin. The Georgians were not pleased by the statue, nor by their main square being named for the Soviet leader. Ken Stanford later said, "I was surprised by the strength of the anti-Soviet sentiment I found. The people I met were very much in favor of becoming an independent country."

Wylene Bryant said " A very old Georgian woman started crying when I was introduced to her as an American visitor. 'All my life I have wanted to see an American,' she said. 'Now I can die happy.'"

The ambassadors were also unprepared for the enormous generosity of the Georgian people. Bob Stauffer reported that when he expressed a desire to see more of their Georgia, his hosts and four other families joined together to rent a helicopter so he could tour much of the countryside from a bird's vantage. "That was just one example of their overwhelming hospitality," Bob said.

Republic of Georgia hosts rented this helicopter so Bob Stauffer could see more of their beautiful country.

Most ambassadors were also surprised and delighted to find that Americans were very much liked and admired. "We represent the freedom they want so badly," Wayne Waddell said. "They want to be free of the USSR. They long to self-govern." Waddell and his wife

Barbara also related a unique experience, but first the background story.

For almost six years Wayne Waddell once languished in various prison camps in North Vietnam. If someone had told him back then that he would one day travel to a Soviet republic on a mission of friendship, he would have dismissed the idea in less than polite terms. But those days were back in the 1960s and early 1970s and these were the 1990s. And, as the retired Air Force Colonel of Marietta, Georgia, can attest, time changes things.

Dads of two Georgias share a toast. Wayne Waddell (left) and Guram Otkhmezuri of Tbilisi.

Barbara Waddell shows a Soviet woman how a Polaroid photo 'develops' right before her eyes.

While in Tbilisi, the Waddells were taken to a school where their hostess, Marina Shubashvili, taught music. After visiting the music department, they met Djoni Saralidze, director of music, and his singing partner Yuri. After the two men gave a wonderful impromptu singing performance the Waddells gave parting gifts to the friendly serenaders. Djoni rummaged through his desk and produced a pen to give in exchange. However, Yuri was caught unprepared—but only momentarily. Then his face brightened as he carefully removed his prized Soviet Army medal from his coat and pinned it to Wayne's jacket.

No one could have understood the significance of this gesture better than a fellow military man. Wayne Waddell knew well the sacrifice Yuri made when he parted with such a cherished symbol of personal honor, bravery and patriotism. Waddell promised Yuri that he would wear the medal on his own military uniform and then the formerly bitter opponents sealed the promise with a toast.

Later on, Waddell remembered an ancient proverb reflecting the Georgian people's wise attitude toward worldly possessions: *If a person holds on to something too closely, it will be lost forever; if it is given to a friend it will never depart from the giver.* (Paraphrased*)*

A footnote to the story: A few months later, Wayne Waddell donned his dress Air Force uniform, complete with rows of medals. The occasion was a reunion of former Vietnam prisoners of war held in San Diego. Fellow veterans in attendance were accustomed to seeing lots of medals, but no one had ever before seen the large medal pinned on the right side of Colonel Waddell's uniform. When they asked about it, Waddell told them about Yuri and his medal that would never be lost and of the truth discovered in an old Georgian proverb. (Waddell has since sent one of his own medals back to Yuri.)

Other ambassadors were also deeply impressed by the love that Georgians freely demonstrate for their families and friends. They were openly affectionate, and teen-agers were seen in the streets holding hands with their mother or father. It was hard to imagine this happening on the streets of cities in the US and many ambassadors expressed a yearning for more family affection to be demonstrated in their homes.

Georgians of the World, Unite!

Back in Georgia USA, the Georgian ambassadors also experienced hospitality, southern-style. For one of the two weeks they were here, my husband and I hosted two young men, Kakha Abashidze and Vaja Kakabadze. They quickly became family. Both were twenty-nine and Kakha was an eye surgeon. Vaja was an engineer, working in a government plant which manufactured concrete blocks.

The first afternoon of their arrival, we were sitting on our deck looking out at a peaceful mountain lake reflecting the blue mountains in the background. They compared the scene to one in the Caucasus Mountains in their own Tbilisi. Suddenly one of our aggressive humming birds zoomed by our heads on its way to the feeder. Vaja and Kakha both screamed and ran inside. We coaxed them back outside, explaining it was only a bird.

"Oh, a bird," Kakha said in breathless relief. "We have been told that everything is bigger in America. We thought it was a mosquito!"

We erupted in laughter and so did they. In fact, that was the beginning of a very merry week with "our boys." Toward the end of the week, Kakha said, 'You're just like my mother!'

We learned a lot about their dreams during late-night talks, including their strong desire for independence. They were part of a growing movement to tear down the big statue of Lenin. They were very pleased that under Gorbachev they were beginning to have greater independence, but the memory of what happened on April 9, 1989, still evoked painful memories and deep anger. (On that date nineteen men and women were killed and scores of others were injured when a peaceful hunger protest turned into a nightmare of swinging clubs, bullets and poison gas at the hands of Soviet soldiers.)

They brought us gifts of Georgian wine and Russian vodka. The first evening they were in our home, we asked them about their custom of toasting. They told us that the head of the table is called the *tamada*. He begins the toasts, often praising his children, telling them how much he loves them and how important they are to him. Kakha said that these toasts are often made between dinner courses, often extending a meal over many hours.

Vaja and Kakha then produced a bottle of cognac and the toasting began. After many toasts, they began toasting our unborn great-grandchildren. We knew then it was past time to go to bed.

Our guests had two requests: Vaja wanted to see a local concrete block plant operation and both wanted to see a gun shop. We obliged and first went to nearby Ellijay where we asked the owner of a local plant if we could walk around and inspect his operation. He was delighted and told us to look at everything and to feel free to ask any questions. Vaja was shocked to learn that this family owned business, operating with only a few employees, made far more and better quality blocks than the government-operated plant where he worked. "And our plant has several hundred workers," he moaned. The notion of ownership appealed to Vaja very much. Everywhere we went, he would point out a building and ask 'private or government?' Of course, almost all were private.

We took many photographs and when the two went on group tours, we loaned them our camera so they could take their own photos. At the end of the week, we had the film developed and discovered that most of the photos they had taken were of automobiles.

We went to a sporting goods store where guns were sold. The owner of the shop allowed Kakha and Vaja to hold several guns as they posed for photographs. They were thrilled. We asked if they had played with toy guns when they were children. Vaja made an imaginary gun with his thumb and one finger and Kakha said "only with make-believe guns.'

On a visit to a large discount store, we temporarily lost our guests. We finally found them in the toy department, giggling like two grade-school boys. They were captivated by the large selection of toys. Each bought something for their nieces and nephews and they each bought for themselves one small toy, a water pistol.

Vaja and Kakha tour an automobile dealership

Toward the end of the week, Kakha became homesick. He thought his parents might be very worried about him because he had not spoken with them in several days. We tried several times to get a call through and finally it happened. Kakha carried on a spirited conversation and after the call he was in high spirits again. We asked if they were worried about him. He grinned sheepishly and replied: "No, they were having such a good time with their American guests until they have forgotten all about me!"

In serious moments, Kakha told us that up until a few years ago, the government led them to believe that if they somehow managed to get out of the Soviet Union and make their way to the United States, they would be shot as soon as they were on American soil. "Even then, we did not take that statement very seriously and now we can't wait to go home and report that the only thing you wanted to shoot us with was a camera!"

The longer these two young men were with us, the more we could see how much we had in common. We could scarcely wait until we could visit their country, a wish that would soon be granted.

Six months later, Dave and I were ready to travel to Tbilisi where we would be hosted by Guram and Manana Abashidze, Kakha's parents. It was perhaps the most memorable trip we have ever made.

On October 15, we left Atlanta bound for Tbilisi, where we would take part in the second Georgia-to-Georgia exchange. Our flight to Amsterdam on a KLM Boeing 747 was smooth and pleasant, but when we transferred to a chartered Aeroflot plane, we were soon informed that it had developed mechanical difficulties. We spent the night of October 16 in an Amsterdam hotel.

We finally arrived in Tbilisi at 1:30 a.m. on October 17, to a warm welcome from our worried hosts. Luggage was quickly collected and we breezed through customs and were whisked away to our hosts' apartment. The exterior of the building was dingy and the entrance equally dark and gloomy.

This banquet was waiting at 2:00 a.m.

We took the elevator to the eighth floor and stepped into a dimly-lit hallway. However, upon entering the apartment, we were amazed to see a lovely, bright home with beautiful furnishings and a cheery dining room set for a banquet! This would be one of many feasts shared with our hosts and their friends and family. It was almost four a.m. when we went to bed, but we weren't so tired anymore. Our host family had made us feel relaxed and very much welcome in their home.

This was our introduction to Georgian life in the Soviet Union. Repeatedly we discovered that many of these clever, energetic people lived in lovely homes which sharply contrasted with the drab, rundown exterior of the state-owned buildings. Time and again, we also discovered that the almost-empty state markets offered a bleak contrast to the bustling private farmers' markets where almost everyone goes to shop. One Georgian explained communism's fatal flaw in simple terms: "When everyone owns something, no one owns it," he said. "How can anyone care about something no one owns?"

The next morning Manana Abashidze, our hostess, served a wonderful breakfast that included a national dish called *khachopuri* (khacho means fresh cheese; puri means bread). This bread looked very much like a small pancake except it was stuffed with cheese and baked or fried until golden brown. It was delicious and *khachopuri* became my favorite Georgian food.

As we enjoyed that first breakfast, talk turned to politics and the upcoming election scheduled for Sunday, October 28. Excitement was mounting as the date drew nearer—and with good reason. This would be the first free election held in Georgia since 1918, when they gained their brief independence (1918-21).

The collapse of tsarist rule in 1917 enabled Georgia to declare its independence on May 16, 1918. With the withdrawal of Allied forces and the collapse of Deniken's anti-Bolshevik White Russian army, the Soviet government intervened in February 1921, and Georgia was forcibly incorporated into the Soviet Union.

Although Joseph Stalin was born in Georgia, he was just as cruel to his countrymen as to those in the rest of the country. In fact, during the purges of 1936-37, a higher proportion of the intelligentsia and professional classes perished in Georgia than anywhere else in the European part of the USSR. "You will have to break the wings of this Georgia!" declared Stalin. "Tear them apart!"

Our host Guram Abashidze was only three when KGB agents knocked on the door one night and took his parents away. His mother was in prison for ten years and his father was jailed for seventeen. They were gifted, educated people and were never told why they were arrested and thrown into jail. When they were finally released, they were given the equivalent of a month's salary and told to forget they were ever in Siberia.

Our first day in Tbilisi, we discovered that the hated statue of Lenin had been torn down the month before.

Lenin Square in Tbilisi. (Now Freedom Square.)

Today, only a grassy median remains, and Lenin Square has been renamed Freedom Square. Yura, our driver, spoke little English, but when we first drove past the square, he happily nodded toward the little green oasis and said, "Lenin, *kaput!*"

We asked Liza who removed the statue and were surprised to learn that it was the Soviet government. When we asked Liza what influenced them to do this, she smiled and said, "Well, we kept insulting the statue until they took it away." And how does one insult a statue? Liza said people wrote 'bad insults' all over the monument, using spray paint.

Thanks to the tremendous effort of Guram Abashidze, we saw quite a bit of Georgia.

Manana and Guram Abashidze

Travel within the country is not easy and it was evident that Guram had spent a lot of time before our arrival, arranging for cars, drivers, translators, accommodations, meals and local hosts in several cities. We first traveled west and spent four days traveling and sightseeing. En route, we saw Stalin's birthplace in Gori and took photos of his statue.

One of the first places we visited in the west was Tskaltubo, a resort area well-known for its mineral springs. People flock to the hotels and "sanitariums" located there, seeking cures for a variety of maladies. Our host told us that for years the facilities at Tskaltubo had been open only to Russians, but they were able to book our party of ten into one of the sanitariums. We were told that all other guests were Russians.

It seemed that the Georgians make their economy work by buying food from the farmers' market; they earn extra money on the side and items that are non-existent in the shops can be purchased on the black market, which always thrives in the absence of a free market.

Georgians have been Christians since A.D. 300. It is traditionally believed that the evangelist who brought religion to Georgia was a slave girl named Nino. Georgia became a bastion of Christianity in the East, and the people have kept their faith in good times and bad. Under communist rule, the churches suffered from neglect and all those we visited had been stripped of furniture; their ancient religious frescoes had been vandalized or whitewashed over. The people were trying to restore their houses of worship, but it was obviously a slow process because of a lack of money and materials.

We continued on to the mountain resort of Borzhomi, also famous for its mineral waters. "Like vichy with a little vodka added,'" our genial host told us. We drove from Borzhomi to the fabulous cave city of Vardzia near the Turkish border. Built during the golden age of Queen Tamar in 1156, it has hundreds of rooms, including a chapel, banquet halls and wine cellars, all carved in a cliff of solid rock.

The city took over fifty years to build and once had nineteen stories. An earthquake shook that part of the world for three days in 1253 A.D. and the top stories of the city were destroyed. Today nine stories still exist, connected by labyrinthine passages and stairways.

On the return trip to Tbilisi, Dave mentioned that he had driven all over the world, but he did not want to take the wheel in the madcap lanes of Georgia. Our interpreter explained the traffic system very easily. "You see, we have no rules—only exceptions," she said cheerfully, never flinching as our driver narrowly averted another head on collision.

"No rules, only exceptions" seemed to fit many aspects of Georgian life under Soviet rule. For example, Georgians are fond of saying, "There is no food, but we are well fed; there are no clothes, but we are well dressed; there is no gasoline, but we all drive cars."

How do they accomplish this? They simply disregard the government's rules and make their own exceptions. Consequently we saw two existing economies—one dictated by the government and one operated by the people.

It was also strange to see that people worked unusual hours. They might go in at ten a.m. and return at noon. Perhaps they would return to work at two p.m. and perhaps they would not. This seemed to take place on a large scale. When we asked Liza, our wonderful translator, about the work schedule, she laughed merrily and said: "We pretend to work and they pretend to pay us!"

When we arrived back in Tbilisi, I looked up at the statue of Mother Georgia on the hill. Her metallic robes shone brightly as she stood holding a cup and a sword—both fitting symbols. We were there as friends, so the cup of hospitality had been extended to us by everyone we met. Georgians use the sword as a last resort to defend against those who seek to harm and to enslave. As I looked up at Mother Georgia, I thought of our Lady Liberty.

After two days back in Tbilisi, we left for the wine country in the East, where the famous poet Rustaveli had attended school. We had hosts waiting to take us to their private wine cellar where we sampled the new wine. We later learned that the tasting of a vintner's new wine is normally reserved for special friends only.

After a night of feasting in our host's home where many toasts were made to us, to their independence and to "Wine" Smith (they have trouble pronouncing "Wayne). We left Telavi the following morning to be back in Tbilisi on election day.

There was a huge turnout and before the day ended, ninety percent of the Georgia voters had cast their ballots. Dave accompanied Manana Abashidze to the polls and took photos of her voting. She cast her ballot for fifty-one-year old Zviad Gamsakhurdia's coalition party called Round Table Free Georgia. Gamsakhurdia's campaign cry had been "Let the Lord bless Georgia."

Two day's later we learned that Mr. Gamsakhurdia's party had won fifty-four percent of Sunday's vote and the Communist Party only twenty-nine percent. Little did Georgians realize that their leadership choice would prove to be first divisive, then bloody.

Georgians believed that independence was inevitable. We found ourselves hoping with them, because in two short weeks we had come to love and admire them very much. The second day we were there we met five year old Georgi, whose mother Nana was the sister of our hostess. We all toured together for a day and that evening little Georgi went home and told his grandmother, "I've been with those Americans all day long and I love them immensely!"

We understood, because we now loved Georgi and his wonderful countrymen who had treated us like brothers and sisters.

We hoped fervently that the Lord would bless both our Georgias and keep our people free forever.

A Bridge Called Georgia-to-Georgia

Manana Abashidze votes in the first free election she has known.

213

In Tbilisi children are openly affectionate toward their parents, a trait which Americans envied greatly.

Chapter 19
A MAGIC FORCE?

A strange force and so necessary! The key to all doors, passport to all addresses. A lift for all sad hours. A cure for broken hearts. In friendship there was written the most beautiful pages of human conquests.
—Dr. Odilon Machado, Araraquara, Brazil

Just six months after the Iron Curtain lifted, the first Friendship Force exchange was set between Southwest Connecticut and Czechoslovakia. There were a lot more 'firsts' associated with this exchange, according to Bill Lamkin, writing in *Friendship* magazine.

"In addition to this being the first time Friendship Force ambassadors had stayed in Czechoslovakian homes, it also was the first time most of the hosts had engaged in conversation with people whose mother tongue was English. And when the group went to Prague for four days, it was the first time Americans had stayed in the hostel there."

Lamkin said his host was Josef Liba, a twenty-seven-year-old athletic coach. He was assisted by his girl friend Luba Daxnerova, also a coach. Josef turned his apartment over to Lamkin and he and Luba spent the nights with friends. Josef also arranged for Lamkin to tour Slovakia over a four-day, seven hundred mile trip. Along the way, they visited relatives of Josef and Luba. In Kosice, they visited Josef's father and on a walking tour of Kosice, they noticed a wedding taking place in an old downtown cathedral. A few blocks away, another wedding was just ending and Mr. Liba told the bride and groom that his American journalist friend would like to take their picture. Later, the film was processed in Bratislava and Lamkin sent several of the photos to the newlyweds. "Of course, I had to close with our well known reminder that "A world of friends is a world of peace," he said.

In Poprad, Lamkin and Josef visited Josef's sister's home. Lamkin enjoyed her little girls, ages three and five, who sat in his lap, looking at an English language picture book.

Later on Lamkin told one of the hosts that the Americans were pleased at how flexible all Slovak hosts appeared to be. Martin Sebasta answered and said "We have so many problems in Czechoslovakia, it's easy for us to be flexible." Sebasta, a three-hundred pound former athlete, was called "The Gentle Giant" and Lamkin said, "His gentleness showed forth as he was usually seen with eighty-seven-year-old ambassador Daisy Airey clinging to his arm."

On the last day of the exchange they drove along the Danube River which separates Czechoslovakia and Austria. Until the peaceful revolution the previous November 1989, Josef and his people were not allowed to cross the Danube. When the barbed wire fence was torn down on December 10, Josef kept a piece of the wire. He gave several pieces to others, but a ten-inch piece of the grim souvenir was displayed in his home.

When Lamkin departed, he summarized: "After more than a dozen Friendship Force experiences, I've become friends with people in distant places. We spoke different languages and came from different cultures. There were what might seem to be insurmountable barriers to friendship, but it happened again. Coveted friendships evolved.

"How did it happen? I have only one explanation. The catalyst is the magic that is The Friendship Force."

Katarina Chlapikova wrote about this same exchange, except from a host's point of view. Katarina hosted Joan Mosey and Patricia Evans. Katarina said that she knew it was impossible for the Americans to realize the enormous changes that Czechoslovakia had gone through in just a few months. "I doubt that people who have lived their whole lives in a democratic society can understand what it means to live under a totalitarian system," she said.

The hosts did their best to educate the ambassadors and Katarina said that by the end of the exchange she hoped the Americans had come to understand "the well-known truth that secondhand knowledge is incomplete and the best way to learn and understand is to make the experience a personal one."

On the first day, Joan and Patricia told Katarina, "We are no princesses."

Katarina said "I think in that moment all the fears, all the strain—and maybe mutual prejudices—simply disappeared. And I was very glad. Our apartment was at once full of understanding and there was a wonderful feeling that there are very many people all over the world who think in a similar way and with whom you could resolve all the problems of the world without difficulties."

(It has often been noted by members that in each Friendship Force exchange, there is always one special moment that changes everything. From that moment, the magic of friendship takes over and the exchange is sure to be a success.)

Katarina was able to explain where she and her countrymen were at this point in history. *"Tempora mantantur et nos mutamuc io illis,"* she said, and then translated: "Time changes and we change in it."

"But how?" she asked plaintively. "In what direction? How many years are necessary to get free from totalitarianism, from all kinds of fears and to begin to live normally? Nobody knows.

[We have had] more than forty years of rule by the Communist party and its communist ideology [has left] deep wounds in the life of our nation. I believe it will take several decades to heal some of them.

"Yes, in our country there are many things worth seeing, but a simple tourist cannot discover them in the streets or in the museums. Many of the changes are taking place in the minds and hearts of our people who are returning to our cultural values, our authentic roots. We don't want to ever give up these values again.

"We have a very old Slovak proverb which truthfully expresses the basic nature of our people: *Guest to the house, God to the house.* Maybe that's what our Friendship Force organization promotes among people. We identify with the meaningful concept, *A world of friends is a world of peace."*

By the time we participated in the first Georgia-to-Georgia exchange, Dave and I had become Friendship Force believers. We had hosted English, Germans, Dutch, New Zelanders and Soviet Georgian ambassadors and had helped day-host Egyptians. We had also traveled as ambassadors to England and New Zealand. Once we had two German men and an English couple scheduled to arrive at our house during the same week. We were somewhat concerned, because both couples had unpleasant memories of World War II. However, I had underestimated the power of the Force. The couples got along well and later the English friend jokingly wrote, "I still have no German friends—except for two!"

I had almost forgotten that day when Wayne Smith exhorted us from the pulpit to "hug a Russian." Later on, I confessed my early negative feelings to Wayne, who just chuckled and said nothing.

One Sunday afternoon following a church service, Wayne and Carolyn asked us to drop by their home. Once there, we were introduced to Lee Walburn, editor of *Atlanta* magazine and several other visitors. One was a multilingual Russian journalist, George Katznelson, who was translating.

Lee Walburn later wrote about this afternoon meeting in the tiny mountain hamlet called Big Canoe. Part of his observations and some of my own follow.

"Two men who have never met before sit near a fireplace," Walburn wrote, setting the stage for the drama that was sure to follow. "George Katznelson is translating the exchange between American David Terrell and Latvian Gunar Kirkhe. A second Latvian, a tall, broad shouldered man named Yan Tichenow, nods and sometimes smiles wistfully as if his subtle facial expressions are needed to punctuate the interpreted passions of David and Gunar, each a former prisoner of war at the hands of a Communist government.

"When Gunar, a lithe, graying photographer, was young, Hitler's army invaded Latvia. Gunar was conscripted into the service of his marauding German neighbors. Short years later his country was expropriated by yet another neighbor, Russia, and he was exiled to remote Armur because he wore the uniform of an enemy he had become a part of quite unwillingly.

"David Terrell, on the other hand, spent five years as a prisoner of war in Vietnam.... A dislike for anything communistic has produced a chary attitude toward even someone as tenuously connected as an assimilated Latvian.

"Only the American host, an habitual do-gooder named Wayne Smith, knows the irony of the cautious meeting between the American and the sad-eyed Latvian, two men whose lives were violently affected by the decisions of powerful men they never met and whose faces they recognize only through newspapers, television or history books.

Wayne Smith then spoke.

"I must tell you all this story. For a time, David Terrell was a navigator/bombardier on B-52 airplanes. They had several contingency targets in case war should break out between us and the Soviet Union. One of those targets was your city of Riga, Latvia, Gunar.

"Now here we are in a different setting. All that was just things...abstractions. David didn't know Yan had a son...was a grandfather. I'll tell you now, I know David Terrell doesn't want to bomb Gunar and Yan.

"Shhh, I want everyone to hear something...hear that?" Smith said.

"In the next room the gurgles of an awakening infant, the son of a Russian immigrant and his American wife, softly punctuate the host's next words," Walburn noted.

Wayne Smith said softly, "That baby doesn't hate Russians. That baby has just awakened after spending a half hour or so in my lap."

Smith then looked directly at me and asked if I remembered the day when I vowed I would *never* hug a Russian? Sheepishly, I nodded acknowledgment.

"Well, George here is a Russian...."

I understood. I walked over to George and gave him a big hug.

As Walburn recorded, "A misty curtain lowers as if to hide the emotion and memories behind Gunar Kirkhe's dark eyes. Yan Tichenow puts his arm across the shoulder of another American and embraces her.

"The scene was nothing more than a small sliver of time shared at street level, away from the summit meetings and monuments, pronouncements and world leaders. Nevertheless, an awful lot of ignorance was tossed out with the garbage that day."

In February 1990, The Friendship Force of Norderstedt, (West) Germany, was so encouraged by the destruction of the Berlin Wall and the Iron Curtain that they decided to hold a Sunday matinee to promote the ideals of the organization worldwide. The matinee was held at the town hall. Konstanze Engberg, Vice President of The Friendship Force of Norderstedt said "We wanted people of our area to know more about The Friendship Force around the world as well as about our local club and its current engagements.

"A local band welcomed our visitors with jazz and western music and numerous helpers served drinks and pretzels to help everybody feel comfortable. Our club representatives were busy for hours afterward, talking with our guests. They enthusiastically explained the main idea of 'friendship around the globe' by telling about their own experiences as hosts and ambassadors.

"In a separate room we had prepared an exhibition of photographs along with reports about past exchanges, information about future exchanges and a description of the worldwide Friendship Force organization. In another room there were video and slide shows depicting Friendship Force activities.

Kamilla Konez displays a U.S. flag at her home in Bogacs, Hungary.

Honorary Chairman Peter Kurd Wuezbach, a member of the German Parliament and former first secretary to the Minister of Defense, took part in the event. As a gift to The Friendship Force of Norderstedt, he brought a concrete piece of the Berlin Wall, which for a quarter of a century symbolized high and unjustifiable barriers between people," Engburg said.

"Public configurations that lead to such a barrier between people are partly based on misconceptions and misunderstandings, the lack of friendship and confidence," Herr Wuezbach said. "If organizers like The Friendship Force had existed some fifty or sixty years ago, maybe things that caused so much pain in my parents' generation and in mine, would not have occurred."

Exotic and mysterious India was the setting for a Friendship Force Festival, "a time for the West to meet the East," as Florence Stahl reported in an article for *Friendship* magazine.

"When you alight from a bus and are greeted by two painted elephants, their trunks raised high in salute and a silken banner draped across their backs emblazoned with the words: WELCOME FRIENDSHIP FORCE! you know something very different and very wonderful is about to happen," Stahl said.

This was the beginning of a very fruitful occasion in Jaiphur for friendship and learning. Florence Stahl recorded many things that she and 111 other Friendship ambassadors from around the world learned together. "We learned that India is the largest democracy in the world, a nation of eight hundred million people in a space about one-third the size of the US. In the words of Amarish Trivedi, the Friendship Festival's director and coordinator, 'India is a great country with great problems.' We also learned that India is composed of twenty-five states, has more than fourteen major languages and at least seven hundred recognized dialects. It is a multi-religious, but predominately Hindu, country, with an illiteracy rate of about sixty percent. Although officially outlawed, the caste system is still practiced, much to the despair of the educated modern Indians.'

"Trividi now heads the Indian Association of The Experiment in International Living and devotes himself to organizations dedicated to the betterment of humankind," Florence explained.

In Trividi's letter of welcome to the delegation, he wrote: "Our duty is to help you know, understand and appreciate the Indian ways and views of life from the inside. Be quick to observe but slow to judge, otherwise you might miss our rhythm, and above all, remember the 'P' word, PATIENCE."

In 1990 the Optimist Clubs of Georgia chose Dr. Wayne Smith as the Georgian of the Year. Smith was nominated for this special recognition by the Jasper Optimist Club. Dr. and Mrs. Smith were guests of the Atlanta Braves and Optimist Clubs on June 9th at the Atlanta-Fulton County Stadium. During pre-game activities, Dr. Smith was recognized as 1990 Georgian of the year.

Smith thanked the Optimist Clubs for the honor and then joked, "Of course, I had expected it all along." Smith predicted a turn-around for the Braves in 1991. "They will soon be on top," he predicted. Not even those who had nominated him for the Optimist Club award were *that* optimistic in 1990.

In 1990, The Friendship Force received some unexpected publicity in a feature in *Atlanta* magazine by Michele Cohen Marill entitled "Would You Buy Peace From This Man?" Before the article was written, Wayne Smith challenged Marill to "follow" him for awhile. He meant it and she accepted, traveling with Smith as an observer as well as an interviewer. She had not counted on such a rigorous schedule, a normal one for Smith.

The article begins: "The Friendship Force's Wayne Smith has the naive notion that peace talks start in kitchens and living rooms of ordinary people. Before you scoff, better check out the holy boldness of the world's greatest salesman."

Smith and Marill flew to South Africa for Smith to "pitch his dream to the esteemed Archbishop Desmond Tutu of South Africa. Confidence is Smith's calling card," Marill noted. After greeting the Archbishop, Smith gave Tutu regards from Jimmy Carter and Andy Young. Marill records Smith's next words: "The purpose of my courtesy call is just to tell you a little bit about us, and some of our plans for South Africa. And to see if you have any suggestions for us."

After Bishop Tutu looked over a small brochure about The Friendship Force, he asked Smith to tell him more about the organization. Smith's response: "What we believe is that one of the biggest problems we have in the world today is ignorance. We're ignorant of other situations. We know about people, but we don't know people. Ignorance breeds fear. We have a tendency to be afraid of things that we don't know about. Fear breeds hostility, hatred, animosity, violence, warfare. So we try to attack this at its roots by putting ordinary people in touch with each other."

Smith explained further. "I want to take a planeload of 344 Atlantans, a biracial group, and put them in black townships and white neighborhoods in South Africa. We'll break all the rigid rules of segregation, but we'll match them by occupation...a taxi driver with a taxi driver, a teacher with a teacher, a carpenter with a carpenter."

Marill wrote: "His idea is stunning in its naiveté."

Smith also told Bishop Tutu that he already had a plane ready. Marill noted that Tutu listened without giving any sign of his support. However, when Smith rose to leave, the Bishop spoke.

"We need a great deal of friendship in the world. People have tried to solve problems with the other kind of force. We need more of your force. God bless you."

To Smith, that meant Tutu gave his support and he acted on it accordingly.

As the trip continued, Marill recorded her musings about this man Wayne Smith.

"When people hear the story and sermon of Wayne Smith, there is one natural question: Is he for real? Someone who talks about love and friendship, then turns those abstract, ephemeral concepts into tangible goods that he can export and import to countries. Someone who is brash enough to ask for an audience with the world's great leaders."

This article was news for many readers of *Atlanta* magazine, but it was no surprise to Friendship Force members who already shared Smith's dream. Marill quoted Jimmy Carter, who said, "Wayne Smith is really the originator of the Carter human-rights policy, and he's also the originator of the Panama Canal treaty and he's also the originator of normalization of relations with China. And the Salt II treaty. What Rosalynn and Wayne taught me about dealing with other people is what I tried to put into practice when I became president of the United States. So anything you like about these projects, give Wayne the credit. And anything you don't like about those projects, please also give Wayne the credit."

Soon Marill and Smith were in Israel, headed for the mostly Arab town of Shefar'am, where they met another peace-seller, Elias Jabbour. On the flight, Smith told Marill that he always carried a photograph of himself with George Bush, who was President at that time. (Smith has met every United States President since John F. Kennedy.) He said carrying a picture of himself and the current President of the USA usually hastened customs agents who insisted on checking his bags. He also told Marill that this visit meant breaking new ground, because he wished to sell his version of peace to more Arabs. He had already started with Elias Jabbour and a handful of Jabbour's friends.

In Shefar'am, Wayne told Elias that he wanted him to do more in the cause of The Friendship Force in his city.

"Yes, yes" Elias said. "We have a saying in Arabic: *To make enemies is easy. To make friends is so difficult.* Believe me, it *is* difficult."

Jabbour knows the difficulty first hand. Born in Galilee, He gave up his job as an educator in 1978 to devote his life to peace. He founded The House of Hope in Shefar'am where he works to bring Arabs and Jews together to settle their differences with words instead of bullets. Most of his success has been with the younger generation. Among the older Arabs and Jews, he draws much criticism.

Marill recorded the following conversation:

"It takes people like you with great courage," Smith says to Jabbour. "You will be misunderstood."

"You're right," Jabbour said.

"It could cost you your life."

"I'm aware of that."

"It's dangerous, but you are ready."

"It is so important for us to visit each other. All the barriers will fall. Our ignorance is our enemy."

The peace-seller and the journalist left Shefar'am in the night and traveled to Tel Aviv where they met with Moshe Gazit. Gazit was difficult to convince about an exchange with the Arabs. He said many of his people were afraid to go to a mostly Arab village.

"Smith remained firm," Marill noted. "Six couples would go to Shefar'am on April 20, for a weekend, six Arab couples would come to Kiryat Ono, a Tel Aviv suburb."

Once they were back in Atlanta, Marill noted that "the staff and a host of volunteers were working feverishly on all the details of many exchanges."

This is a normal thing. I, too, have been in the Atlanta office and felt the kinetic energy flying around like unseen lightening bolts. Sometimes the demands of implementing Smith's ideas prove to be too stressful for his beleaguered staff. Workers leave and new ones come to be trained. At times, this turnover places even more hardship on the overburdened staff at Friendship Force International.

The problem—and the blessing—is that Wayne Smith is nothing short of an idea factory. He spews forth new ideas which seem to pop out of his head like popcorn over a very hot fire. Sometimes an harassed employee will mumble, "Nothing is impossible to the man who doesn't have to do it himself!"

Smith is nonplussed by these reactions. He has confidence in his staff and they know it. That's the only reason they keep on carrying out Smith's seemingly impossible missions.

"The thing I hate," one frustrated staffer told me, "is the times when I've worked on one of his impossible ideas for weeks and have finally figured out how to make it work and he comes in and says breezily, 'Oh, forget that! I have a much better idea.'

"He doesn't realize that we can't change gears as fast as he does."

Marill waited in the office until Smith finished dictating messages, faxes and letters to his assistant Wilma Gray. Then they were off to Cape Town to meet with the mayor and to tour the impoverished areas of Crossroads and Hanover Park.

Upon arriving, Smith skipped dinner to prepare for a speech on organizing a Friendship Force club in South Africa. He had earlier vowed to Marill that The Friendship Force would not make an exchange "just to be in touch with only *white* South Africans."

Next Smith was off to be interviewed on South African television. Afterward, he wanted to go to Soweto, but was told to forget it. It was too dangerous, advisors told him. Smith was unconvinced. He sent for a taxi driver named Samson and after a bit of touring, Samson realized that this man Smith was actually interested in him as a person. Finally, Samson pulled into his own driveway and invited Smith to come in and meet his family.

Smith proceeded to convert Samson and his family to The Friendship Force philosophy and before he and Marill left, Samson and his wife were asking about the weather in Atlanta and when they would have to pay their fee and who would they be staying with when they got there.

After returning to Atlanta, completely exhausted by the rigors of Wayne Smith's schedule, Marill needed to rest for a few days. Before the reporter recovered from jet lag and excitement overload, Wayne Smith was off to another country halfway around the world. Michele Marill said she could easily see why Carolyn Smith won't even try to keep up with her globe-trotting husband.

Another big first in Friendship Force history was the hosting of Ambassadors from former East Germany by The Friendship Force of Greater Des Moines. Two of those wide-eyed Germans were Joerg and Kerstin Haehnar. They told of their dream come true, a dream which began when they read about the exchange in a Saxony newspaper. They were skeptical, but since they were planning to be married, they thought this Friendship Force exchange to the United States would be an ideal honeymoon trip. They wrote to The Friendship Force of Berlin and were accepted immediately.

"The many years we were not allowed to travel to the west were over," they said. "The beautiful things in life were no longer forbidden." Joerg and Kerstin were married on March 14, 1990, and they departed from Frankfurt, Germany, on March 20.

"Our reception in Des Moines exceeded all expectations," Joerg and Kerstin said. "Our hosts, Jane and Ken Shipley made us feel at home from the first moment. They received us lovingly and made us feel comfortable in this new country."

At the end of the exchange, the newlyweds said, "All of us from eastern Germany had a totally different picture of the USA. We were moved by the mentality of the people, the joy they express in being alive. A spark of this gusto for life was transferred to us and caught fire in our hearts."

Chapter 20
You Can Make A Difference

There is no power on earth that can neutralize the influence of a high, simple and useful life.
—**Booker T. Washington**

You *can* make a difference! This Friendship Force motto is sometimes forgotten and it is often doubted, even by some of the volunteer "ambassadors" of the organization. When trouble erupts around the world on a daily basis, it's easy to throw up our hands and say, "We tried, but obviously our efforts didn't count."

Another of Wayne Smith's parables addresses the amazing power of the individual.

"While I was in Brazil, I heard a beautiful story," Smith said. "It seems that lightning had hit a tree in the Amazon jungle and set the tree afire. A small bird had its nest in the tree and was terrified that it would lose its home.

"The bird began to shriek out a cry to its neighbors for help. But since the other birds didn't live in the threatened tree, they ignored the cries of their neighbor. They didn't believe that flames would eventually spread to their nests.

"The little bird then flew off to a nearby lake and filled its beak with water, then flew back and dropped the tiny globule of water on the blazing tree. Then it flew back to the lake for another sip of water to drop on the fire.

"Exhausted, but still making its round-trips of desperation, the bantam bird was challenged by a parrot perched in a nearby tree.

"You silly bird! Don't you know you'll never put out that fire?"

"That may be," replied the distressed bird as it set off on yet another trip to the lake, "but I'm doing what I can."

Smith can talk for hours about many incidents when only one Friendship Force volunteer made a great deal of difference. Stories like the one about George and Pat Montross of Winterset, Iowa, who applied to be part of a Greater Des Moines an A.R.M.S. visit to the Soviet Union in late 1989. There were no openings, but the Mission

Director Lucy Gutenkauf contacted Friendship Force International and the Montrosses were placed with a group from Dayton, Ohio.

This group went to the Soviet Republic of Turkmenistan for an eight-day home-stay with hosts in the capital of Ashkhabad, just north of the border with Iran. More than four million Turkmen live in central Asia in the area surrounding the Kara-Kom desert east of the Caspian Sea. In addition, 2.5 million live in Turkmenistan and 1.2 million live in Iran. Another four hundred thousand reside in Afghanistan. Turkmenistan is landlocked on every side by Islamic republics.

The Turkmen come from a nomadic tribal past, but they were forcibly united as a country under Russian tsarist rule in 1881. (Turkmenistan remained a Soviet Republic until its independence in 1990.) Turkmen in Turkmenistan are almost all Sunni Muslims, while those in Iran are Shi'ites.

The Montrosses were sent on to Chardzhou to stay two days in homes on a collective farm. There they lived with a couple and their very sick little girl named Ola. Ola's poor health was the result of a serious illness she suffered as a baby. She had since almost died on two occasions. She was on a waiting list of four to eight years for surgery outside the Soviet Union, but the chances were slim that she would last that long.

Once they were back in the United States, Pat Montross began to check with hospitals where surgery might be performed. Two were excellent candidates. Pat's next big problem was red tape. On the other end, Guila, the child's mother, made five trips to Moscow. Finally the arrangements were made and the Soviet government actually paid for flying Guila and Ola to Washington. The government also gave them extra money for medications.

A friend of the Montrosses, Charles Ihler, obtained four inexpensive tickets for George and Pat Montross and the mother and child to fly to Des Moines. He paid for the visitors' tickets himself. Congressman Jim Ross Lightfoot arranged for an interpreter to meet the party at Dulles Airport and the interpreter took them all on a sightseeing tour of Washington.

Later in Des Moines, Dr. John Jay examined Ola and made arrangements for Dr. Stephen Phillips, a children's heart surgeon, to operate. The doctors and Mercy Hospital made no charge for their services. The Montrosses were at the hospital daily to provide loving support for the child and her mother. Finally, the two were allowed to make a brief visit to the Montross home before they returned to their country.

John Schmidt who wrote the story said, "The Friendship Force isn't always that dramatic—not every exchange is life-saving. But they all do something to make life better, here and abroad."

In October 1990, Edith Haraughty of The Friendship Force of Oklahoma wrote about an amazing woman. Upon arriving in Lampang, Thailand, Edith discovered that she would be staying in the home of a "family" of forty! The family was headed by a woman known as Maelek, a beloved native who continued to do much for her country. It was later explained that the woman's actual name was *Lek* and that *Mae* means mother. Maelek had been caring for others over the past thirty years. The American women were surprised to learn that Maelek was seventy-two years old and that most Thai families have an average of eight children. The average Thai family lives on about two hundred dollars a year.

Shortly after Edith and Sue Simpson of Oklahoma and Mary Clary of North Carolina met Maelek, their hostess excused herself to attend a friend's funeral. They were left in the hands of Sommatra Troy, another of Maelek's many house guests.

When Edith and her two friends arrived at Maelek's home they saw an old teakwood house built high above the ground in typical Thai style. Four bathrooms had been added to accommodate Maelek's children and her many visitors. These children all needed some kind of help. Some stayed until they were grown and able to find jobs.

At the first opportunity Maelek took the three Americans into town where they saw motorcycles, pushcarts, horse-drawn carriages and some cars and trucks. They were told that most of the merchants lived in the rear of their shops.

After the tour, they returned to the house where they discovered a tub of hot water, already prepared so they could soak their feet and relax with a Coke. Then they were given a foot massage. Following this pampering, they visited Maelek's dressmaker who lived next door. Maelek had arranged for them to select material to be made into Thai dresses to be worn at a banquet scheduled later in the week.

Maelek then called for a carriage to take her three guests on another tour around Lampang. "It was a real treat to be riding in an open, flower-decorated carriage behind a clip-clopping horse as the beautiful colors of the sunset filled the sky," Edith recalled.

In addition to her other chores, Maelek was involved in many outside activities and the three visitors accompanied her when she went to a college where she made the keynote speech. "We were beginning to realize that Maelek was almost beyond belief," Edith said. "She arose at five a.m., exercised, wrote an article for her newspaper, packed pickles all day with a crew of young people and then was the main speaker at a banquet honoring her friend. And the day wasn't over yet. After we watched the lovely dancing girls, ate wonderful Thai food and said good-bye to our friends, Maelek asked her driver to take us into the country to a small village where people were gathered inside a Buddhist temple. We removed our shoes and joined the crowd. Maelek then introduced another remarkable lady to the assembly. To our surprise it was Sommatra Troy whom we had met upon arrival.

"Although we had spoken briefly to Sommatra, we did not know much about her. At the temple, Maelek told us that Sommatra was a nurse. She was educated in Scotland before becoming a resident of the USA for twenty-eight years. She then returned to Thailand to educate her people about AIDS, teaching them the facts about the deadly virus and giving them advice on how to combat the danger. Maelek was Sommatra's sponsor and both women worked together," Edith said.

Later the ambassadors learned that one village high up in the mountains had been blessed by Maelek in several ways. She had negotiated for a road to be built to the village with a population of about one thousand and she paid for the construction of a building so villagers could process tea for shipment to Japan. In exchange, the leader of the village had promised that no more girls would be sold into prostitution. It became apparent that Maelek believes that one person can make a difference," Haraughty said. "She has set out to save the young girls of the hill people in northern Thailand from being sold. Formerly, young women were often sold by their families only to end up in Chaing Mai or Bangkok as prostitutes."

At another village, they learned that Maelek had moved all the residents from another place to this new village where the soil was more fertile. They also learned that Maelek had organized a rice "bank" to serve collectively five mountain farming villages. If one group has a poor harvest, they can draw on this bank to feed their people. If the harvest is good, rice is returned to the bank.

From village to village, The Friendship Force ambassadors traveled with Maelek. As they approached each place, villagers of all ages dropped what they were doing and ran toward them, crying delightedly: "Maelek! Maelek! Maelek!"

The three American women made many friends in Thailand and they returned home greatly inspired by little Maelek, a loving, energetic, seventy-two-year-old woman who is making an enormous difference in distant Thailand.

On November 1, 1990, a group of Friendship Force ambassadors from the United States left for the very first visit to South Africa. Wayne Smith and his staff had tried to accomplish this since 1980, but government officials in both countries feared "mischief-making by extremists" and were not willing to chance such problems.

All but one person in the group were seasoned Friendship Force travelers, but not one of the ambassadors really knew what to expect. Some suffered occasional pangs of anxiety, recalling televised news of riots in the streets.

Once they arrived, anxiety was quickly wiped away by warm greetings from host families, who were all delightful people and most hospitable. Ambassadors quickly discovered that The Friendship Force in Cape Town was totally integrated, as were most places of employment and the society in general.

Nathan Bushnell III said " ...despite Friendship Force caution to avoid politics, the principal subject on the minds of virtually every person we met was politics. And that's what they wanted to talk about—not passionately, but quite frankly." Bushnell said that under President F.W. DeKlerk, many apartheid laws had already been rescinded and all such laws were widely ignored. He also reported that the South Africans exhibited great pride in their country.

The country is breathtakingly beautiful, as the ambassadors learned through tours provided by their hosts. From Parliament Square in Cape Town to well-planned communities at the foot of Table and Lion Head Mountains, they saw a vibrant country. Hosts also showed off beautiful beaches on both the Indian and the Atlantic Oceans.

Bushnell said "One of the eye-opening highlights was a tour of Crossroads and Khayelitsha, two of the fastest-growing Black townships in South Africa, now housing in excess of half a million immigrants from the Black homelands and neighboring independent states. More are pouring in, seeking employment at the rate of twenty thousand per month. Shelter in these huge areas ranges from tents provided by the government to crudely-built shanties, to well-built small cottages and tenements, renting for about eight dollars a month for a two-room cottage."

On the long trip back home, Bushnell reflected on all the group had learned. "How uninformed we had been about this great country just a few days earlier," he marveled. "This may turn out to be one of the most significant exchanges in the history of The Friendship Force. It certainly was the most significant of the seventeen in which I have participated as either an ambassador or host.

"Each of our eighteen ambassadors went home determined to spread the news of all we had learned about the friendly people of South Africa.." Bushnell said. "And I learned anew the truth of The Friendship Force motto: 'You *can* make a difference.'"

In May 1991, Friendship Force activity in Ireland included hosting a mini- Friendship Force Festival. For two weeks, the Irish hosted twelve ambassadors from Tbilisi, Republic of Georgia. This was the first East-West visit of its kind in Ireland. The exchange director Tsisana Gabunia was Professor of English at the Institute of Foreign Languages in Tbilisi. The Georgians were hosted by four Friendship Force clubs: Bantry in County Cork, Kildare, Tubbercurry and Dublin. During the same two weeks, seventy additional ambassadors from Wisconsin, Iowa, Arizona, California, Tennessee and Georgia also participated in the mini-festival.

In June 1991, a powerful earthquake shook parts of the Republic of Georgia. The Friendship Force teamed with five other organizations to provide tents for the victims. Fifty-two ambassadors from Atlanta on an exchange to Tbilisi in August delivered sixty tents, each one weighing thirty-nine pounds. It was quite a sight to see all those big boxes being shoved through the Atlanta, New York, Moscow and Tbilisi airports. In Tbilisi, they were met by Georgia Greens of The Friendship Force of Tbilisi, who distributed the tents to needy families. Barbara Bruegger led this exchange of friendship and mercy.

The Friendship Force Begins in Ghana, West Africa
In April 1991, Dr. Wayne Van Tilburg and his wife Eleanor traveled from their home in Ridgefield, Washington, to Accra, Ghana, in West Africa, to help a group of Ghanaians establish a Friendship Force Club. The Van Tilburgs had read about the days when this West African nation swarmed with Portuguese, British, Danes, Dutch and Germans, all searching for the precious metal that gave the Gold Coast its name. However, no amount of study could fully prepare the Van Tilburgs for their developmental excursion on behalf of The Friendship Force. When they left for Ghana, one name was given to them by Bobbie Jones of Friendship Force International: Prince Baffour Awuah Gyanu.

"First we flew into Nigeria," Dr. Van Tilburg said. "The terrain looked pretty desolate and we were wondering if Ghana would be the same. We were relieved to see that, from the air, Ghana looked brighter along the coast. We deplaned on the tarmac and walked into the tiny airport in Accra. The heat and humidity enveloped us instantly, plastering clothing to our bodies. The first thing we saw was a very large sign, maybe fifteen feet long. It had a strong, simple message: IMMUNIZATION. Thank goodness, we had received all our shots before leaving the States and our papers were in order.

"Then we went to customs," Eleanor Van Tilburg said. "It looked as if we were going to be inspected thoroughly, because they asked me to open my luggage. Fortunately, I always travel with a supply of small United States flags and they were readily visible when I opened my first bag. Everyone in customs wanted one, so after I distributed several flags, our luggage received no further scrutiny."

"In the lobby we were greeted by Prince Baffour and his entourage. We were a bit confused as to who the others were, but they were obviously very important and respected people. Prince Baffour directed us into a small room to meet a man who wore a draped headdress. They said he was an Ashanti and was in the employ of Dr. Otumfuor Opoku Ware II, known as the *Asantehene*. The Asantehene is revered as king and chief statesman of the Ashantis, one of the most powerful and respected groups in Ghana. He is revered throughout Ghana and he alone governs the Ashantis. He is also guardian of The Golden Stool, symbol of national unity. According to Ashanti tradition, The Golden Stool came down from Heaven and alighted gently on the knees of their hero-founder Osei Tutu in about 1695. This sacred object is decorated with bells and effigies of slain enemies. So sacred is it to the people that no one—not even the Asantehene—must ever sit on it.

"The current military dictatorship rules Ghana, but there seems to be an unwritten law that allows the Ashantis to self govern, although they make up only thirteen percent of the population of Ghana. The Ashantis live mainly in Ghana and they speak a dialect of the Twi people. When we were there, the dictator was Jerry Rawlings.

"At the time we met Prince Baffour and the others, we were still very much in the dark about the government and leadership in Ghana," Wayne Van Tilburg said. "Prince Baffour greeted us and spoke with us for a few minutes before we were ushered into still another room where about fifty people were waiting for us. They were there to shake hands with us—all fifty of these smiling Black people. We were touched that they had waited there just to greet us and make us feel welcome," Dr. Van Tilburg said.

"Everywhere we went, we had an entourage of at least fifteen to twenty people—all Black and all men. As we traveled about in Accra, we saw a spacious city with broad avenues, public gardens and sandy beaches. Despite modern buildings and squares, Accra retains its tropical atmosphere with fruit trees growing in profusion.

"We soon learned that Prince Baffour and other key people who wanted to start a Friendship Force Club had waited for us to arrive so they would have an easier time of selling the idea of bridging the world's great divides simply by making friends. Now that we were there, they were determined to use our visit to gain access to the highest places in the government.

"The first place that Prince Baffour asked us to go was to the United States Consulate General in Accra. We did pay a call on the Consulate General and she told us that very few Ghanaians receive visas to travel to the United States. She also said that each interview for a visa cost the Ghanaian applicant fifty dollars. We explained The Friendship Force concept and she finally promised us that she would 'be on the lookout for a group applying for visas to go on a Friendship Force exchange,'" Dr. Van Tilburg recalled.

Eleanor Van Tilburg told of the hours they spent with the committee members who were working to establish a Friendship Force Club in Ghana. "We spent a great deal of time answering their many questions," she said. "We went over every detail, covering how to put an exchange together, how to handle the finances, how to recruit members—all of those things and more.

Wayne Van Tilburg said, "While we were there, we stayed in private homes. Our first hosts were a young man and his wife. They lived in a beautiful home and we were treated very kindly. We learned that after a few days, we were scheduled to go to another home. When the second host arrived, our first host did not want us to leave. An argument ensued and after two hours of heated debate, we realized that neither side was budging. I sat in our room and listened to the argument going on outside. Finally, I decided to intervene."

"I didn't want him to go outside," Eleanor said. "I was very frightened for Wayne's safety. I listened with my heart in my throat as Wayne walked outside and said calmly, 'This must stop. We will go to the other home, as planned.'

"To my great surprise, they agreed and the argument stopped immediately."

"We went on to the other home," Dr. Van Tilburg said. "It was also the first time this family had ever home-hosted and they were really excited about a Friendship Force exchange. While we were there, they were already thinking about how they could make Western ambassadors comfortable. They were aware of the dangers from mosquito-borne malaria, so they were talking about putting netting over the beds."

"The people were just beautiful," Eleanor said. "I remember one day when I sat on the bed with several Ghanaian women and we had a great time, laughing and giggling like school girls. We talked about our families, our hobbies and our husbands. It was just like being with a bunch of my friends in the United States. Those women mothered me and treated me like one of the family. They even ordered Ghanaian style dresses made for me. They were such genuine people. They readily allowed me to share their kitchens and to learn about their food and their recipes."

Eleanor Van Tilburg and
April, a new friend in Ghana

Ellen, Adwor, Daniel
and Maggie

"We also visited Cape Coast, a town in Ghana on the Gulf of Guinea," Dr. Van Tilburg said. "We met with the Central Regional Secretary who received us at his office. We told him about The Friendship Force. Following the visit, his protocol officer escorted us on a tour of Elmina Castle and Cape Coast Castle. We returned to the Governor's legislative dining room for dinner."

Soon Prince Baffour told the Van Tilburgs that he wanted them to accompany him to Kumasi where one of his wives lived. His other wife lived in Accra. On the drive to Kumasi, Prince Baffour told the Van Tilburgs that virtually all trade between southern and northern Ghana passes through Kumasi and that after World War I, Kumasi was largely rebuilt according to a 'garden city' plan. The population of Kumasi is approximately 261,000.

"When we arrived in Kumasi, the very first thing we did was to pay a visit to the Asantehene. He was expecting us. Prince Baffour explained that this was quite an honor, because the Asantehene normally makes a public appearance only one time each year and at other times, he grants few appointments."

"As we left to meet with the Asantehene at Manhia Palace, Prince Baffour and his entire entourage went with us. They were dressed in their finest garments and had coifed their hair elaborately. The children wore frilly dresses and it became plain to us that all were expecting to see the great Asantehene," Dr. Van Tilburg said. "However, when we arrived at the palace, everyone was turned away except Eleanor, myself, Prince Baffour and the man whom we first met at the airport. There may have been one of two more who were allowed inside, but only a very few were invited. I felt terrible about that, because I sensed the acute disappointment the others felt at being turned away. I still feel terrible each time I think about it."

"It was very impressive to meet the Asantehene," Eleanor Van Tilburg recalled.

"Yes," her husband agreed. "We first had to sign a book and present ourselves.

The Van Tilburgs were told that the Ashantis were actually sitting on top of a gold mine since they control all the gold in that part of Ghana. After a brief lecture by Prince Baffour, they were ushered into a large room and were seated.

"When the Asantehene entered, he was wearing a richly-colored robe made of a shimmering material, somewhat like satin, only heavier. It was worn draped over one shoulder in the manner of a Roman toga. He sat on a low carved chair ornamented with gold. He was a soft spoken man in his fifties and he spoke English well. We presented gifts to him and we mentioned President and Mrs. Carter's affiliation with The Friendship Force. In reply, the Asantehene told us that Carter had been to visit him sometime earlier. We already knew that the Carters were held in very high esteem in Ghana," Dr. Van Tilburg said. "We later learned that the Carter Center, through some funding from Ryoichi Sasakawa, had provided a new drought and disease resistant maize to Ghanaian farmers. In Ghana today, the maize is called Carter-Sasakawa corn .

"After we presented our gifts, we were invited to speak about The Friendship Force.

The Van Tilburgs admire the "Carter-Sasakawa Corn."

Dr. Wayne Van Tilburg presents gifts to the revered Asantahene, Dr. Otumfuor Opoku Ware II, at Manhia Palace in Kumasi, Ghana.

The Asantehene said nothing to us after we spoke, but he had listened with apparent keen interest and he also appeared to be extremely interested in the ideals of the organization. He spoke privately with Prince Baffour at the end of our visit and Prince Baffour later disclosed that the Asantehene said to him: 'This Friendship Force is an important organization and we must be careful and hold it tight so it does not slip away.'

Following the meeting, Prince Baffour told the Van Tilburgs they would travel with him to his village. Along the way he told them how Ghana gained independence in 1957, and became the pioneer of black nationalism in Africa. Although Ghana has gone through some rough periods of economic instability, the Van Tilburgs had already observed a thriving farming industry, saving Ghana from the mass starvation so prevalent in Somalia, Djibouti, Ethiopia, Eritrea, Sudan, and other crop-poor and strife-torn African nations.

Along the way, Prince Baffour stopped and bought a loaf of bread. By the time they arrived, it was late afternoon. As the Van Tilburgs got out of the car, they heard the slow beating of many drums, announcing their arrival. As they passed through an entrance into a courtyard Prince Baffour gave the loaf of bread to Dr. Van Tilburg and asked him to present it to Baffour's mother.

"I gave her the bread, which is apparently a gesture of respect in Ghana, and we spoke to this elderly woman who said little. We were introduced to her and shook her hand. The other women present were also introduced as Baffour's second, third and fourth mothers. This was his way of telling us that his father had four wives, who all lived together in the compound," Dr. Van Tilburg said. "Prince Baffour's other wife also lived in the same compound with Baffour's four mothers.

"We followed Baffour to the village center," said Eleanor Van Tilburg. "We were seated and all the elders of the village were seated around us. We then stood and walked slowly around the circle and shook hands with everyone. We sat down again and they all solemnly filed around us and shook our hands. Then they produced a homemade alcoholic brew, which we quickly discovered was far too strong for us. By then, it was getting very dark and the only light came from flickering oil lamps. The scent of oil was so strong that we felt we had actually tasted it," she added.

"The dancing began," said her husband. "It was an exotic and beautiful experience to be there in a small village in Ghana, West Africa, somewhere near Kumasi...two white Americans seated among an all-black cast of dancers who performed for us into the night. It was surreal then and it still seems so today. Only with The Friendship Force could such a thing happen!"

"We concluded our business over the next day or two and went back to Accra where we ran afoul of customs officials," Eleanor Van Tilburg said. "Earlier in the visit, someone had taken our passports to get a required police stamp as permission for us to leave the country. When our passports were returned, we never checked for a stamp. As we went back through customs, we were told the necessary stamp was missing. Finally, I realized it was going to take more than words to enable us to leave, so I pulled out what looked like a lot of money—actually just a roll of one dollar bills. After I peeled off several of those, the obstinate customs employee became a lot less interested in the lack of a police stamp. We were allowed to go at last. Of course, Ghana is not the only country where a small 'bribe' is sometimes expected," she said.

After the Van Tilburgs returned to their home, they received a warm letter from Prince Baffour Awuah Gyanu. It read:

Dear Dr. and Mrs. Van Tilburg,

This comes from me and my wives to thank you from the very abyss of our hearts for the gifts you gave us. My acknowledgment could not be filled earlier, because I had to go to my village for my senior mother's funeral immediately after we saw you off at the airport. My own mother also suddenly collapsed as a result of her sister's transition. This kept me at Kumasi for over a month, but, thank goodness, she recovered and then I had to proceed to my farm to see to the cropping as we now have only one major cropping season in Ghana.

Our very best compliments to you and your family. We will remember you always.

In love and friendship,
Prince Baffour Awuah Gyanu and Family.

(Note: Baffour's title is inherited and is passed down to the eldest son in each generation.)

The Van Tilburgs made another friend, a man from Kumasi, an Ashanti named Oheneba Mensah Oppong Kyekyeku, treasurer of the local Friendship Force club. The Van Tilburgs' friendliness and openness impressed the treasurer, but the Americans had no idea just when or how his appreciation would manifest itself. In August 1991, they found out when a letter arrived from their new African friend.

Dear Dr.,

We have had quick results regarding the establishment of The Friendship Force in Ghana from headquarters, Atlanta, and I know you are part of our success. Thank you. I shall never forget the mini-exchange we had with you. You both have become part of my life, thanks to The Friendship Force.

I am happy to announce to you that my second wife brought forth a child on the 6th of April 1991, and I have named him after you. He is Van Tilburg Osei Oppong-Bonsu. The naming of my child after you is the beginning of many things to come. I hope to establish a long and eternal friendship with you, Sir.

I am an orphan. My father died on October 6, 1954, and my mother died on May 5, 1955. I have had to strive hard to gain a scholarship before I went to high school. I did my best and entered Kumasi Polytechnic for my degree as a member of the Chartered Institute of Secretaries.

By 1970, I had three children by different girls. Nobody warned me. An orphan as I am, I was left to myself. Later I married three wives and they brought forth three children each. Twelve children, one died, leaving eleven. I married my fourth wife. The first three left me. I have stalls where I sell records, hence I added one more wife and then another to take care of my three Record-Shops. These wives also brought forth two children each. One wife left for London and I married yet another...whose second child...I have named after you.

I am now grown and have realized my folly. I am praying to God that I will be left with only one wife, or at most, two. I was too young to know the burden of child caring. Therefore, I am left with a heavy responsibility of taking care of eighteen children.

Personally, I neither smoke nor drink. My hobbies are music and reading and I am very good in trading.

In short, this is the life history of your friend, the treasurer.

I appreciate everything you are doing for us. Dr., thank madam for me. She made your visit complete. She played a most important role. My children told me to express their gratitude to you and your family for the love and kindness shown to them. They thank you all.

I am happy to announce that the Kumasi Community of which I am the President provided most of the patrons for the club and our number now far exceeds that of the Accra club. We have very active members. We are supposed to have our first exchange on the 8th of October this year. I shall keep in touch for more of your useful advice and you may expect to receive progress reports.

The workshops I had with you have been helping me a lot. We thank you Doctor. You have left sweet memories in Ghana.

Hoping to hear from you soon.

Yours faithfully, Oheneba Mensah Oppong Kyekyeku

Prince Baffour and Dr. Van Tilburg

Eleanor Van Tilburg's snapshot of Prince Baffour and her husband, shown in a warm farewell embrace, won first place in a *Friendship* magazine photo contest. It made the cover of the magazine's third quarter 1991 edition.

After the magazine reached Ghana, their friend Oheneba Mensah Oppong Kyekyeku wrote a touching letter of congratulations. These were a few of his words:

"Dear Doc,

I write to congratulate you on the award winning photograph. The whole wide world has seen you. Your humble visit to Ghana was historic. God has linked Ghana and America together in a special way. We hope you shall never regret coming to Ghana. We are a poor African country but we have untapped potential and we live in a land rich in gold and minerals. It is historic that Ghana and America were linked in friendship through you and your wife. God bless you."

And in another note, Oheneba Mensah Oppong Kyekyeku said, "Thanks to your favourable recommendation to Friendship Force International representatives, the Ghana Friendship Force will forever remember you: You are the father of the club. Your wife is the mother."

Dr. Van Tilburg also reported that Prince Baffour had purchased a large parcel of land outside Accra. "He has donated approximately thirty hectares of the parcel to The Friendship Force of Ghana. His dream is to build a Friendship Park. He is quite serious about this project."

The 15th annual Friendship Force International Conference met in Daytona, Beach Florida, in October 1991. The theme was "Waves of Friends—Florida Style" and hosts were Joe and Ruth Nathan of East Central Florida.

Among delegates who attended were thirteen representatives of five Friendship Force clubs in Eastern and Central Europe. Prince Baffour Awuah Gyawu and Dr. Kwesi Oyenam Panford. came from the newly established Friendship Force of Ghana:

David Luria, Executive Vice President of Friendship Force International, said, "One of the Bulgarians, Dr. Emil Peitchev, delighted the delegates by singing *La Bamba* in Spanish at the Saturday evening banquet."

Another delegate responded: "Only in The Friendship Force would you find a scene like this. People gathered in friendship from twenty nations, listening to a calypso band from Jamaica playing background music for a dentist from Bulgaria who is singing a Mexican song in Spanish."

You can make a difference—and sometimes in unexpected ways. For example, back in 1989, an exchange inbound from Germany to the United States included a woman who was a Lutheran minister. On her application, she asked to be placed in a home of those practicing a different religion than her own. Her preference was a Jewish family.

When the German ambassadors arrived in a southern city in the United States, the minister was pleased to learn that she would be living in the home of a Jewish rabbi.

The exchange director feared that the German minister and the Jewish rabbi might not be at all compatible, but each time they were present at group events, both seemed happy and expressed no complaints. It was two years later before the exchange director learned what had happened.

Before the week was out, the Lutheran minister told the Rabbi that she was born Jewish, but that the Nazis had sent the rest of her family away. She was saved by a kind-hearted Lutheran family who had risked much by taking her into their home. She never knew where her parents and siblings were taken and that had always troubled her, especially as she grew older.

The Rabbi listened with growing amazement. When she finished telling him about losing her parents, he said softly, "I, too, was sent away by the Nazis...to a place of death called Auschwitz. I knew your mother and one sister because they were there. I can tell you that they did not live until the war was over. I saw them for the last time in 1944," he said gently.

Somehow the news was both devastating and comforting. The Jewish rabbi and the Lutheran minister grieved together. Then came a measure of relief and release for the minister. At last she knew the truth and could finally stop the self-torment of wondering if somehow her family might have survived the war.

Another first in 1991, was a Friendship Force exchange to Bulgaria. Pat Cunningham was the Exchange Director, and she called the trip to Sofia, Bulgaria, on July 1, 1991, "the ultimate."

Pat told of the good fortune of having a recent emigrant from Sofia living in her part of Iowa. "When I told her about the upcoming exchange, she seemed puzzled and remarked, 'Why would anyone want to go there? My family and I left...because conditions were so bad.'" After she understood that Pat and the others were not seeking "places," but "faces," the former Bulgarian said, "Oh, then you will not be disappointed, because you will love the people."

Before the departure, the newspapers were filled with grim accounts of shortages in Bulgaria, even for necessities such as food and fuel for heating and operating vehicles. The War in the Persian Gulf was another worry and the Atlanta club heard fears from volunteers who said they were reluctant to travel anywhere. Nevertheless, fifteen ambassadors signed up to travel to Sofia.

How were they received? Pat Cunningham said, "Our hosts rearranged their lives to insure that we were comfortable. As we were shown the sights of Sofia and the surrounding countryside, we learned about Bulgarian history, and I began to recall long-forgotten names from my high school days—Macedonia, Thrace, Trimontium, Philippopolis. These places either are—or were—part of Bulgaria. In the National History Museum in Sofia we saw the magnificent nine-piece set of vessels fashioned of pure gold from the Thracian empire. We walked the yellow brick road to the Alexander Nevsky Cathedral and heard the heavenly music of its choir. We visited a monastery in Rila that dates back to the 13th century; the monks kept the Bulgarian culture alive during the five hundred years of Turkish domination.

"We saw a veritable kaleidoscope of colorful scenes of mountains, orchards, tobacco fields and donkey carts loaded with loaves of bread. Suddenly the landscape changed to stark sandstone hills and vineyards as we approached the tiny town of Melnik near the border with Greece."

Although the Americans witnessed the hardships endured by the Bulgarian people, they were "impressed by the way the members of The Friendship Force of Sofia meet each day with dignity, grace, a zest for life and a marvelous sense of humor."

In fall of 1991, Donna Malacic, President of The Friendship Force of Belgrade, Yugoslavia, visited Friendship Force International offices to begin her training in preparation for organizing exchanges to and from her country. Those plans were shattered when civil war broke out in Yugoslavia immediately after Donna returned to her home. In a letter to The Friendship Force in 1992, Donna wrote of the war and of her prayers for peace.

Dear Friends,

I was so glad to receive your New Year's greeting (1992) with the photograph. I'm not sure if you will receive this letter. I'll try also to send a fax. I used to send faxes from my friend's office, but unfortunately he is now at the battlefield—his office closed. I hope he will return soon, alive and well.

We are at war now and what a war! The most dirty war that could be imagined in the 20th century—and in the middle of Europe.

People who suffer most are those who never brought communism to this country. I guess you can't very well understand what's really going on here. No wonder. It's so maddening that most of us can't understand either.

I really feel guilty for not being able to do more about the creation of The Friendship Force club in Belgrade, but believe me, we are living in an awful period. Although there is no bombing in Belgrade as yet, everybody has somebody at the battlefield. If men are not sent already, they expect to go any day now. People simply are not in the state of mind to think of anything else but war...and survival.

Anyway, men over eighteen are not allowed to leave the country. We fear that the war is going to escalate and spread. We all expect much from the United Nations and hope the blue helmets are coming soon. If they don't come we are lost. We will be exterminated.

I'll tell you briefly the history of my family so I think you will realize how complicated and sad this situation is for me and for many others.

I come from an old Serbian family from Belgrade. After the Second World War my parents, who were not communists, were considered a bourgeois element, and that in itself was enough to cause them to be considered an enemy of the regime. Our family home was taken from us and we were allowed to live in a very small part of it.

Then my father was labeled as a dissident and after many persecutions, he was put in prison for having criticized President Tito. The poor man spent eight years in prison. He died in 1984 and never lived to see the collapse of communism and the destruction of Tito's myth.

I was born during the Second World War and was educated as a Yugoslav. I felt much more Yugoslav than Serb; most of us did. We were brainwashed with the idea of 'brotherhood and unity.' Now people from different republics are vilifying each other in the most atrocious ways.

This hatred all seemed to come so suddenly. It is beyond me. My husband is also a Serb, but he has strong national feelings. He always considered himself a Serb and he told me I was wrong to believe in brotherhood between the Serbs and the Croats. He never forgot that Croatian people joined the fascists during the war and committed genocide of Serbian people and of Jews. They were never tried for these crimes after the war.

Tito was a Croat so he had a big part in it. Maybe during the Second World War there was reason to hate these crimes, but as we have been living together in one country for fifty years, I thought it was over. But alas, it is not!

My stay in Atlanta was the last nice thing that happened to me. The war started just at the end of my stay there. I think of those days often and hope that we can meet again. I send much love and friendly thoughts to all the wonderful people I met in Atlanta.

The 16th International Conference was held in Niigata, Japan, in 1992

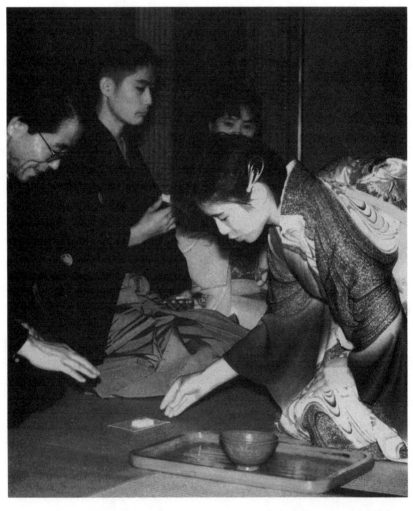

Delegates to the Conference are treated to the beautiful tea ceremony.

Chapter 21
A Bridge Called Friend-to-Friend

Blessed are they that have the gift of making friends, for it is one of God's best gifts. It involves many things, but above all, the power of going out of one's self and appreciating what is noble and loving in another.
—Thomas Hughes

By the end of 1991, Russia society was changing rapidly and irrevocably. A coup attempt had failed in October and communism was collapsing. The vast empire of Lenin and Stalin was breaking up. Viewed up close, the Iron Curtain was in tatters. It was history in the making and part of that history involved The Friendship Force.

This dramatic photo by Tomaz Tomaszewski depicts the break-up of the old USSR. The men are happily removing busts of Stalin to a warehouse. (Photo appeared in National Geographic in March, 1991. Used by permission.)

Beginning at Thanksgiving, twenty-five groups of Americans were scheduled to visit cities in and around Moscow, St. Petersburg, Riga, Tbilisi, Minsk and other locations. And this time, the exchanges would include *home-hosting* of the Americans and other westerners.

Smith was too busy planning these hard-won exchanges to bask in victory. He realized the new-found freedom in the former Soviet Union was very fragile and that unless the people had assistance and training in the free enterprise system, they might not survive the inevitable currency devaluation and shortages of food and other essential goods. He wanted The Friendship Force to be one of the first to offer such aid.

It was announced that these early exchanges in the "new" Russia were excellent vehicles for friendship, but also that "each ambassador, representing his or her family, and a minimum of three other families in the ambassador's neighborhood...will take four boxes of scarce food supplies as a goodwill gift for their host family and three neighboring families—a total of a hundred pounds. Thus a one-week visit by a twenty-five-member delegation will align a hundred American families in the US with 100 families in Moscow, or one of the other cities."

But that would only be half the program: Those Americans who home-hosted inbound ambassadors from the former Soviet countries would send the same amount of food parcels with their guests when they returned to their respective countries. This new program would be called *Friend-to-Friend* and Smith hoped that by the end of the winter more than ten thousand American families would be linked with ten thousand families in Russia.

It was a huge undertaking, considering that the average Soviet made the equivalent of eight dollars US a month. If they couldn't afford food, how could they afford airline tickets? Smith thought he could arrange for their travel to be subsidized. Immediately he made travel arrangements with Delta Airlines for the first series of exchanges between Atlanta and Moscow. Publicity was arranged with WXIA-TV who agreed to send reporters on the first exchanges.

George Brown, then head of the Department of World Citizen Exchanges for The Friendship Force, said: "The Atlanta Community Food Bank provided valuable assistance in determining what food should be sent and how it could be collected without interfering with ongoing food drives for the local needy."

Cash donations were also solicited to help with needed subsidy expenses. It was an exciting time for The Friendship Force and Wayne Smith was delighted to see so many volunteers building bridges of friendship where once an impenetrable Iron Curtain separated people.

Smith wanted to do everything possible to keep in place what he called "the change from *nyet* to *da*."

"I made my first visit to Moscow in January of 1981," Smith recalled. "My memories of that trip revolve around the thoughts of "repression," "atmosphere of fear," "cold," "*nyet*."

"As soon as the coup failed last August, I got myself over to Moscow as quickly as I could. I wanted to see if there was anything The Friendship Force could do to help strengthen the forces of freedom at work in that giant nation," Smith said.

"I proposed my plan to two members of our International Advisory Council: Foreign Minister Eduard Shevardnadze and Dr. Syvatoslav Fyodorov, the internationally renowned eye surgeon. They told me their people were facing a very difficult winter, with food and fuel in short supply. Shevardnadze expressed his belief that the fate of the former Soviet countries would depend on how well the impending crisis was resolved. Both men responded enthusiastically to the plan.

"On my last evening in Moscow, I attended a grand reception in the Kremlin. Dr. Fyodorov was there and he took me to speak with Mikhail Gorbachev about this new Friendship Force plan. This time I really had a chance to share my ideas with him. He listened as the interpreter relayed my plan. And then he responded with '*Da, da*.' I don't understand much Russian, but I didn't need an interpreter to know he meant 'Yes, yes.' After so many years of hearing only '*nyet*' from Russians, this was music to my ears."

But how would the Russians respond to the Friend-To-Friend program? Would they, too, say *da, da*. Vladimir Ulyanov was not certain. Here is part of what he felt, as later reported in *Friendship* magazine.

"Year 1991. Russia is shocked by a decrease in production and the closing of plants. We feel disillusionment and uncertainty. For the first time in many years people face fear of unemployment and lines for bread.

"August 1991: The *putsch* (coup attempt) shook the whole country. After three dramatic days, there was victory for freedom and people. After the victory, there was a period of destruction of the old system, its monuments, and the KGB and police offices. Most Russians were tired of everyday problems, tired of revolutions and of demonstrations. They wanted stability, guarantees, support, warmth and friendship.

"By October, we expected Friendship Force groups from Marshalltown and Des Moines, Iowa. We were excited and scared at the same time.

"How will it work out when a 'stranger' will stay with our family? Will we be able to find a common language? The mountain of doubts fell off our shoulders at the moment American 'strangers' came off the bus. The gloomy faces of Muscovites blossomed. Flowers, smiles, handshakes and hugs pushed the last doubts from our hearts," Vladimir said.

"Then we had another serious test in December when Wayne Smith presented a surprise: a grandiose "Friend-to-Friend" program. Every week a group of thirty ambassadors of Friendship came to Moscow to share for a week the lives of a Russian family. They were coming to show support for us and to make friends.

"We were inspired and excited by the idea and the scale of the program, but we were confused about where to start and how to transfer wonderful words into real life.

"We placed a small piece of information in the morning newspaper on Tuesday, and by six p.m. that day, four hundred volunteers came to our office and within three weeks we had more than three thousand application forms requesting to host Americans. We did not expect that."

Meanwhile, Dave and I gave no thought about traveling to Moscow at any time, much less in winter. I was working hard to complete extensive research on a book and felt that I could not afford any delays. On a bright cold Sunday morning in December 1991, the Reverend Wayne Smith was in the pulpit at Big Canoe Chapel. He told the worshippers that he and his wife Carolyn and their daughter Susan were moving to Moscow in January to live there for a year. (Susan Smith was already working for The Friendship Force.) He passionately described the plight of the Russians and told of the very fragile state of the country's economy. Wayne Smith was determined to do everything in his power to insure that the Friend-to-Friend exchanges would go as planned and he explained that this was a major reason they were moving to Moscow in the middle of winter. "Come by to see us when you're there," he said, and I laughed with the rest of the congregation.

Suddenly, Dave whispered to me and said, "Let's go in February."

"Sure," I said sarcastically, thinking he was joking.

He was not.

We left on Valentine's Day, but I was not thinking romantic thoughts and I admit, my original misgivings lingered heavily on my mind. As our plane made its way across the Atlantic, I was having a long conversation with myself while Dave slept peacefully.

I pondered the question as to why I, who almost froze to death watching the movie *Dr. Zhivago*, would voluntarily agree to travel to Moscow in February? This nagging question was on my mind as crystals formed on the windows of the jet, hinting at the polar conditions we were likely to face when we landed in Moscow on February 15, 1992. We, along with twenty-one other Americans, had each agreed to deliver one hundred pounds of food staples to families in Moscow. We had further agreed to live in Russian homes as ambassadors of The Friendship Force. I was pleased that The Friendship Force would soon be formally nominated for the Nobel Peace Prize and I was happy to be a part of such a noble idea, but...Russia...in winter?

As the plane headed down through gray clouds toward Sheremetyevo International Airport, we got our first good look at the starkly white landscape below. I shivered and braced for icy weather, however, the first chilly greeting did not originate with the elements: it came in the first slow-moving queue when it was my turn to face the uniformed passport control officer.

The sullen young man snatched my entry papers and stared at me as if to say, "Surely, you don't expect a shrewd spy spotter like me to believe you and this younger, long-haired person in the passport photo are one and the same?"

Obviously my clever disguise as a middle-aged woman from an unmapped—and no doubt fictitious—Georgia village was not about to fool him. Not if he could help it. He stared some more. I contemplated Siberian *gulags* when he telephoned someone and carried on a conversation punctuated by a lot of loud *nyets*. He hung up the phone and abruptly shoved my passport and visa thorough the window and reluctantly waved me through. I smiled at him in relief and was rewarded by another scowl.

The encounter with the official did nothing to lift my spirits or change my ideas about "the evil empire," but then the queue abruptly ended and people spilled into an open area. Waiting there were our shy, but smiling Russian hosts who held placards bearing our name. A tall man and a pretty woman in a white fur hat held a sign with our names imprinted. Soon Yuri Gladkey and Irina Demianova took us under their protective wings and before we knew it, our luggage and two hundred pounds of food were stored on the bus.

Moscow: A Gloomy Giant

As we rode through the huge city, we peered at the somber sprawling, landscape of white snow, black tree skeletons, gray skies and grayer buildings and brown slushy streets and sidewalks everywhere. It was like looking at a photo album filled with sepia toned prints. After more than an hour, we arrived at Yuri and Irina's tiny apartment where we met their only child, a delightful nine-year-old boy named Alosha, and his equally delightful pet, Kusha, the cat

Yuri and Irina   **Alosha and Kusha the cat.**

The apartment was on the fifth floor of a standard, drab building, identical to all those around it. The foyer and small elevator were dark, dirty and sour-smelling, but their four little rooms were more personal and a lot cleaner. Nevertheless, they were decorated in monotonous tones: brown flowers on the peeling wallpaper; brown designs on the curtains; brown coverlets on the beds. The Muscovites have surely cornered the world market on brown dye.

Cold Weather; Warm Hosts

Our learning adventure started with our host family. Irina, age forty-five, is a mining researcher who enjoys art and literature. Her husband Yuri, fifty, is an electronics engineer and computer expert. Alosha is in the fourth form in school and enjoys sports. Kitty Kusha enjoys playing with Alosha and with anyone else who will join in. Yuri and Irina both work and their combined monthly salaries equal fifteen dollars. We saw a lot of food in Moscow, but prices have skyrocketed while salaries increased only marginally. Muscovites eye the food longingly, but they simply can't afford it. Irina was gone each day while Yuri served as our teacher and guide. We first thought she was working, but we later realized she was standing in long lines to buy provisions for our dinner. The long lines form for occasional "cheap" food each time a few items appear briefly in government shops. We were told the longest lines were for cheap wine.

Ballet and Burgers

Irina, Yuri, Alosha and Kusha were all cheery contrasts to their surroundings. Yuri and Irina had exhibited reserve at the airport, but when we reached home we were soon laughing and trying to communicate through pantomime, phrase books and dictionaries. For the next week, they saw that we got a crash course in daily Moscow living, plus a taste of history and culture. They were successful, although we spoke only a few words of Russian and they spoke about the same amount of English. Somehow they managed ballet tickets and fares to the Pushkin Museum. We responded by treating them to dinner at the world's most famous restaurant: McDonald's. It was a happy exchange. As we looked at the wonderment on Alosha's face when we entered the restaurant, it made our hearts sing and ache at the same time. We thought about how much our children and grandchildren take McDonald's as a normal part of life. Our hosts had never entered the land of Golden Arches. After all, our meal cost as much as half their combined monthly salaries.

First time at McDonald's for Yuri, Irina and Alosha

Equality in Russia

We were shocked to learn that Yuri and Irina's advanced degrees did not mean they earned more than a factory worker or laborer. The communist theory means that for everyone to be equal, earnings must be equal. "This makes us all equally poor," one Muscovite admitted.

When Dave asked Yuri why he bothered to get an engineering degree when he could make the same salary in a factory and with less effort, our host was perplexed. He mulled the puzzling question for a moment and said in shorthand English, "I not like factory."

Moscow By Metro

On our second day in Moscow, Yuri introduced us to the Metro. Moscow's population is estimated at nine million and most travel by subway trains, giant bulimic beasts, constantly swallowing up mouthfuls of people only to disgorge a similar mass of fur-clad Muscovites , upholstered in their woolliest winter layers. When train doors open they slam shut again in less than thirty seconds. Trains roar through stations every minute or two. Running for trains while wearing twenty pounds of heavy clothing makes after-work jogging an unnecessary pastime for most Russians.

Muscovite Mushrooms?

Russians learned long ago what most army privates quickly discover: it is unwise to call attention to oneself. Moreover, they know it is especially unwise to outshine anyone else. An English observer once noted that communism made mushrooms of everyone. When pressed by a Russian to explain the comment, he said: "Why, it's simple, old chap. Your government keeps you in the dark, feeds you a lot of manure and when a head pops up above the ground, they chop it off!"

We saw a changing system with heads beginning to cautiously pop up without being chopped, but seventy-five years of communism, added to centuries-long struggles against cruel rulers from within and invaders from without have left the Russian people wary. Ancient Russian proverbs reflect this attitude: "God is too high and the tsar is too far," says one proverb. "If only one evil woman lived on earth, every man would claim her as his wife;" "Light a candle for the Devil, too—you never know; "The little one is too small; the big one is too big; the medium one is just right—but I can't reach it" or "Fear life; not death."

Negative attitudes among ethnic groups have been slower to change. We heard a story about a Jewish woman who feared a return to the old purges and persecutions of the Stalin era. Her son wanted to be a physicist , but she begged him to become a doctor until he relented and enrolled in medical school. Her reasoning was that when Russian Jews were all taken to the camps someday, he would be spared because "they will need doctors." This tortured logic didn't seem abnormal against the backdrop of communism's past. Even friendship is a novel idea for many Russians. Not so long ago, friends and informers were difficult to tell apart. Friendships, like entry papers, needed much scrutiny and forgeries of either could prove hazardous to one's health.

A People of Great Contrast

As the week passed, our prejudices began to fall away. We could testify to the bitter cold of a Russian winter, but we had also learned that many Russians are warm, courteous, hospitable and generous with the little they have. And yes, it is true that many Russians are fond of drink, but it is also true that many, like our hosts, drink moderately, if at all. Are they all smokers? No, our hosts did not smoke. Yes, it is true that many Russians have not been to a church service in their lifetime, but hundreds of thousands are now flocking to crowded services in those churches which have reopened. Scaffolding on many other church buildings hints at an all-out religious revival. (Ironically, the only lines longer than those for cheap wine were those to get in the Baptist Church services.)

Tough People in Troublesome Times

Life is hard in Moscow; winters are cold and lines are long. The ruble as a currency fluctuates wildly and is nearly worthless outside Russia and the other republics. Even GUM, the huge state department store, has many shops where only US dollars and other hard currencies are accepted. The distribution system is a shambles; the housing shortage acute. Twenty percent of the people cannot get adequate housing. This has led to communal life with three families often sharing an apartment. Each family has its own room and they all share the kitchen, corridor and toilet. Many Russians still harbor a deep uneasiness about the West, but many more welcome what the West has to offer.

Irina and Yuri asked dozens of questions about our lives and confessed their lifelong dream was to visit America. We found the Russian people and their culture to be like the painted wooden eggs they exchange at Easter—eggs which nest inside each other, growing more gorgeous as they grow smaller. The closer we looked, the more we liked the spirit of our hosts and their friends. We saw enough to realize that our friends were not atypical, but were truly representative of a strong people who have survived many scourges. From the Mongol invaders and Ivan the Terrible to the Nazi invaders and Joe Stalin, Russians have endured. They are no strangers to famines, cold, revolutions, plagues and purges, and they should not be written off now as hopeless because of this present crisis, grave as it is. After all, the Yuris and Irinas of Russia are still around while Lenin lies dead in his Red Square mausoleum, preserved, yet no longer widely revered, feared or even respected enough to merit a queue. The snowy day we were in Red Square, not a soul was near his tomb.

Yuri and Irina said of their system, "It's still a carousel: we go around and around in workday routine, but we never get anywhere. We see signs of change and we hope Alosha will someday benefit from a new system; however, we don't expect to see it in our lifetime."

When it was time for us to go, our hosts said in halting English, "We very like you Americans." We very like you too, Yuri, Irina, Alosha and Kusha, and our hope is that you WILL see new and better changes in your lifetime. And perhaps it will be the Force that makes that difference.

Irina and Yuri were later selected to travel to America in the Friend-To-Friend program. They were on separate exchanges. We hosted each for a week and enjoyed showing them our part of the world. We look forward to the time when they can come here together and bring Alosha with them. It is impossible to measure the good that flows from these exchanges, but one thing we can say for sure: At least two couples are convinced that the people in Moscow and the people in Georgia, USA, do not hate each other, fear each other or wish to go to war against each other.

It's a small step, but it's in the right direction.

In March 1992, The Friendship Force celebrated its fifteenth anniversary. With the enthusiastic support of many who had participated as ambassadors and hosts, the organization was nominated for the Nobel Peace Prize by Ed Jenkins, US Congressman from the Ninth District of Georgia. In making this nomination, Jenkins said, "There is evidence and testimony that The Friendship Force, while devoid of actual political activity, has had an influence on the collapse of the Berlin Wall, the advance of democracy in the former

Soviet Union and the promotion of peaceful solutions to problems in the Middle East and China."

Wayne Smith was nominated for another award by his alma mater West Virginia State College. The award was for the outstanding black alumnae of the year. Although Smith is Caucasian, he received the award for his mission of global understanding and friendship.

When pressed for his formula for success at West Virginia State, later as a Brazilian missionary and now as president of The Friendship Force, Smith said: "God led me to those places at the right time. there is no question about that. He uses me as a pawn on a chess board. He picks me up and sets me down beside a king, a queen or a bishop, then uses me for his purpose and moves me to some other place. It will always be that way.

More than 360 Friendship Force members from nine countries gathered in Atlanta for celebrations at the Carter Center. They were also hosted by Governor and Mrs. Zell Miller at a reception at the Governor's Mansion, and enjoyed a gala anniversary banquet at the Omni Hotel. It was time to celebrate fifteen years of world friendships

Wayne and Carolyn Smith returned from Moscow for the occasion. At the banquet, the Smiths were delighted to learn that the first two exchange directors in 1977, Alan Redhead of England and Walter Drake of Atlanta, were present.

In a letter from the president of the United States, George Bush offered best wishes for future success for The Friendship Force. He also said: "Motivated by the belief that each of us can play a role in helping to create a more peaceful world, the volunteers of your organization are making important contributions toward the growth of international understanding and friendship. By exchanging one-week home visits with families of other nations, the "citizen ambassadors" of The Friendship Force have built bridges between people—bridges that transcend differences in language and culture. Indeed, your efforts demonstrate that through people-to-people contacts, we can gain a deeper awareness of the hopes and dreams that form a common bond among members of the human family."

During the banquet program, it was announced that Helga Ponischel of Sarasota, Florida, who was presently on an exchange to Brazil, was the 100,000th ambassador. Another milestone took place at the same time: the 2,000th exchange which was between Miyagi, Japan, and Greater Orlando, Florida.

Honorary Chairperson Rosalynn Carter said: "Wayne Smith dreams big; he doesn't put boundaries on his vision. If he can dream big, I can dream big too, We CAN change the world."

Zagorsk. Russia, February, 1992

Chapter 22

Job Description For Ambassadors of Friendship

As a member of The Friendship Force, I recognize that I have a mission. That mission is to be a friend to the people of the world. As I embark upon this adventure, I know that others will be watching me. I know that through my example to my own fellow citizens and the people of other countries, the cause of friendship and peace can be furthered.
—The Friendship Force Pledge

What is it that kindles a friendship? Some think it takes ideal conditions and perfectly matched people to forge long-lasting friendships. Naturally, such unrealistic expectations are often not met and many tourists who demand ideal conditions become unpleasant travelers who gripe incessantly because the country they are in is not exactly like their own.

Flexibility and Adaptability: Two Key Words In The Language of Friendship
In February, 1991, fourteen hardy ambassadors from the Big Canoe/North Georgia Friendship Force left for England. It was during the coldest winter in years and the ambassadors' plane landed on the eve of Great Britain's worst snowstorm of the century. Moreover, the exchange occurred during the tense times of the Persian Gulf War.

Elovoyce Greer was one of those hardy ambassadors who later described the conditions in England. "Airport runways had been cleared just a few hours earlier and we had to exit the airplane down icy steps because the jetway to the terminal was frozen. It had been uncertain whether our exchange directors, Bob and Terri Gamble, would be able to get to us with the chartered coach because the snow was still falling when they left from Bournemouth at 3:30 a.m.," she said.

However, the exchange directors made it and hosts and ambassadors were quickly matched. Later in the exchange Elovoyce noted: "Not only were we received as friends in the true Friendship

Force fashion, but also embraced as comrades as we shared our thoughts about the war—and thoughts about an even greater conflict which made us allies half a century earlier.

"For Bill Maxwell of Calhoun and Bill Bellamy of Dahlonega, this was a sentimental journey of sorts, back to the area where they were stationed as servicemen during World War II," Elovoyce said. "It was where Bellamy spent two and a half months in a hospital recovering from combat wounds.

"We soon learned that these folks who took a chance on us during a bleak period in history, in the depth of winter, were warm, sincere and fun-loving and were committed to friendship at a time when the world was so in need of friends."

The weather did not stop this exchange and it did not prevent the magic that always occurs when true friendships are made. The hosts took their guests "to pubs, Westminster Abbey, Christchurch, Pool, Stonehenge, City Hall at Manchester, Wigan Pier and small fairy tale villages in between."

Elovoyce said that they "...ate Yorkshire pudding, visited pottery and china outlets, attended covered-dish dinners and were entertained by Scottish dancers. We also learned to play skittles (much like our bowling), went to a Working Man's Club where we played bingo and where beer was served in pints. We walked the Roman Wall, met a Lord Mayor and were students in a 19th century classroom.

"But the human side of every Friendship Force experience is really what sticks in our hearts and minds the most—the extending of other people into our lives. We recall the open hearts and homes that accepted us just as we are. Our mission of friendship was accomplished."

On yet another exchange, a group from Brazil traveled as ambassadors to a city in West Virginia. Two of these ambassadors were sisters and they were matched with a widow who lived out in the country. The day they arrived, the Brazilian sisters were horrified to see the home they would be living in for the next week. It was a small dilapidated house with sagging floors and lumpy beds and the only light provided was from a single bulb dangling from the ceiling at the end of a cord. Their hostess was a farm woman and she was obviously exhausted. She told her guests that she had to go to bed early because tomorrow she would have a very busy day on the farm. She explained wearily that she made a living by growing flowers to market commercially.

The sisters spent a miserable night and they could not wait until they joined the group tour the next day while their host stayed behind. The lady farmer took them to town to meet the bus and went back home to work. The Brazilians went directly to their leader and insisted that they be moved to a better home that very day.

"However," one sister told me years later, "our exchange director was a wise person with a lot of Friendship Force experience. He asked us to stay at our present home for only one more day and night. Reluctantly, we agreed and as we bumped along in our hostess' old beat-up pickup truck that evening, we were not looking forward to another night in her home.

"What a difference twenty-four hours makes! When we arrived at the farm, our hostess had prepared a lovely meal for us and she seemed rested and fresh. She took us through her large plots of lovely flowers and explained all about her work. She knew so much about horticulture and the things she told us were fascinating. She did have time for us the next day and we had the most fun! We saw a part of rural America we never knew existed and it was a beautiful experience.

Wilma Gray, an early volunteer with The Friendship Force who later became a full time Friendship Force International employee, expressed her opinion of what it takes to be a good Friendship Force ambassador: "They are those who not only complement the positive in their host's country but who represent the positive in their country.

"When our family visited a family in Newcastle upon Tyne, England, we were the first Americans to enter those homes. Our hosts, like many people in other countries, received their impressions of our country through American television. They expected my husband to be like John Wayne and for me to be like "I Love Lucy" and for our children to be spoiled. It is an awesome feeling to realize that the impressions we make are the ones which will transfer to all Americans.

Although Wayne Smith is a warm, enthusiastic man by nature, his countenance clouds and his blue eyes become flinty when he hears complaints from would-be Friendship Force ambassadors who have somehow missed the point of an exchange.

Using the "Friend to Friend" column in the second issue of the magazine, Smith wrote the following classic response to those who travel for all the wrong reasons:

"About a dozen years ago Lynn Anderson recorded a best seller titled. *I Never Promised You a Rose Garden*. The Friendship Force is going to have to play that song at our outgoing orientation sessions for Friendship Force ambassadors. From the very beginning, our organization always has said it doesn't matter *where* you go in The Friendship Force, it only matters *why* you go.

"We are not a tourist organization. We are engaged in people-to-people diplomacy. We have pointed out that it may be necessary, when placed in a home away from one's own home, even to live in an igloo in the Arctic or sleep on a dirt floor in the Tropics. Friendship Force ambassadors need to have the attitude that they're willing to live anywhere under any circumstances for the sake of gaining a friendship across the barriers that divide persons. Those barriers can sometimes be the living conditions of the new friends we are making.

"On one of the first Friendship Force visits between a Latin American nation and a city in the Northeast USA, two American women flew together to their Latin American destination. They were assigned different hosts. Jane lived in an apartment in the heart of the capital city. The family had three maids and a chauffeured Mercedes-Benz. Polly was assigned to a family fifty miles away in the countryside. There were thirteen members in her host family who shared three bedrooms. There was no indoor plumbing and Polly once took a shower out in the open under a tree with the water falling thorough a five-gallon can wedged between the limbs above her head.

"When Polly and Jane met the second night at a party given by all of the hosts for all of the guests, Polly was sorely tempted to ask her exchange director to place her somewhere else. She couldn't bring herself to do it, though. She kept thinking about "her" family and the great disappointment which they would have if she were to leave them over such a minor and transitory matter as the physical condition of their home—the home in which they lived 365 days a year. To her great credit, Polly returned to the farm with her new friends. She learned to live with the conditions and came to know that friendship isn't a matter of the hearth, but a matter of the heart.

"Prior to departure, all ambassadors are told where they are going and some of the conditions they are likely to face. No one is promised a rose garden. Some get a rose garden, as far as living conditions are concerned, but a few may be assigned to a home with a dirt floor. Some of those who get the dirt floor hardly notice it; they are too busy looking into the smiling eyes of their new friends, who are overjoyed that an American would be willing to come to their country and share their common life with them for a few days. Any other reaction brings dishonor upon themselves and discredit to the high ideals of The Friendship Force. In effect, it would be telling the host families that their home is unfit for an American to live in.

"Once a woman was a guest in an American home and after she returned to her own city abroad she hired an attorney to see if she could get her money back because the American family to which she had been assigned had not lived up to her expectations of hospitality and entertainment.

"Folks, The Friendship Force doesn't promise you a rose garden. Think twice before you sign up to participate in one of our experiences. The Friendship Force is not for everyone. But, for those with an adventurous spirit who are willing to go anywhere and who place people above places, it can be one of life's most rewarding experiences."

A Good Sense of Humor is a Must

Sometimes misunderstandings do occur and some are caused by language; however, any temporary chaos is often relieved by humor.

Several years ago, Wayne Smith recalled a few examples of the difficulty in translating our complicated English. One example was a sign in a Moscow hotel which advised: "If this is your first visit to the USSR, you are welcome to it."

In an airline ticket office in Copenhagen, someone spotted this sign: "We take your bags here and send them in all directions."

These translations point out the difficulty involved in the English language, which is the primary language used by Friendship Force volunteers. Smith says we should "pity the poor Chinese man who posted this sign outside his tailor shop in Hong Kong in an effort to lure English-speaking customers: 'Ladies may have a fit upstairs,' the message suggested. And then there was this sign posted by a Hong Kong dentist: "Teeth extracted by the latest Methodists."

And in a Scandinavian bar, another sign admonished: "Ladies are requested not to have children in the bar."

A notice in a laundry in Rome offered this interesting advice: "Ladies, leave your clothes here and spend the afternoon having fun."

Sometimes the American version of English does not translate properly in England and vice versa. One English couple directed their American ambassadors to the guest bedroom the first night of their homestay. Since the husband in the host family had to go to work the next day and the ambassadors also needed to rise early to attend a Friendship Festival workshop, the thoughtful man turned to the wife of the American ambassador and said, "My dear, may I knock you up in the morning?"

When he noticed the expression on her face, he misread her reaction, thinking she did not wish to burden him with another responsibility, so he said, "Really—it will be *no* trouble at all."

Near the end of the week, the Americans finally explained to their English friend that his question in American slang meant something far more personal than knocking on the bedroom door. Both couples had a big laugh and the double entendre became "their" joke.

When ambassador Bettye Brown of Ridgefield, Washington, completed her application to go on an exchange to Mexico, under "allergies," she wrote "yellow jackets." Bettye did not know that the pesky bees are unknown south of the border. She learned much later that when the Mexican exchange director met with the host families before the Americans arrived, he cautioned them against wearing a yellow blouse or coat because "as strange as it seems, an American woman is *allergic* to yellow jackets!"

During that same stay in Mexico, the Browns once requested to be seated in an area reserved for non-smokers. The cheerful waitress said, "No problem! In this restaurant, you can non-smoke anywhere you wish."

Once in Africa, a native stared at Harold Brown for some time and then asked, "Please tell me, sir—why do you wear your earrings *inside* your ear?" After Brown stopped laughing, he explained that the "ornaments" were not earrings, but hearing aids.

Dutch guests in a home in Georgia (USA) didn't understand something their host said in jest. The wife told them, "Don't worry about him, he's just pulling your leg." The guests quickly raised the tablecloth and looked under the table at their legs. When the hosts finally stopped laughing, the slang was explained and the Dutch guests immediately appropriated it as their very own, frequently using the term throughout the week.

Another example of how humor can diffuse an otherwise tense situation occurred when the former world heavyweight champion boxer Muhammad Ali flew into Atlanta with his wife and small child. Ali was ending a hectic schedule and the flight arrived at 1:30 a.m. Wayne Smith met Ali and his family and took them to a downtown hotel. A porter took their bags and Wayne went along as the guests were escorted to an upper floor to locate the assigned room. Alas, the key did not fit, so the porter left to fetch another.

Shortly afterward, Ali told Smith that he had an urgent need to visit the toilet. Smith spied an open door several rooms down the hallway.

He went to the door, called out to see if anyone was inside. There was no answer, so Smith turned on the light to make certain it was empty. He told Ali to use the bathroom in that suite, since it was not occupied. Just as Ali went inside, a man, obviously intoxicated, lurched out of the elevator. He gave Wayne Smith and Ali's wife and child a fierce scowl and then marched to....yes, you guessed it...the room that the heavyweight boxing champion of the world had just entered.

As the man entered, the first thing he saw was the back of a huge black man. The rightful occupant erupted in fury. He put his hand roughly on Ali's shoulder and attempted in vain to swing him around. As the drunk yelled, "Just who the !*#** do you think you are?!" Ali slowly turned to face his accuser. With a big smile, he calmly answered in that famous soft voice: "I'm Muhammad Ali...but who, sir, are *you?*"

Slack-jawed and astonished, the man backed away, stared at Ali and shook his head. As he stumbled inside the room, they all heard him say, "That does it! I really *am* gonna give up drinking this time."

––––––––––––––

Tom Eubanks of Pickens County, Georgia, tells of an hilarious mix-up due to language. "I was not a part of The Friendship Force at the time this happened, but a friend was responsible for meeting a group of Egyptian ambassadors at the Atlanta airport," Tom explained.

Tom's friend, the exchange director, had arranged for a bus to be waiting to transport ambassadors and their luggage to communities fifty miles north of the city. He asked Tom to go to the gate and meet the Egyptians while he checked to see if the bus had arrived.

Everything went smoothly, but while Tom and the ambassadors were waiting for luggage from their flight to appear on the carousel, the leader of the group, Mrs. Boussaina Farid, approached Tom and told him that everyone was very thirsty. Tom told her they would stop on the way and get something to drink. That wouldn't do; they wanted to purchase soft drinks right then.

Tom reluctantly escorted them to a snack bar and waited while they all purchased large plastic cups of Coca Cola.

They returned to the baggage claim area to wait for their luggage. Mrs. Farid approached Tom again and said, "Mr. Eubanks, we have a question."

"I'll try my best to answer," he responded.

"Can you tell us why they put so much ice in these drinks?"

Wanting to be as truthful as possible, Tom decided to admit that the more ice in the cup, the less room there was for the cola. As tactfully as possible, he said "Well...first of all, it's the...*profit motive.*"

Mrs. Farhid opened her eyes very wide and backed away. She whispered his answer to the others, who also seemed a bit astonished. Finally, she stepped forward again. She cleared her throat and looked around a bit nervously. Then in a hushed voice she said, "Mr. Eubanks, can you please tell us just what the *Prophet Moses* has to do with our drinks?"

When Dave and I were in Tbilisi, our excellent translator was a lively and witty woman called Liza. Liza's husband Robert was a charming little man with an impish sense of humor. Although Liza's English was almost perfect, Robert was struggling to learn a few phrases. Gregarious by nature, Robert was often frustrated when he could not communicate without his wife's help.

One morning Robert showed up in a very jolly mood. He told us haltingly that he had "learned" some English. "Today," he said confidently, "I speak English!" Then he balanced on tiptoe for a moment, sighed deeply and began to recite every English phrase he had learned the evening before, not by meaning, but by rote: *Good morning, my dear! Good-night, my darling. May I have this dance? I am most honored to meet you.* **Shut up Robert!**

We broke into laughter over his last phrase and after we regained our composure, by gestures and pointing, we asked Robert who taught him these wonderful English expressions.

Finally, Robert understood. He beamed with pride and said in fractured English: "Liza, my vife. She teached me."

The New Zealanders are known for their wry humor and one Friendship Force ambassador, reported this message inscribed on a plaque in his New Zealand hosts' home:

Guests must arise at 6:00 a.m.
We need the sheets for tablecloths.

Friendship Force ambassador Anne Skelley of Southwestern Virginia recalled that in 1992, the fifteenth anniversary of The Friendship Force, each exchange during the year was given a title. For example Anne's club was assigned an exchange called "Nature Lovers Exchange to New Zealand and Australia".

"Imagine the giggles this produced in our host countries since 'nature lovers' in the lands 'down under' means *nudists*," Anne said.

On a more poignant note, Inger Rice of Virginia, recalled the time when two Friendship Force ambassadors were hosted in a home where only the husband spoke English. Early in the exchange the ambassadors asked permission to telephone their adult children to let them know they had arrived safely. Each time, before bidding their children good-bye, the ambassadors told them that they loved them.

Shortly afterward, their host said something in his language to his wife. She burst into tears and left the room and her husband hastily followed. The puzzled ambassadors were very concerned, fearing they they had inadvertently said or done something to offend.

When their host returned he smiled and told them not to worry. "You see, from the time my wife and I were small children, our marriage was arranged by our parents," he explained. "It is an old custom which I resented. Nevertheless, I now value my wife who has many virtues. On impulse, I followed your example and told her I loved her. It was the first time she ever heard me say those words."

"When in Rome do (somewhat) as the Romans do."

Another incident involved a teacher from West Virginia who was very excited about becoming a Friendship Force ambassador to an European city. She was new to The Friendship Force and was naturally a little bit anxious. She had been assured that she would be matched with a woman who shared her interests and who was from a similar profession. When the ambassador arrived, she was met by an attractive woman about her age. The first day was a day of rest and on the second day, the European remembered that all hosts had been asked to take their ambassador to their workplace. It was about 10:30 or 11:00 p.m. on the second day when she said to her guest, "Well, it's time to go to work. Let's go!"

The surprised West Virginian said, "Don't tell me you have to you teach at this hour!"

"Teach? Well...you might call it that," she laughed. "Let's go."

The American was very puzzled and perplexed. "Where are we going?" she asked.

"We're going out on the street," was the reply. "I'm a *prostitute*. Aren't you?"

Of course the American was very embarrassed and explained that she was a school teacher and had been led to believe that her host was of the same profession. The story could have ended with the American storming out in anger and demanding to be taken to another home. Although she was taken aback, this was not the ambassador's response. She remained in the home because she genuinely liked her new friend, in spite of her profession.

However, the ambassador never went to work with her new friend and she's still trying to find out who in her local club decided to "match" her with the European "teacher."

Good Ambassadors Value Faces, Not Places

Another experience involved an early exchange, one where ambassadors signed up without knowing their destination until the final briefing. An exchange from Costa Rica to the United States was announced. The Exchange Director was Juan Edgar Picado, who started the first club in Costa Rica. Before the envelope was opened to reveal their destiny, he asked the assembled ambassadors, "Where do you think you're going in the United States?"

Some guessed New York, others, San Francisco and some said Orlando, but the answer was, "You are going to *Pocatello, Idaho*."

"What! Where? You mean we've paid our money to spend ten days in Pocatello, Idaho?"

There was a bit more grumbling, but go they did.

The next year, Wayne Smith was in Costa Rica. He told the same group that he remembered that when he was there a year earlier there was not a lot of enthusiasm about their destination. "I told them I had been thinking about where they might like to go this year," Smith said. "I quickly added that I could assure them that it would NOT be Pocatello, Idaho".

"One man jumped to his feet and yelled, 'What do you mean it's not Pocatello, Idaho? You told us we could have a reciprocal exchange and that we could go back to the same destination for the second time. I WANT to go back to Pocatello, Idaho. In fact, I insist on going there," he said.

A stunned Wayne Smith asked the man why he was so adamant.

"Last year I was in the home of a potato farmer," he explained. "I admit, the first couple of mornings were strange. They'd get up at 4:30 or 5:00 a.m. and they'd get me up, too. They were farmers and I understood them, because I'm also a farmer. We'd go out and shovel manure until about 7:30 a.m. and come back in and have our breakfast. Now, it's fertilizing time again back in Pocatello and my friends are waiting for me. I want to go back there and help them shovel manure. They *need* me," he said proudly.

Chapter 23
Friendship: A Space Where Change Can Take Place

...hospitality...is primarily the creation of a free space where the stranger can enter and become a friend instead of an enemy. Hospitality....is not to change people, but to offer them space where change can take place. Hospitality is not a subtle invitation to adopt the lifestyle of the host, but the gift of a chance for the guest to find his own.
—Henri Nouwen.

Friendship is evidenced through hospitality and hospitality just comes naturally for most Friendship Force members. However, friendship-generated hospitality becomes a remarkable thing when it creates "a free space where the stranger can enter a home and become a friend instead of an enemy." This is the real test of the force of friendship, a test that passed scrutiny during the first Friendship Force exchange ever between Arabs and Jews in July 1990.

Elias Jabbour has already been introduced in chapter ten, but more needs to be said about this intense man with dark lively eyes that flash with passion and determination. Perhaps it took someone like Jabbour to drive the first nail in the shaky bridge of friendship reaching across the troubled region we call the Holy Land. You see, Jabbour can be described by very conflicting names: he is an Arab—a Palestinian—an Israeli ...and a Christian.

Elias Jabbour and Wayne Smith, two extraordinary men of peace, became instant friends the day they met and Jabbour happily assisted in the formation of The Friendship Force of Shefar'am. This club had hosted American clubs in years past, but in July 1990, an historic exchange took place when Shefar'am hosts opened their doors and their hearts to members of Kiryat Ono, Israel club. On August 25, 1990, the Kiryat Ono club reciprocated by hosting members of the Shefar'am Club.

Elias Jabbour and his friends waited anxiously in the hot July sun. They were expecting a bus bringing Jewish ambassadors from Kiryat Ono, Tel Aviv and Ashkelon. Finally, the bus arrived at the square in

Shefar'am, a city dating back three thousand years. Stepping out onto the narrow cobbled street, twenty-four nervous Jewish ambassadors, squinting in the bright sunlight, were received warmly by their Palestinian hosts. Girls from the House of Hope presented corsages of red and white flowers to each ambassador.

Hosts and ambassadors gathered in the large vaulted hall of the House of Hope where the guests were welcomed. Banners displaying words of welcome in Hebrew and Arabic festooned the walls. Yehuda Levy and Moshe Gazit spoke a few words on behalf of the Jewish group. Time was allowed for people to meet, enjoy refreshments and chat before ambassadors were paired with their hosts for the day.

At the end of the exchange, a beaming Elias Jabbour said, "I don't know what happened in the homes; I can only guess. But whatever happened must have been wonderful, judging by the smiling faces when everyone again assembled at the House of Hope. The Jewish delegation expressed gratitude for the hospitality they received and the hosts responded, expressing warm feelings for their new Jewish friends.

"My heart was glad," Jabbour said. "It has been many years since four different religious communities lived in peaceful coexistence in my ancient city. I hoped that today the first step was taken to restore that same peaceful time once more. Whatever the future may hold, I was certain that I had witnessed something very special that day.

"Six weeks later, we received an invitation for a reciprocal visit from the Kiryat Ono club. We accepted. We sent twenty-four ambassadors from Shefar'am—youth, children and adult couples were all represented," Jabbour said. "We were very impressed when the Mayor of the town turned out to greet us. We visited with our hosts at the Labour Club during a short formal reception.

"Once again, at the end of the exchange when we were assembled again at the Labour Club, Palestinian families shared beautiful memories and deep impressions of the wonderful hospitality of their Jewish hosts. It seems that the hosts not only competed with the hospitality offered earlier in Shefar'am, but they exceeded it!

"As we were waiting there, Jews and Palestinians alike suddenly became quiet. All eyes were on Jewish children and Palestinian children playing happily together. There were no barriers of any kind separating them because they had not learned to hate," Jabbour said with much emotion. "We should not forget that these exchanges took place in Israel when tensions and confrontations were far more common than peace and understanding. The most significant thing....was that these exchanges proved to the world that in spite of the tremendous difficulties we face, our people are ready to break through the barriers of hatred and overcome hardships to pave the way for friendship and for peaceful human interaction as an alternative to distrust, hostilities and wars" Jabbour said. "I agree with my friend Wayne Smith who says we must once again make our region 'The Holy Land' instead of 'The Horror Land.'"

Nina Bahar, writing about the exchange from the Jewish club's viewpoint, said "...we were welcomed warmly in Shefar'am. Yehuda Levy, Moshe Gazit and Elias Jabbour all praised the feelings of friendship and closeness between the two ethnic peoples who live on the same piece of Holy Land and who have, whether they wish it or not, the same joint destiny."

Bahar noted that the exchange made the two groups realize that "if we, as Friendship Force representatives, were willing to go around the world to make friends with people of different cultures, traditions and ways of thinking, then why should we not begin to do the same on our own doorstep. Where is friendship needed more than in our tumultuous and dangerous area, in this country that has ...developed and done so much and that has known so many wars."

Bahar told about hosts and ambassadors who had lunch in private homes during the day-long exchange. "Over the tables, hearts opened, hands reached out in friendship; prejudices were forgotten and very close relations began to develop. Arab hospitality is well known and we enjoyed all of it."

Bahar also spoke movingly about what happened when the reciprocal exchange brought Palestinians to Kiryat Ono. "As soon as they left the bus, we all fell into each other's arms," she reported. "Embraces and kisses were the first contact. These were happy faces because now we were old friends. Then we dispersed throughout Kiryat Ono, Kfar Azar and Ramat Et'al where Jewish families hosted their Arab friends. Jewish hospitality and warmth also are well known."

Twin sisters Mary and Martha Pace were introduced to Elias Jabbour and the House of Hope when they participated in the Atlanta-Israel exchange in 1991. In March 1992, the sisters went back to the House of Hope, this time to volunteer their services for a three-month period. The sisters kept busy organizing files, handling correspondence, typing articles for publication, updating form letters, preparing copy for the newspapers, affixing stamps and labels to 1,400 envelopes for mailing the newsletter and serving as hostesses to many visitors.

At the end of their work, the twins commented: "Our experience at the House of Hope has strengthened our conviction that the type of person-to-person diplomacy practiced by Friendship Force ambassadors and hosts can have a strong influence on bringing about a more peaceful world."

Marie Haisova, a writer, lived in Prague, Czechoslovakia. In 1992, she wrote a witty and honest account of her first Friendship Force experience. She and her husband had never traveled, "thanks to the Communist system." She said they were led to believe that they lived in Paradise together with all the eastern (Soviet) countries and that all countries west of Czechoslovakia were "imperialist devils."

Mrs. Haisova's Czechoslovakia was cobbled together after World War I from provinces of the defeated Austro-Hungarian Empire. In 1989, Czechs and Slovaks rejoiced in their victory over forty-one years of communist rule. Their victory was a bloodless triumph dubbed the "Velvet Revolution," a peaceful revolt led by the chief intellectuals of the country.

In May 1991, the Haisovas were visited by Pavel Faltysek, a friend. He asked them if they would consider hosting some Americans who were coming to Prague with The Friendship Force. He told the Haisovas that the organization was a wonderful way for people to really get to know each other and to build a bridge of understanding so friends could cross back and forth at will.

Marie was enthusiastic, but her husband was totally against the idea. He told his wife that he was not excited about the prospect of having people from a foreign land, speaking a foreign language, coming to live with them in their small apartment. He said, "I know everything from books and from movies. I can imagine everything. I have my own fantasies. I don't need more experiences." Marie was unmoved. She wanted to host Americans.

"My husband's second argument was taken from the famous German philosopher Immanuel Kant. Kant lived all his life in Konigsmark; he never left this small town yet he was the founder of an important new philosophical direction. And he did all this without traveling. He appreciated two things about the world—stars in the sky above him and moral law within himself. His writings convinced my husband that all our happiness comes from within ourselves," Marie

Haisova said.

But Marie prevailed and in September 1991, they welcomed the first Friendship Force group to Prague. The people who were hosted by the Haisovas were Ann and Gene Johnson from Winston-Salem, North Carolina. The open door of hospitality at the Haisovas small apartment created a big space for friendships to grow.

"What we had imagined two years ago was so different from what we experienced when the Johnsons arrived," Marie said. "We had a wonderful time with them in Prague. They are marvelous people."

The Haisovas traveled to the USA in 1992 to visit their new friends. Marie wrote to The Friendship Force from their hosts' home. "We knew the USA only from communist advertisements which told about the troubles that you have. And now we see a beautiful country, houses in the parks and gardens and such friendly, open and sincere people! Flying over in the airplane, we could see how the earth is small and that after several hours we could visit another continent. Thanks to this personal experience we understand better our responsibility for saving life on this planet. Thanks to The Friendship Force we have enriched our lives with the knowledge of new friends, new countries and new understanding. This awareness we could never learn from local experiences or great books.

"Thanks to The Friendship Force for broadening our awareness. Thanks to Ann, Gene, Bill, Betty, Nancy, Martha, Buck and many other friends that we have met and for others that we hope to meet. We learned more during several days here than we could have learned in forty years from books alone."

(On New Year's Day, 1993, the union called Czechoslovakia dissolved, becoming the Czech Republic and the Slovak Republic. The "Velvet Divorce" was not good news for everyone, but the wiser Czechs and Slovaks had seen what happened to their neighbors in Yugoslavia and were relieved when their separation was a peaceful one.)

Chapter 24
Friendship In Action

*It is one of the most beautiful compensations of this life that no man
can sincerely try to help another without helping himself.*
—Ralph Waldo Emerson

As friendship after friendship built connecting bridges, it became
apparent that some of those bridges needed extensions and extra
fortifications if they were to last. Rosalynn Carter made reference to
one such need when she spoke at the fifteenth anniversary celebration
of The Friendship Force in 1992.

"The purpose of The Friendship Force is expressed in our motto,"
she said. "That was Wayne Smith's vision from the beginning. We
have seen that dream come true."

Then she challenged the delegates to do something about urgent
social problems in their own communities. "When you go home, get to
know one of those people in your community who is different," she
suggested. "—maybe a juvenile delinquent... or a homeless person.

"It is not easy to cross the chasm that separates us from the poor,"
Ms. Carter explained in her impassioned plea, "but I think it can be as
exciting and as rewarding as coming to know and understand those
from other nations whom we meet through The Friendship Force."

Later in 1992, Wayne Smith said that Rosalynn Carter's charge "to
improve the lives of people less fortunate than ourselves, at home and
overseas," came at a time when he, too, saw the need to take friendship
a step further. After living in Moscow, Smith had seen the challenges
facing the Russian people who were bewildered by the sudden changes
wrought, as communism was seemingly all but swept away in the
aftermath of a failed coup attempt. The new freedom thrust upon those
who had never truly known what freedom meant was both exhilarating
and scary. Smith knew that Russians and those in the former republics
were not only in need of the "basic necessities of life—food, medicine,
housing—but also for compassion, concern AND professional,
educational and technical advice from their newfound friends in the
West."

Foremost in Smith's mind was that Russia and the other republics of the old USSR were increasingly finding themselves operating in the dark as they sought to make economic sense out of a dismantled system. Smith knew a lot about Russian history and he thought of the 1917 popular revolution, which was hijacked by Lenin and his Bolsheviks. At that time, a dynamic industrial base had been established, making the country one of the world's economic leaders. (Russia ranked fifth among world economies.) After Lenin's death, Joseph Stalin took over and by the 1930s, nothing of value remained in private hands.

By the early 1970s, communism was beginning to strangle the country, like a giant, malevolent vine, slowly killing its host. New programs were touted, but productivity declined. By 1986, under Mikhail Gorbachev, real reforms were instigated, but even Gorbachev did not realize that the *glasnost* (openness) he offered to the people would hold up a world mirror to Russia and her republics, allowing the citizenry to see clearly the rotten fabric of their system as they beheld better conditions in the West. With old props removed, the whole communist structure—the Iron Curtain and the empire—came crashing down under its own weight.

What former Soviet citizens needed now was friendship in action. For as long as most citizens could remember, their government had programmed them on what to do in their private and public lives. Suddenly, that type of government was gone and citizens had to make decisions on their own. They also had to find a way to make a living in a new and frightening time. They slowly realized they were now playing by new rules, rules that no one had explained.

The Carters and Wayne Smith saw a need for a new kind of Friendship Force exchange. They envisioned a program which would send teams of social service volunteers to meet their counterparts in the former Soviet Union "to create long-term institutional linkages. For example," Smith said, "the director of a community food bank from Denver, Colorado, can help his or her counterparts in Russia to establish a similar voluntary food distribution center.

Smith gave other examples of recent humanitarian efforts which had gone beyond the normal Friendship Force mission:

"When an earthquake occurred in Tbilisi last year, we raised over $6,000 among former Georgia-to-Georgia participants to purchase badly needed tents and shelters," he recounted.

"When our former Board Chairman Jim Wise charged The Friendship Force members to 'become citizen diplomats involved in improving the human condition,' The Jim Wise Club Development

Fund was created in 1991 to assist Friendship Force clubs in economically developing countries.

"Through our Friend-to-Friend program established in 1991, over one thousand American ambassadors delivered forty-five tons of food and medical supplies to their Russian host communities, purchased with fifty thousand dollars in funds contributed to The Friendship Force," Smith said.

"We are now interested in recruiting teachers, health workers, child care specialists, professionals, including professionals in women's advocacy, and civic club leaders. We want your help in building a tradition of volunteerism in a society recovering from communism. Let's build upon the half million friendships already created...and now, as Bridgebuilders, let us create a better world for our friends and for ourselves."

From these experiences, a new program called Bridgebuilders emerged within The Friendship Force. Some wondered if The Friendship Force would actually be allowed to carry out this hands-on approach of taking friendship a big step further, especially in the former Soviet Union. Whatever doubts were harbored were mainly put to rest when on May 2, 1992, Moscow's famous May Day Parade included four hundred United States Friendship Force ambassadors.

Many of the Americans marched arm in arm with their Russian friends, carrying both Russian and American flags. The experience was later described as "overwhelming."

The May Day march ended in a rally where different leaders spoke to the huge crowd. Among the speakers was Wayne Smith. As he stepped forward, Smith must have thought about the many trips he made to the Soviet Union in the 1980s—days when he was constantly thwarted by a system replete with bureaucratic red tape, frightened citizens and stern laws. On this May Day 1992, Smith must have been pleased that he had endured those unfruitful times. This parade, little more than a decade after his first visit, took place when the Union of Soviet Socialist Republics had ceased to exist. Smith no longer was in Moscow to knock on closed and bolted doors.

The participation in the big parade originated with George Brown who has served in many capacities at Friendship Force International, beginning in 1983. Brown has a Ph.D. in International Relations and has considerable professional experience with various international programs. "George Brown has undertaken every job I have asked him to do," Wayne Smith said. "And he has always carried out his responsibilities expertly and timely."

However, Wayne Smith knew that new bridges wrought by thousands of Friendship Force volunteers, could quickly collapse if Russia collapsed or if disagreements between factions led to Civil War. Even without its former republics, Russia remains the largest country in the world, being almost twice as large as the United States. Smith knew that this unfamiliar freedom was a new and heady drink to Russians. He also knew that the political situation might produce a nationalist demagogue who could bring down the aspiring new democracy.

President and Mrs. Carter advised Wayne Smith that the birth of democracy amid the rubble of communism would be a difficult time. They knew help would be needed and that friendship might not be enough. The Russian people were tough, but they needed knowledge and they needed teachers to give them this knowledge. The leaders of The Friendship Force thought that the new program called "Bridgebuilders" might be part of the answer. They believed this program would unite Soviets and Americans in projects fostering democracy, free enterprise and volunteerism. They all knew it would take a strong bridge to reach the developmental needs of the former USSR republics and Russia itself. They realized that when Russian cupboards were bare, people might be eager to trade freedom for the mere promise of bread.

The Bridgebuilders program was defined as "a movement within The Friendship Force to use individual friendships as the base for strong linkages between people with similar interests." Although the concept would first be applied to the former Soviet Union, it was relevant anywhere in the world. After she returned from living in Moscow for eighteen months, Susan Smith, daughter of Wayne Smith, became the Director of Bridgebuilders. Speaking about the new program, Susan emphasized that all Friendship Force clubs are invited to propose Bridgebuilders exchanges that match a particular interest of a club or of community members. "The Bridgebuilders exchanges are extensions of the traditional Friendship Force exchanges in that they offer the participants not only an opportunity to live with a friend, but also to work with this new friend on a project of mutual interest. The Bridgebuilders approach to an exchange is also an effective way to attract new members to the club who might not have otherwise sought an international friendship experience," Susan said.

A first step was taken when a group of doctors and medical technicians traveled to Moscow in July 1992. The twenty-nine member delegation was organized by Senator Gib Armstrong, a long-time Friendship Force supporter. In the group was Ray Clark of Pennsylvania, an X-ray engineer, who was on crutches at the time. Clark quickly learned just how badly his assistance was needed. At the Russian Children's Clinical Hospital in Moscow, he found the physicians to be well-trained and talented, but they simply had little to work with—few supplies and only worn, outdated equipment.

"When they made X-rays, they were blasting patients and personnel with too much radiation because they didn't have radiation meters or test equipment to calibrate properly," said. Clark, president of an MRI imaging center and a specialist in pediatric radiology.

Clark worked to solve this problem together with his counterpart and host Dr. Kirill Vasiliev, an oncologist and surgeon at the Children's Hospital, and his wife Olga, an X-ray technician. As he worked with Dr. Vasiliev, plans were in place for the doctor and his wife to travel to Pennsylvania in November where Clark had arranged for his new friends and colleagues to attend training sessions on calibration and maintenance of X-ray equipment. These sessions would be held at Georgetown University Medical School.

As other doctors made rounds with their counterparts at the Russian Children's Clinical Hospital, they discussed the hospital's most critical needs and explored possible joint efforts to fill them. The Pennsylvania team delivered about a ton of medicine, medical supplies and equipment.

Following the exchange, Susan Smith said, "These are the kind of bold leaders needed for the Bridgebuilders program, We need many others to work on projects not only in medicine, but in agriculture, distribution, education, small business development and other vital areas."

On May 14, 1993, two groups of nurses traveled to Moscow to aid their counterparts in a hospital there. They took medical supplies as part of their luggage, including Tylenol, bandages, aspirin and other first aid supplies. They toured St. Alexis, a ninety-year-old general surgical hospital and taught classes related to new equipment and treatment methods.

Following this Bridgebuilders exchange, one of the nurses, Bonnie Hull, of Douglasville, Georgia, succeeded in building a strong bridge linking Douglas General, her community hospital, to St. Alexis Hospital in Moscow. Bonnie said she had felt "at home" with the medical staff at St. Alexis, inspiring her to initiate several projects with her host, Elena Pereverseva, chief of anesthesiology. First, Bonnie and Elena identified specific needs at St. Alexis and after she went home, Bonnie headed a drive at her hospital to collect these items. And collect they did: 270 boxes of much-needed supplies and equipment. After some difficulty and expense, a shipment was on its way in the fall of 1993. The shipment was forwarded thorough the Congress of Russian-American Aid in New York, an agency which handles medical shipments to all parts of Russia. Shipping charges were still very expensive. Bonnie has since discovered that medical supplies can be shipped all over the world through our own State Department.

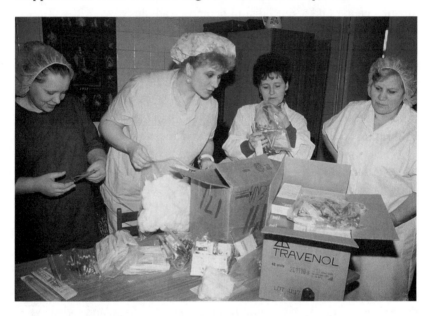

Medical staff at St. Alexei unpacking medical supplies.

Bonnie and others from her exchange hosted a group from St. Alexis in November 1993. The Bridgebuilders project created such enthusiasm that it became a hospital-wide endeavor at Douglas General. In March 1994, a delegation of twenty-three people, mostly from Douglas General, went to Moscow and were hosted by their counterparts at St. Alexis.

Bonnie's husband Jim, a surgeon, has also been heavily involved with the medical staff of St. Alexis and has introduced new techniques and equipment to the surgical staff. "We sponsored several Russian surgeons, allowing them to be able to study at our hospital," Bonnie said. "My husband taught a course in laparoscopic surgery especially for them. Dr. Yuri Panin was one of the surgeons and he later said that he appreciated being treated as an equal by my husband and the other doctors. He had feared that might not happen and he was very happy that his worries had been in vain.

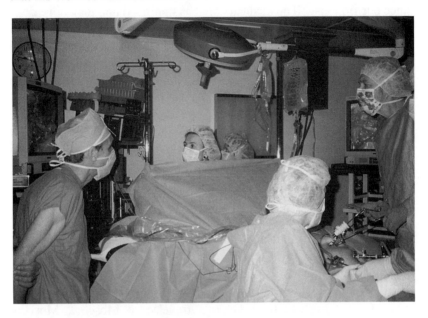

Dr. Hull demonstrating new procedures to Russian doctors.

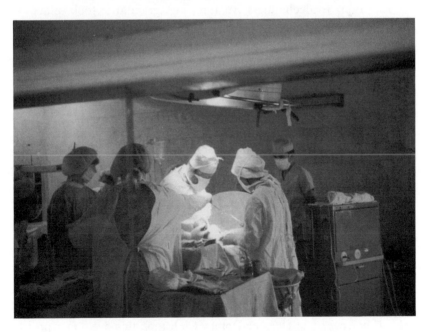

American doctors watching a procedure in a Russian operating room

"I can tell you that the friends we have made through these Bridgebuilders exchanges will be friends for life. It has also been very rewarding to see the positive changes that have been made at St. Alexis since our first visit. The medical care has improved and they have done some much-needed remodeling. The surgeons are using more up-to-date procedures and the morale of the entire staff is very high," Bonnie said.

"Two years ago I saw Senator Sam Nunn in an interview on CNN. He was talking about Russia and the relationship between our two governments. He said that Russia and the United States will stay friends as long as people at the grass roots level are friends. He said that a friend-to-friend approach makes an enormous difference. After our participation with some wonderful doctors and nurses at St. Alexis, I certainly agree with him."

Bonnie hopes that the ongoing exchange between the two hospitals can continue. As of September 1996, Bonnie's group of doctors and nurses had just sent half a semi-truck load of supplies and equipment to a city near Chernobyl.

In June, bicyclists from Georgia traveled to Moscow; Moscow bicyclists reciprocated by sending a group to the United States.

The first Bridgebuilders venture in agriculture took place in September 1993, when a group of eight Pennsylvania poultry industry representatives traveled to St. Petersburg. Each member of the delegation was hosted by an individual family associated with one of five poultry farms. Thirteen members of the St. Petersburg host families from the original exchange participated in a return exchange to Lancaster, Pennsylvania, the following April. They visited a 750,000 bird egg operation, a hatchery and a broiler processing plant. They also visited pullet and broiler operations, a feed mill and an egg processing plant.

In 1993, Bill Funk, principal of Decatur High School, led forty teachers on an exchange to Moscow, where they visited teachers at the English High School. Students with a propensity for learning languages attend the English High School. These teachers hosted a return group of teachers, including the principal of the English High School. Both groups agreed that students would benefit enormously from direct communication with each other.

Unfortunately no computer equipment was available at the Moscow school; however, the Decatur Rotary Club took this need as a project and provided funds for the Russian school, enabling the students to have a computer. Now with an e-mail link-up, the students at each school are able to talk to each other daily.

The Friendship Force's first Bridgebuilders' exchange to Russia for attorneys was a resounding success. Thirty-one Georgia lawyers participated in the exchange in September 1993, which was organized in partnership with the Institute for Continuing Legal Education in Georgia and was hosted by the St. Petersburg Lawyer's Association. Each ambassador was hosted by an attorney or judge. The participants gained an insider's view of the restructuring of the Russian legal system. They spent time in visiting the courts, prisons and local bar association. Among the results was a business partnership between the American participants and their Russian hosts formed to ensure proper representation for Russians marketing their technology and goods on the international market.

In February 1994, a follow-up exchange took place when St. Petersburg attorneys traveled to Atlanta. Many of the Russians were hosted by the American colleagues they had befriended in September. They attended a hearing before the Supreme Court of Georgia and visited other courts with their hosts. The group was honored at a luncheon given by the legal counsel at the Coca-Cola Company. They were also greeted by the dean and faculty of Emory University Law School.

In September 1994, Rosalynn Carter announced another Bridgebuilders' exchange. This exchange would link radio stations in cities in Russia, Georgia and Belarus with United States stations in Georgia, Ohio and Minnesota.

The first phase of the eighteen-month project began in November, as nine US radio staffers traveled to visit their "sister stations." US broadcasters participating in the program were WHIO, Dayton, WGST, Atlanta; WUGA, Athens (Georgia) and Minnesota Public Radio.

"We're looking to build long-lasting relationships between these stations," Harriet Kuhr said. "On a technical level, we want to establish a learning place for American stations to help their sister stations in the former Soviet states. However, there is also an important personal element. The real goal is to begin an interaction that will continue...."

Radio personality Jackie Daye of WHIO said he learned that "Jocks are jocks, no matter what corner of the world they are from. I was really surprised to learn that people bitten by the radio bug are the same everywhere. We all seem to have a genuine passion for what we do."

"Economic decline and impoverished conditions may hinder the advancement of commercial radio in the Republic of Georgia," said Jan Banker, WGST special projects director, who visited Tbilisi-based Georgia State Radio. "There was little electricity and no water or heat," she says. However, "... there is a spirit of hope that makes them believe that things will improve."

In April 1994, Glenda Willis participated in the second annual "Spring Break in Moscow," an exchange for teachers. Glenda was prepared to share her skills with teachers she met in Moscow, but she was unprepared for what she learned.

"My life-altering moment was an unexpected one," she said. "I had spent time with my hosts, toured Moscow and environs and was escorted to the circus by my gentlemanly teenage host. We were just settling down to dinner one evening and my hostess was preparing a special soup with mushrooms she had gathered and dried in the summer. Usually I am a person in control, but I was suddenly overcome with emotion and had to leave the room."

Naturally, Glenda's hostess was distressed and asked if she were ill or homesick or afraid.

It took several moments before Glenda could answer. "As I tried to grasp the reason for my emotion, all that came to mind was the word 'shame.' Suddenly, I realized that I was ashamed for all I have—all many of us have and take for granted. I was ashamed that with all our American luxuries and conveniences we often wish for more and we squabble with our friends and families over trivial matters.

"I explained to my hostess that although they saw themselves as poor, I felt the richness of their hospitality and the wealth of kindness shown to me by their friends and family.

"This was a gift I never expected to receive," Glenda said. "It is a gift awaiting all Americans who visit Russia to extend their hands and hearts in friendship. While Russia is a country in economic chaos, there is much to touch and nurture the human spirit."

Lounette Nicol had participated in the April 1993, "Spring Break in Moscow" exchange. Lounette, an art teacher to the disabled met her counterpart and host Vladimir Erokhin. The two developed an idea of exchanging their student's artwork. A year later fifty American and fifty Russian students prepared their own work to send as a gift to another student on the other side of the ocean. Some of the students were unable to draw or paint with their hands, so they used their feet and mouths to create on canvas. Each student's work was sent along with a biography. The work was displayed in Moscow and Atlanta and then distributed to the students as a gift.

A centerpiece of the Bridgebuilders' exchange programs was called "Sisters Embracing a Dream." In May 1994, The Friendship Force sponsored an exchange and conference in Moscow that focused on women's issues. Eight professional women from the US spent ten days in Moscow, meeting with women there who were involved in Moscow's fledgling organizations attempting to fight violence against women and children.

At the new Moscow Sexual Assault Recovery Center, the eight Americans helped train hotline volunteers. The enthusiasm which grew from this program led to "Sisters Embracing a Dream," a training program made possible by a grant from the United States Agency for International Development through the Academy for Educational Development. This grant enabled The Friendship Force to provide training to women from Armenia, Russia and the Republic of Georgia. These women were able to immerse themselves in classes, workshops, outings and lectures.

Fifty-four women (and one man) arrived in Atlanta on September 18, where they began a thirty-day program on the subject of violence against women and children. According to Sandye Mullins, Project Director of the training program, "The goal was to introduce the participants to American management techniques and to familiarize them with some of our methods for organizing private institutions and nonprofit agencies. In the Atlanta metro area, many of the attendees worked as interns in shelters for battered women, in rape crisis centers and at abuse hot lines.

Volunteerism and nonprofit agencies are very novel concepts in the former USSR. Networking and methods of fundraising are equally new ideas. As Sandye Mullins said, "...private organizations in the former USSR are often greeted with suspicion by a populace accustomed to the expectation that it is the government's role to meet their needs. There is much ground to cover in terms of advancing the status of women in the former USSR, especially in the area of abuse against women and children."

In the former Soviet bloc, laws against rape exist, but are rarely enforced, according to Dr. Peg Ziegler of Grady Memorial Hospital's Rape Crisis Center in Atlanta.

Dr. Lola Karimova of Moscow told the group about a fourteen-year-old Moscow girl she had recently treated after the girl was raped. "People told her she'd been shamed enough," Dr. Karimova said bitterly. "They said, 'You don't have to go for medical help....You know the system; you can't prove a thing,'"

The "Sisters Embracing a Dream" training program was deemed a big success by the leaders and participants alike. Galina Startseva, program coordinator for a women's center in Russia, said that sitting down and talking with women throughout her own country had been a revelation. "They all talk about their problems. Now I am beginning to realize the scale of the catastrophic changes that are occurring," Startseva said.

The trainees also lived with Atlanta host families and were given a big dose of American culture through these homestays. Highlights of the month-long program included a meeting with Rosalynn Carter at the Carter Center. At the end of the program, the participants traveled to Washington, DC, to meet with key representatives of women's groups throughout this country.

Tom Eubanks and his wife Barbara of Georgia, led a group of architects and historic preservationists to St. Petersburg, Russia, in October 1994. They focused on the beautiful eighteenth century architecture of St. Petersburg, city of the tsars, and were able to see first-hand the ongoing work to restore St. Petersburg's architectural treasures to their original splendor. Their St. Petersburg hosts were Valery Lukin, Chief Architect of the Hermitage renovation, and his wife Irina. It was a surprise for the Eubanks to find that the chief architect of the largest museum in the world lived in average housing. The Eubanks soon learned that what they might consider average was far above average for Russia. However, it was the people and their culture that made the trip so memorable for Tom and Barbara. "Everyone was so very kind to us," Tom said. "For example, one of the restoration architects who works for Valery surprised me with a gift. It was one of the lovely Delft blue tiles that had been made to replace those that were originally in Peter the Great's Winter Palace."

The Lukins and their friends made certain that the Eubanks and other Friendship Force participants saw as much as possible of Peter the Great's city. As fresh snow fell, they marveled at the architectural wonders built by a succession of tsars and tsarinas who ruled for over two hundred years. Tom noted that "During this period of great architecture, it must have seemed to Russians that each new wonder was replaced by yet another building of an even grander magnitude. This all stopped with the rise to power of the 'red tsar,' Nikolai Lenin. Lenin moved the capital back to Moscow in 1918. Peter the Great's city had been the capital of Russia since 1712. During World War I, Tsar Nicholas changed its name to Petrograd. Under Lenin, the city became Leningrad, a name which was thrown out by the new Russian Parliament in 1991. Without any fanfare, the name reverted to St. Petersburg. There was no protest. Most felt that St. Petersburg was the logical choice, honoring the man who created a glowing city of architectural treasures out of the Baltic swamps."

Between the wonders of the beautiful mosaics in the Church of the Resurrection, the classic columns of Kazan Cathedral and the wonders of Catherine's Palace in the nearby town of Pushkin, the ambassadors received quite a history lesson. In Pushkin, the Eubanks met assistant director Nikolai Nagorsky. He explained, "The palace was burned during the Siege of Leningrad and is now being restored. The stunning domed chapel has been almost restored to its original glory. The great ceiling paintings are being restored by four artists who are laboring to recreate *The Marriage of Bacchus and Adriadne.* The huge *Triumphe of Russia* painting has been recreated. It is the largest ceiling painting in Europe," Nagorsky concluded with obvious pride.

Their heads spinning by all they had seen and heard, the Eubanks soon learned other lessons in the home of their hosts. Barbara Eubanks recalled that they had taken along some popcorn. To their surprise, popcorn was unknown in Irina and Valery's household. "They looked at it, but had no idea what it was," Barbara said. "I couldn't explain it to Irina, so finally I told her that I would demonstrate. I found a pan to use for popping the corn. Their cat slept on top of the vent hood and when the corn started popping, the poor cat ran away. Valery and Irina were fascinated by the change in the corn after it was popped. They thought it tasted delicious.

"Slowly, we began to realize that so many things we take for granted, Irina and Valery would consider a luxury. Let me give you an example," Tom continued. "Valery had a car. There was parking somewhere around their apartment building. Each morning, hordes of people were in the main boulevard, heading for their cars or the Metro, a good two miles away. We had not seen Valery's car during the first two days, but we were curious about the battery we saw in the corner of the bathroom. The first day, we walked to the Metro.

"After we were back in their home that evening, one of their friends arrived. John was an American who spoke perfect Russian. He explained that the reason we traveled by Metro was because the night before, Valery had forgotten to get the battery from the bathroom before we went to bed. He didn't wish to disturb us by going through our bedroom to the balcony where he kept a charger. You see, each night, the battery was removed from the car to prevent it from being stolen and also to make certain it was charged during the night. The very cold winters take a heavy toll on batteries unless they are protected in this manner.

"John explained that Irina had already retrieved the battery charger so that would not be a problem the next morning. Sure enough, the battery was over in the corner being charged as hydrogen gas was pumping into the atmosphere in our bedroom. I told Barbara to leave the door ajar. All night long we heard that battery boiling away.

"At breakfast the next morning, Irina said, 'Tom, would you like to go with Valery to get the car?'"

Tom agreed and proceeded to don his coat and gloves. Valery was looking for a flashlight, but when it was located, it would not function. The flashlight discarded, Valery put a handle on the heavy battery and carried it downstairs. It was about six a.m. and the first signs of dawn streaked the otherwise somber sky. Tom assumed that the parking garage was nearby. It was not. After a long hike, they turned into a construction site and then walked across wooden boards to the edge of the Gulf of Finland. Between the road and the beach were row upon row of little buildings, similar to Quonset huts. The huts were within a large enclosed area. Tom and Valery entered the enclosure and walked down a narrow street until Valery stopped at one of the huts.

"He turned the key in an enormous lock and there was his car, parked head first into this little building," Tom Eubanks marveled. "Valery, with battery in hand, barely squeezed by the car and suddenly I realized the importance of the missing flashlight. Valery raised the hood and fumbled to attach the battery—in the dark! Finally, after some loud outbursts in Russian, he succeeded. He got in the car, inserted the ignition key and...nothing. The car refused to crank.

"By hand signs, he let me know that we had to push the car out of the garage. Not only was it a very tight squeeze to get in the garage, but there was a sill we had to push the car over, so we had to 'rock' the vehicle to coax it over that sill. It was not a tiny car, but one of the larger Russian models.

"The car finally popped over the sill and Valery quickly jumped in and coaxed the vehicle into the street. He tried the ignition several more times and finally shrugged. The car was not going to crank.

"At last, a man who parks two garages away cranked his car and came over to talk to Valery. The neighbor opened his trunk and pulled out...no, not jumper cables. He pulled out a length of nylon rope, similar to ski rope. He went to the front and tied the rope to towing hooks. Valery was about to be towed so that hopefully, his car would crank. They headed out in a cloud of smoke," Tom said. "And then an awful thought came to me. Here I am all alone, standing a hundred yards from the Gulf of Finland with the sun barely peeking over the horizon. I was pacing about nervously when Valery returned in about fifteen minutes. The stubborn engine had started. He got out and locked the building. Meanwhile, the car engine went dead. Luckily, it fired back up on the first try.

"Can you imagine? Every day Valery and thousands of others go through that same routine," Tom said. "If they are lucky, the car engine is not so cold that it won't crank. Even if the car is easily cranked, they still have to go through the battery ritual every time."

"We will never forget how difficult everyday life was in St. Petersburg, nor how heroically the hardships were borne by our hosts and their friends," Barbara Eubanks said. "The week with these wonderful people passed all too quickly."

Several Atlanta Hospitals participated in an exchange program with Hospital Number Two in Tbilisi. The educational program was sponsored by the United States Agency for International Development. The exchange brought hospital personnel from Tbilisi for educational internships at Grady Hospital. Grady personnel, assisted by USAID, have visited Tbilisi for on-site teaching of hospital management and various medical procedures.

Grady, Emory and Morehouse Schools of Medicine and the Georgia State School of Nursing have donated a large library of medical videotapes. English classes are being taught to Tbilisi's nurses, doctors and administrators.

Norma Hassinger, of Atlanta, a long-time Friendship Force member and supporter, raised funds to buy video players with monitors to send to Tbilisi so they were able to use the tapes.

Wayne Smith often spoke warmly about Friendship Force board member Joe Ritchie of Chicago. "We met in a roundabout way through Senator Sam Nunn, who knew that both of us were working in Moscow to help people with the transition from communism to free enterprise. We finally got together in Chicago and I learned that Joe was brought up in Afghanistan, the son of Christian missionaries.

"After a successful career in commodities research, Joe went to China to see if there were business opportunities. He was not encouraged at the time, so he went to Moscow. He is now in partnership with a former Communist bureaucrat in a company dealing in personal computers and software. The business has grown dramatically and provides several thousand jobs.

"If I could pick someone to take The Friendship Force to great heights, it would be Joe Ritchie. I would select him for his priceless assets of a great mind and a great heart. We are very fortunate to have Joe Ritchie on our board of trustees," Smith said. "There is no one I admire or respect more."

Joe Ritchie

Chapter 25
Ordeal or Opportunity?

Just because a person can't do everything that needs to be done, that is no excuse for doing nothing.
—Wayne Smith

Carolyn Smith was ill and after three months of a long Moscow winter, her doctor advised her to return to the United States. Wayne Smith and daughter Susan remained in their Moscow apartment. With each passing day they saw signs of great need all around them. Daily they saw a growing number of beggars "... huddled in the cold and snow in the passes of the Metro underground system."

Wayne Smith returned to the United States in early 1993. Susan Smith had returned by May of the same year. She confirmed that reports of widespread need were all true. "I would see people standing on a street corner in the morning trying to sell a single toothbrush or one bottle of vodka. Often they would still be standing there when I passed by that same corner in the evening. They would be half-frozen and the expression on their faces was completely blank," Susan recalled, grimacing at the memory. "But by June of this year, two thousand Americans will have participated in the Friend-to-Friend program and over seven hundred Russians will have traveled to America. Through these exchanges, we estimate that about seventy-five tons of food were delivered direct to Russian families. In this time of upheaval...you can't imagine what a big difference the Friend-to-Friend program has made," Susan said.

Despite positive stories like Friend-To-Friend, many prospective Friendship Force hosts and ambassadors fail to pursue international friendships. Their reasons all come from a single root cause: fear. The same is true of nations. As far back as 1981, Wayne Smith said: "The biggest problem between America and Russia is fear. That fear comes from ignorance. We know a lot about each other, but we don't *know* each other."

Smith told of an incident that occurred in January of 1982. It was the first interchange. One hundred and eight Americans traveled to Moscow, Leningrad and Kiev. "The Americans were farmers, teachers, school children, owners of small businesses and persons who were fascinated with the prospect of being able to do just a tiny bit about the gigantic problems that existed between their beloved country and the Soviet Union," Smith said.

"Many of the Soviets were far from 'ordinary.' One of the first meetings was held in the House of Friendship in Moscow. This place was a factory of pro-Soviet propaganda and we knew it when we went there. About fifty Soviet intellectuals attended a tea in our honor at the House of Friendship. There weren't too many Americans who visited Moscow in those days and we must have been quite a sight for those Soviets to see. The spokesman for the Soviets gave a greeting that was both laughable and offensive to most of us. It went something like this:

Welcome peace-loving Americans, to our beloved homeland. We are happy you are here to see for yourselves the truth of the world situation. We are distressed that your country has a warmonger for its President. But our wise and noble leader, Leonid Brezhnev, is working tirelessly for world peace. You are invited to join us in this noble effort by telling your own people the truth when you return home.

"Wow!" Smith said. "Now it was my turn to respond to this 'welcome.' I stood and thanked our host for his welcome and told him how glad all of us were to be in Moscow. Then I shocked him by asking him a question.

"Do you have a dog?" I said.

"Why do you ask?" the host replied, obviously flustered by the simple question.

"Do you have a dog?" I repeated. "I have one. His name is Snowball. Here is a photograph of Snowball. I love this little dog with all my heart. So, please tell me, do you have a dog?"

"Well, yes," the Russian responded warily. "My dog's name is Bimka."

"Great!" I said. "Let's talk about our dogs and how we grow roses and what we eat for breakfast and whose poetry we like to read. Perhaps if we start off this way as we try to know each other, we can abandon the kind of polemic which speaks of 'peace-loving versus warmongering.' You should know that all of us love our country and believe in its international policies, in the main part. When we disagree

"Do you have a dog?"

with our politicians we throw them out of office and get new ones who will do what we want.

"And frankly, with the fear that exists between our two nations at this time, we are quite delighted that our government has strong weapons to defend us from what we perceive as a threat from your government. But if we can discover that Soviets and Americans love dogs and roses and poetry, then just maybe we can learn to trust each other so that both governments can disarm."

Even today, with the Iron Curtain gone and a solid record of amazing friendships which have occurred under The Friendship Force banner, fear still plagues many. They remain woefully myopic, seeing only the possibility of a fearful ordeal looming before them instead of looking for an opportunity to befriend people.

Fear could have been used as an excuse during the first half of the decade of 1990, when there were many Friendship Force "firsts." One of those included a journey from the San Francisco Bay Area to Kyrgyzstan in Central Asia. Much earlier, others had traveled to Uzbekistan, but few Americans knew anything about the Kyrgyz (also spelled Kirghiz) people.

Even the etymology of the name *Kyrgyz* is not clear; however, most Turcologists believe it is a compound of two Turkic words: *girgh* (forty) and *qiz* (girl). According to the Kyrgyz, the name means "descendants of the forty maidens."

Prior to departure, the ambassadors learned that Kyrgyzstan was poor in oil and gas and was far away from foreign markets. The country has an estimated population of 4,500,000, of which 2,500,000 were Kyrgyz. Almost 200,000 Kyrgyz live in neighboring Uzbekistan. This mountainous nation seems to face an uphill economic battle; however, the country is reported to have sufficient minerals, arable land and industrial infrastructure to build a modern nation.

Of the five Central Asian republics, once part of the Soviet Union, Muslim Kyrgyzstan has the oldest and most explicit democratic tradition. They also have one of the few heads of state who did not rise through the former political system. Kyrgyzstan, independent since 1991, was the first of the five to abandon the ruble and establish its own currency, the *som*.

Since the middle of the 18th century, the Kyrgyz have occupied the Pamir-Altai ranges in the former Soviet Union and the Kunlun and Tien ranges in China. For centuries, the Kyrgyz were nomadic, wandering from grassland to grassland with herds of sheep, goats, yaks, cattle, camels and horses. The people often say "To be Kyrgyz is to be Muslim;" however, they have also retained a strong and ancient belief in spirits.

The Kyrgyz have long been known as superb horsemen, but their country's natural beauty may prove to be its greatest asset. Steppes, mountains, desert, glaciers, river valleys, lakes and forests offer varied and spectacular views. Pobeda Peak in the Tien Shan Mountain range is one of the world's highest and Issyk Kul in the northeast is the world's second-largest mountain lake. Opportunities for mountaineering, skiing, white-water rafting, hunting and birding are abundant.

Not really knowing what to expect, twenty-nine adventuresome ambassadors passed through Moscow's airport on the way to Bishkek, Kyrgyzstan, carrying with them twenty-four boxes of food and pharmaceuticals. Once the group arrived in Bishkek, they were warmly greeted by Jamal Tashibekova, President of the Kyrgyz Friendship Society.

Allen Shelton said in an account in *Friendship* magazine, "Every time we entered a home we were overfed—champagne, cognac, soups, breads, sausages, shashlik and a special dish of noodles and vegetables, made only by the men..

"One evening our hosts and their four children served us a traditional dinner on the floor—huge lamb bones, boiled potatoes and sausage—all to be eaten with the fingers and washed down with tea and cognac. Afterward we were flooded with gifts and the daughters sang and played stringed instruments.

"The warmth and hospitality of the Kyrgyz were unlimited!" Shelton said. He also added that the Kyrgyz "were very interested in America and were working hard toward establishing a free economy. They need and deserve help in developing joint enterprises."

Shelton said, "One highlight of our stay in Kyrgyzstan occurred when the hosts took the American ambassadors high in the mountains to picnic in the snow. The hosts heated *shashlik* and tea on a long griddle. Fuel for the fire consisted of corn cobs. Afterward many ambassadors joined their hosts in vodka and cognac toasts and then rode horses in the forest."

Shelton also reported that Kristin Gustavson, the youngest of their group, spoke Russian and was "interviewed and taped by news media in both countries." Her language skills proved invaluable when a local dentist had questions about a particular pharmaceutical he was given by an ambassador. Kristin was able to translate the information on the label. The dentist planned to use the medication to treat a very important patient—his own son.

The group went on to Uzbekistan and enjoyed visits to Samarkand and Tashkent. They were delighted with visits to a Tashkent kindergarten and a tour of one of the collective farm greenhouses, where even tropical plants were grown.

This group reached out to people in lands with strange names and they found friends, not problems. These friendships are impossible to measure, but they are a start toward halting future problems before they develop. As Wayne Smith said, "If something is not done now; we could have a recurrence of strife greater than was experienced during the cold war. While meeting the challenge of helping the people living in the Newly Independent States (NIS) and eastern Europe, we must continue to provide opportunities for people to make friends all over the world."

A group of twenty-two ambassadors, mostly from Colorado, traveled to Hyderabad in south central India. Sue and Bill Edelstein wrote about their experience and came to a typical Friendship Force ambassador's conclusion.

They said "despite the many miles and vast cultural differences, our welcome couldn't have been warmer.... Our 'family—they will always be family to us—was a three-generation extended group of eleven.

Sue Edelstein added, "Little was held back. Together we examined business contracts, discussed politics, religion, marriages and earthquakes. We picnicked; visited a yogi to consult about the timing of submission of a family member's Ph.D. dissertation and we were taken on a two-day trip to visit (and be blessed at!) a Hindu shrine at Sri Sailam. We shared some computer secrets while experimenting with their new PC; met family members; shopped and talked, talked, talked. The children, five teens and preteens, had a welcome warmth and curiosity."

The Edelsteins found their trip to be an adventure and thoughtfully noted that "India and other Asian countries have growing numbers of well-educated, intelligent people who, with the advent of the 'information highway,' will be increasingly part of our lives." They quickly adapted to the differences in culture and looked at these differences with pleasure and without even a hint of superiority. There was no bragging about the way things were done back home.

On the long trip home, the Edelsteins stopped over for two weeks in Thailand. As they reflected on the past weeks in India, and later in Kathmandu, Nepal, they came to a surprising conclusion. "Although we had a fascinating visit in Thailand, we realized that it would be very difficult for us to ever again visit a foreign culture—*without the benefit of a homestay.*

In 1993 a group of forty-two ambassadors journeyed to troubled South Africa, although a State Department advisory recommended against travel to that country. Furthermore, the ambassadors' insurance would not be valid due to possible dangers looming ahead. All signed a waiver and left on an adventure into the unknown.

Robert L. Balfour later told of this adventure in *Friendship* magazine:

"We reached Johannesburg on the day of the funeral for assassinated African National Congress leader Chris Hani," he said. The group was not allowed in Soweto so they checked into the Johannesburger Hotel in Hillbrow, located in what Balfour said was "one of the most dangerous districts in the Johannesburg area."

Mrs. Jean Young (now deceased), wife of Andrew Young, former ambassador to the United Nations, led the group. Thanks to her, the group was received at Mr. and Mrs. Oliver Tambo's Villa Rosa estate and mansion. Tambo was Nelson Mandela's law partner and became Secretary General of the African National Congress in 1955 and was Deputy President in 1958. Tambo fled to England and then Sweden after Mandela was imprisoned. He was in exile for thirty years and was referred to by his countrymen as "our African Moses." When Mandela was freed, Tambo returned..

Mrs. Tambo, a cousin to the wife of Chris Hani, took the ambassadors to the home of Mrs. Hani. "We spent two hours sharing the grief of Mrs. Hani and her three daughters," Balfour said. "It was in the driveway of this home where Mr. Hani was assassinated while his youngest daughter watched.

"Two days after our meeting with the Tambos, Oliver Tambo died of a heart attack." Balfour said.

The group traveled to Cape Town where they arrived to a musical greeting by forty bagpipers. They were then given a special welcome at the African Methodist Episcopal church. Bishop and Mrs. McKinley Young led a large group in welcoming the ambassadors. (Bishop Young was once pastor of Big Bethel AME Church in Atlanta.)

Robert Balfour said that he and Mrs. Azira Hill of Atlanta and Max Moroz of Marietta "were hosted by Donovan and Matilda Forbes and their son Lehton and daughter Adelaide. They drove us to their home in Kensington in their BMW. They live in a very comfortable three-bedroom, two-bath home with cable TV and a stereo. A Morris mini-car and a Caravan trailer were parked in their driveway.

"Mr. and Mrs. Forbes and their children are coloureds. In addition to 28.4 million blacks and 5 million whites in South Africa, there are three million coloureds," Balfour said. He also noted that because of their mixed race, they are not totally accepted by either whites or blacks.

"Mr. Forbes was a school principal when his wife was a teacher in Cape Town fifteen years ago. Suddenly they were told they had to move to a suburb called Kensington. Mr. Forbes and nineteen other coloureds systematically saved their money over a period of several years, then went to a banker for advice and a loan to begin business. The banker recommended a catering business and lent the group the balance needed to get started. Mr. and Mrs. Forbes continued to teach school while working to make a success of the business. They also bought a twelve-room hotel and a butcher shop. Theirs is a success story showing what can be accomplished when a group pools its resources and then works hard," Balfour said admiringly.

"The Forbes family couldn't do enough for us," he continued. "I've never been entertained more lavishly and Mrs. Hill, Mr. Moroz and I are hoping to reciprocate when the Forbeses make their promised visit to the United States."

However, Balfour acknowledges that South Africa is still "a powder keg." While he was there, Balfour noted newspaper accounts of shootings and warnings for school principals and hospital authorities to be "on the alert for possible hand-grenade attacks." Bombings, shootings and mob attacks are all too frequent occurrences.

In spite of the bad news, Balfour declared: "I'm betting on the future of South Africa. And I'm convinced that our mixture of white and black Friendship Force ambassadors and hosts traveling together throughout the country left an indelible impression on both whites and blacks. We were seen traveling, eating, shopping and living together and enjoying each other's company. None of us were harmed, ridiculed, embarrassed, mocked or scorned.

"It was a fantastic experience and I'm glad I chanced it."

After the people of the Republic of Georgia elected Zviad Gamsakhurdia and brought the beloved Georgian flag out of mothballs, something went terribly wrong. First the South Ossetians (in Georgia) and the North Ossetians (in Russia), always ethnic powder kegs, exploded in violence. Within weeks, civil war raged. After the 1991 coup attempt against Gorbachev, which South Ossetian leaders supported, the situation became worse. The violence and bloodshed grew. Gamsakhurdia and his cohorts holed up in a bunker and the parliament building was first under siege, then torched. In the clash, more than a hundred Georgians died at the hands of fellow Georgians. National Guardsmen then ousted Gamsakhurdia and claimed power under a military council, which promised new elections. Gamsakhurdia fled the city. Later reports said he committed suicide. When it was over many of Tbilisi's landmarks were in ruins along a mile-long strip of Rustaveli Avenue and Liberty Square.

Meanwhile, back in Georgia, USA, many in The Friendship Force who had traveled or hosted during the first Georgia-to-Georgia exchanges, were very worried about their friends in Tbilisi. Mail service in and out of Georgia was almost non-existent and the telephone service was usually equally unreliable.

In late May 1992, Donnis Bauman, one of those worried Georgians, banded together with about fifteen others and headed for Moscow, where they planned to go on to Tbilisi. "We wanted to see first-hand how the civil war had affected 'our' families since we saw them in 1990," Donnis said.

"After spending one night in Moscow, we went to the airport for our flight to Tbilisi. Upon arriving at seven a.m., we were told that we had no reservations because they had not been confirmed. We would have to fly stand-by, they said.

"We were shown to a corner of the airport filled with men, who looked rather menacing to some of us. A large TV was turned on full blast. As the day progressed, one couple and several of the men in our group were put on flights.

"By late afternoon we realized it would be two more days before we were all in Tbilisi. We were becoming desperate, not to mention tense. We agreed to put up at least a hundred dollars each to see if someone would agreed to get us out of Moscow. Our group included Bill Lamkin, editor of *Friendship* magazine, Mike Buffington, General Manager of the Jackson County Herald, Zurab, the Georgian who had come to Moscow to meet us and four others, myself included. Zurab, Bill and Mike went off to see what could be done. Forty-five minutes later they returned with the news that a cargo plane carrying used tires (black market items) to Tbilisi was making a clandestine flight about 11:30 p.m. Bill Lamkin, who had flown in World War II, checked the plane out and said he thought we should take it. That was all the encouragement we needed. We unanimously voted to go. Besides, the pilot only wanted fifty dollars each.

"The mood of the group was no longer grim. Our spirits were now buoyant and we were all talking, laughing and joking. We left as directed, down a flight of stairs, thorough a dark walkway, where we were met by a van to take us to the far side of the plane. The plane looked okay from a distance, but we weren't too sure about the driver of the van. We arrived as planned and boarded. The plane was filled with tires. There were no seats, no overhead room, only tires, with the smallest of passageways through the plane to the front. They supplied us with four folding chairs and we sat in those right behind the cabin. Bill rode with the pilot and Mike and Zurab sat on tires in the galley.

"Two hours and fifteen minutes later, we arrived in Tbilisi. For most of us, our families were still there to greet us, clutching bouquets of long-stemmed roses they had brought for us. They had been there since 3 p.m. and it was now 1:30 a.m.

"We were so happy to see each other again. They were thrilled to know that we still cared for them and loved them enough to risk such a flight just to see if they were in good health and had enough to eat. We learned that they had been very fearful for our safety, knowing the difficulty we had in Moscow. It was a jubilant reunion, reminiscent of the first exchange to Tbilisi.

"It wasn't until later that we fully realized the risk we had taken. Several weeks later, a similar plane was shot down," Donnis said.

"I'm still eager to return again to see my dear friends in Tbilisi. Maybe next time, we'll go through Istanbul!" she added.

This was a flight to remember for a determined group bound for Tbilisi.

Chapter 26
Enemies No More

━━━━━━◆━━━━━━

*Travel is fatal to prejudice, bigotry and narrow-mindedness, and
many of our people need it sorely.... Broad, wholesome, charitable
views ...cannot be acquired by vegetating in one's little corner of the
earth.*—**Mark Twain**

There have been hundreds of "firsts" for Friendship Force clubs
around the world. An important one was an exchange between
Hungary and Zutphen, the Netherlands. Peter Jahn, exchange director
of the Hungary club, said "After the Berlin Wall was torn down and
Soviet soldiers went back to their own country, our Friendship Force
club finally had an opportunity to visit our 'enemies.' We had been
taught for the last forty years that everyone outside the grip of the
USSR fell into the enemy category.

"The seven days we spent in The Netherlands proved that everyday
people are not enemies at all. We learned that like us, the Dutch people
live on the same continent and their way of thinking is much like ours."

The group from Hungary included many ambassadors still in their
teens. These young people were living away from their home for the
very first time. "All they knew about the Netherlands was that it is a
country with windmills, flowers and cheese," Peter Jahn reminisced.

The Hungarian ambassadors visited farms, factories and forests.
They were impressed by the industrious nature of the Dutch people,
evidenced by the cleanliness of the country. "The people work hard
and make a lot of effort to keep everything in order. We now realize
that we have to learn how to work hard day by day, because this is the
only route that will make us truly a part of Europe. Political changes
are not enough: more efficient work is necessary with less waste and
improved quality. We have similar technology and machinery in
Hungary, but it is not as well made. This showed us that we need to do
things differently. These lessons were very important results of our
wonderful Friendship Force experience."

The Hungarians also enjoyed Holland as they boated on scenic
canals and window shopped in Dutch cities. They were very surprised

to see thousands of Dutch riding bicycles. When asked why, a Dutch host explained, "Bike riding is a healthy and cheap way to get around." The Hungarians were impressed by the pragmatism of their hosts.

"A farewell party was held in an old mansion where the Dutch and Hungarians danced and sang songs, hand in hand in a large circle," Peter Janh said. "Our Friendship Force exchange proved that stupid ideologies cannot separate people of goodwill."

More than six thousand ambassadors participated in 274 exchanges during 1994 and in January 1995, forty-eight Siberians traveled to the United States. Viktor Kozlov of The Friendship Force of Irkutsk, Siberia, told of his impressions of Atlantans in *Friendship* magazine. Viktor, being a tour guide, paid a special compliment to those in charge of activities by saying the tours "were well-planned and scheduled" so that they were "numerous, but not exhausting."

Viktor enjoyed the World of Coca-Cola and said that Coke is now well-known in Siberia. He also commented that the CNN Center was "... quite a different thing. To most of us, CNN seemed to be the very embodiment of the American spirit of free enterprise, with its highly developed technology and very business-like manner."

Viktor wryly observed Georgia lawmakers at work at the State Capitol. "It was a surprise to me to discover—from the point of view of an outsider—how an American governmental body was similar to those in Russia. The politicians we happened to communicate with were all very charming and clever people, and one felt it would be only right to vote for them in the next election. However, the general turmoil going on during passage of a bill—when most of the lawmakers were preoccupied with something more amusing than voting—was very Russian-like."

Like thousands of other ambassadors, Viktor concluded that the most important experience was living with an American family. "My hosts, Ron and Cheryl Matson and their charming three-year-old daughter Monika, are my friends now," Viktor said. "The two weeks I spent in their home was the best time I've had in years. They were helpful, considerate and tactful. I'm very happy to have met such people."

When he rejoined his fellow ambassadors at the airport on the return flight home, Viktor was surprised to learn that his friends were insisting that *they* had the best hosts. However, Viktor remained unconvinced and is still certain that his host family was the best.

Viktor said, "I do hope that Friendship Force International will keep in touch with Siberia. There are quite a lot of people who really appreciate the idea of establishing heart-to-heart relations with the American people."

On March 17, 1995, The Friendship Force celebrated anniversary number eighteen. Mrs. Carter reviewed the remarkable history of organization and told those gathered for the celebration that preparations were underway for the day when The Friendship Force could send a group of everyday citizens to live in the homes of their counterparts...in Iraq! "Sometimes it is possible for ordinary citizens to create an environment for peace that makes it easier for governments to work out their problems," she said. "I am very proud to be the Honorary Chairperson of The Friendship Force and to serve on its Board of Trustees. Not only I, but my children, my mother and brother all have been involved actively in this wonderful program. Jimmy's mother, Miss Lillian, also traveled as an ambassador.

"Let me take this opportunity to commend The Friendship Force to any who have not tried it. And if you have, I encourage you to continue your involvement. Indeed, our motto is true: 'A world of friends is a world of peace.'"

Again, Wayne Smith was ahead of the times. He was serious about asking Friendship Force volunteers to travel to Iraq to meet with ordinary people. Smith noted that the CIA had released a report saying it was likely that over a million Iraqis would die of starvation or malnutrition in 1995.

"It is easy to be a friend to those who have no serious problems," Smith declared. "It will not be so easy to befriend those who are in desperate straits in Iraq, but few people anywhere need friends more than the Iraqis. The Friendship Force is looking for an opportune time to have its first exchange of citizen-ambassadors with citizens of Baghdad," he said. "The purpose of our first Friendship Force exchange to Iraq is simple: It is to extend a hand of friendship to the people of Iraq by ordinary citizens from other parts of the world. We have been invited to do this by the Women's Federation of Iraq, an organization not directly affiliated with the government of that nation."

Calling this first future exchange 'Desert Peace,' Smith warned that it would not be an easy experience. "But it will be one that all will remember—and relate to their grandchildren—for the rest of their lives."

David Luria, former Executive Vice President and Chief Operating Officer of Friendship Force International, was born in Hamburg, Germany. He emigrated to the United States with his family when he was only two years old. Luria tells several favorite stories so well that they are quoted here almost in their entirety.

Ambassadors from Gelsenkirchen, Germany, had just arrived the previous evening to begin a week's exchange in Auckland, New Zealand. They welcomed the chance to relax and get to know their hosts at a small restaurant in downtown Auckland.

A number of the ambassadors were in their sixties and seventies, and after a few drinks they began reminiscing about their experiences in World War II. At this point, one of the New Zealanders said he had served on a British frigate during the war and the closest he had ever come to being killed was on January 3, 1941, in the North Sea.

"We were being chased by a German destroyer," he told them. "My God, she was fast! She was lobbing shells that almost blew us out of the water. Fortunately, we were able to lay down a smoke screen that morning and we lost the destroyer in the smoke screen. Otherwise, we would have been dead!"

The German guest suddenly turned to his host and said, *Zaht vas you?* You were on that ship? I remember that battle, because I was a crewman on the German destroyer! We were so angry because you got away. I can't believe I am being hosted by the man I was shooting at fifty years ago!"

And this is just one of many incidents that occur frequently in The Friendship Force, where people are constantly discovering that peace is made—and scars are healed—one handshake at a time.

For me, as a child of Germany whose family escaped from the Nazis because of our Jewish heritage, it was especially important and moving to observe first hand how individual people, through friendship, can heal fifty-year-old wounds of war, intolerance and hatred. I was particularly struck, for example, by another incident that occurred in Orlando, Florida, in 1990.

An ambassador from Berlin—a man in his sixties—was being hosted for a week by an elderly widower in Orlando. They had a few drinks in the back yard one evening, and the conversation drifted around the one event they had in common: the Second World War, the most significant event in the lives of most men of their generation.

"'What were you doing during the war?" the German asked.

"Oh, I was a pilot on a B-17 bomber operating out of England," his host replied.

"You were? Is that so? Tell me, do you remember what you were doing on May 3, 1944?"

"No, I can't remember every day of the war," his host replied. "But wait; I have my war diary in the bedroom. Let me get it."

He retrieved the diary and sat with his German guest at a table under an orange tree as he looked through the pages. Sure enough, there was an entry for May 3, 1944.

"It looks as though we made a bombing run over a village called Zossen, south of Berlin," he told his guest. "I remember that there was a German armored tank unit based there."

And once again: *Zaht vas you?* The German stood up, his eyes filled with tears. *Zaht vas you?* My God, I was a seventeen-year old boy that night. I was riding my bicycle along the road in Zossen when the bombs fell. YOU ALMOST KILLED ME!"

The American was dumbfounded to discover that he was hosting a man he had almost killed half a century before.

Seeking to break the tension, he went over to an orange tree, picked an orange up from the ground and said: "Well, I missed you in 1944, but I won't miss you this time." And with that he threw the orange at his guest. The German caught the orange, but it broke open and spilled sticky juice all over his shirt. He laughed and immediately hurled the orange back at the American's stomach. Both laughed and cried, stared at each other and then embraced. United by a common link to a terrible event both had shared, they have since become best friends.

Perhaps the most extraordinary incident of all occurred in 1992, when thanks to The Friendship Force, seventy-seven-year-old Karl Schugart of Limburg, Germany, received back the wartime diary he had lost in the desert of El Alamein as a sergeant with the Afrika Korps fifty years earlier. The diary had been found in 1942 by Phil Andrew, a young soldier from New Zealand. For years he had tried to decipher the cryptic handwriting in hopes he could return the diary to its owner. It was not until 1992 when Phil met a delegation of ambassadors from Wolfsburg, Germany, at his home in Gisborne that he was able to get the diary translated and return it.

One of the ambassadors was Hans-Joachim Kieselbach, a police inspector in Wolfsburg, who agreed to do the detective work necessary to find Mr. Schugart. He was able to track Schugart through a priest, former neighbors, church records and relatives. He found the German veteran alive and well in Holzheim, a village near Limburg, and delivered the diary to him just as Schugart was completing work on his own personal life history. Needless to say, he was amazed and gratified and has now struck up a correspondence with his former enemy, Phil Andrew."

David Luria pointed out that these are a few stories that "demonstrate this IS a small world, after all, and that The Friendship Force IS a force of positive change. It's not just for Germans, Americans or New Zealanders: we are showing that PEOPLE with similar hopes and dreams can get along very well with each other, if they just try!"

Keiko Marui, President of The Friendship Force of Tokyo, wrote movingly about an exchange between her country and Korea. Though close in proximity, the nations have traditionally not been friendly.

Keiko said that "The anti-Japanese sentiment resulted from bitter experience in past history." (The Japanese occupied Korea after the Russo-Japanese War of 1904-5. In 1919, the Koreans staged a passive resistance campaign known as the March First Independence Movement, which resulted in serious retaliation by the Japanese government. There were many deaths and imprisonments. Korea was liberated in 1945.)

After decades of chilly relations, the Japanese Friendship Force clubs decided to bridge the divide with an exchange with Korea on March 17, 1995. Twenty-four Korean ambassadors from Kwangju arrived at Narita Airport. Keiko said "Ambassadors usually show up with a big smile on their faces and with their arms open wide, but not this time. Their stiff expressions were impressive. Most of the ambassadors over sixty years old could speak Japanese better than we usually use in our daily life. I experienced very mixed feelings that day. But, as time went on, I found we ate the same rice and drank the same tea and we began to take to one another. The guests in my home were a university student and her mother."

Keiko and her fellow hosts had a lovely time with their Korean ambassadors and three months later, a reciprocal exchange was arranged. Keiko traveled this time as an ambassador.

"To see our new friends again in Kwangju made our visit all the more wonderful. It was a very good idea to have a return exchange. This time we ran up to each other and held hands and hugged. It was quite different from the first time we met at Narita Airport. At the farewell party, singing songs of Korea and Japan as we stood hand in hand, I couldn't help wishing that both countries could someday become close in friendship."

On July 18, 1995, Ryoichi Sasakawa died of a heart attack in a Tokyo hospital. He will always be remembered by The Friendship Force for his generosity, encouragement and wise counsel.

Bill Lamkin has covered many Friendship Force stories, but one of his best involved an exchange between Pearl Harbor, Hawaii, and Hiroshima, Japan.

The story was personal because Lamkin graduated from high school in Arcadia, Louisiana, in 1938, making him the right age to go marching off to war shortly after the bombing of Pearl Harbor by the Japanese. Lamkin became a radio operator-mechanic on a combat cargo plane parachuting supplies to ground troops in Burma.

During his first months overseas, Lamkin was based in Assam province, India, noted for having one of the heaviest annual rainfalls in the world. Combat cargo planes flew despite the monsoons.

Lamkin returned from overseas on May 5, 1945, just two days before Germany surrendered. He became a news reporter in his home state. On August 6, 1945, he recalled the banner headlines announcing the atomic bomb had been dropped on Hiroshima and eight days later, another headline told of the second atomic bomb dropped on Nagasaki.

Little did Lamkin know that one day he would go back to Hiroshima and actually meet a survivor of the atomic blast.

Lamkin went to Japan because his reporter's nose smelled a good story. Americans from Pearl Harbor, bombed by the Japanese, were going to Hiroshima, destroyed by the first atomic bomb ever used in warfare. Americans would actually stay in the homes of the people of Hiroshima, just like all other Friendship Force exchanges.

When the exchange director learned of Lamkin's desire to meet a survivor of the bomb, he arranged for him to meet Fumie Katayama at Hiroshima University.

At the university they were met by two professors and several graduate students who would serve as interpreters and who were keenly interested in hearing what Mrs. Katayama and Lamkin both had to say.

First, Mrs. Katayama produced posters depicting the horror that followed the atomic blast. "Through an interpreter, I learned that she and her grandmother had been standing about 900 meters away from the epicenter of the explosion," Lamkin said. "Fortunately, a high wall saved them, allowing Fumie Katayama to live past the age of 60." (Lamkin was there in 1985. He noted that Mrs. Katayama had no disfiguring scars or skin disease problems, despite her proximity to the blast.)

She told how she and others hid in nearby mountains after the blast, but they had no idea what they had just witnessed. After about half an hour, she said, "As a survivor of nuclear bombing, I feel that I must try to convince as many people as possible—in the Soviet Union, too—that governments must desist from building nuclear arsenals."

Lamkin then told her about The Friendship Force and of the first ambassadors from the republic of Georgia who had just completed the first-ever visit to the United States where home-hosting was allowed. She agreed that this was an important step down a road toward real peace in the world.

When the interpreter told Bill that Fumie Katayama had not wanted to meet with him at first, but changed her mind because she wanted him to know how she feels about nuclear arms.

Bill said: "The agony in her voice as she told about the ordeal that she and thousands of others endured touched a sympathetic chord in me. I found myself wanting to ask for forgiveness, but words wouldn't come. I choked up. Tears began to flow and it took several minutes for me to regain my composure.

"She came and sat in front of me, took my hands and said something in Japanese. I didn't hear the translation, but the tone of her voice and the way she stroked my hands told me she understood and wanted me to feel better. She wanted me to know that I didn't need to ask for forgiveness and, best of all, she wanted to be my friend.

"Finally, I said to her, "Both Hiroshima and Hawaii suffered through surprise bombings. The tragedy of nuclear war was dramatically reinforced yesterday during my visit to the peace museum. I just had to vent to my feelings."

The next day, Mrs. Katayama attended the farewell party for the Americans and she was at the train station the next day to tell them good-bye. She had a special message for Bill Lamkin. "Next time you come to Hiroshima," she said through a translator, "you must stay at my house."

Seventeen months later, after an International Conference in Hong Kong, Lamkin stopped at Hiroshima and did just that.

Bill Lamkin said he agreed with Ryoichi Sasakawa who often declared, "The most horrible sin on earth is killing, with war being the paramount example."

Chapter 27
Vietnam: A Bridge Too Far?

◆

Never does the human soul appear so strong and noble as when it
forgoes revenge and dares to forgive an injury
—E.H. Chapin

It is not always easy to extend the hand of friendship. When The Friendship Force offered veterans and civilians of the Vietnam War era a chance to return to Vietnam, my husband's answer was a flat "No." When Wayne Smith asked him directly if he might consider it, all Dave said was, "I was there once and I didn't like it."

Wayne just smiled and said, "Okay."

Others took the first trip back to Vietnam, many for personal reasons as much as for the goal of making friends. One of those was Jill Hubbs whose father, Navy Commander Donald Richard Hubbs, went to Vietnam in 1968 and never returned. Jill was ten years old.

Now thirty-six, Jill felt compelled to go to Vietnam, hoping to heal the wounds that now-distant war had inflicted on her soul. She went, admitting that she had no idea just what personal demons she might confront there. Later Jill wrote movingly about what happened to her when she took that searching Friendship Force trip back to Vietnam.

"To my surprise, I discovered that there is no trace of war in Vietnam," Jill said. "It is a beautiful country with many special aspects. One of those is the people—something I didn't expect to discover. I arrived in Vietnam with the burden of a lifetime of suspicion, mistrust and dislike for the country that had taken my father away. I had not counted on the people being so warm and friendly and accepting of me. They welcomed me into their homes and made me feel like a special guest."

Jill told of how her father had loved children and during his first tour in Vietnam in 1964, he had taken pictures to send back home —pictures of the countryside and of the people, including many children.

"While he was in Vietnam, he spent time going to orphanages and schools. He felt sorry for the Vietnamese children because he felt they were the innocent victims of a war they had no control over," Jill said.

"When he was stationed in Saigon, he lived at the Brink Hotel while working on General Westmoreland's staff. Every day he would pass out candy to children outside his quarters. We would send peppermint candy so he could give it to the children," she recalled.

"The Vietnamese children knew his routine and would eagerly wait every day for the 'Candy Man' to return to the Brink Hotel. This daily ritual was a bright spot in my father's life in Vietnam and became a treasured memory for him," Jill said.

One of the highlights of Jill's visit was a trip to the Brink Hotel. She sought and found her father's old room. "I was able to find a feeling of peace I hadn't known in many years. I felt my father's presence there and I know he was smiling as I handed out peppermint candy to the children I found outside the building."

Jill, a teacher herself, visited a school in Hanoi where she shared teaching materials, books and maps with the Vietnamese faculty. She delivered pen-pal letters from students at the elementary school in Florida where she taught. She also took back responses from Vietnamese children.

Once she was home again, Jill shared all she had learned with her students. She showed them interesting pictures and souvenirs and even arranged a Vietnamese dinner. At the dinner, Jill wore a traditional Vietnamese costume called *alzai,* which was tailored in Vietnam.

"We listened to Vietnamese music, learned a few simple Vietnamese words and phrases and looked at pictures of our pen pals and their beautiful country...."

A Lesson In Peace

"I learned that children are the same everywhere—whether it's Jacksonville, Florida, where I live, or halfway around the world in Vietnam," Jill reflected. "When you become acquainted with a person and form a friendship, you can no longer be enemies. The children in Vietnam showed me that despite our many cultural differences and the scars of war that both countries bear, we have many things in common. A future of friendship and understanding between our countries is possible if we only follow the example of the children.

"My experience in Vietnam was very healing for me. It also had a positive effect on the Vietnam veterans from my city, who followed my journey closely and have spent hours talking with me and reliving some of their experiences in Vietnam. Many of the veterans are now expressing a strong desire to make their own journey back to the country that has so greatly impacted their lives.

"I will always have some sad memories of Vietnam," Jill admitted, "but now I have new memories that I will always treasure. Memories of smiling faces and new friends. Memories of a journey of the heart—a journey to Vietnam."

Still, no home hosting was available in Vietnam and the planned exchanges were like the early missions to the former Soviet Union. And would the government ever allow a Vietnamese delegation to come to the United States to be home-hosted? That remained to be seen, but Susan P. Respess of *The Florida Times-Union* wrote: "If the Vietnamese follow through with The Friendship Force exchange and permit Vietnamese residents to make similar trips to the United States as guests of American families, the force of friendship could only bring more healing on all sides.

"And," she added, "it would push the potential for future confrontations farther into the distance."

A Rare Glimpse of Vietnamese Home Life

Unexpectedly, reporter Julie Allinder of Atlanta's Newsradio WGST, traveling with her father Myrl Allinder over Thanksgiving, 1994, found themselves invited into a Vietnamese home. They were visiting a coffee shop owned by a photographer. After admiring some of his work on display, Julie asked if she could visit the ladies' room. She was ushered out a door and into the family's living area.

"A large bed with no mattress took up most of the space," Julie said. "On it sat five people. Others stood around the room, all completely absorbed by a television screen, beaming a foreign film that was dubbed in Vietnamese .

"Passing through another door, we entered a much larger room where a teenage girl washed pots and pans in a bucket on the floor, while several women worked to prepare the family's Sunday dinner. I asked if I could photograph them and they smiled and agreed.

"Speaking flawless English, one of the women, who later told me she was a professor at the University of Hanoi, asked me if I realized that what I was doing was virtually unprecedented. "Americans," she said, "have never been in the homes of average Vietnamese in Hanoi—ever.""

Like Jill Hubbs, Julie Allinder came away from Vietnam with a lot of memories. They both agreed that the people were what they would remember most.

Heidi Schuh also spent that Thanksgiving in Vietnam. Heidi had reservations, like the others. "I desperately wanted to go but I was very scared. I had not forgiven the people who had killed our men and tortured our prisoners.... I also had not forgiven our government for the mess they created," Heidi admitted honestly. "I knew God was taking me on this trip for a reason, so I went not with my own agenda, but with an open heart."

With that attitude, Heidi was certain to be a great Friendship Force ambassador and the results were typical. "Fortunately, I loved Hanoi. I felt welcome from the moment I got off the plane. I had not been prepared for this and it really shook me," she said, still a bit in awe. "I had almost wanted them to hate me because I was an American, but it didn't happen that way. The people were kind and caring. My three host friends greeted me with flowers and bought me clothes to wear until our luggage arrived.

"Admittedly, not everything was as sanitary as we would expect in the US, but we were in one of the poorest countries in the world. I usually just ate or drank what they gave me and prayed to God, saying 'Please don't let me get sick. I am trying to be nice and I don't want to insult them.'" (Heidi suffered no ill effects.)

After learning that Heidi would soon begin medical school, Hong , one of her hosts, took her to a hospital where he worked as an endocrinologist. "I was greeted by six doctors when we arrived," Heidi recalled. "They told me they had no X-ray machine, no narcotics and very little antibiotics and anesthesia. I couldn't believe this until I was given a tour. I saw rats in ICU and people without heart monitors or respirators. In the nursery there were no working incubators and babies had tubes in their noses made out of old tire rubber.

"I even walked into an operation with my street clothes on. Why not? They have no sanitizing equipment. I watched them saw off a man's leg with an old rusty saw. He was not under anesthesia, but was drunk and passed out. His arm was swollen and already infected where the IV was placed because he was the third patient who had used it. That's right. They use all needles at least three times before they are allowed to throw them out," Heidi reported.

Heidi came back from Vietnam a changed person and like so many Friendship Force ambassadors, she came home in a very thankful frame of mind. "I will never again sit at a Thanksgiving table and not know exactly what I am truly thankful for. I am thankful for every opportunity my parents have made for me, and I am thankful for my family. The Vietnamese lost so many during the war. I didn't meet anyone who had not lost a family member," she said.

"In Vietnam I even learned how to forgive the 'enemy' by watching them forgive me. I realized that the people of Vietnam are victims. They cannot vote their government out of office. They can only sit quietly and suffer."

Heidi said that although she and her new Vietnamese friends did not cause the war, they "...were all affected by it. The talks we had helped each of us to come to some kind of peace within ourselves. The more we talked and helped each other, the stronger our friendship grew.

"And I have The Friendship Force to thank for this wonderful gift," she concluded.

Dave and I read with interest about the Friendship Force ambassadors, including veterans of the Vietnam War, who began to travel to Vietnam. They even went to Hanoi, the oldest capital in Southeast Asia, founded in AD 1010. We heard about how they walked into the heart of Hanoi and saw the Lake of the Restored Sword. They dodged thousands of bicycles on the main avenues and poked about in narrow streets with curious names like Sweet Potato Street, Tin Street, Jewelers Street and Broiled Fish Street. Some sought out the old Hoa Lo Prison. They were Americans, mostly flyers whose planes were shot down during the long conflict. They went to the infamous prison to take another look at the place where they had spent some of the worst days of their lives.

But things were changing in Hanoi and Hoa Lo prison was to be torn down. News reports said it would become a luxury hotel. Former POWs chuckled at the irony and said they would bet that the new hotel would *not* be called the Hanoi Hilton. It was amazing to them that they were in Hanoi and free to travel about as they pleased. After all, the war ended only two decades earlier.

When the first Friendship Force visitors left Vietnam, most predicted it would be another two or three decades before the ruling communist government allowed any Vietnamese to travel to America for any reason, much less to be hosted in private homes.

However, in May 1995, word came that a Friendship Force delegation of twenty Vietnamese was coming to Georgia in June.

Colonel Wayne Waddell (USAF retired) outside the Hoa Lo prison.

About half were musicians, singers and dancers in a folk music group. Nothing was said about the others.

For us, the news brought back a host of memories, especially for my husband Dave.

On January 14, 1968, Dave Terrell was on his ninth mission during a second tour of duty in the Vietnam. He was a navigator on a US Air Force EB-66, providing electronic countermeasure support for F-105 fighter-bombers by jamming enemy radar.

On this fateful day, Dave's aircraft was suddenly ripped by an enemy missile. The crew had no choice but to eject.

After evading the enemy for two days, Dave was captured at gunpoint and transported to the infamous Hoa Lo prison, sarcastically called the "Hanoi Hilton" by American prisoners of war. From the time he landed in the dense bamboo jungle, Dave Terrell would not enjoy freedom again for five years and two months.

The long ordeal of captivity, harsh treatment and deprivation was physically draining, but Dave's love for his country, his strong character and his faith in God remained intact.

As Dave and several hundred fellow prisoners were shifted about from year to year among various dreary prison camps, they never dreamed they would ever want to return to Vietnam once they were free, but very recently many veterans and former POWs did go back to take another look—this time without having to dodge sniper fire and missiles. But my husband—now retired Colonel Dave Terrell—was not among them.

Several of Dave's former POW friends made the journey and found the experience to be interesting and surprisingly healing. "It was like writing the final chapter of an unfinished episode," one said.

Dave watched the videos and heard the stories after their return. "It's all very interesting," he said. "But Vietnam remains far down on my list of places to go."

"We said that about the Soviet Union," I reminded him, "but we've been on exchanges to Tbilisi, Georgia, and Moscow—in February! And we enjoyed both visits very much."

Dave said nothing more about Vietnam until a call came from Friendship Force International, asking the Big Canoe/North Georgia club, to host Vietnamese in our homes during their last four days in the state.

Would Dave and I consider hosting? Our schedule would only allow us to participate from Sunday until Tuesday. When another family agreed to host for the final two days, we decided to participate. Were we apprehensive? Yes; we were not sure what to expect. Others in our club feared that hosting a Vietnamese might be too painful in light of Dave's experience. Dave himself admitted it was "a big step," but he firmly believed it would not be a problem.

Secretly, I was still apprehensive and slept poorly—until I remembered these words from Ecclesiastes:

> *To every thing there is a season, and a time to every purpose under the heaven;...a time to kill, and a time to heal; a time to break down, and a time to build up; ...a time to love, and a time to hate; a time of war and a time of peace...."*

It was comforting to dwell on those ancient words of wisdom, and I began to sense that Dave was right: this visit was *not* going to be a problem.

On Father's Day, June 18, we attended Big Canoe Chapel. The Reverend Dr. Wayne Smith introduced two members of the Vietnamese delegation who had arrived in North Georgia a day early: Tran Minh Quoc, Deputy Secretary General of the Vietnam Union of Friendship, and Luong Van Hung, a hotel and restaurant manager.

I wondered what they were thinking as Dr. Smith said, "Today we come here in friendship, one of our gifts from God...." The men were stoic at first, but when the congregation applauded their introduction, they smiled a little, then a little more, and finally they were openly grinning in pleasure—and perhaps in relief.

Later that afternoon, the rest of the ambassadors arrived, including our guest, pretty Pham Hoang Van, an intelligent young woman who spoke excellent English. Van was not born until a year after the American POWs were released.

Atlanta Channel 5-TV sent a reporter and cameraman to cover the event and Van was the interpreter. The interview took place at our home. Those interviewed were Dave and Duong Duc Hong, Director of the International Press and Communications Cooperation in Hanoi. Hong was a teenager when he fought with the Vietnamese army against the French in the decisive battle at Dien Bien Phu. He was a TV reporter during the Vietnam War.

Van skillfully interpreted Hong's remarks, but the reporter was intent on guiding him toward a sensational rehash of the Vietnam War. She had her own agenda which reality would not change. She tried the same technique when she interviewed my husband, but without success. Dave is always plain spoken and he stopped the camera while he explained that The Friendship Force is an organization founded to make it possible for ordinary citizens of many countries to find common ground in order to communicate and learn more about each other. After she asked him if had been tortured, he responded: "Questions designed to elicit debate on controversial subjects are not relevant and are not appreciated. This is not the time to justify or condemn, but a time to heal."

When the news team left, the incident was pushed aside. We relaxed on our deck with beautiful Lake Petit and hazy blue mountains in the background and chatted with Van and Mr. Hong. Suddenly, Mr. Hong lifted his glass and made a toast: "To no more war," he said firmly. He was smiling but there were tears in his eyes.

That evening we shared a meal at our home with the Big Canoe hosts and their Vietnamese ambassadors. It was a time of spirited questions and answers, of learning and teaching. There was no more controversy and no talk of war. Instead the conversation turned to jobs and family, children and grandchildren, hopes, dreams, common problems and common worries and universal pleasures in the simple things of life. As we sat in the shadow of ancient mountains, a wish came to mind—a wish that all people everywhere could be simultaneously enjoying this same peaceful interlude.

The next day we had the opportunity to talk with Mr. Quoc during a pontoon boat cruise. "What has been your biggest surprise during this visit?" I asked.

He was pensive before replying. "It is small things that have surprised us," he said. "For example, we are very surprised by the spirituality of the American people. We thought that was a thing of the past in this country. We are also surprised by your direct approach to so many things. Most of all, we are surprised by your hospitality and your overall cheerful nature. All surprises—very nice surprises."

Later that day, the community center at Big Canoe was packed for a covered dish dinner, followed by a performance by the folk musicians. Everyone watched in wonder as big trunks were opened and many strange instruments were assembled. Most were fashioned from bamboo, and all were unfamiliar to us. The musicians and dancers were dressed in native costumes of a bygone era.

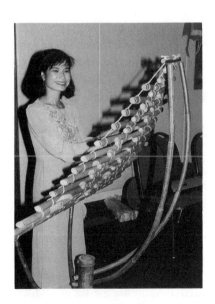

Folk musicians were part of the first ever in-bound exchange from Vietnam.

Pretty Pham Hoang Van, a teacher, spoke excellent English.

Dave and I were proud of Van, who introduced each performer in English. She did so with poise and grace far beyond her twenty years. The performance depicted an exotic and ancient culture.

At closing, one musician played a large bamboo instrument that he had invented. Using techniques similar to playing the xylophone, Van Huu Thinh hammered out the strains of "O, Susannah." and then he surprised everyone by playing soft, familiar strains of "Amazing Grace." Just as softly the audience began to hum along. It was a moving climax to a very special evening.

Again, I wished that people everywhere could be part of this lovely and peaceful scene. If this could be, perhaps The Friendship Force story would be the sensation of the evening news, replacing coverage of cruelty, war, famine and crime. I could almost see the lead story rolling across the TelePrompTer:

THE FRIENDSHIP FORCE CONTINUES TO WAGE PEACE, ONE FRIENDSHIP AT A TIME. OLD ENEMIES ARE "KILLED WITH KINDNESS." IT IS PREDICTED THAT SOON THERE WILL BE NO ENEMIES REMAINING, BECAUSE THEY HAVE ALL BECOME FRIENDS.

Amazing Grace indeed.

The story did not end that evening in June. Van captivated us with her sweet nature, intelligent questions and kind words. She and Dave had a talk about Vietnam, but not about the war. He told her that perhaps when she returned again, he would talk about his prison experience. For the present, he did not want to waste time talking about the past. He wanted to know about Van's work, her family and her ambitions. He learned that she lived with her parents and two sisters. The parents are retired. Van is working on an advanced degree and teaches English. She also worked for the Vietnam-USA Friendship Society. More than once, she invited us to come to visit her and her family.

We promised to keep in touch and Van did the same. In her first letter, Van asked if we minded if she called us her "American Dad and Mom." We were touched by the request and told her we had no objections at all. She signed her first letter—and all the letters which followed—as "Your Vietnamese Daughter."

Now when asked if he will go back to Vietnam one day, Dave says, "Maybe........to see my Vietnamese daughter."

Chapter 28
Urgent Missions to Troubled Lands

*We are now faced with the fact that tomorrow is today. We are
confronted with the fierce urgency of now. In this unfolding
conundrum of life and history there is such a thing as being too late.
Procrastination is still the thief of time....*
—Martin Luther King, Jr.

Friendship Force leaders are very serious about meeting current
challenges in the face of an ever-changing world. For a number of
years, The Friendship Force Board of Trustees has looked at new
challenges and new missions, many involving children and young
people. Questions of how to get more youth involved and how The
Friendship Force might be able to help suffering children are
frequently discussed and studied. These challenges also involve much
new development in areas like Africa, South America, the Middle East
and South East Asia.

In a recent *Friendship* magazine editorial, Wayne Smith told of two
of his own encounters with suffering children.

"In Brazil, a country that I love, I recently saw some of these
suffering children," Smith wrote. "I was sitting at an outside table on
the mosaic sidewalk overlooking the beautiful Bay of Guanabara. I
ordered a pizza. During the hour I was there at least a dozen 'street
children' approached me, begging for 'crumbs from the rich man's
table.' It wasn't as if I were dining at Maxim's in Paris. It was just a
pizza that cost a couple of dollars. But for those children it was the
difference between having a mouthful of food or going hungry. And as
incredible as it seems, many of those children were under the age of six
and had no parents or guardians.

"Merchants have found the street children to be detrimental to
business and have hired off-duty policemen to keep them away from
their establishments. On more than a few occasions, some of those
policemen, in acts of frustration and cruelty, have taken children in a
boat into the bay and dropped them overboard to drown."

The other suffering children Smith wrote about were in Iraq, a very unlikely place for an American to visit. However, in April, 1995, he visited a children's hospital in Baghdad. What he saw there horrified and saddened him. Children who were dying daily could have lived if basic medicines had been available. Children who needed surgery had to endure operations without anesthesia. On top of these horrors, the air-conditioning system was not functioning and, as an added torment, flies swarmed through open windows.

After learning that a few simple parts were all that was needed to repair the cooling system, Smith left sweltering Iraq, determined that if nothing else could be done, at least he would somehow get permission to send the needed parts to the children's hospital. Despite the international embargo against the government of Iraq, Smith thought there must be a way to help the suffering and dying children languishing in that hellish, fly-infested inferno.

"The temperature was 107 degrees Fahrenheit when I was there in June," he recalled. "In July and August, it can rise to 150 degrees. Children, already ill, dehydrate quickly in such suffocating heat."

Smith began working on the problem. He soon learned that it was not easily solved and that severe penalties awaited any individual or institution who ignored the provisions of the strict embargo. After much investigation, he determined that no legal avenues were open. Time passed, but Smith did not forget the suffering children.

It takes compassionate people to attract other compassionate people and while Wayne Smith fretted over the plight of the suffering Iraqi children, another man was struggling in another desert, trying to help an entire nation regain their homeland and to stay alive in the meantime. That man is Christopher Winchilsea of England. In his country, he is known as Lord Winchilsea, the Earl of Nottingham and Winchilsea, although he prefers to be called 'Chris' by his friends.

Since 1985, Lord Winchilsea has been working to help the Saharawi people return to their home territory in the Western Sahara on the coast of Africa, just south of Morocco. Once called the Spanish Sahara, Spain relinquished its rule of the area in 1975, promising the people that a referendum on their future would be conducted under the auspices of the United Nations. Meantime, Mauritania invaded the Western Sahara from the south and Morocco invaded from the north.

Thousands of defenseless Saharawi women and children were subjected to aerial attack. Horrible weapons rained down upon them: napalm and phosphorous and cluster bombs. The Saharawis had no choice but to flee into the desert, leaving their homes and possessions behind. As they made their way across the vast and inhospitable desert, they were pursued by enemy aircraft. Miraculously, many finally arrived at their present sanctuary across the Algerian border, hundreds of miles away from their homeland.

"When they arrived, they were ill, dehydrated, starving and exhausted," Winchilsea said. "They had nothing except the tattered clothing on their backs. About sixty children were dying every day. Additional refugee camps were established around the Algerian town of Tindouf.

"As the Saharawis began to arrive in Algeria, the Algerian Red Crescent (Red Cross) provided what they could, preventing 200,000 innocent people from perishing in the desert. With this aid, four clean and well-organized camps were established, each accommodating about 50,000 Saharawis," said Winchilsea "Every child now goes to school, from kindergarten to age sixteen and beyond. They built their schools with their own hands and trained their teachers. A National Health Service has developed hospitals, clinics and day centers which are staffed by nurses trained in the camps and with doctors sent overseas for training.

"The remarkable Saharawis have successfully greened over 150 acres of barren desert where nothing ever grew before. It is a surprise to see such a huge garden with rows of cabbage, carrots, potatoes, melons, grapes and pomegranates thriving in that parched and dusty land. They also have three long buildings near this garden, housing 75,000 hens which produce about 20,000 eggs a day. Computers control the ventilation, lighting, food and water." (Western relief agencies provided the technology for deep wells and pumping equipment after they learned of the need through Chris Winchilsea.)

Twenty years later, the Saharawis are still in the desert, waiting for the long- promised referendum from the United Nations. Their plight is generally unknown to the rest of the world, but Lord Winchilsea is slowly changing that. Since 1985, he has sent hospital equipment, educational materials, clothing, medicines, vehicles and spare parts.

In 1991, Lord Winchilsea met Ron and Camilla Laybourne, both long-time Friendship Force supporters. Ron Laybourne has been Friendship Force Volunteer of the Year and Ron and Camilla have both served as president of The Friendship Force of Newcastle upon Tyne. With the Laybournes help, a convoy was organized, including three vehicles supplied by money raised from individuals, commercial organizations and local businesses, mostly from the Newcastle upon Tyne area.

Ron Laybourne accompanied Lord Winchilsea on the convoy and was amazed to see how much the Saharawi people have accomplished.

Tent cities in the harsh desert

Sandstorms often cause respiratory and eye problems.

He was also struck by how they were surviving with only basic medical facilities and tents for housing. "We throw more stuff in the trash than these people have," Laybourne marveled.

Ron Laybourne came away from the experience determined to bring the plight of the Saharawis to the attention of Friendship Force International. In a letter, he wrote: "While I feel that The Friendship Force must not get involved with the political argument that caused this problem, I also believe that it is totally wrong that these people have had to endure such an existence for such a long time, largely ignored by the rest of the world."

Since his first visit to the desert camps, Laybourne has returned on another convoy together with his wife Camilla. He agrees with Lord Winchilsea who says: "The Saharawis want nothing more than the right to live in their own country, in their own homes, with their own families, unmolested by anyone else. They don't hate anyone, not even those who invaded them. They are peaceful, decent, law-abiding people who have been shamefully treated. Do we continue to ignore them, or do we accord them with basic human rights?"

Susan Smith, Director of Bridgebuilders, attempted to join the convoy to see first-hand the plight of the Saharawi people in 1995; however, a strike in France grounded her connecting flight and she was unable to find other suitable transportation.

Nevertheless, the compassionate Lord Winchilsea soon met Wayne Smith. Little did Winchilsea realize that he was about to play a significant role in another desert country.

It all began when Wayne Smith told Ron Laybourne about the children's hospital in Iraq and explained how he had been unable to find a legal way to ship the parts needed to fix the air-conditioning units. In May, 1996, Ron Laybourne went to Iraq to have a look at the situation for himself. After he returned, he said, "I was in the Saddam Children's Hospital in Baghdad, looking down at a child with meningitis, and I knew she was going to die because there were no medicines to treat her. I thought of my own grand-daughter, Claire who was just a month old at the time. There were lots of babies in the hospital, most of them suffering from gastroenteritis and diarrhea. Even the most basic medical supplies were not available. Distilled water was all they had to sterilize the syringes.

"Since I've been back in England, some people have said to me, 'It's their own fault!' But how do you say that to a mother who is watching her child die. These children weren't even born when the Gulf War was on. The sanctions may be needed to prevent war again, but these people have a humanitarian right to drinking water, basic medicines and food."

Ron Laybourne told Chris Winchilsea about the need to repair the air-conditioning at the hospital. Winchilsea was moved by his friend's description of the suffering children and in August, 1996, the two men legally entered Iraq through Amman, Jordan. They had secured approval from the UN to take the air-conditioning parts and to see that the equipment was repaired. Through The Friendship Force, a private donation earmarked for use in providing humanitarian relief for a children's hospital anywhere in the world, was sent to purchase the spare parts in England.

Laybourne and Winchilsea were soon off on a mission "to rebuild as new, six of the air-conditioning cooling pumps and one of the main water supply pumps." This was the minimum required. The men discovered that all the pumps were almost completely worn out; however, in temperatures of up to 69 degrees centigrade (155 degrees Fahrenheit), the system could cope with cooling three of the six floors. Ron Laybourne asked what was needed to bring the air-conditioning up to full capacity, enabling the hospital to cool all six floors. The Iraqi technician in charge kept insisting that they were more than happy if cooling was available to only three floors and to ask for more would appear greedy.

The two men finally talked the technician into telling them what was needed to make the second system operational. He responded that it could require three large electric motors and eight cubic meters of filament. Ron Laybourne assumed these materials would have to be purchased in the U.K. and he mentally estimated the overall cost to be as high as $7,500. The engineer surprised him by saying the motors could be bought through a local dealer. They went to the dealer, found the motors and agreed upon a price of 50,000 Iraqi *dinars* ($550). The parts were transported back to the hospital in an ambulance!

The story had a very happy ending. Ron Laybourne and Lord Winchilsea returned to England with the satisfaction that they had not only accomplished their mission, but had done much more than they had set out to do. When they left, the sick children and hospital staff were enjoying mercifully cool air. The two friends were justifiably proud of their significant accomplishments, and Wayne Smith was very pleased to receive a fax detailing the extent of their success in what could have easily been a very difficult and dangerous mission.

Smith also received a letter sent to The Friendship Force by Dr. Nazan Ahmed El-Abbaki, Director of the hospital in Baghdad. In part, the letter read:

I would like to thank you most sincerely for making these repairs possible and for sending Ron and Chris, who have worked so hard in temperatures of more than 60 degrees centigrade, to help us restore the air-conditioning to the only children's hospital in Iraq.

Finally, I would like to offer you an open invitation to visit my hospital. It would be an honour for me to meet you personally and I will show you the improvements in the operating conditions at the hospital which resulted from these repairs.

If you would seriously consider my invitation to visit the hospital, we could use that happy occasion for you to tell us all about The Friendship Force, with a view to possibly starting The Friendship Force of Iraq.

Compassionate people do indeed attract other compassionate people and the results can touch and heal in miraculous ways.

The Friendship Force ventured into the Middle East as early as 1978 when 800 ambassadors traveled with the New Haven, Connecticut, club to Tel Aviv, Israel. The first exchange with Egypt came in 1983. In 1996, The Friendship Force leadership targeted the Middle East for expansion. In April, forty-four ambassadors of friendship from around the United States flew on a Royal Jordanian jet to Amman, capital of Jordan, on a Friendship Mission. Wayne Smith, along with Sam and Louisa Ayoub joined them there.

The Egyptian-born Ayoubs left their country years ago to seek political asylum in he United States. Sam Ayoub soon was employed by a company which was eager to use his unique combination of international finance and management talents. That company was The Coca-Cola Export Corporation, the international arm of the famous Atlanta beverage giant. Mr. Ayoub has retired from his job as Senior Vice President and Chief Financial Officer; however, he is spending his retirement managing Seaboard Management Corporation and The Ayoub Group. Mr. Ayoub is a member of The Friendship Force Board of Trustees.

In Amman, the ambassadors visited a high school for gifted youth called the Jubilee School. This center of education is of special interest to American-born Queen Noor. The Queen met with Wayne Smith and pledged her personal support to The Friendship Force. She also initiated discussions about possible educational exchanges between American and Jordanian high school and university students and faculty members.

Her Majesty Queen Noor of Jordan with Sam Ayoub and his wife Louisa.

The Friendship Force is now seeking financial support for this educational exchange program. It is seen as the first of many such exchanges around the world. The importance of these exchanges was underscored by Sam Ayoub who said, "Working now to develop love-centered values in our future leaders ensures that peace is within our reach."

This Friendship Mission also launched a Friendship Force Club in Jordan, with leadership by Liela Diab and support from Mirele Abujabar.

After leaving Jordan, the group traveled to Syria and on to Israel, visiting Jerusalem, Galilee and Jericho. They made friends along the way and found the people eager to establish lasting friendships.

While Friendship Force ambassadors were in Amman, a delegation representing the Iraqi Women's Federation traveled from Baghdad to spend the day with the American ambassadors. It is hoped that this meeting might serve as a future linkage, allowing The Friendship Force to participate in an exchange or mission to Iraq.

The Friendship Force Foundation was established in 1996 to build an endowment fund to provide long-term financial stability for The Friendship Force and to supply funding for selected projects, resulting in an expansion of exchange programs involving new people and new locations.

**Rosalynn Carter, Lord Winchilsea and former President Jimmy Carter.
Lord Winchilsea is a trustee of The Friendship Force Foundation.**

The Foundation is led by Board Chairman Hulett C. Smith, a former Governor of West Virginia and one of the original Trustees of The Friendship Force. Day-to-day operations are currently guided by Boyd Lyons, President of the Foundation. George Brown replaced Lyons as Executive Director of The Friendship Force. Brown was already serving as Director of the New Development Program. The versatile Brown made the change from department head to executive director with ease. Wayne Smith said of the new director: "His past knowledge of the evolution of The Friendship Force and of the functions of all departments at Friendship Force International are only some of the invaluable assets he brings to the job of executive director and to our entire organization. I have worked directly with George for over a decade and I have great respect for him. He will do a fine job."

Of course, 1996 in Atlanta meant the Centennial Olympic Games. The Friendship Force played an important role in the Games through a community-wide partnership with AT&T, a principal corporate sponsor. Friendship Force International provided the management for the project, which involved homestays for the families of athletes from 197 countries.

"The Olympic Games represented the largest and most universal peacetime gathering in the world," Executive Director George Brown said. "The next Summer Games will be held in Sydney Australia, in the year 2000. The Friendship Force has a very strong presence in Australia, and we are anxious to continue the family homestay program with the Sydney Olympic Games.

"It is too soon to know if this will be possible, but we are not waiting for official decisions to be made in 1997," Brown explained. "The Friendship Force will sponsor a series of special exchanges from Atlanta to Australia, providing this year's host families the opportunity to visit Sydney and then to enjoy a week's homestay with one of our Australian Friendship Force families."

One of the happiest stories of 1996 came from Judith Citron of the North Shore-Boston Friendship Force club. During the previous July, Judith traveled with other ambassadors to Irkutsk, Siberia. She was hosted by Yuri and Evgenia (called "Genia"), parents of Evgenie, age nine, and Anna, who was only one year old.

Judith was thrilled with her Siberian adventure, including boating on Lake Baikal, the world's oldest and deepest lake. It holds one-fifth of the world's fresh water and eighty percent of the former Soviet Union's. "We spent two nights at a tourist camp, hiked, drank tea made with Baikal's water, sang by the campfire and toasted the gods with vodka. We drove through a *taiga* (sub-arctic evergreen forest), visiting small towns and observing everyday life," Judith said. "The sightseeing was incredible. I quickly learned that Siberia is not a frozen wasteland: it is green and lush and in summer, the weather is as warm as it is back home."

One day they passed the local children's hospital. It was then that Yuri and Genia told Judith that baby Anna was in serious need of urological surgery, but they were too fearful to submit her to surgery there because of "substandard sanitary conditions." Judith said, "I sympathized with them and saw the deep concern in their faces, but what could I do?" Before the two weeks had ended, Judith knew that sympathy wasn't enough and when she left for the United States she carried Anna's X-rays to take to Children's Hospital in Boston.

Judith called the hospital as soon as she got home and was asked to send the X-rays. She did better than that—she personally drove from her home in Peabody to Boston, taking the X-rays and a letter explaining everything that Yuri had told her about Anna's condition.

"Yuri said she was born with a kidney disease that restricts the flow of fluids from her body, causing infections and high fevers," Judith explained. "In three days, the hospital called to confirm that Anna needed the surgery and that they would do it, but the Shirokovs would have to apply for free care."

After much effort on the part of Judith and of Anna's parents, on November 8, 1995, Anna was approved for free care and twenty days later, the costs for surgery and anesthesiology were waived.

"The parents had acquired visas by this time, but the difficulty was in getting a visa for Anna. Yuri phoned to say that Genia was in tears and asked if there was there anything I could do to help?"

Through a phone call to her senator, Judith received information listing the steps the Siberian couple must take to properly submit numerous documents to support the required affidavit. She faxed the information to Irkutsk and waited.

"On Christmas Day, Yuri called with the good news that the visas were all ready," Judith said. "I called the hospital and the dates were set. Suddenly, I realized that I had some scurrying to do to prepare for a month's home-hosting for a Siberian couple and their twenty-month-old baby. I needed diapers, a high chair, car seat, toys, stroller...."

Judith called local stores and told them the story. Many were touched and offered support. The results were overwhelming and soon Judith received gift-certificates and donations to cover most of their needs.

After the flight was delayed due to stormy weather, the Siberians finally arrived and were seen at the hospital two days later. To Yuri and Genia's great surprise, the hospital staff already knew Anna's story and she was welcomed as a celebrity. On February 7, Anna was taken to surgery and Judith spent those tense hours with Yuri and Genia. Finally, the doctor came to tell them that Anna was fine and the surgery had gone well!

Anna was soon playing in the hospital's activity room for toddlers and in a few more days she was allowed to go to Judith's home to recuperate fully.

Yuri and Genia left for Siberia. They were thrilled with new clothing they received for the entire family, plus many toys and books for the children.They also left with the most precious gift they could ever wish for: the miracle of good health for their little daughter, thanks to their friend, Judith Citron, another outstanding example of friendship in action.

Chapter 29
Winning the Peace

The bravest person is the one who brings peace, not the one who makes war. —**Elias Jabbour**, Shefar'am, Israel.

Susan Smith, Director of the Bridgebuilders program, decided if there was no existing bridge to lead her to battered Bosnia, then she would walk a tightrope to get there. Why? To develop exchanges to help rebuild the war-torn land and to create long-term linkages for the future.

"This has already started on a diplomatic level and on a trade level," Susan explained. "The problem is, there has been no involvement at the grass-roots level of ordinary citizens-to-citizens. Here at Friendship Force International we are ready to provide leadership for a series of *Passages To Peace* exchanges, which will give ordinary citizens the chance to get involved and to rebuild a bridge between Bosnia and our country.

Susan told me these things as we sat in her cheerful office on the ninth floor of the Healy Building in Atlanta. She had just returned from Sarajevo. When asked who arranged her contacts, she smiled and said she went in "cold."

"I didn't do much advance communication to people in Bosnia because it's difficult due to the extensive war damage and because of the language difference. I just went over...and showed up," she said.

The idea was to lay the groundwork for an initial exchange between the people of Sarajevo and the people of Dayton, Ohio, the city which hosted the peace talks that produced the Dayton Accord only a year earlier. We have told the people of Dayton that now instead of hosting the diplomats, they have a chance to BE a diplomat by staying in a home in Sarajevo and establishing a community link on a person-to-person basis. We will look for teachers to go to the homes of teachers; doctors to go to other doctors...in other words, it will be a normal Bridgebuilders exchange taking place amid the ruins of war.

Now, back to the tightrope. Susan arrived in Dubrovnik, once the jewel of old Yugoslavia, and met with a contact she found through a Moscow connection. "That worked out beautifully," she said. "In fact, during this trip, I began to believe a Divine hand was guiding me. Each time I made a phone call, the person was there, and each time I asked for assistance or cooperation, the answer was 'yes.' Everyone I talked to became very enthusiastic about the idea of a Bridgebuilders exchange."

Susan Smith's journey began in Dubrovnik.

"I boarded a bus and headed for Sarajevo. I didn't know what to expect or just how an American would be perceived along the way. I knew the route the bus would take would be protected by the peace-keeping troops, but I still didn't know how I might be received when I arrived," she said.

"The bus had been on the road for about an hour before we crossed the border into Bosnia-Herzegovina. I began to notice a burned-out house here and there...maybe one in about every thirty houses we passed. Soon, one in twenty houses was destroyed; then one in ten. By the time we got to Mostar, everyone on the bus had tears in their eyes. It was a very heavy feeling, because Mostar was completely destroyed. You can imagine the ethnic cleansing that went on there. I read that during the siege, captives were taken to school buildings where they were tortured and killed. Now the schools are still standing and some of the kids are going back to the very place where their fathers were killed. A horrible thought.

"All I could think of was *why* did this happen? Why did everyone allow this to happen? These were not soldiers who were killed. These were innocent people. It made me so sad to witness the destruction and to realize the human pain it represented. It was something I will never forget. How can we prevent this sort of thing from happening again? It's something we must all ask ourselves. We must find a solution. I thought that if we in The Friendship Force could get to know people by staying in their homes, then perhaps if anything else happens, if we can't stop it, at least we could get our friends out of harm's way."

Susan said that once they arrived in Sarajevo, it was easy to see what had happened. "You see," she said, "Sarajevo is in a valley, surrounded by mountains, so the troops surrounded the city and rained destruction upon them from the vantage of the mountainside. The people were trapped.

"As I walked around town, it was cloudy and overcast, and the dreary weather reflected the mood of the people. It seemed to me that the people were no longer aware of the destruction around them. They were walking around, obviously dazed, and numbed to the destruction evidenced on every street.

"Most businesses were not functioning. I walked into a travel agency and asked if they booked city tours.

"No," the agent said. "We are only able to rent homes. Nobody comes here anymore, so we don't have city tours. Once we did and maybe we will again...someday."

However, there were signs that people were slowly trying to put their lives and their city back together. Susan soon met people who really wanted to reconnect and become part of the international community again. She said most of the people consider themselves to be Europeans and remember with great pride when they hosted the Winter Olympic Games in 1984.

Susan went to the International Council for Volunteers in Sarajevo. They gave her the names of some very reputable people in town and Susan said she just started "cold calling."

"The organization I was referred to was called *La Benevolencia*, Spanish for 'benevolence.' It is connected to the synagogue and is led by the Jewish community. They had a meeting place, faxes and organizational capability. This was exactly what I had hoped to find. I learned that *La Benevolencia* and Director Jacob Finci, are highly respected in Sarajevo. They supplied enough food to many citizens during the war. Mr. Finci introduced me to one of those people, Safeta Kovacevic, a widowed pensioner, who agreed to host me for two days. She fed me potato soup, potato cakes and potato casseroles. Water rations were limited to a few hours in the mornings and late at night. Most of the windows, like those of my hostess, were covered with plastic provided by a United Nations committee.

During these two days, Susan learned that Safeta's husband was killed during the war. She also met Safeta's daughter, who had also lost her husband. Her sisters had already moved to other countries. "The daughter was very depressed." Susan said.

Susan Smith and Safeta Kovacevic in Sarajevo

All buildings were damaged.

"I met the rabbi of the synagogue. He is highly respected in town and he referred me to several people, including a young girl named Svetlana who spoke excellent English. She is going to help us," Susan explained.

"I made a number of excellent contacts in a short time and I am convinced the exchange will be very well received," Susan said. "I think the world community needs to come to the people in Sarajevo now. During the war, we felt there was nothing we as individuals could do. We couldn't even understand the complicated history which spawned such a tragedy. In fact, most Americans still don't understand who was fighting or why.

"We want to take the first step to show the people we care. The first exchange from Dayton will consist of thirty ambassadors. We all believe that we, as compassionate human beings, have a remarkable opportunity to actively support the restoration of peace in Bosnia," Susan explained. "The people I have talked to in Dayton are very enthusiastic. The Exchange Director is Doris Ponitz and she has already started to work. We will begin with this small exchange. Just as new ground is often won step by step during wars, peace can be won the same way. For twenty years The Friendship Force has been proving that ordinary people can be a part of the peace process by taking time to know and understand people from other cultures. And no people today need our support and understanding more than the Bosnian survivors who are trying to rebuild their cities and their lives." she added.

Susan reported that government and relief organizations are sending food and materials. "People can give the Bosnians something that organizations cannot. We can show the people of Bosnia that there are caring people in another country who understand their plight and have come to stand beside them to offer encouragement and help—people who have come to live in their homes and be their friends."

Friendship in a Shattered Land

In December, 1996, a group of thirty-five adventuresome travelers set out from Dayton, Ohio, bound for Sarajevo, Bosnia-Herzegovina. These people, ranging in age from 19-80 and coming from many walks of life, had observed the terrible war which destroyed Yugoslavia, but only from the comfort and safety of their living-rooms. Now they were headed for Sarajevo to see first hand the results of a conflict which had raged for four long and bloody years.

With the knowledge of land mines still buried in the streets, hillsides and even the cemeteries, plus the occupation of the land by international peace-keeping forces, this small band of travelers hoped to make a difference in the lives of Bosnians who were awaiting their arrival. The Americans could not understand the war or the long-simmering hatreds behind the conflict. They were non-political, non-judgmental and non-military. They were ordinary people who believed they could actually do something to alleviate suffering and somehow comfort the shattered survivors who were trying to pick up the threads of their former lives out of the charred rubble of their once-beautiful city. The delegation simply went in friendship.

After an eight hour flight to Frankfurt and a long layover, the weary travelers headed to Zagreb, the capital of Croatia and on to Split where they boarded a bus bound for Sarajevo. It had snowed a few days earlier and they shivered as they waited for transportation. Traveling the same road which Susan Smith had traveled earlier, the Friendship Force ambassadors soon witnessed mile after mile of destruction heaped upon the land by mortar, rockets, bullets and bombs. Over and over, they found themselves asking the same questions Susan had pondered: "Why? Why should such destruction ever occur? Does the ruin of a country and the death of thousands

The Other Side of the Mountain

accomplish anything beyond mindless destruction?" Would the ambassadors find answers in Sarajevo?

Journalist Carol Jennings and her husband Max, editor of the *Dayton Daily News*, were part of the delegation. They were met by their hosts, Lidumil Alikafic and his wife Vera. Lidumil, called Braco, is a well-known architect, having designed the complex for the stadium and ice rink built for the 1984 Winter Olympics. Once the Jennings were in the Alikafic's apartment, Braco became very animated as he told the Jennings of their ordeal.

"He jumped up and started toward the door in his living room and partly closed it, showing us how he had been holding a candle to light his way one dark night during the war," Jennings said of his host. "He told us it was not ten seconds after he went through the door that a rocket came through the window and exploded in the living room, destroying their apartment and most of their possessions, including Braco's beloved art collection.

"He still has the collection," Jennings said. "He showed it to us, but it was no longer in frames. It was mere pieces of paper and canvas in a stack. Every piece was peppered with holes, some as big as marbles, where red-hot pieces of shrapnel had burned through. One by one, he showed his damaged treasures, hoping, I suppose, that we could imagine how they had once been. His wife Vera said to us in English, 'That art was his life.'

"Carol and I, like most Americans, had read about the horror of this war many times, but it was never brought home until we sat with Braco and Vera, he a Muslim, she a Croatian. They sadly confessed that they also could not understand a war that suddenly turned Muslim against Croat against Serb

Sarajevo has long been a mixed city. Ambassador Andrew Bosworth discovered that in the apartment building of Armin Teskeredzic, his host, the Muslim Teskeredzics lived above a Catholic Croat family and below a Bosnian Serb family whose son was killed serving in the predominantly Muslim Bosnian army.

As the ambassadors made their way around the city with their hosts, they began to fully realize the extent of the death and chaos that rained down during the shelling of Sarajevo. Max Jennings wrote about the experience, using this closer-to-home example:

"Imagine what it would be like if an artillery division set up its heavy guns on the hills of Huber Heights and Kettering and began to blast away at the city of Dayton, lying helpless below. The gunners could take their time, aiming carefully, picking their targets, their goal to break the backs and the spirits of the people below," he said.

As the Jennings and their fellow travelers were shown the sites of deaths and the effects of four years of bombing, they learned of something even more detrimental to the rebuilding of Sarajevo. That something was the Bosnian brain drain. Thousands of intellectuals and highly skilled professionals of all types had fled the country even before the siege began. They may never return.

One night the hosts and ambassadors gathered for a new exhibit in an art gallery and Max Jennings struck up a conversation with a Bosnian who had recently lived in the United States. "Look around you," the Bosnian said of the 200 or so persons packed into the frigid gallery. "Multiply this by three or maybe four and that's all the intellectuals left in this country. How long will it take us to train engineers to help rebuild?"

Yet, amid the debris, the ambassadors also saw hope and they began to envision ways to help the people long after this visit ended. This help had already begun with each ambassador bringing along an extra suitcase filled with warm clothing, medicine and toys. "Thirty-five suitcases of foreign aid may not make much difference in an entire nation, but they made a huge impact at the modest Institute for Special Education for Children where we dropped them off," Jennings said.

Jan Rudd of Dayton said she planned to establish a program to help support refugees. Others wondered aloud if perhaps Habitat for Humanity or similar organizations might help rebuild damaged housing. Most contemplated ways they might make their hosts' lives more bearable, including raising money to bring some of the host families to the United States. Fledgling plans began to develop for collecting medicine and supplies to ship back to Sarajevo.

Ralph Dull, a lifelong farmer in the Brookfield area, learned from Professor Zahid Causevic that an estimated $4.5 billion damage to agriculture was another terrible result of the siege. Grain is now scarce in the Muslim-Croat half of Bosnia. Dull promised to donate fifty-five tons of seed corn.

Tom Wolford told about Almir, the twenty-two year old son of his host. An epilectic, the young man was injured during the war and now his seizures strike five or six times a day. Wolford, a retired Lutheran pastor, noted that Amir was uncommonly solicitous of his grandmother and of the 71-year-old Wolford. "He fetched my slippers when he entered the house and insisted on tying my shoes when it was time to leave. He took my arm when we were outside on the icy street and ever so often, he would come and put his hand on mine and say, 'I'm glad you're here.'"

The ambassadors all agreed that they too were glad they were in Sarajevo even in the cold weather and with the many inconveniences necessitated by the war. When they arrived in Dubrovnik on their way home, the media were there to question them. "Do you really believe your small group actually made any difference in Sarajevo?" one asked. "Is this just a meaningless do-gooding excursion by a few naive citizens?" queried another. One cynic suggested that the group had not accomplished anything except to provide stories for their next cocktail party.

Editor Max Jennings responded: "I know my own answer. I have new understanding and new friends whom I intend to help in any way I can, and I believe people-to-people contact really works better in some ways than government-to-government ever can. Now I can say with certainty that I believe we must never abandon these people who have already suffered so much for so long.

Oliver Wendell Holmes said, "Man's mind stretched to a new idea never goes back to its original dimensions." The thirty-five citizen ambassadors to Sarajevo discovered Holmes' observation anew. So have thousands and thousands of others who have stretched their minds to encompass the idea of spreading genuine friendship around the world and have happily found their lives forever changed in the process. In fact, as of January, 1997, over 136,000 ambassadors and 400,000 hosts have participated through 3,300 exchanges, touching the lives of over two million people and bringing to life The Friendship Force motto: "A world of friends is a world of peace."

You, too, can make a difference.

For information about The Friendship Force or the address of the
club nearest you, please write or telephone the international office:

The Friendship Force
57 Forsyth Street, NW
Atlanta, GA 30303 USA
Telephone: (404) 522-9490
Fax (404) 688-6148

NOTE

Since the information in the next section is a compilation of names of people, clubs and places, these are not repeated in the index.

FRIENDSHIP FORCE LEADERS AND FACTS

Before each Friendship Force exchange takes place, many details must be dealt with by the hard-working staff at the Atlanta office. These dedicated men and women are often unsung heroes, yet it is they who work to insure the success of each exchange. They have enormous responsibilities and often deal with mind-boggling logistics.

The following people were staff members as of January 31, 1997:

Claude Armendariz
Shirley Bagwell
Shields Blankenship
John Box
Perry Brice
George Brown
Kathy Castricone
Allison Cloud
Linda Ector
Clara Diedrich
Delois Edwards
David Faulkner
DeFrieda Howard
Bobbie Jones
Won Kim

Harriet Kuhr
Boyd Lyons
Jean Lyons
Ketevan Mennenoh
Claudia Park
Martha Parr
Susan Smith
Wayne Smith
Vickie Sterling
Marnie Sturgeon
Levy Tavares
Gerald and Helen Weekes
Barbara Williams
Courtney Williams
Sarah Wynn

During the first twenty years of The Friendship Force, the following staff members served three years or longer at some time during this period. (Current staff members are not repeated.)

Ashley Allen
Elizabeth Asbury
Stoncil Boyette
Sean Dammann
Betty Dougherty
Karen Harrell
Stan Humphries
Betty Hull
Alice Josephson
Stephen Y.S. Kim

Bill Lamkin
Becky Lynch
Beverlie Reilman
Mary Beth Reilman
Patrice Reynolds
Angelica Smith
Doug Stamps
Kathy Thomas
Susan Weldon
Pam Whiteside

1977-1997
The Friendship Force Board of Trustees

(Those serving on the Board as of January, 1997, are in bold type..)

Francisco Aguilar-Hernandez	Cuernavaca, Mexico
Kazuo Aichi	Tokyo, Japan
Jimmy Allen	**Big Canoe, Georgia**
Jerry Apodaca	Santa Fe, New Mexico
Bahaman Armajani	Chicago, Illinois
Gibson E. Armstrong	Lancaster, Pennsylvania
Sam Ayoub	**Atlanta, Georgia**
Ralph Birdsong	Atlanta, Georgia
James A. Bishop	Brunswick, Georgia
Landrum R. Bolling	Washington, DC
Helena Z. Benitez	Manila, The Philippines
Cairo Campante	**Sao Paulo, Brazil**
Rosalynn Carter	**Plains, Georgia**
Tony Coates	**Newcastle, England**
Robert Coggin	Atlanta, Georgia
Clarence Cooper	Atlanta, Georgia
Thomas Cousins	Atlanta, Georgia
Paul Dillingham	Atlanta, Georgia
Richard Falk	**Wilmar, Minnesota**
Boussaina Farid	Cairo, Egypt
Alice Freeman	Kenly, North Carolina
Ronda Furgatch	Marina del Rey, California
Joseph G. Grubbs	Raleigh, North Carolina
Robert Halyburton	Charlotte, North Carolina
Joan Herraman	Adelaide, Australia
Hanns-Peter Herz	Berlin, Germany
Carlton T. Hicks	St. Simons Island, Georgia
Stanley C. Humphries	Atlanta, Georgia (ex officio)
Carolyn Hunt	Lucama, North Carolina
Bunkichi Itoh	Niigata, Japan
Lyun Joon Kim	Seoul, Korea
Yong Song Kim	**Seoul, Korea**
Bert Lance`	Calhoun, Georgia
Auseklis Lazdinsh	Riga, Latvia
Eckard Lehnart	Nooderstedt, Germany
Jeanne Tchong Koei Li	Taipei, Taiwan ROC

Margo Lindl	**Madison, Wisconsin**
Bert W. Lindsay	Albuquerque, New Mexico
Francis Luk	New York, New York
Charles MacCormack	Brattleboro, Vermont
William F. McSweeney	Washington, DC
Harvey Mars	Atlanta, Georgia
Arthur L. Montgomery	Atlanta, Georgia
Edward E. Noble	Atlanta, Georgia
Gerry Phillips-Hughes	Bristol, England
Robert Ray	Cedar Rapids, Iowa
Joe Ritchie	**Batavia, Illinois**
Stephen H. Rhinesmith	Washington, DC
Inger Rice	Richmond, Virginia
Marion Ruscoe	Wanganui, New Zealand
Theresa Russell	Newcastle upon Tyne, England
Ryoichi Sasakawa	Tokyo, Japan
M.B. Seretean	Boca Raton, Florida
Yuri Smirnov	Moscow, Russia
Hulett C. Smith	Beckley, West Virginia
D. Wayne Smith	Big Canoe, Georgia
Maureen Takacs	**Carmichael, California**
A. Wayne Van Tilburg	Vancouver, Washington
Anthony R. Volk	St. Louis, Missouri
John A. Wallace	Atlanta, Georgia
Barbara Weinberg	Manchester, Connecticut
Kanitha Wichiencharoen	Bankok, Thailand
James Wise	Des Moines, Iowa
Andrew Young	Atlanta, Georgia

The Friendship Force International Advisory Council Members
1981-1997

The International Advisory Council was established by the board of Trustees in 1981. The following distinguished citizens from around the world have been on the Council at one time or another, agreeing to have their names associated with The Friendship Force. The Council does not meet as a group but serves as a "board of reference" for The Friendship Force. There are 21 members as of January, 1997. Their names are in bold print..

Francisco Aguilar-Hernandez	Cuernavaca, Mexico
Kazuo Aichi	**Tokyo, Japan**
Muhammad Ali	**Berrien, Michigan**
Jeffrey Archer	**London, England**
Datin Akiko Aw	**Singapore**
Helena Z. Benitez	**Manila, Philippines**
James Callaghan	**Cardiff, Wales**
Kirk Douglas	**Beverly Hills, California**
Y.W. Fong	Hong Kong
Svyatoslav Fyodorov	**Moscow, Russia**
Georgy M. Grechko	**Moscow, Russia**
Nageb Halaby	McLean, Virginia
Armand Hammar	Los Angeles, California
Mark Hatfield	**Washington, DC**
Luis Herrera-Campinas	Caracas, Venezuela
Thomas W. Kaufman	**Moscow, Russia**
Lyun Joon Kim	**Seoul, Korea**
Martin Luther King, Sr.	Atlanta, Georgia
Leanne Tchong Koei Li	**Taipei, Taiwan ROC**
Ernesto Pereira Lopes	Sao Carlos, Brazil
Paulo Maluf	Sao Paulo, Brazil
Juan Edgar Picado	San Jose, Costa Rica
Juan Edgar Picado, Jr.	**San Jose, Costa Rica**
Ivo Pitanguy	**Rio de Janeiro, Brazil**
Inger Rice	**Richmond, Virginia**
Ryoichi Sasakawa	Tokyo, Japan
Max Schmeling	**Hamburg, Germany**
David Shalikashvili	Tbilisi, Republic of Georgia
Eduard Shevardnadze	**Tbilisi, Republic of Georgia**
Dietrich Stobbe	Bonn, Germany
Wan-San Tae	Seoul, Korea
Youssef Abu Taleb	**Cairo, Egypt**

Ted Turner   **Atlanta, Georgia**
L. Douglas Wilder   Richmond, Virginia
James Wright   Washington, DC
Andrew Young   **Atlanta, Georgia**

THE FRIENDSHIP FORCE VOLUNTEER OF THE YEAR AWARDS

1981-	Norma Hassinger, Georgia
1982	Henny Willemsen, Netherlands
1983	Father Jorge Diaz, Mexico
1984	Inger Rice, Virginia
1985	Dr. Boussaina Farid, Egypt
1985	James Wise, Iowa
1986	Isamu Sahara, Japan
1986	Ruth and Joe Nathan, Florida
1987	Trevor Pollitt, England
1987	Jeanne Comer, Ohio
1988	Cairo Campante, Brazil
1988	Alice Freeman, North Carolina
1989	Bunkichi Itoh, Japan
1989	Gerry Ernest, California
1990	Julia Cesar Cifuentes, Mexico
1990	Wayne and Eleanor Van Tilburg Washington
1991	Marianne Miehe, Germany
1991	Mary Garner, Georgia
1992	Michiko Nakano, Japan
1992	Janice Wenger, Pennsylvania
1993	Ron Laybourne, England
1993	Bettye Brown, Washington
1994	Kim Moon Suk, Korea
1994	Gloria Griffin, North Carolina
1995	Kevin Meagher, Australia
1995	Brenda Unti, North Carolina
1996	Horst Neumann, Germany
1996	Bill Hagen, Ohio

USA Friendship Force Clubs as of January, 1997

(1.) **Alabama:** Birmingham, Huntsville Area, Montgomery; (2.) **Alaska:** Anchorage, Fairbanks; (3.) **Arizona:** Central Arizona; (4.) **California**: Greater Sacramento, Kern County, Los Angeles, Napa Valley, Orange County, San Diego County, San Francisco Bay Area; San Luis Obispo, Santa Barbara; (5.) **Colorado**: Colorado Foothills, Greater Denver, Northern Colorado, Rocky Mountains, Southern Colorado, Western Colorado; (6.) **Connecticut**: Connecticut, Southwestern Connecticut; (7.) **District of Columbia**: National Capital Area; (8.) **Florida**: Central Florida, Daytona Beach, East Central Florida, Florida Suncoast, Greater Orlando, Lee County, Northeast Florida, Sarasota, Southwest Florida, Spring Hill, The Treasure Coast; (9.) **Georgia**: Albany, Atlanta, Atlanta Northwest, Atlanta South, Big Canoe/North Georgia, Coastal Georgia, Greater Augusta, Lake Hartwell, Macon, West Georgia; (10.) **Hawaii**: Honolulu, Kauai, Maui; (11.) **Illinois:** Chicago, Northern Illinois; (12.) **Iowa**: Cedar Rapids-Iowa City, Central Iowa, Dubuque, Greater Des Moines, Quad Cities; (13.) **Kansas**: Kansas; (14.) **Kentucky**: Louisville, Western Kentucky; (15.) **Louisiana**: Baton Ruge; (16.) **Massachusetts**: North Shore-Boston, The Pioneer Valley; (17.) **Michigan**: Greater Detroit, Lansing-Satellite, Northwest Michigan, Western Michigan; (18.) **Minnesota**: Lake Superior, Minnesota-Twin Cities, South Central Minnesota; (19.) **Mississippi**: Jackson; (20.) **Missouri**: Greater Kansas City-Satellite, Missouri-St. Louis; (21.) **Montana**: Billings, Flathead Valley, Great Falls, Helena, Western Montana-Missoula; (22.) **Nebraska**: Eastern Nebraska, Lincoln; (23.) **Nevada**: Las Vegas, Reno-Tahoe; (24.) **New Hampshire:** New Hampshire Seacoast; (25.) **New Jersey**: Northern New Jersey, Southern New Jersey; (26.) **New Mexico**: New Mexico; (27.) **New York**: Greater Binghamton, Long Island, Southeast New York State; (28.) **North Carolina**: Charlotte, Colonial Carolina, Durham-Chapel Hill, Greater Winston-Salem, Raleigh, Shelby, Western North Carolina, Wilson-Rocky Mount; (29.) **Ohio**: Central Ohio, Dayton, Greater Cincinnati, Northeast Ohio; (30.) **Oklahoma**: Oklahoma; (31.) **Oregon**: Oregon's Willamette Valley; (32.) **Pennsylvania**: Greater Harrisburg, Lancaster; (33.) **South Carolina**: Orangeburg; (34.) **Tennessee**: Knoxville, Memphis, South Central Tennessee; (35.) **Texas**: Austin, Dallas, Ft. Worth, Houston, Rio Grande Valley, San Antonio; (36.) **Utah**: Utah; (37.) **Virginia**: Charlottesville, Danville, Richmond, Southwestern; (38.) **Washington**: Columbia Cascade, Eastern Washington-Northern Idaho, Lower Columbia, Olympia, Puget Sound, Sea-Tac, Whidbey Island; (39.) **West Virginia**: Charleston; (40.) **Wisconsin:** Greater Milwaukee, Wisconsin; (41.) **Wyoming:** Cheyenne.

(The total number of USA clubs listed above is 129.)

FRIENDSHIP FORCE INTERNATIONAL CLUBS
AS OF JANUARY, 1997

(1.) Australia: Adelaide, Brisbane, Bundaberg, Cairns, Casterton, Central Coast, Currumbin-Gold Coast, Glasshouse Mountains, Hobart, Ipswich, Kempsey, Mount Barker, Mount Gambier, Murray Bridge, Newcastle, Perth, Salisbury, Sydney, Tamworth, The Sunshine Coast, Tweed Valley; **(2.) Austria:** Krems, Vienna; **(3.) Belarus**: Belarus; **(4.) Belgium**: Brussels-Pajot, Flanders, Limburg, Maas & Kempen, South Flanders; **(5.) Belize**: San Pedro; **(6.) Brazil**: Araraquara, Belem, Belo Horizonte, Brazilia, Brazil (Office), Campinas, Cascavel, Curitiba, Engenheiro Beltrao, Greater Sao Paulo, Ilha Bela, Itajuba, Itanhaem, Joao Monlevade, Jundiai, Mandaguacu, Natal, Ouro Preto Do Oeste, Piracicaba, Porto Alegre, Recife, Ribeirao Preto, Rio Branco, Rio de Janeiro, Salvador-Bahia, Santo Andre, Santo Angelo, Sao Carlos, Sao Jose Dos Campos, Sao Jose do Rio Preto, Sao Miguel do Iguacu, Sete Lagoas; **(7.) Bulgaria**: Sofia-Center; **(8.) Canada**: Lethbridge, Ottawa Region, Quebec Region; **(9.) Chile**: Serena, Santiago, Vina del Mar; **(10.) Colombia**: Bogata, Cali; **(11.) Costa Rica**: Alajuela, San Jose; **(12.)Cyprus**: Cyprus; **(13.) Czech Republic**: Bohemia, Prague; **(14.) Egypt**: Cairo; **(15.) Estonia**: Tallinn; **(16.) France**: Compiegne, Pau, Remiremont; **(17.) Germany**: Berlin-Brandenburg, Bockhorn. Braunschweig-Peine, Chemnitz, Cottbus, Freiburg-Umkirch, Gelsenkirchen, Germany (Office), Halle-Saale, Hamburg, Hannover, Herne, Jena, Kiel, Schleswig-Holstein, Lubeck, Magdeburg, Merseburg, Norderstedt, Rheinhessen-Mainz, Varel, Wolfsburg; **(18.) Ghana**: Accra, Akosombo, Ho-Volta Region; **(19.) Hungary**: Budapest, Pecs, Szekesfehervar; **(20.) India**: Hyderabad, India; **(21.) Indonesia**: Bandung, Indonesia, Malang, Manado, Semarang, Southeast Asia (Office), Surabaya, Ujungpandang, Yogyakarta; **(22) Ireland**: Dublin, Tubbercurry; **(23.) Israel**: Ashkelon, Givatayim, Raanana, Shefar-Am, ; **(24.) Italy**: Piacenza, Piza; **(25.) Japan**: Ehime, Fukuchiyama-Kyoto, Fukuoka, Gifu, Japan (Office), Koriyama, Kumamoto Mie, Miyagi, Nagasaki, Niigata, Oita, Osaka, Ota Gunma, Saitama, Shizuoka, Tokai, Tokyo, Western Tokyo, Yamaguchi; **(26.) Kenya**: Nairobi; **(27.) Korea**: Kwanju, Pusan, Seoul; **(28.) Latvia**: Latvia; **(29.) Liberia**: Monrovia; **(30.) Mexico**: Altotonga, Guanajuato, Mexico City, Puebla, San Christobal, Toluca, Tula, Tuxtla Gutierrez; **(31.) Moldova**: Moldova; **(32.) Netherlands**: Arnhem, Friesland, Middleburg, Noord, Rijnmond, Zutphen; **(33.) New Zealand**: Auckland-North Shore, Christchurch, Gisborne, Hamilton, Horowhenua, Howick, Kapiti Coast, Manawatu, Marlborough, Napier, Nelson, New Plymouth, New Zealand (Office), Paeroa-Hauraki, Rotorua, South Taranaki, Taupo, Thames-Coromandel, Wairarapa, Wanganui, Wellington, Western Bay of Plenty, Western Waikato, Whangarei, **(34.) Norway**: Bergen; **(35.) Peru**: Ariquipa,

Lima, Lima-Dos, Trujillo; **(36.) Philippines**: Manilla; **(37.) Poland**: Olsztyn, Warsaw; **(38.) Republic of Georgia**: Tbilisi; **(39.) Russia**: Irkutsk, Korolev, Moscow, Nizhny Novgorod, Novgorod, Russia (Office); St. Petersburg; **(40.) Singapore**: Singapore; **(41.) Slovakia**: Bratislava; **(42.) South Africa**: Cape of Good Hope, Cape Town Atlantic, Pretoria: **(43.) Sweden**: Helsingborg; **(44.) Taiwan R.O.C.**: Kaohsiung, Taichung, Taipei, Taiwan (office); **(45.) Thailand**: Bangkok, Chiang Mai, Lampang, Mae Hong Son, Nakhon Ratchasima; **(46.) Turkey**: Ankara, Izmir; **(47). Ukraine**: Kiev, Lugansk - SE Ukraine; **(48.) United Kingdom**: Bristol, Cardiff, Causeway Coast, Cleveland County, County Durham, Derbyshire, Devon, Hampshire, Hertfordshire, Isle of Wight, Manchester, Newcastle upon Tyne, Northumbria, Sussex, Wessex, West of Scotland.

(The international clubs listed above total 243.)

FRIENDSHIP FORCE INTERNATIONAL CONFERENCES
1977-1996

Year	Location	Hosted By
1977	Washington, DC	Rosalynn Carter, Honorary Chairperson
1978	Washington, DC	Rosalynn Carter, Honorary Chairperson
1979	Atlanta, GA	Wayne Smith, President
1980	West Berlin, Germany	Hanns-Peter Herz, National Director
1981	Newcastle, England	Tony Coates,Chairman The Friendship Force of Newcastle upon Tyne and Alan Redhead Associate Director of Development
1982	Asheville, NC	Carolyn Hunt, State Chairperson
1983	Las Vegas, NV	Capt. "Mac" McKinney, President, The Friendship Force of Las Vegas
1984	Rio de Janeiro, Brazil	Levy Tavares, Regional Director
1985	Des Moines, Iowa	Members of The Friendship Force of Greater Des Moines
1986	Hong Kong	Eddie Lam

Friendship Force Leaders and Facts

Year	Location	Hosted By
1987	Richmond, VA	Inger Rice, State Director
1988	Veldhoven, Netherlands	Henny Willemsen and The Friendship Force, Netherlands
1989	Portland, Oregon	Bettye Brown and The Friendship Force Clubs of The Pacific Northwest
1990	Adelaide, Australia	Joan Harraman and The Friendship Force Clubs of South Australia
1991	Daytona Beach, FL	Joe and Ruth Nathan and The Friendship, Force Clubs of Florida
1992	Niigata, Japan	Bunkichi Itoh and The Friendship Force of Niigata
1993	Acapulco, Mexico	The Friendship Force Clubs of Mexico
1994	Denver, Colorado	The Friendship Force Clubs of Colorado
1995	Atlanta, Georgia	The Friendship Force Clubs of Georgia
1996	Montreal, Canada	The Friendship Force Clubs of Canada and the City of Montreal

FRIENDSHIP FORCE CLUB OF THE YEAR AWARD 1987-1996
UNITED STATES CLUB OF THE YEAR

1987	Atlanta, Georgia
1988	Greater Des Moines, Iowa
1989	Wisconsin
1990	East Central Florida
1991	Richmond, Virginia
1992	Denver, Colorado
1993	Western North Carolina
1994	Sarasota, Florida
1995	Oklahoma
1996	Lincoln, Nebraska

INTERNATIONAL CLUB OF THE YEAR 1987-1996

1987	(None Awarded)
1988	Tokyo, Japan
1989	Taipei, Taiwan
1990	Tweed Valley, Australia
1991	Arnhem, Netherlands
1992	Hannover, Germany
1993	Christchurch, New Zealand
1994	Haale-Saal, Germany
1995	Bratislava, Slovakia
1996	Irkutsk, Russia

Place Name and Surname Index

A

Aaron, 160
Abashidze, 204, 207, 208, 210, 212, 213
Accra, 232, 233, 234, 239, 240
Adelaide, 176, 297
Afghanistan, 228, 290
African National Congress, 296, 297Afrika Korps, 305
Airey, 216
Alabama, 14, 65, 77, 78, 79, 82, 90
Albuquerque, 77, 78
Alexander Nevsky Cathedral, 243
Algeria, 321
Algerian Red Crescent, 321
Alikafic, 336
Alitus, 107
Allen, 17, 31, 294
Allen Foundation, 17
Allinder, 311, 312
Almalyk, 171, 172
Alosha, 252, 253, 256
Altengamme, 55
Alytus, 107
Amman, 324, 325, 326
Amranand, 99
Amsterdam, 73, 144, 207
Andropov, 163, 166
Arab, 37, 38, 102, 103, 223, 224, 269, 271
Arafat, 33, 36, 37, 38, 39
Araraquara, 215
Arcadia, 307
Areshidze, 110, 112, 117, 119
Arizona, 232
Armendariz, 62, 77
ARMS, 109

Armstrong, 121, 279
Arnhem, 105, 154
Asako, 191
Asantehene, 233, 236, 238
Ashanti, 233, 239
Ashkhabad, 228
Ashley, 86, 88
Atabaeva, 173
Athens, 283
Atlanta, 8, 9, 12, 15, 16, 17, 21, 23, 24, 26, 27, 32, 33, 40, 51, 53, 65, 75, 77, 82, 88, 93, 110, 111, 112, 117, 119, 124, 125, 127, 130, 139, 142, 149, 154, 160, 161, 166, 167, 174, 183, 189, 200, 207, 218, 221, 223, 224, 225, 232, 243, 245, 248, 257, 264, 265, 271, 283, 285, 286, 289, 297, 311, 316, 325, 327, 328, 331
Atlanta Constitution, 51, 125
Auschwitz, 243
Austin, 27, 30, 104
Australia, 78, 86, 106, 153, 176, 192, 328
Austria, 123, 129, 130, 153, 216
Ayoub, 325, 326
Aytutthya, 99

B

Baghdad, 303, 320, 323, 324, 326
Bagley, 21
Bahar, 271
Bahasa, 131
Baidukov, 170
Balfour, 296, 297, 298
Baltic Sea, 125
Bangkok, 99, 106, 230
Bantekas, 20
Bantry, 232

Place Name and Surname Index

Baton Rouge, 104
Bauman, 298
Bay of Guanabara, 319
Bayonne, 131
Beahm, 77
Beckley, 178, 179, 180
Bedouin, 103
Beeson, 200
Beirut, 33, 34, 36
Belgrade, 244, 245
Bell, 19, 144, 145
Bellamy, 260
Bengfort, 75
Benghazi, 130
Benzel, 77
Bergen, 105, 188
Bergman, 174
Berlin Wall, 88, 188, 199, 219, 220, 256, 301
Berner, 185
Bethlehem, 33, 38
Biarritz, 131
Biederman, 49
Big Bethel AME Church, 297
Big Canoe, 109, 110, 112, 113, 118, 120, 121, 143, 146, 147, 174, 176, 189, 194, 195, 218, 250, 259, 315, 316, 317
Binghamton, 104
Birdsong, 16, 23
Bishkek, 294
Blackmon, 14, 65, 77, 90
Blue Ridge Mountains, 110, 113, 174
Bogacs, 220
Boise Peace Quilt, 107
Boldrini Children's Hospital, 64
Bolshoi Theater, 163
Bonnie Prince Charles, 15
Boortz, 23
Boriesienne, 107
Borzhomi, 211
Boston, 78, 104, 328, 329
Bosworth, 336

Bournemouth, 259
Bowers, 28, 29
Braniff, 53
Brasilia, 4, 6, 7
Bratislava, 215
Brazil, 4, 6, 7, 8, 9, 10, 13, 21, 51, 64, 96, 98, 128, 133, 141, 149, 192, 195, 196, 215, 227, 260, 319
Brea, 104
Brezhnev, 53, 111, 292
Bridgebuilders, 277, 278, 279, 280, 282, 283, 285, 323, 331, 332
Bristol, 178, 179, 180
Brown, 3, 27, 28, 29, 74, 88, 101, 104, 123, 126, 248, 264, 277, 327, 328
Broyles, 8, 21, 71, 111
Brugger, 124
Bryant, 202
Budapest, 130, 134
Buffington, 299
Bukhara, 171, 172
Bulgaria, 242, 243
Busbee, 17
Bush, 195, 196, 223, 257
Bushnell, 231, 232
Byrne, 47

C

Cairo, 91, 92, 152
Calcutta, 176
Cali, 50, 51, 53, 67, 105
California, 103, 104, 145, 156, 179, 190, 232
Camden, 41, 42
Camp David Accord, 38
Camp Wheeler, 79
Campinas, 4, 5, 6, 64
Canada, 21
Cape Coast, 235

Place Name and Surname Index

Cape Town, 224, 231, 297

Caracas, 24

Carey, 23

Carolina, 14, 51, 57, 74, 81, 105, 118, 154, 183, 184, 187, 229, 273

Carrington, 137

Carter, 8, 9, 10, 11, 12, 13, 14, 15, 16, 17, 20, 23, 24, 25, 26, 27, 28, 30, 33, 38, 52, 62, 68, 89, 93, 94, 96, 105, 110, 111, 112, 123, 124, 139, 140, 141, 143, 148, 149, 155, 156, 160, 180, 182, 222, 223, 236, 237, 257, 258, 275, 278, 283, 286, 303, 327

Caspian Sea, 228

Castro, 196

Catherine's Palace, 287

Caucasus Mountains, 201, 204

Causevic, 337

CCN, 104

CELEBRATE, 158

Centennial Olympic Games, 327

Central Asia, 293, 294

Chadwick, 40

Chapel Hill, 121

Chapin, 309

Chardzhou, 228

Charkviani, 110, 112, 116, 118, 127

Charleston, 1, 3, 4

Charleston University, 3

Chattanooga, 114, 115, 116

Chernobyl, 282

Cherry Hill, 41

Chester, 112

Chiapas, 62, 78

Chicago, 134, 290

Children's Home Society, 66

Children's Palace, 160

Chile, 130, 191

China, 82, 83, 86, 87, 88, 105, 131, 153, 158, 159, 160, 171, 185, 223, 257, 290, 294

Chlapikova, 216

Christchurch, 260

Church of the Resurrection, 287

Churchill, 126

CIA, 6, 303

Cinnaminson, 42, 47

Citron, 328, 330

City of York, 144

Ciuffardi, 21

Clancy, 101

Clarke, 15, 16, 21

Clary, 229

Clawson, 103

CNN Center, 302

Coates, 82, 84, 93, 94, 95, 96, 140, 155

Collins, 1, 192

Colombia, 50, 51, 53, 57, 58, 67, 133

Communist Party, 96, 212

Condon, 21, 77

Connecticut, 14, 142, 154, 215, 325

Consett, 144

Cooper, 119

Copenhagen, 34, 106, 263

Coptic, 152

Cork, 102, 232

Coronet Industries, 17, 114, 115

Costa Rica, 9, 21, 32, 77, 268

Cousins, 9, 11, 17, 21, 69, 70, 71

Coventry, 103

Covington, 57

Crabapple Middle School, 158

Creech, 118

Croat, 245, 336, 337

Cuba, 193, 194, 196

Cunningham, 118, 243

Czech Republic, 273

Place Name and Surname Index

Czechoslovakia, 215, 216, 272, 273

D

Daroff, 41, 42
Darragh, 17
Davis, 19
Daxnerova, 215
Daye, 283
Dayton, 51, 53, 57, 58, 228, 283, 331, 334, 335, 336, 337
Dayton Accord, 331
Dead Sea, 169
Dean, 34, 35
Deardorff, 21
Debo, 197
Debrecen, 134
Decatur, 16, 19, 31, 33, 282
Decatur High School, 282
DeKlerk, 231
Delta Airlines, 17, 21, 23, 248
Demianova, 251
Denmark, 21, 32, 34, 100, 106
Dentsu Corporation, 68, 76
Denver, 145, 276
Des Moines, 24, 67, 68, 73, 75, 99, 100, 225, 227, 228, 249
Desert Peace, 303
Dien Bien Phu, 316
Disney, 174
DMZ, 151
Do Xuan Ohne, 195
Domenico, 156, 157
Dorfman, 130, 131
Douglasville, 279
Dover, 104
Drake, 17, 21, 257
Draper, 116
Druze, 35, 102, 103
Dublin, 24, 32, 62, 101, 102, 232

Dubrovnik, 331, 332, 338
Duffie, 102
Duke University, 121
Dull, 337
Dulles, 30, 158, 194, 228
Duncan, 68
Duong Duc Hong, 316
Dussault, 112, 119, 120
Dutch, 132, 183, 217, 232, 264, 301, 302
Dutch East Indies, 132
Dworetz, 21, 40, 53
Dzhaparidze, 110, 117, 121

E

Eagen, 40
Earnest, 190, 191
Eastern, 26, 31, 144, 193, 242
Eaves, 23
Edelstein, 295, 296
Egypt, 21, 38, 89, 91, 92, 152, 325
Eigner, 129
Eisenhower, 163, 169, 194
El Alamein, 305
El Chiconal, 78
El Paso, 104
Ellijay, 205
Elmina Castle, 235
Emerald Buddha, 99
Emerson, 275
Emory University Law School, 283
English High School, 282
Erickson, 130
Eritrea, 238
Erokhin, 284
Ethiopia, 238
Eubanks, 176, 265, 266, 286, 287, 288, 289
Europe, 1, 16, 26, 57, 110, 171, 242, 244, 287, 295, 301

Place Name and Surname Index

Evans, 216
Evtushenko, 109
Eyman, 113

F

Falk, 14, 77, 197
Farid, 265
Fedosov, 53, 65, 67, 74
Ferrari, 44, 46, 48
Finci, 333
Finland, 74, 75, 151,
    152, 288, 289
Fisher, 2
Florida, 49, 110, 133,
    184, 192, 196, 242,
    258, 304, 310, 311
Foote, 176
Forbes, 297
Fouzik, 158
France, 15, 21, 32, 130,
    323
Frankfurt, 225, 335
Franklin, 115, 121
Freedom Square, 209
Freeman, 75
Friedman, 40, 41, 43
Friendship Force Board
    of Trustees, 27, 90,
    319, 325
Friendship Force
    Festival, 51, 52, 161,
    220, 232
Friendship Parade, 140,
    141, 144
Frost, 21
Fuller, 200
Funabashi, 76
Funk, 282
Fuqua Industries, 17
Fyodorov, 249

G

Gabunia, 232
Gaeddert, 68
Galbraith, 145
Galilee, 103, 169, 223,
    326

Gallagher, 153
Gamble, 259
Gamsakhurida, 212,
    298
Garner, 127, 167
Garst, 77
Gazit, 224, 270, 271
Gelsenkirchen, 165,
    304
Genghis Khan, 171
Genoa, 26
Gentillet, 131
Geordie, 15
Georgetown University,
    279
Georgi, 170, 212
Georgia, 8, 9, 11, 12,
    13, 16, 17, 20, 32,
    53, 71, 79, 82, 90,
    109, 110, 111, 112,
    113, 114, 116, 118,
    119, 121, 122, 123,
    125, 127, 143, 145,
    146, 156, 158, 160,
    167, 168, 188, 194,
    199, 200, 201, 202,
    203, 204, 207, 208,
    210, 211, 212, 217,
    221, 232, 251, 256,
    259, 264, 265, 276,
    279, 282, 283, 284,
    285, 286, 289, 298,
    302, 308, 315, 316
Georgian Friendship
    Societhy, 110
Georgian Orthodox
    Church, 201
Germany, 21, 31, 32,
    54, 55, 57, 59, 77,
    78, 81, 88, 90, 103,
    130, 133, 141, 156,
    157, 165, 184, 188,
    189, 191, 197, 198,
    219, 225, 226, 242,
    304, 305, 307
Ghana, 232, 233, 234,
    235, 236, 238, 239,
    240, 241, 242
Gifu, 191
Gisborne, 305
Gladkey, 251
Go Riju, 124

Place Name and Surname Index

Godwin, 106

Golden Stool, 233

Gorbachev, 113, 128, 145, 146, 147, 161, 163, 164, 165, 192, 195, 205, 249, 276, 298

Gori, 210

Grady Memorial Hospital, 286

Graham, 145

Gray, 82, 200, 224, 261

Great Wall of China, 159, 160

Greater Des Moines, 225, 227

Greece, 33, 244

Greer, 259

Griffiths, 179

Grizzard, 125

Grossinger, 21, 23

Grubbs, 14

Guasalia, 110, 112, 117

Guatemala, 32

Gulf of Finland, 288, 289

Gustavson, 156, 295

Gutenkauf, 228

Gyanu, 239

H

Haack, 57

Haan, 154

Hada, 134, 135

Hadrian's Wall, 155

Haehnar, 225

Hahn, 59, 60

Haisova, 272, 273

Hall, 23, 45, 68, 107, 201, 260

Hammer, 17, 21, 23, 32, 52, 53, 68

Hangyang University, 30

Hani, 296, 297

Hannover, 104, 105, 188

Hanoi, 109, 194, 195, 310, 311, 312, 313, 314, 316

Hanoi Hilton, 109, 194, 195, 313, 314

Haraughty, 229, 230

Hare, 17

Harris, 160

Harrisburg, 59

Hartford, 24, 26, 142

Hassinger, 17, 200, 289

Hatfield, 21, 67

Hausrath, 107

Hawaii, 104, 307, 308

Hayes, 102

Heaster, 3

Helsinki, 75

Hendrickson, 54

Hermitage, 286

Herraman, 176, 178

Herz, 54, 77

Hill, 41, 121, 159, 183, 297

Hillbrow, 296

Hinshaw, 81

Hiroshima, 307, 308

Hiroshima University, 307

Hoa Lo Prison, 194, 313

Holland, 90, 94, 154, 156, 180, 182, 301

Holmes, 338

Holy Land, 269, 271

Holzheim, 305

Home Depot, 174, 175

Hong Kong, 153, 263, 308

House of Hope, 103, 104, 223, 270, 271, 272

Howrah, 176

Hubbs, 309, 312

Huber Heights, 336

Hudgins, 17

Hughes, 179, 247

Hugo, 11

Hull, 17, 40, 279, 281

Humphrey, 175

Humphries, 27, 30, 40, 48, 77

Place Name and Surname Index

Hungary, 130, 134, 220, 301
Hunt, 14, 57

I

Idaho, 107, 268
Ihler, 228
Illinois, 134
India, 11, 56, 100, 105, 176, 178, 220, 221, 295, 296, 307
Indian Ocean, 131
Indonesia, 131, 132
Infui, 198
Ingram, 108
International Council for Volunteers, 333
Intourist Hotels, 67
Iowa, 14, 24, 67, 73, 74, 99, 134, 143, 145, 197, 227, 232, 243, 249
Iran, 102, 228
Iraq, 303, 320, 323, 324, 325, 326
Ireland, 1, 21, 24, 40, 90, 101, 102, 130, 137, 141, 191, 232
Irkutsk, 302, 328, 329
Israel, 21, 36, 37, 38, 102, 103, 223, 269, 270, 271, 325, 326, 331
Italy, 1, 2, 21, 32, 40, 41, 42, 45, 191
Ivan the Terrible, 256

J

Jabbour, 103, 104, 223, 269, 270, 271, 331
Jackson, 17, 160, 299
Jahn, 301
Japan, 38, 68, 69, 71, 76, 105, 124, 139, 184, 191, 230, 246, 258, 306, 307

Japanese Shipbuilding Foundation, 70
Jasper, 17, 125, 221
Jenkins, 256
Jennings, 336, 337, 338
Jericho, 38, 326
Johannesburg, 296
Johnson, 78, 100, 174, 175, 196, 273
Jolly Boy, 29
Jones, 17, 40, 77, 82, 92
Jordan, 35, 38, 89, 104, 169, 324, 325, 326
Jordan River, 104, 169
Josephson, 200
Jubilee School, 325
Judge, 14, 119
Jugsujinda, 99

K

Kakabadze, 204
Kalmus, 196
Kant, 272
Kanyar, 134, 135
Karimova, 286
Katayama, 307, 308
Katznelson, 218
Kauai, 104
Kazakhstan, 170
Kazan Cathedral, 287
Kenmare, 102
Kennedy, 223
Kensington, 297
Kent, 94
Kenya, 153, 154, 184
Kettering, 17, 336
KGB, 167, 208, 249
Khayelitsha, 231
Kiev, 156, 157, 158, 292
Kikvadze, 110, 116, 121
Kildare, 232
Kim, 29, 66, 77, 99, 125
King, 15, 17, 99, 135, 319
King and Spaulding, 17

Place Name and Surname Index

King Bela III, 135
King George II, 15
Kirkhe, 218, 219
Kiryat Ono, 224, 269, 270, 271
Kissinger, 145
Kiwi, 174
Kohl, 188
Konetschny, 156
Konez, 220
Konigsmark, 272
Konorezov, 111
Korean Airlines, 90
Kosice, 215
Kovacevic, 333, 334
Kozlov, 302
Krakow, 83
Kremlin, 113, 136, 161, 163, 249
Krems, 129, 153
Ku, 17
Kuhr, 283
Kumasi, 235, 236, 238, 239, 240
Kura River Valley, 201
Kusha, 252, 253, 256
Kuznetsova, 119
Kyekyeku, 239, 241

L

La Benevolencia, 333
Lady Liberty, 212
Lake Baikal, 328
Lamar, 23
Lamb, 51
Lamkin, 89, 99, 100, 102, 119, 125, 140, 215, 216, 299, 307, 308
Lancaster, 58, 59, 60, 67, 94, 96, 97, 282
Lane, 5
Las Vegas, 179
Latin America, 11, 183, 262
Latvia, 218
Lavony, 43, 44, 45, 47
Laybourne, 321, 323, 324

Lebanon, 33, 34, 35, 36, 100, 169
Lee, 1, 14, 28, 81, 156, 218
Leftwich, 179
Lenin, 201, 205, 209, 247, 256, 276, 287
Lenin Square, 201, 209
Leningrad, 67, 75, 77, 125, 145, 287, 292
Leroy, 107
Levy, 96, 127, 128, 149, 183, 195, 270, 271
Liba, 215
Liberta, 47
Libya, 130
Lieber, 152
Lievonen, 151
Life of Georgia, 17
Lightfoot, 228
Limburg, 305
Lincoln, 102, 131, 132
Linda, 90, 91
Lion Head Mountain, 231
Lithuania, 107, 125, 192
Little, 1, 179, 212, 296, 307, 323
Liza, 209, 211, 266
Locri, 1
Lord Mayor's Parade, 140
Los Angeles, 191
Louisiana, 104, 145, 307
Lourdes, 131
Low, 68
Luehring, 156
Lukin, 286
Luong, 316
Luria, 242, 304, 306
Luxembourg, 21
Lyon, 130
Lyons, 77, 327

M

Macedonia, 243

Place Name and Surname Index

Machado, 215
Macon, 79, 188, 200
Macon Telegraph and
    Post, 188
Madison, 90, 192
Maelek, 229, 230
Maguire, 101
Malacic, 244
Mandela, 297
Manhia Palace, 236
Marcos, 40, 149
Marechall, 185
Marill, 221, 222, 223,
    224, 225
Marshall Trust, 17
Marshalltown, 249
Marui, 124, 306
Matson, 302
Maui, 104
Mauritania, 320
Maxwell, 260
McCarty, 117
McDonald, 57, 90, 100,
    167, 253
McGill, 1
McGovern, 77
McNamara, 145
McTaggart, 156
Melnik, 244
Mercy Hospital, 228
Mexico, 14, 40, 62, 65,
    78, 90, 103, 191, 264
Mexico City, 40, 62
Miami, 12
Middle East, 89, 137,
    257, 319, 325
Mierendorff, 78, 79, 81,
    82
Milan, 43, 142
Miller, 90, 257
Minneapolis, 58, 197
Minnesota, 14, 66, 74,
    77, 83, 100, 103,
    197, 283
Minsk, 197, 248
Missionaries of Charity,
    176
Missions to Moscow,
    90, 125
Missouri, 74
Mongol, 170, 256

Montana, 14, 57, 76,
    99, 100
Montross, 227, 228
Moody, 27
Moon, 80, 81, 82
Moore, 133
Morgan City, 104
Morocco, 89, 320
Moroz, 297
Morris Harvey College,
    3
Moscow, 65, 68, 75, 90,
    107, 123, 125, 126,
    142, 145, 156, 161,
    162, 168, 180, 192,
    228, 232, 248, 249,
    250, 251, 252, 253,
    254, 255, 256, 257,
    263, 275, 277, 278,
    279, 280, 282, 284,
    285, 286, 287, 290,
    291, 292, 294, 298,
    299, 315, 331
Mosey, 216
Mosier, 76
Mostar, 332
Mother Georgia, 212
Mount Holly, 47
Mountain Lakes High
    School, 156
Mtsuzavishvili, 112,
    113, 120
Muhammad Ali, 21, 22,
    23, 264, 265
Mullins, 285
Munich, 56
Muscatello, 1, 2
Muschiol, 188
Muslim, 132, 294, 336,
    337
Mustafa, 34

N

Nagasaki, 307
Nagorsky, 287
Nagy, 134
Nairobi, 153, 184
Nana, 212
Nathan, 231, 242

Place Name and Surname Index

National Geographic,
247
Nazareth, 103
Nebraska, 50, 66, 88,
102, 103, 131, 132
Netherlands, 21, 78, 84,
94, 191, 301
Neuschwanstein Castle,
56
New Delhi, 105
New Haven, 325
New Jersey, 41, 105,
156, 158
New Mexico, 14, 78,
90, 103
New York, 34, 104,
145, 232, 268, 280
New Zealand, 84, 85,
86, 153, 156, 161,
174, 175, 176, 191,
192, 217, 266, 304,
305, 306
Newcastle Civic Centre,
141
Newcastle upon Tyne,
15, 140, 261, 321
Newly Independent
States, 295
Newman, 145
Nicol, 284
Nigeria, 90, 233
Noor, 325, 326
Norderstedt, 219, 220
North Carolina, 14, 51,
57, 74, 105, 118,
154, 229, 273
North Dakota, 54, 55,
56, 57
North Ossetians, 298
Northern Ireland, 130,
137
Nouwen, 269
Nunn, 200, 282, 290

O

Obear, 115
Ohio, 11, 51, 53, 57,
74, 193, 228, 283,
331, 335

Okajima, 191
Oklahoma, 14, 68, 106,
138, 229
Olympia, 26, 27
Olympic, 327, 328, 333
Omaha, 66, 86, 153
Omni, 10, 13, 257
Ono, 145, 224, 269,
270, 271
Opelika, 78, 82
Optimist Clubs of
Georgia, 221
Orlando, 258, 268, 304
Ortiz, 183, 184, 185
Osanae, 124
Otkhmezuri, 203
Oxenham, 85

P

Pace, 200, 271
Palestine, 33, 34, 38, 39
Palestine Liberation
Organization, 33, 34
Palumbo, 14
Panama Canal, 223
Panford, 242
Paris, 195, 319
Park, 48, 88, 224, 242
Parker, 77, 121
Parliament Square, 231
Partners of the
Americas, 9
Pau, 130, 131
Pawlik, 90
Pearl Harbor, 307
Peitchev, 242
Peking, 86
Penna, 132
Pereverseva, 280
Pernambuco, 9, 13
Persian Gulf, 243, 259
Peter the Great, 286,
287
Petrograd, 287
Pham Hoang Van, 316,
317
Philippines, 40, 78
Philippopolis, 243
Phillips, 17, 179, 228

Place Name and Surname Index

Piacenza, 40, 41, 42, 43, 44, 45, 46, 47, 48
Pioner Valley, 104
PLO, 33, 34, 35
Po Valley, 42
Pobeda Peak, 294
Pocatello, 268
Poland, 61, 82, 83, 90, 91, 197
Pool, 125, 126, 260
Popaloo, 176, 178
Porch, 125
Portman Center, 160
Post, 188, 189
Postar, 191, 192
Prague, 215, 272, 273
Prince Philip, 19
Prometheus, 201
Prouty, 153
Prychka, 158
Puerto Rico, 183, 184, 185
Pushkin Museum, 253
Pyrenees Mountains, 131

Q

Quaddafi, 130
Queen Elizabeth, 19

R

Radulovic, 100
Rae, 180, 182, 183
Raleigh, 118, 121
Ramat Et'al, 271
Rawlings, 233
Ray, 14, 28, 101, 143, 279
Reagan, 72, 77, 98, 128, 145, 146, 161, 163, 164, 165, 188
Ream, 156
Red Square, 256
Redhead, 40, 52, 95, 143, 257
Reidsville, 79, 82

Reilman, 17, 40, 51, 53, 61, 63, 74, 77, 78, 180, 199, 200
Respess, 311
Rhinesmith, 27
Rice, 14, 40, 106, 119, 267
Rich, 17, 201
Richmond, 4, 26, 68, 106, 118
Ridgefield, 232, 264
Riga, 218, 248
Rila, 243
Rio de Janeiro, 4, 105
Ritchie, 290
Roberts, 115
Robertson, 158, 159, 160
Rockefeller, 14, 27
Rome, 103, 263, 267
Rudd, 337
Runnels, 90
Ruskin, 69
Russell, 18, 77, 95, 106, 143
Rusteveli Street, 201
Ryan, 62

S

Saddam Children's Hospital, 323
Sahara, 320
Saharawi, 320, 323
Sailor, 23
Salas, 185
Salt Lake City, 32, 67, 91, 92
Samarkand, 171, 172, 295
Sammons, 68
Samson, 225
San Diego, 104, 179, 204
San Francisco Bay, 104, 191, 293
Sao Carlos, 51
Sao Paulo, 51, 96, 97, 128, 196

Place Name and Surname Index

Sarajevo, 331, 332, 333, 334, 335, 336, 337, 338

Saralidze, 203

Sarkar, 50

Sarkis, 35, 36

Sarner, 200

Sasakawa, 68, 69, 70, 71, 72, 82, 107, 123, 124, 139, 143, 236, 237, 307, 308

Sata, 184

Schmeling, 54, 189

Schmidt, 60, 229

Schugart, 305

Schuh, 312

Scolzhauer, 187

Scotland, 15, 32, 230

Sea of Galilee, 169

Seal, 13, 15, 16, 21, 22, 24, 25, 26, 27

Seattle, 29

Sebasta, 216

Semenikhina, 180

Senate Foreign Relations Committee, 113

Seoul, 26, 29, 30, 66, 105

Seretean, 21, 23, 26, 77, 114, 115, 116, 143, 193

Shanghai, 86, 88, 160

Shaw, 129

Shefar'am, 103, 104, 223, 224, 269, 270, 271, 331

Shelley, 58

Shelton, 294, 295

Sheremetyevo International Airport, 251

Shevardnadze, 249

Shiite, 35

Shipley, 225

Shubashvili, 203

Siberia, 209, 302, 303, 328, 329

Silk Route, 171

Simpson, 229

Sisters Embracing a Dream, 285, 286

Skelley, 266

Slovak, 216, 217, 273

Slovakia, 215

Smirnov, 180

Smith, 1, 2, 3, 4, 6, 7, 8, 9, 10, 11, 12, 13, 14, 15, 16, 17, 18, 19, 21, 22, 23, 24, 25, 26, 30, 31, 32, 33, 34, 35, 36, 37, 38, 39, 40, 52, 53, 62, 65, 66, 67, 68, 69, 70, 71, 72, 73, 74, 75, 77, 82, 85, 86, 89, 90, 91, 92, 94, 96, 105, 107, 109, 110, 113, 120, 122, 123, 125, 127, 137, 139, 141, 142, 143, 145, 146, 149, 161, 162, 163, 165, 166, 167, 169, 176, 178, 179, 180, 182, 183, 187, 189, 190, 193, 194, 195, 196, 199, 200, 212, 218, 219, 221, 222, 223, 224, 225, 227, 231, 248, 249, 250, 257, 258, 261, 263, 264, 268, 269, 271, 275, 276, 277, 278, 279, 290, 291, 292, 295, 303, 309, 316, 319, 320, 323, 324, 325, 327, 331, 332, 334, 335

Smith family, 7, 8

Smithfield, 118

Smithfield Senior Center, 118

Smoketown, 58

Sofia, 243, 244

Somalia, 238

Somerdale, 156

Somers, 23

South China Sea, 131

South Jersey, 41, 42, 43, 158

South Korea, 48, 95, 151

South Ossetians, 298

Place Name and Surname Index

South Wales, 52
Soviet Georgia, 110,
111, 113, 116, 119,
121, 127, 168, 200,
217
Soviet Union, 52, 65,
67, 68, 73, 74, 89,
90, 107, 113, 118,
121, 122, 125, 128,
142, 145, 153, 157,
158, 163, 164, 165,
166, 170, 180, 200,
206, 208, 218, 227,
228, 248, 276, 277,
278, 292, 294, 308,
311, 315, 328
Soweto, 225, 296
Spain, 21, 320
Speed, 27
Split, 335
St. Alexis, 279, 280,
282
St. Basil's Cathedral,
162
St. Louis, 34, 105
St. Petersburg, 248,
282, 283, 286, 287,
289
Stahl, 220, 221
Stalin, 208, 210, 247,
255, 256, 276
Startseva, 286
Stauffer, 202
Sterling High School,
156
Stonehenge, 260
Strathclyde, 52
Sudan, 238
Sudhikam, 106
Sugamo Prison, 69
Summers, 124
Summit, 158, 161, 163
Sundanese, 132, 133
Sunni, 228
Supreme Soviet, 163,
172
Switzerland, 21, 32, 47
Sydney Olympic
Games, 328
Sykes, 192
Syria, 38, 326

T

Tacoma, 26
Tae Wan Son, 77
Taguatinga, 4, 5, 6, 7
Taipei, 133, 185
Taiwan, 133, 180, 185
Tajakistan, 170
Tambo, 297
Tasama, 53, 57, 58
Tashibekova, 294
Tashkent, 171, 172,
173, 295
Taupo, 175
Tavares, 96, 127, 128,
149, 183, 195
Tbilisi, 53, 110, 114,
117, 119, 120, 121,
127, 128, 199, 201,
203, 204, 207, 209,
211, 212, 214, 232,
248, 266, 276, 284,
289, 298, 299, 300,
315
Tel Aviv, 24, 26, 224,
325
Telavi, 212
Tereskova, 163
Terrell, 109, 218, 219,
314, 315
Teshabaiev, 170
Teskeredic, 336
Thailand, 82, 99, 100,
106, 153, 192, 229,
230, 296
Thatcher, 59, 60
Thompson, 50
Thrace, 243
Tichenow, 218, 219
Tien Shan Mountain,
294
Tito, 245
Tokyo, 57, 70, 76, 123,
124, 139, 184, 306,
307
Tokyo Broadcasting
System, 124
Tomaszewski, 247
Tran Minh Quoc, 316
Trebor Foundation, 17
Trimontium, 243

Place Name and Surname Index

Tripoli, 130
Trivedi, 221
Troy, 229, 230
Truman, 9
Trust Company Bank,
  17, 32
Tsar Nicholas, 287
Tskaltubo, 210
Tubbercurry, 232
Turkmenistan, 170, 228
Tutu, 222, 233
Twain, 301
Twin Cities, 130

U

UK, 52, 82, 84, 95, 179
Ukraine, 198
Ulyanov, 249
Union Theological
  Seminary, 4
United Kingdom, 15,
  31, 40, 137
United Nations, 37,
  180, 245, 296, 320,
  321, 334
United States, 1, 3, 6, 8,
  11, 16, 23, 24, 30,
  34, 35, 38, 39, 52,
  54, 62, 67, 68, 73,
  83, 93, 94, 106, 117,
  118, 122, 126, 128,
  129, 130, 133, 134,
  142, 145, 149, 158,
  166, 169, 170, 179,
  180, 189, 192, 194,
  195, 206, 223, 225,
  228, 231, 233, 234,
  235, 242, 257, 268,
  277, 278, 282, 283,
  285, 289, 291, 298,
  302, 304, 308, 311,
  325, 328, 337
United States
  Consulate, 234
University of Hanoi,
  311
University of
  Tennessee, 116

US, 2, 3, 14, 21, 23, 26,
  31, 34, 39, 51, 57,
  73, 77, 90, 99, 110,
  119, 130, 165, 166,
  167, 193, 204, 221,
  248, 255, 256, 285,
  312, 314
USA, 12, 53, 57, 65,
  67, 77, 82, 86, 88,
  89, 90, 91, 111, 119,
  127, 153, 156, 158,
  161, 163, 165, 167,
  174, 198, 199, 201,
  204, 223, 226, 230,
  256, 262, 264, 273,
  298, 318
USSR, 52, 71, 75, 76,
  77, 78, 83, 89, 90,
  98, 109, 118, 122,
  126, 127, 161, 163,
  165, 166, 167, 193,
  197, 198, 199, 202,
  208, 247, 263, 276,
  278, 285, 301
USSR/USA Society,
  163, 165
Uzbek Friendship
  Society, 170
Uzbekistan, 170, 171,
  173, 293, 294, 295
Uzbeks, 170

V

Van Tilburg, 27, 28, 29,
  30, 74, 123, 129,
  151, 152, 170, 171,
  173, 232, 233, 234,
  235, 236, 237, 238,
  239, 240, 241
Vance, 145
Vancouver, 29, 169,
  170
Vasiliev, 279
Veldhoven, 180, 182
Venezuela, 21, 24, 32,
  92
Vienna, 130
Vier Lande, 55

Place Name and Surname Index

Vietnam, 193, 194, 195, 196, 203, 204, 218, 309, 310, 311, 312, 313, 314, 315, 316, 318

Vietnam Union of Friendship, 316

Vilnius, 107, 125, 192

Viondi, 23

Virginia, 1, 3, 4, 7, 14, 16, 21, 40, 73, 106, 118, 145, 178, 179, 257, 260, 266, 267, 327

Volunteer of the Year, 106, 321

Von Schmeling, 189

W

Waddell, 202, 203, 204, 314

Wages, 23

Wagner, 57

Walburn, 218, 219

Wales, 52, 179

Wallace, 16, 23, 25

Wanganui, 85

Ware, 233, 237

Warren, 14, 106

Washington, 14, 24, 27, 28, 30, 48, 51, 52, 57, 61, 62, 72, 74, 88, 94, 107, 118, 119, 120, 129, 145, 146, 151, 161, 163, 166, 169, 170, 227, 228, 232, 264, 286

Washington State, 14, 48, 74, 88, 151, 169, 170

Washington, DC, 30, 51, 52, 61, 74, 118, 119, 161, 163, 166, 286

Wattles, 23

Wayland, 58

Wayne, 1, 2, 3, 4, 5, 6, 7, 8, 9, 10, 11, 12, 13, 14, 15, 16, 17, 18, 19, 21, 22, 23, 24, 25, 28, 29, 30, 31, 32, 33, 34, 36, 39, 40, 48, 52, 53, 57, 62, 65, 67, 68, 69, 70, 71, 72, 73, 74, 75, 76, 77, 82, 85, 86, 89, 90, 91, 92, 94, 96, 105, 107, 109, 110, 113, 114, 120, 122, 123, 125, 127, 129, 137, 139, 142, 143, 145, 147, 149, 161, 163, 166, 169, 170, 173, 176, 178, 180, 182, 183, 187, 189, 190, 193, 194, 195, 199, 200, 202, 203, 204, 212, 218, 219, 221, 222, 223, 224, 225, 227, 231, 232, 233, 234, 237, 248, 250, 257, 258, 261, 263, 264, 265, 268, 269, 271, 275, 276, 277, 278, 290, 291, 295, 303, 309, 314, 316, 319, 320, 323, 324, 325, 327

Weekes, 84, 85, 86

Weihrauch, 197

Weinberg, 14

Welch, 9

Welcome Point, 56

Wells, 144

West Berlin, 30, 54, 88, 130, 185, 187

West Virginia, 1, 3, 4, 7, 14, 16, 21, 73, 145, 178, 179, 257, 260, 267, 327

West Virginia State College, 3, 257

Westborough, 104

Westchester, 34

Western Sahara, 320

Westminster Abbey, 260

Westmoreland, 310

WGST, 283, 284, 311

WHIO, 283

Place Name and Surname Index

White House, 10, 12,
13, 24, 25, 106, 128,
139
Whitfield, 121
Wichiencharoen, 99
Wick, 166
Wigan Pier, 260
Willemsen, 84, 94, 156
Willis, 284
Winchilsea, 320, 321,
323, 324, 327
Wisconsin, 77, 90, 145,
192, 232
Wise, 276
Witmer, 58
Wolford, 337
Wolfsburg, 133, 305
Woodward Academy,
110
World Citizen
Exchanges, 248
World War I, 54, 55,
69, 110, 116, 117,
118, 121, 127, 132,
134, 182, 188, 189,
217, 236, 260, 272,
287, 299, 304
World War II, 54, 55,
69, 110, 116, 117,
118, 121, 127, 132,
134, 182, 188, 189,
217, 260, 299, 304

Wright, 21, 124
Wuezbach, 220
WUGA, 283
Wyoming, 11, 93

Y

Yamano, 76
Yancey, 15, 121
York Minster, 144
Yorkshire Dales, 144
Young, 66, 134, 149,
222, 296, 297
Youngblood, 66
Yugoslavia, 100, 244,
273, 331, 335
YWCA, 176

Z

Zagorsk, 258
Zagreb, 335
Zarubina, 73, 74
Ziegler, 286
Zima, 89
Zolotukhin, 52
Zossen, 305
Zurab, 299
Zutphen, 301